EUROPEAN COMMUNITY COMPETITION LAW IN PRACTICE

Inns of Court School of Law

BLACKSTONE
PRESS LIMITED

First published in Great Britain 1998 by Blackstone Press Limited,
Aldine Place, London W12 8AA. Telephone (020) 8740 2277
www.blackstonepress.com

© Inns of Court School of Law, 1998

First edition, 1998
Second edition, 1999
Third edition, 2000

ISBN: 1 84174 005 5

British Library Cataloguing in Publication Data
A CIP catalogue record for this book is available from the British Library.

Typeset by Montage Studios Ltd, Horsmonden, Kent
Printed by Ashford Colour Press, Gosport, Hampshire

FOREWORD

These manuals are designed primarily to support training on the Bar Vocational Course, though they are also intended to provide a useful resource for legal practitioners and for anyone undertaking training in legal skills.

The Bar Vocational Course was designed by staff at the Inns of Court School of Law, where it was introduced in 1989. This course is intended to equip students with the practical skills and the procedural and evidential knowledge that they will need to start their legal professional careers. These manuals are written by staff at the Inns of Court School of Law who have helped to develop the course, and by a range of legal practitioners and others involved in legal skills training. The authors of the manuals are very well aware of the practical and professional approach that is central to the Bar Vocational Course.

The range and coverage of the manuals have grown steadily. All the practice manuals are updated every two years, and regular reviews and revisions of the manuals are carried out to ensure that developments in legal skills training and the experience of our staff are fully reflected in them.

This updating and revision is a constant process, and we very much value the comments of practitioners, staff and students. Legal vocational training is advancing rapidly, and it is important that all those concerned work together to achieve and maintain high standards. Please address any comments to the Bar Vocational Course Director at the Inns of Court School of Law.

With the validation of other providers for the Bar Vocational Course it is very much our intention that these manuals will be of equal value to all students wherever they take the course, and we would value comments from tutors and students at other validated institutions

The enthusiasm of the staff at Blackstone Press Ltd and their efficiency in arranging the production and publication of these manuals is much appreciated.

The Hon. Mr Justice Elias
Chairman of the Board of Governors
Inns of Court School of Law
December 1999

CONTENTS

CONTENTS

TABLE OF CASES AND COMMISSION DECISIONS

TABLE OF UK LEGISLATION

TABLE OF EUROPEAN COMMUNITY TREATIES

TABLE OF EUROPEAN COMMUNITY SECONDARY LEGISLATION

ONE

INTRODUCTION

1.1   What the Manual is Intended to Do

The EC has, among its aims, the raising of living standards and a harmonious development of economic activities (Article 2, EC Treaty). It seeks to achieve these aims largely through the mechanism of a common market. To this end, certain specific tasks (or 'activities') are imposed on the Community in Article 3, EC Treaty; primarily (for our purposes) a 'system ensuring that competition in the internal market is not distorted'. In Part Three of the Treaty, under 'Title VI. Common rules on competition, taxation and approximation of laws', you find 'Chapter I. Rules on Competition'. This is divided into two sections:

Section 1. Rules applying to undertakings
Section 2. Aids granted by States

We are mainly concerned here with those Articles which deal with undertakings, that is, Articles 81–86 (ex 85-90) and, in the space available, we shall concentrate almost exclusively on the 'substantive' competition laws: Articles 81 (ex 85) and 82 (ex 86). The European Court of First Instance has described these Articles as 'independent and complementary provisions designed, in general, to regulate distinct situations by different rules'.

These Articles are interpreted and applied primarily by the European Commission. Article 83 (ex 87), EC Treaty, requires the EC Council to pass legislation to give effect to the principles set out in Articles 81 (ex 85) and 82 (ex 86): it refers explicitly to the need to 'define the respective functions of the Commission and of the Court of Justice in applying' the legislation. This is taken further in Article 85 (ex 89), EC Treaty, which states that, as soon as the Commission takes up its duties, it shall ensure the application of the principles laid down in Articles 81 (ex 85) and 82 (ex 86). The Commission is to investigate cases of suspected infringement. If proved, the Commission is to propose appropriate measures to bring the infringement to an end.

In addition to the relevant Articles in the Treaty, the competition rules of the European Community are found in regulations issued under the authority of the Treaty by the Council or Commission and in case law, that is, decisions of the Commission made in individual cases and the judgments of the Court of Justice and Court of First Instance. The Commission also issues notices from time to time indicating its policy on certain topics (e.g., the Notice on Agreements of Minor Importance).

The first piece of secondary legislation to appear pursuant to Article 83 (ex 87) was Council Regulation 17/62 (in force from 13 March 1962). This sets out in detail the powers and duties of the Commission in the field of competition. It will be examined in detail later (see **Chapter 7**).

The recital to Regulation 17 makes the point that all decisions taken by the Commission under the Regulation are subject to review by the Court of Justice of the European Communities (ECJ), in accordance with the Court's jurisdiction as laid down by the

Treaty. This allows the Court to review the procedural or substantive merits of a decision. Now, the *initial* judicial review will be undertaken by the Court of First Instance (a more recent creation, which first sat in 1989).

For ease of reference, Articles 81 (ex 85) and 82 (ex 86) and Council Regulation 17/62 are printed in full at **2.1**, **5.1** and **Appendix 1**, respectively. Other measures are not printed in full but are set out in the text as appropriate (e.g., Articles from the 'block exemption' on exclusive distribution, Regulation 1983/83 (see **Appendix 2**).

It was said above that we are going to concentrate on Articles 81 (ex 85) and 82 (ex 86): the 'competition' rules. However, it is also important to be aware of related topics which sometimes interact with or are relevant to the operation of those Articles. So **Chapter 10** looks briefly at the rules governing free movement of goods throughout the Community, and includes a short explanation of intellectual property rights.

1.2   Brief History of the European Union and its Institutions

1.2.1   THE CREATION AND MEMBERSHIP OF THE EUROPEAN UNION

The European Community grew out of the movement towards international cooperation after World War II. The Council of Europe grew from the same impetus.

The foundations were laid by Robert Schuman, the French Foreign Minister at the time, in his declaration made on 9 May 1950. He set out a plan he and Jean Monnet had devised to combine the European coal and steel industries in a European Community for Coal and Steel. The European Coal and Steel Community (ECSC) was established a year later by the signing of the Treaty of Paris on 18 April 1951 and came into force in 1952.

The European Economic Community and the European Atomic Energy Community (Euratom) were formed by the same original six states (France, Germany, Italy, Belgium, The Netherlands, Luxembourg) signing the Treaties of Rome (EEC Treaty and Euratom Treaty) on 25 March 1957.

The United Kingdom, Ireland and Denmark joined on 1 January 1973 and Greece entered in 1981. Spain and Portugal followed in 1986, and most recently Finland, Sweden and Austria, so that total membership is now 15 States, with a combined population of some 370 million people. Moves are now going ahead for the further enlargement of the EU to a possible 26 Member States. Negotiations are reported to be in place with Hungary, Poland, Romania, Slovakia, Latvia, Estonia, Lithuania, Bulgaria, the Czech Republic, Slovenia and Cyprus. Any enlargement is unlikely before the year 2000.

There is not just one European Community (although from 1 July 1993, the EEC has been known as the European Community). Three separate Communities have existed since the entry into force of the Treaties of Rome, each based on its own foundation treaty. No formal merger of the three Communities has ever taken place although the three now share a single Council and a single Commission. Regardless of their differences, the three Communities are regarded as one unit. They share the same basic objectives expressed by the same Member States and share the same legal structure and institutions. All three Communities are by common usage referred to as the European Community. Under the ECSC Treaty the Community has the task of administering the coal and steel industries. The European Atomic Energy Community concerns the utilisation of atomic energy within the Community and research connected with it.

On 1 January 1993, the (then) 12 Member States of the European Community evolved into the 'European Union' (EU) as the result of the Treaty on European Union signed at Maastricht on 7 February 1992. The original EC Treaty of Rome continues in force, though, as amended over the years since 1957, so we need not put aside the idea of the European Community and its laws just yet. (We should also note that the other two 'European' treaties — those establishing the ECSC and Euratom — continue to exist as well.) The Treaty on European Union made some changes to the EC Treaty but the institutions created in 1957 carry on into the European Union and often continue to derive their functions from the EC Treaty. In particular, Article 2 of the TEU states that the EU will 'maintain in full', 'respect' and 'build on' the *acquis communautaire* (or the acts of the EC as interpreted and applied since the beginning). The TEU does go further than the Treaty of Rome in one salient respect, though — in Article 6 the EU states that it will 'respect fundamental rights, as guaranteed by the European Convention for the Protection of Human Rights and Fundamental Freedoms [1950] . . . and as they result from the constitutional traditions common to the Member States, as general principles of Community law'.

Without wishing to confuse the reader too much, we should also remember that on 1 January 1994, the Agreement on a European Economic Area (EEA) came into effect. This brought together, as a single territory, the Member States of the European Community with those countries belonging to the European Free Trade Association (except Switzerland) in many important economic areas, for example free movement of goods and rules governing business competition. Extra institutions have been created for the EEA, together with new rules, but any examination of them in this Manual would make it unduly long and complicated; it should also be remembered that three members of the EFTA subsequently joined the EU (see above), leaving Iceland, Lichtenstein and Norway outside the EU but within the EEA.

1.2.2 WHAT ARE THE TASKS OF THE EUROPEAN COMMUNITY?

The underlying goals for creating the European Community are set out in the preamble of the EC Treaty, as amended. They are mainly economic but also include social goals, and even political ideals such as laying 'the foundations of an ever closer union among the peoples of Europe' and 'pooling their resources to preserve and strengthen peace and liberty'. These ideals are continued and expanded in the preamble to the Treaty on European Union.

The European Community was formed to create a single European market uniting the national markets of the Member States and in which goods and services could be offered and sold under common conditions, usually in a free, competitive market. Freedom of movement for capital and labour were also to be secured.

In order to evolve the common economic market, the national economic policies of the Member States were to be gradually harmonized insofar as they fell within the EC's jurisdiction.

The Community's tasks are outlined in the EC Treaty:

Article 2 (as amended):
The Community shall have as its task, by establishing a common market and an economic and monetary union and by implementing common policies or activities referred to in Articles 3 and 4, to promote throughout the Community a harmonious, balanced and sustained development of economic activities, a high level of employment and of social protection, equality between men and women, sustainable and non-inflationary growth, a high degree of competitiveness and convergence of economic performance, a high level of protection and improvement of the quality of the environment, the raising of the standard of living and quality of life, and economic and social cohesion and solidarity among Member States.

To facilitate the establishment of the market, the Community is to engage in the following activities:

Article 3 (as amended):
For the purposes set out in Article 2, the activities of the Community shall include, as provided in this Treaty and in accordance with the timetable set out therein:

(a) the prohibition, as between Member States, of customs duties and of quantitative restrictions on the import and export of goods, and of all other measures having equivalent effect;

(b) a common commercial policy;

(c) an internal market characterised by the abolition, as between Member States of obstacles to the free movement of goods, persons, services and capital;

(d) measures concerning the entry and movement of persons as provided for in Title IV;

(e) a common policy in the sphere of agriculture and fisheries;

(f) a common policy in the sphere of transport;

(g) a system ensuring that competition in the internal market is not distorted;

(h) the approximation of the laws of Member States to the extent required for the functioning of the common market;

(i) the promotion of coordination between employment policies of the Member States with a view to enhancing their effectiveness by developing a coordinated strategy for employment;

(j) a policy in the social sphere comprising a European Social Fund;

(k) the strengthening of economic and social cohesion;

(l) a policy in the sphere of the environment;

(m) the strengthening of the competitiveness of Community industry;

(n) the promotion of research and technological development;

(o) encouragement for the establishment and development of trans-European networks;

(p) a contribution to the attainment of a high level of health protection;

(q) a contribution to education and training of quality and to the flowering of the cultures of the Member States;

(r) a policy in the sphere of development cooperation;

(s) the association of the overseas countries and territories in order to increase trade and to promote jointly economic and social development;

(t) a contribution to the strengthening of consumer protection;

(u) measures in the spheres of energy, civil protection and tourism.

In all other activities referred to in this Article, the Community shall aim to eliminate inequalities, and to promote equality, between men and women.

These activities are developed in more detail in later provisions of the EC Treaty.

The EC Treaty extends to social matters including *inter alia*:

(a) cooperation between Member States on employment, labour law and working conditions, vocational training and social security;

(b) prevention of occupational accidents and diseases and improvements in occupational hygiene;

(c) the right of association and collective bargaining between workers and employers (Article 140 (ex 118)); and

(d) equal pay for men and women (Article 141 (ex 119)).

The Community has by the EC Treaty assumed competence in all of these areas. However, the founding treaties have not given the Community power to deal with all aspects of national sovereignty so that matters like defence, diplomacy, education and culture remain outside the Community's jurisdiction. Even so, the Community has partial competence in some of these areas (e.g. diplomacy and education).

The Single European Act 1986 (SEA) amended the EC Treaty. It provided additional objectives and thus enlarged the scope of Community competence. The SEA was signed by all 12 Member States. Incorporation into UK law was brought about by the European Communities (Amendment) Act 1986.

The SEA provided for a formal framework for political cooperation between Member States which had not been covered by the EC Treaty (see below). It set out new goals for economic and monetary cooperation, health and safety of workers, regional policy, research and technological development and environmental protection. It made procedural changes which accelerated progress towards a single internal market by 1992 and moved Member States nearer to European integration. The scope of the Treaty as amended by the SEA was very broad and was expanded much further by both the TEU and the Treaty of Amsterdam, as can be seen in the amended Article 3 above. The Community has been given competence to deal with important areas of economic and social activity which had hitherto been within the sole competence of Member States.

A Community law point may arise in cases involving any of these areas.

1.2.3 THE INSTITUTIONS OF THE EUROPEAN COMMUNITY

The three Communities share common institutions which carry out their tasks. The major ones are: the European Parliament, the Commission of the European Community, the Council (formerly called the Council of Ministers), the European Court of Justice (ECJ) and the Court of First Instance (CFI). In addition to the Economic and Social Committee, which has a purely consultative role, the more recent, and perhaps more minor, community institutions are:

- The Court of Auditors.

- The European Investment Bank.

- The Committee of the Regions.

- The European Ombudsman.

- The European Monetary Institute.

- The Office for the Harmonization of the International Market (perhaps strictly an 'agency' rather than an institution).

An enormous amount of material about the institutions is accessible on the Internet, at http://europa.eu.int/inst-en.htm. See also **Appendices 6** and **7**.

1.2.3.1 The function and powers of the European Commission

The Commission, sometimes called the 'guardian of the Treaties', consists of 20 members (Commissioners) who are appointed by the governments of their own Member States and agreed to by all the Member States. The Amsterdam Treaty 1997 declares that there will be only one Commissioner from each Member State in the future; those countries which at present have two Commissioners (Germany, UK, France, Italy and Spain) will give up their second Commissioner. They do not represent their own countries as they are supposed to be above national loyalties and their independence should be beyond doubt. In performance of their duties they must 'neither seek nor take instructions from any government or any body'. A breach of this principle by a Commissioner would mean his or her compulsory retirement which the ECJ would request the Commissioner to take. See generally Article 213 (ex 157), EC Treaty, as inserted by the Treaty on European Union.

The function of the Commission is threefold:

(a) It is to initiate proposals on any matter provided for under the Treaty (Articles 208 (ex 152) and 308 (ex 235), EC Treaty).

(b) It acts as the Community watchdog. Article 10 (ex 5) of the EC Treaty states:

Member States shall take all appropriate measures, whether general or particular, to ensure fulfilment of the obligations arising out of this Treaty or resulting from action taken by the institutions of the Community. They shall facilitate the achievement of the Community's tasks.

> *They shall abstain from any measure which could jeopardise the attainment of the objectives of this Treaty.*

The Commission investigates (and takes to the ECJ) any Member State which infringes the EC Treaty, under Article 226 (ex 169). It also has the task of administering and enforcing EC competition policy. It can impose fines and penalties on individuals and companies who are in breach of this policy.

(c) The Commission also acts as the manager and executor of Community policies. If the Council makes a policy decision, it falls to the Commission to carry it out. This usually means adopting further, detailed, legislation to implement the policy.

Subject to any review by the European Court, the European Commission is the investigator, judge and jury in competition 'trials'. A complaint was made in *Musique Diffusion Française* v *Commission* (100–103/80) [1983] ECR 1825 (the 'Pioneer' case) that this multiplicity of roles was a breach of due process of law, contrary to Article 6 of the European Convention on Human Rights. The complaint was rejected by the Court of Justice, which indicated that the Commission was not a tribunal within the meaning of Article 6 of the Convention. The same point was raised subsequently before the European Commission on Human Rights in *Société Stenuit* v *France* [1992] EHRR 509. The Commission felt that the nature of investigations under Regulation 17 was such that Article 6(1) of the European Convention should apply to them. The Commission on Human Rights said that, regardless of the procedural safeguards that competition proceedings now have, the European Community Commission is both plaintiff/prosecutor and judge, there is no presumption of innocence and the burden of proof on the EC Commission is only to a civil standard. It was felt that none of these elements complied with Article 6(1) of the Convention. There have been suggestions that there should be an independent 'Competition Authority', distinct from the Commission. For example, in October 1994 the head of the German Cartel Office recommended that the competition decisions which are currently made by the Commission should instead be made by an independent authority so that political interference might be reduced (see *Financial Times*, 3 October 1994; and Alan Riley, 'The European Cartel Office: A Guardian Without Weapons' [1997] ECLR 3). However, this is unlikely to be created in the short to medium term. Indeed, the head of DG IV, Dr Claus-Dieter Ehlermann, has expressed the opinion that the Commission, rather than the Council of Ministers, possesses the fundamental power in the matter of competition policy.

The Commission investigates either on its own initiative or following a complaint made to it, using its own officials to elicit information; it then decides whether the law has been infringed. If it finds that there has been an infringement, the conduct is prohibited and the Commission either requires termination of the conduct and/or imposes a fine or (under Article 81 (ex 85) only) grants an exemption.

1.2.3.2 **The functions and powers of the Council of the European Union**

The Council ensures the coordination of the general economic policy of the Member States and has the final power to make decisions in the decision-making process of the Community. Its final say is subject usually to consultation with the Parliament. Any legislation it adopts must first, however, be proposed by the Commission. The Council decides some matters by qualified majority voting, while others require unanimity (it depends under which enabling Article of the Treaty the proposed legislation is introduced). Under the Amsterdam Treaty, the weighting of Member States in the Council will be adjusted so that a majority decision of the Council will represent a similar proportion of the population of the EU.

Each Member State has one member on the Council but the identity of the actual delegate fluctuates and will depend on the topic being decided. The actual member will be the Head of Government for important issues or the appropriate government minister on specialist issues.

As the Council is not a permanent body and meets for only a few days each month, the day-to-day work is done by the Committee of Permanent Representatives, COREPER, and a system of Management Committees.

1.2.3.3 The European Parliament

The European Parliament was originally called the Assembly in the EC Treaty (formally changing its name in the SEA 1987). It has over 600 members, including 87 from the UK. The Amsterdam Treaty of 1997 sets a ceiling of 700 members of the European Parliament (or MEPs). This figure is intended to remain the ceiling for some time, even after the probable expansion of the EU from the present 15 Member States up to 20. The Parliament represents the political and other views of all the peoples of the Member States.

The Parliament's powers have been expanded considerably by the Treaty on European Union. For example, Article 251 (ex 189b), EC Treaty (inserted by the EU Treaty) not only involves the Parliament fully in the procedure for the adoption of an act, but allows Parliament to veto such adoption (i.e. it can prevent proposed legislation from becoming law). Article 252 (ex 189c) (an alternative procedure for the adoption of acts) contains no such veto. Under Article 192 (ex 138b) (again inserted by the EU Treaty), the Parliament may initiate the legislative process by requesting the Commission to submit proposals on topics that Parliament considers require legislation.

1.3 National Use

The extent to which national courts make use of Articles 81 (ex 85) and 82 (ex 86) varies from State to State. This was examined by the Commission through a questionnaire sent to the Member States in 1985. Although the response was very patchy (due to an absence of systematic gathering of information) the Commission concluded that:

> ... in principle, there are no fundamental obstacles to the application of Community competition law by national courts.... Until now it is clear that the Community competition rules have generally been pleaded as a basis for obtaining an injunction or other interim relief or as a defence to an action for breach of contract. There does not appear, to the Commission's knowledge, to be any case in which damages have been awarded by a national court for a breach of either Article 85 [now 81] or Article 86 [now 82] of the EC Treaty. (16th Report on Competition Policy, 1987.)

In 1993, the Commission issued Guidelines for national courts when applying Articles 81 (ex 85) and 82 (ex 86) in 'domestic' litigation. The use of Articles 81 and 82 in English courts is examined in **Chapter 8**.

It is also now possible in some Member States for their competition authorities to use Articles 81 (ex 85) and 82 (ex 86) (or suitably amended variants) against undertakings whose activities do not attract the attention of the European Commission. In the United Kingdom this is not currently the situation. However, when the relevant parts of the Competition Act 1998 are brought into force (expected to be in March 2000), the Office of Fair Trading (OFT) will be able to apply statutory rules, virtually identical to Articles 81 and 82, to anti-competitive actions which may affect trade within the United Kingdom. The previous mélange of statutes which provided the regulatory framework for competition affairs in the United Kingdom will largely be replaced (for example, the Resale Prices Act 1976, the Restrictive Trade Practices Act 1977 and some parts of the Competition Act 1980). The European Commission is keen to delegate work to bodies in the Member States, where appropriate. Guidelines for cooperation between the Commission and national competition authorities were issued in 1997 and it is possible for the Commission to find that a complaint made to it lacks Community interest but should be referred to the appropriate national authority (in the UK, this is usually the OFT). Currently, OFT officials assist those of the European Commission when they investigate cases in the UK and, in such circumstances, the OFT can exercise the investigative powers vested in the European Commission by EC Regulation 17/62. The Competition Act 1998 allows High Court judges to issue search warrants, backing up the investigative actions of the Commission. The 1998 Act also makes it a criminal offence for anyone intentionally to obstruct a Commission (or OFT) official executing such a warrant (punishable by imprisonment). See **7.3**.

The influence of the EC competition rules can be found in rather unexpected areas in the United Kingdom. Recently, the London Stock Exchange was found (by the Minister for Corporate Affairs) to be in breach of Article 86 (now 82) by virtue of its rules on the dissemination of news about companies. Under the Financial Services Act, the Minister is empowered to direct the Stock Exchange to take specific action if he considers that its conduct conflicts with the Community obligations of the United Kingdom.

1.4 What is an 'Undertaking'?

'Undertakings' is a term that will be referred to many times in this book. There is no definition of it in the EC Treaty, nor in the secondary legislation, although Regulation 17/62 gives some clues as to the probable scope when it deals (in Article 11) with requests to undertakings for information. Article 11 imposes a duty (to supply information) upon:

(a) the owners of undertakings (or their representatives);

(b) the authorised representatives of legal persons, companies or firms;

(c) the authorised representatives of associations which have no legal personality.

It seems in practice that any form of entity which engages in economic activity will be considered by the Commission (and the European Court) to be an undertaking.

Examples have included:

(a) individuals (e.g. *AOIP/Beyrard* [1976] 1 CMLR D14 — an inventor who gave exclusive rights in his invention to a commercial organisation; franchisees like Mrs Schillgalis in *Pronuptia*; even opera singers — *RAI/Unitel* [1978] 3 CMLR 306);

(b) corporations — even of non-EC origin (*Europembellage Corp. and Continental Can Co.* v *Commission* (6/72) [1973] ECR 215; *Ahlström Oy* v *Commission* (89/85 et al.) [1993] 4 CMLR 407 — the woodpulp cartel);

(c) partnerships (*Re William Prym-Werke* [1973] CMLR D250);

(d) non-profit-making organisations which operate to collect artists' royalties commercially (e.g., *GVL* [1983] ECR 483 — a German society which collects copyright royalties); and

(e) organisations which are part of the 'State', where they carry on economic or commercial activities (an example in the UK might be the Post Office).

1.5 The Competition Articles

It should be noted that the Treaty of Amsterdam created a consolidated version of the EC Treaty. The consolidated version can be found, for example, in Foster, *Blackstone's EC Legislation*. The Treaty of Amsterdam came into effect on 1 May 1999 and the Articles containing the competition rules were re-numbered. The two main Articles are (now) Articles 81 and 82. In decisions or regulations of the Commission or Council, or judgments of the European Court, which precede 1 May 1999, you will find these Articles referred to as Articles 85 and 86 respectively. For ease of reference, the current Article numbers are added in square brackets.

1.6 Preliminary Work

Before reading anything else, turn to **2.1** and **5.1** and read the text of Articles 81 (ex 85) and 82 (ex 86) of the Treaty.

TWO

ARTICLE 81(1): ANTI-COMPETITIVE AGREEMENTS

2.1 Introduction

The purpose of Article 81 (ex 85) is to ensure that competition is not restricted, prevented or distorted within the common market as the result of two or more undertakings agreeing to do (or not do) something which runs counter to the normal, competitive, working of the market.

Article 81 (ex 85) is divided into three paragraphs. Paragraph (1) sets out the prohibitory rule itself:

> 1.   The following shall be prohibited as incompatible with the common market: all agreements between undertakings, decisions by associations of undertakings and concerted practices which may affect trade between Member States and which have as their object or effect the prevention, restriction or distortion of competition within the common market, and in particular those which:
> (a)   directly or indirectly fix purchase or selling prices or any other trading conditions;
> (b)   limit or control production, markets, technical development, or investment;
> (c)   share markets or sources of supply;
> (d)   apply dissimilar conditions to equivalent transactions with other trading parties, thereby placing them at a competitive disadvantage;
> (e)   make the conclusion of contracts subject to acceptance by the other parties of supplementary obligations which, by their nature or according to commercial usage, have no connection with the subject of such contracts.

Paragraph (2) simply states the legal effect of such prohibition:

> 2.   Any agreements or decisions prohibited pursuant to this Article shall be automatically void.

Lastly, paragraph (3) creates an exemption for certain agreements etc. which would otherwise be prohibited and void. In order to be exempted, these agreements must comply with certain requirements:

> 3.   The provisions of paragraph 1 may, however, be declared inapplicable in the case of:
> —any agreement or category of agreements between undertakings;
> —any decision or category of decisions by associations of undertakings;
> —any concerted practice or category of concerted practices;

which contributes to improving the production or distribution of goods or to promoting technical or economic progress, while allowing consumers a fair share of the resulting benefit, and which does not:

    (a) impose on the undertakings concerned restrictions which are not indispensable to the attainment of these objectives;

    (b) afford such undertakings the possibility of eliminating competition in respect of a substantial part of the products in question.

We shall look in detail at Article 81(3) (ex 85(3)) in **Chapter 3**. The rest of this chapter will focus on Article 81(1) (ex 85(1)) — the prohibitory rule.

Article 81(1) (ex 85(1)) can be split into several elements, each one of which needs to be satisfied before the prohibition will take effect.

First, there must be a meeting of minds between two or more undertakings to do (or refrain from doing) some act. This may take the form of a written agreement or may be something much less formal. This will be considered in **2.2**.

Secondly, the 'agreement' must have an actual or potential effect on trade between Member States of the European Union. This will be considered in **2.3**.

Thirdly, the parties to the 'agreement' must intend that their agreement shall prevent, restrict or distort competition. Alternatively, it is enough if the 'agreement' does in fact prevent, restrict or distort competition within the common market. This will be considered in **2.4**.

What sort of things might be caught by Article 81(1) (ex 85(1))? Maybe the most obvious example would be the activities of a *cartel* — that is, a group of companies that should be competing with each other under normal competitive conditions but who decide to substitute cooperation for competition. The cartel may decide to split up territories between its members, so that each member has an exclusive area where it faces no effective competition (its 'home' market). Or the cartel may decide upon a common pricing structure for the product, with a view to lessening (or removing entirely) competition in terms of the price charged for the product. The effect of these decisions is to decrease the level of both active and passive competition.

The Commission and the European Court have seldom spoken in practical terms about the way their ideal, competitive, market should work. But the message seems clear that there should be competition between companies operating in the same market: that competition should be reflected in different prices being charged, different services being offered (lots of knowledgeable staff available to advise customers prior to purchase, or self-service and no staff, for example).

2.2 Agreements, Decisions of Associations and Concerted Practices

2.2.1 INTRODUCTION

Article 81(1) (ex 85(1)) distinguishes between three forms of collusion:

- agreements between undertakings

- decisions by associations of undertakings, and

- concerted practices

all of which are described as being 'incompatible with the common market' when they prevent, restrict or distort competition. In practice, the Commission and the Court do not maintain hard and fast divisions between the three. There may be differences as to ease of proof between the three: a piece of paper bearing the word 'Agreement' on its head in gothic script may do the job more swiftly than the detective work that may be needed to demonstrate a concerted practice but there is no magic in the labels themselves.

2.2.2 AGREEMENTS BETWEEN UNDERTAKINGS

A legally-binding contract will be covered. So a patent licence will suffice, as will an exclusive dealership, a tied public house, a fast food franchise agreement. A less formal agreement will also be covered: a morally-binding (or gentlemen's) agreement will fall within Article 81(1) (ex 85(1)). According to the Court of First Instance in *Hercules* v *Commission* (T-7/89) [1991] ECR II-1711:

> ... it is sufficient if the undertakings ... have expressed their joint intention to conduct themselves on the market in a specific way.

The agreement may be between specific parties for a stated period of time. Alternatively, it may have a changing membership with different parties active over different periods. Although this presents problems of proof, this may still be an 'agreement'. Where the Commission investigates such a 'rolling' agreement, it will need to adduce sufficient evidence to show that any particular company was a party to the agreement; the Commission will also need to adduce evidence of the *duration* of that company's participation — this will be relevant to the severity of punishment handed down. As the Court of First Instance observed in *Dunlop Slazenger International Ltd* v *Commission* (T-43/92) [1994] ECR II-441:

> With regard to the alleged duration of an infringement, the ... principle of legal certainty requires that, if there is no evidence directly establishing the duration of an infringement, the Commission should adduce at least evidence of facts sufficiently proximate in time for it to be reasonable to accept that infringement continued uninterruptedly between two specific dates.

As to exactly what the parties have agreed to (in the legally-binding contracts referred to above) there should be no problem, but companies do need to be on their guard. In *Sandoz Prodotti Farmaceutici SpA* v *Commission* (C-277/87) [1990] ECR I-45, the Court of Justice held that tacit acquiescence may lead to the incorporation of terms into the contract. In *Sandoz*, a supplier sent out invoices to his customers, containing the expression 'export prohibited'. When a customer raised no protest about this and continued to order supplies, the expression could become a part of an agreement between the supplier and customer within the scope of Article 81 (ex 85) (re-affirmed by the Court of First Instance in *Dunlop Slazenger International Ltd* v *Commission* (T-43/92) [1994] ECR II-441). For an example of an agreement being inferred from behaviour, see *Tipp-Ex* v *Commission* (C-279/87) [1990] ECR I-261.

Although unilateral acts are not covered by Article 81(1) (ex 85(1)), it is important to consider whether an act which is apparently unilateral may have some underlying, collusive, motive. For example, if a producer decides to terminate its relationship with an exclusive distributor, that looks like a unilateral act. But we must ask why the termination has occurred. If it is the result of pressure being brought to bear on the producer by its other exclusive distributors, maybe because the terminated dealer is undercutting the others on price, then we may have an agreement within the scope of Article 81(1) (ex 85(1)). See further on this: *Holleran* v *Daniel Thwaites* [1989] 2 CMLR 917; *Richard Cound Ltd* v *BMW (G.B.) Ltd*, 10 May 1995, unreported; and *Dunlop Slazenger.*

To fall within Article 81(1) (ex 85(1)), an agreement must be made *between* undertakings, not *within* a single undertaking. So one needs to know when more than one undertaking is involved. This can become problematic when a parent company and its subsidiaries are parties to an agreement. The Commission and the Court have said that parent companies and their subsidiaries form a single economic unit: *Hydrotherm* v *Andreoli* (170/83) [1984] ECR 2999. Any agreements between them (sometimes known as a 'bathtub conspiracy'!) cannot fall foul of Article 81 (ex 85). Thus in *Centrafarm* v *Sterling* (15/74) [1974] ECR 1147 the ECJ said:

> [There is no violation of Article 81 (ex 85) by] agreements or concerted practices between undertakings belonging to the same concern and having the status of parent company and subsidiary, if the undertakings form an economic unit within which the subsidiary has *no real freedom to determine* its course of action on the market, and if the agreements or practices are concerned merely with the internal allocation of tasks as between the undertakings. (Emphasis added.)

(Conversely, this idea of economic unity has been used to fine a parent company for the misdeeds of its subsidiary: see, e.g., *Eurim Pharm GmbH* v *Johnson & Johnson* [1981] 2 CMLR 287; see also *Commercial Solvents Corp.* v *Commission* (6–7/73) [1974] ECR 223.)

What constitutes an agreement for present purposes? It is clear that legally binding contracts are included but it seems that the meaning is broader than this. 'Gentlemen's agreements' are included — in *Boeringer* v *Commission* (7/72) [1972] ECR 1281 a quinine cartel divided up the world market and fixed prices, but its contract expressly excluded the common market. The members of the cartel then wrote down a gentlemen's agreement, which extended the application of the contract to the common market. This was held to be an agreement for the purposes of Article 81 (ex 85) even after its operation was suspended by the members, as the prices set under its terms continued to be used. If two or more entities pursue a joint plan then it may not matter that it cannot be classified as an 'agreement' — it may be labelled as a 'concerted practice' (see **2.2.4**) and still be within the net of Article 81 (ex 85).

The polypropylene cartel which was investigated by the Commission in the early 1980s (see OJ 1986 L230) was alleged to be a 'rolling' agreement which lasted some six years. It was asserted that it had a variety of members at any point in time, who sometimes undercut their (covertly) agreed prices and where meetings occurred at different levels of importance ('bosses' meetings and 'experts' meetings). The Commission found that the basic, detailed plan constructing the cartel was an agreement for the purposes of Article 81(1) (ex 85(1)). We should note that, in the present judicial climate, the Commission would be put to strict proof as to who belonged to the cartel and for what period(s) — see the Court of First Instance in its judgments on the polypropylene cartel decision; e.g., *BASF AG* v *Commission* (T-4/89) [1992] 4 CMLR 357. That the Commission has accepted and discharged that burden of proof may be seen in *Re Cartonboard Cartel* 1994 OJ L243/1 where the participants in a series of regular 'secret and institutionalised meetings' were divided into four groups by the Commission, according to the period of their participation.

2.2.3 DECISIONS BY ASSOCIATIONS OF UNDERTAKINGS

Typically, such associations are trade associations but the expression could include other organisations such as cooperatives. Formal decisions which are approved by the members of a trade association would fall within the scope of Article 81(1) (ex 85(1)) (although they could as easily be classified as a collection of agreements between the members: see e.g., *Groupement des Fabricants de Papiers Peints* v *Commission* (73/74) [1976] ECR 1491). Non-binding recommendations made by a trade association to its members may be regarded as 'decisions': see e.g., *FEDETAB* v *Commission* (209/78)[1980] ECR 3125; *Vereeniging van Cementhandelaren* v *Commission* (8/72) [1972] ECR 977.

If two trade associations reach an agreement, the terms of which will affect their respective members, this may be regarded as both a decision of the associations *and* an agreement between the individual members, rendering both members and associations liable to fines if the agreement infringes Article 81(1) (ex 85(1)): see e.g. *FRUBO* v *Commission* (71/74) [1975] ECR 563. A trade association may be liable for its involvement in a cartel, if undertaken separately from the involvement of individual association members. Two examples can be found in the Commission decisions involving (i) a Finnish board mills association, Finnboard, for its participation in a producers' cartel (*Cartonboard* OJ 1994 L243/1); and (ii) the European Cement Association, Cembureau, for its participation in a cartel comprising Cembureau, eight national associations and 33 producers (*Cement* OJ 1994 L343/1).

2.2.4 CONCERTED PRACTICES

2.2.4.1 Coordination

The expression *concerted practice* is intended to bring within Article 81(1) (ex 85(1)) those forms of cooperation which are more amorphous than a formal oral or written agreement. In a case involving a cartel of dyestuff producers (*ICI* v *Commission* (48/69) [1972] ECR 621), the Court of Justice observed that:

> By its very nature . . . a concerted practice does not have all the elements of a contract but may *inter alia* arise out of coordination which becomes apparent from the behaviour of the participants.

The Court of Justice went on to define a *concerted practice* as:

> a form of coordination between enterprises that has not yet reached the point where there is a contract in the true sense of the word but which, in practice, *consciously substitutes a practical cooperation for the risks of competition.* (Emphasis added.)

This may cause difficulties for the Commission, which bears the burden of proof on the issue, but it will also create problems for companies which find themselves suspected of involvement in a concerted practice. Although there is no burden of proof on the company(ies) in the strict sense, it may make good sense tactically for them to offer explanations for their behaviour which are consistent with the absence of a concerted practice (see e.g., *CRAM and Rheinzink* v *Commission* (29 and 35/83) [1984] ECR 1679).

The evidence adduced to establish the existence of a concerted practice may be direct: a company may decide to cooperate with the Commission (cf. the Commission's Notice on the non-imposition or reduction of fines for 'whistle-blowers' in cartel cases, OJ 1996 C207/4), or detailed records of meetings may be found by the Commission on searching through a company's files (see **Chapter 7** for details of the Commission's investigative powers). More often, the evidence is indirect: there may be evidence that meetings occurred and who attended them but perhaps not what was discussed or what the participants disclosed to each other. One then looks at circumstantial evidence to see what may be inferred from the activities of the suspect companies. If there is evidence of:

(a) meetings between companies that should be competing with each other (in the same product market and same territories), and

(b) identical or very similar actions by these different companies, often on the same date (perhaps announcing identical price rises for the product within days of each other),

then a concerted practice may be inferred. However, the Court of Justice has stated that simply producing evidence of parallel conduct will not suffice as proof of a concerted practice unless that is the only plausible explanation for the conduct (*Re Woodpulp Cartel: Ahlstroem Osakeyhtiö and others* v *Commission* (C-89/85) [1993] ECR I-1307). In that case, the Court's experts found that the structure of the market in woodpulp was a more credible explanation for the companies' pricing policies than any attempt at concertation. In a similar vein, Advocate General Mayras observed in the *ICI* case that:

> [I]t is necessary at the least to show: first, that the conscious parallel behaviour is not exclusively or even mainly due to economic conditions or to the structure of the market; secondly, that, where there is no express meeting of minds, sufficiently clear,

unequivocal presumptions lead to the conviction that the parallel conduct was the result of concertation, of a coordinated policy.

It should be easier for the Commission to discharge its burden of proof where the market is not oligopolistic in nature (see also Van Gerven and Verona [1994] CMLR 31, at p. 601).

In the cases concerning a polypropylene cartel, the Court of First Instance in *Rhône-Poulenc SA* v *Commission* (T-1/89) [1991] ECR II-867, set out what companies must avoid doing in order to avert suspicion. What is forbidden is:

(a) to have contact, whether direct or not, with one's competitors;

(b) if such contact is intended to (or does); either

(c) influence the conduct of a competitor (whether actual or potential); or

(d) disclose to such competitors the intended or possible future conduct of one's own company.

According to the Court of First Instance, each company must work out its policies for itself. That does not mean that they cannot adapt their policies intelligently to respond to the existing and anticipated conduct of their rivals.

The best indicator of a concerted practice seems to be if the Commission can adduce evidence of contact between the alleged participants. Again, though, even this can be inferred from the circumstances. An example is found in the *Dyestuffs* case (*ICI* v *Commission* (48/69)), where the correspondence of behaviour showed a high degree of coordination between the various producers. The Court of Justice observed that the dye producers had raised their prices by similar amounts on three separate occasions. The first point to be noted was that the rates of individual price increases were identical in all the relevant countries. Further, with very few exceptions, the price increases applied to the same dyestuffs. The price rises were put into effect on almost — or even exactly — the same day by producers in the different countries concerned. The orders sent out by several producers contained very similar wording, even with some sentences exactly the same, and were sent out on the same day, sometimes simultaneously. The Court was also furnished with evidence of attendance by producers at meetings in Basel and London but that hardly seemed necessary in light of the remarkable series of coincidences that would need to exist for these events to be explicable on any basis other than concertation.

2.2.4.2 Parallel conduct

The Commission's biggest problem occurs when it tries to infer a concerted practice from circumstantial evidence in an oligopolistic market (or industry). It is forced to rely upon parallel conduct (or coincidences) which, in the absence of evidence of contact between the suspected undertakings, may simply be the natural result of having so few players on the market. Where there are 12 or fewer 'in play', economic theory suggests that similar behaviour (perhaps increasing price at the same time, or by the same amount or percentage) by undertakings may just be the way an oligopolistic market operates. The dividing line between mere parallel behaviour and a concerted practice is a hard one to spot but it must be done. In *Re Polypropylene Cartel*, OJ 1986 L230, the Commission stated that while it is not very important to maintain a strict distinction between 'agreements' and 'concerted practices', what matters is distinguishing a concerted practice from the simple parallel behaviour of companies who are not colluding.

2.3 Effect on Inter-State trade

2.3.1 WHY YOU NEED TO CONSIDER THIS

This phrase introduces the intra-Community element into Article 81 (ex 85), an idea similar to that which can be seen in some of the cases on free movement of workers (e.g., *Morson & Jahnjan v Netherlands* (35 and 36/82) [1982] ECR 3723). The idea is that there should be a single common market with goods circulating freely within it. If one's behaviour cannot affect trade *between* Member States, then it is outside the scope of the EC Treaty.

The phrase may be taken, then, as indicating the boundary between the jurisdiction of the EC rules on competition and the competition laws of the Member States. This was certainly the position adopted by the Court of Justice in *Hugin/Liptons v Commission* (22/78) [1979] ECR 1869. However, it is quite limited because the Court usually gives a generous interpretation of those matters which may affect trade between Member States — for example, it will acknowledge the jurisdiction of the Community rules even where behaviour has only an indirect or even potential effect on trade between Member States: see, e.g., Advocate-General Trabucchi in *Groupement des Fabricants de Papiers Peints v Commission* (73/74) [1976] ECR 1491, who suggested that, in time, the idea of 'an effect on trade between Member States' would simply mean that the effect of the behaviour must be '... such as to be significant at Community level', regardless of frontiers or geographic areas.

It has been suggested (by Dr Ehlermann of DG IV) that the inclusion of a requirement of an 'effect on inter-State trade' in Article 81 (ex 85) was an early forerunner of the *subsidiarity* principle (introduced by the Maastricht Treaty to indicate that matters of purely local/national importance should fall outside the scope of the European Community).

Agreements have been found to have an effect on trade between Member States even though they are restricted expressly to cover a single country. Examples are:

(a) *Vereeniging van Cementhandelaren v Commission* (8/72) [1972] ECR 977— price fixing between Dutch cement producers, limited to sales in The Netherlands but which, the Court said, made the Dutch market more difficult for foreign cement producers to operate in or penetrate.

(b) *Papiers Peints (supra)* — loyalty discounts to customers who bought in bulk from Groupement members, but only within Belgium. The Court acknowledged that, in theory, the alleged behaviour could have an effect on trade between Member States, but quashed the decision of the Commission because it was not sufficiently reasoned (and thus fell foul of Article 253 (ex 190), EC Treaty).

This is likely to remain the situation, notwithstanding the view of the Commission that 'agreements whose actual or potential effect [is] limited to the territory of only one Member State' will not come under Community law but will be a matter for national law. The Commission recognises that agreements made between undertakings established in only one Member State may be within Article 81(1) (ex 85(1)) where they concern intra-community imports or exports from that State. Similarly, as the Commission has also noted:

so-called 'national' agreements, in which only the undertakings of one Member State participate and which were created with the sole aim of regulating the production or the marketing of products in that Member State, are covered by Article 85(1) [now 81(1)] when they cover the whole or the greater part of the national territory, because they grant an artificial protection to national industry and therefore impede the economic interpenetration envisaged in the [EC] Treaty.

(Commission Notice relating to the revision of the notice of 3 September 1986 on agreements of minor importance which are not caught by the provisions of Article 85(1) of the EC Treaty, 1996.)

A typical example of a clause which had a direct effect on inter-State trade is found in *Consten and Grundig v Commission* (56 & 58/64) [1966] ECR 299. Specific terms of contracts prohibited exports of Grundig machines from Germany into France other than by the authorised French dealer, Consten. Grundig transferred its French trademark, 'Gint', to Consten. When an unauthorised exporter shipped (cheaper) German Grundig machines into France and undercut Consten's prices, Consten started litigation in France alleging, *inter alia*, breach of its trademark rights. The matter was then brought to the attention of the Commission and subsequently to the European Court on appeal. The insulation of the French market from imports clearly affected trade between Member States.

2.3.2   AGREEMENTS OF MINOR IMPORTANCE

Returning to the remark of Advocate-General Trabucchi that the effect of the behaviour must be 'significant at Community level', it is important to note that not all effects on inter-State trade will fulfil this criterion of Article 81 (ex 85). The Commission has issued notices defining what constitutes economically significant activity for the purposes of Article 81 (ex 85). In the past, these 'notices on Agreements of Minor Importance' have tried to remove small and medium-sized firms from the operation of Article 81(1) (ex 85(1)). The philosophy which underpinned them was that such companies must be encouraged to thrive and expand. Only by doing so might they grow and provide a challenge to bigger, more established, firms. The result would be a more competitive market in the longterm. As recently as 1997, the Commission used a Notice which it originally issued in 1986. This excused agreements from Article 85(1) (now 81(1)) where their effect on inter-State trade or on competition was 'negligible' or which had 'no appreciable effect'. An appreciable effect was defined in terms of market share and turnover. The market share of the contract goods or services could not exceed 5%, and the annual aggregate turnover of the participating firms should be less than ECU 300 million. Both figures might be exceeded by no more than 10% in any two succesive financial years.

In December 1997, the Commission moved away from its rather simplistic aim of protecting small and medium-sized firms through the criterion of turnover. What is important now is just the market share of a firm. Even a large company may now find that its agreement does not have an appreciable effect on competition if its market share is insignificant. In its new Notice on Agreements of Minor Importance (OJ 1997 C 372), the Commission distinguished vertical and horizontal agreements. Horizontal agreements are seen as being a bigger threat to the proper working of a competitive market. Vertical agreements are regarded as a threat to competition only when they foreclose markets or suppliers from their competitors and, generally, their anti-competitive effects are often outweighed 'by the positive influence which such contracts may have on the development of dynamic competition in a single market'.

The distinction between the 'good' vertical agreements and the 'bad' horizontal agree-ments comes in para. 9 of the Notice. The relevant threshold is a market share (for all participating undertakings on any relevant market) of:

(a)   5% ... where the agreement is made between undertakings operating at the same level of production or of marketing (i.e. horizontal); but

(b)   10% ... where the agreement is made between undertakings operating at different economic levels (i.e. vertical).

These thresholds may be exceeded up to a ceiling of plus 10% within two successive financial years. It is also worth noting that the Commission continues to regard price fixing and sharing markets with such disfavour that Article 81(1) (ex 85(1)) may apply to agreements which have either as their object, notwithstanding that the market shares fall below the relevant threshold. However, the normal means of enforcement against such low key infringements will be through the national competition authori-ties or courts.

Consistent with its approach elsewhere to Article 81(1) (ex 85(1)), the Commission recognises that when looking at market share it must first establish the relevant market. To do so, it will be necessary to define a market in terms of product and territory. The relevant product market is decided by looking at:

- the degree of physical similarity between products;

- any differences in the end use to which products are put;

- price differences between products;

- the cost involved in switching between two potentially competing products;

- easily detectable consumer preferences for one type of product over another.

The relevant geographical market is found by determining the area:

- in which the contract goods compete with products from other sources;

- in which conditions of competition are sufficiently homogenous; and

- which is distinguishable from proximate areas because of appreciably different conditions of competition which apply in those areas.

One should look at the nature and characteristics of the products concerned (e.g. perishable; large bulk, low value; consumer tastes); whether there are barriers to entry; significant differences in market shares for an undertaking in different areas; and any substantial differences in price.

The criteria in the Notice will not save individual agreements, where there are parallel networks of similar agreements whose cumulative effect is to restrict competition.

2.3.3 A REASONED TEST?

The determination of an effect on inter-State trade may now be subject to a 'rule of reason' test, in similar fashion to the rest of Article 81(1) (ex 85(1)) (see **2.4.3**). We can draw this conclusion from the decision of the ECJ in the *Delimitis* case (C-234/89) [1991] ECR I-935. The court considered an 'access' clause in the beer supply agreement between the litigants, which purported to allow the customer to purchase beer from other suppliers, including those in other Member States. If it was a genuine clause, and foreign suppliers could have access to the customer, then the effect on inter-State trade of an exclusive purchase agreement could be minimised so that Article 81(1) (ex 85(1)) need not apply. See further **2.4.4.6** on *Delimitis*.

Against this introduction of a 'rule of reason' must be balanced the interesting opinion of both the CFI and ECJ that a contractual clause which has *never* been implemented may nevertheless have an effect on trade between Member States because its existence may create a 'visual and psychological' effect which contributes to a partitioning of the market. See e.g., the CFI in *Parker Pen Ltd v Commission* (T-77/92) [1994] ECR II-0549.

When considering whether there is an 'effect on trade between Member States,' remember that 'trade' has been broadly construed to cover trade in services as well as goods.

2.4 The Object or Effect of Prevention, Restriction or Distortion of Competition within the Common Market

2.4.1 OBJECT

The European Court treats 'object' as separate from 'effect'. If you are concerned with the object of an agreement, you need not analyse the market to see the effects of the agreement — purpose (or intention) alone is enough: see, e.g., *Re Polypropylene*

Cartel (1986), where the Commission was satisfied that the producers' cartel had an anti-competitive object; it was unnecessary to demonstrate that competition had been affected. You should remember, though, that even if a company is found 'guilty' of having an unlawful objective, the degree of any consequential effect may be examined in order to determine the amount of any financial penalty to be imposed on the company.

The ability to prohibit conduct which is *intended* to have anti-competitive effects is vested in the Commission, by virtue of Article 85 (ex 89). Subject to problems of proof, the Commission may act to prevent business plans from coming into effect, or at least stop them at an early stage. This requirement, that parties have the object of preventing, restricting or distorting competition, has been interpreted quite liberally — see, for example, *Consten and Grundig v Commission* (56 & 58/64) [1966] ECR 299: '. . . it is not necessary to take into consideration the actual effects of an agreement where its purpose is to prevent, restrict or distort competition'. The agreements between Consten and Grundig were *designed* to isolate the French market and artificially maintain separate national markets within the Community for products of a widely distributed brand. This meant that there was a distortion of competition within the common market.

These matters were considered by the Court of Justice in the *Sandoz* case (C-277/87) [1990] ECR I-45) where Sandoz raised three objections to the allegation that its conduct had the object or effect of preventing, restricting or distorting competition. Sandoz said:

(a)   the conduct (inclusion of the words 'not to be exported' on an invoice) was void under national (Italian) law;

(b)   there had been no allegation that its conduct had an adverse effect on trade between Member States;

(c)   it had done nothing to enforce observance of the clause by its customers.

All three points were rejected by the Court: it was unnecessary that the agreement be valid in national law — Article 81 (ex 85) was concerned only with the parties' intention; if it appeared that an agreement had the objective of preventing (etc.) competition within the common market, it was unnecessary to have regard to the specific effects of the agreement; the absence of enforcement was not sufficient to excuse the clause from the prohibition in Article 81(1) (ex 85(1)). One can see that the Court of Justice is still determined to take a tough line on 'offenders' by its adherence to a teleological interpretation of the phrase 'object or effect' in Article 81(1) (ex 85(1)). That the Court of First Instance adopts the same attitude can be seen in, e.g., *Solvay v Commission* (T-12/89) [1992] ECR II-907.

2.4.2   EFFECT

The effect must be established by means of a market analysis (and see **2.4.3**). In *Volk v Vervaecke* (5/69) [1969] ECR 295 the Court demanded that there must be an 'appreciable' or not insignificant effect on the market. This means that agreements between undertakings who hold only a small share of the market may fall outside of the scope of Article 81 (ex 85). That idea was first given some formal detail in 1970, when the Commission issued its first *Notice on Agreements of Minor Importance.* Originally set up to facilitate cooperation between small and medium-sized undertakings, the Notice has been amended so that now even quite large companies can get the benefit of it, so long as their combined share of the relevant market is small.

The Court considered the concept of behaviour which has the effect of restricting competition within the common market in *Ahlström Oy v Commission* (C-89, 104, 114, 116–7/85, C-125-129/85) [1993] 4 CMLR 407) (the woodpulp cartel). The defendant undertakings were companies based outside the EC who sold woodpulp to paper manufacturers based in the EC and who had been found guilty (by the Commission) of fixing the prices of these sales by means of agreements and other concerted practices. On appeal, the defendants alleged that they were outside the jurisdiction of the EC competition rules. The Court held that if woodpulp producers established in non-EC countries sold directly to purchasers established in the Community and engaged in price competition in order to win orders from those purchasers, that would constitute competition *within* the common market. Where, as here, those woodpulp producers jointly fixed the prices at which they would sell to EC customers and then sold at such prices: '. . . they are taking part in concertation which has the object and effect of restricting competition within the common market'. This is a very simplistic analysis but is perhaps best explained by the fact that the Court was only concerned with the jurisdiction of the Commission to investigate and fine the non-EC enterprises, rather than the merits of the Commission's decision.

Whilst one should not demean the significance of this element in Article 81(1) (ex 85(1)), the usual finding of the Commission is that competition has been restricted in some way without too rigorous an analysis. This may be because an agreement which infringes Article 81(1) is automatically void (Article 81(2)) unless it is granted an exemption under Article 81(3). According to Regulation 17/62, only the Commission has the power to grant an exemption and it can impose conditions on an undertaking in order to qualify for an exemption. Thus, by finding that an undertaking has infringed Article 81(1), the Commission concentrates a lot of power in its hands.

This simplistic approach to economic analysis for the purposes of Article 81(1) has come under attack on two grounds. First, it is not good enough to perform a full economic analysis under Article 81(3): one can see why the Commission wants to do things that way but there should be a proper analysis initially to determine whether conduct is anti-competitive, whether by purpose or effect. This approach has been advocated by the Court of First Instance: see, for example, its judgment in *Delimitis* v *Henninger Braü AG* (and see **2.4.4.6**). This shift was further reinforced by the reliance on reports by economic experts in the Court of Justice when it heard the *Ahlström Oy* case. The second challenge to the Commission's preferred way of working is the application of a 'rule of reason' — this is examined below.

2.4.3 RULE OF REASON

Examples of behaviour which has been found to have the effect of preventing, restricting or distorting competition and which may be prohibited by Article 81(1) (ex 85(1)) include:

(a) non-competition clauses;

(b) restrictions on use of know-how, patents;

(c) non-challenge clauses;

(d) restrictions on conditions of resale;

(e) price-fixing (other than within a specific contract);

(f) export bans;

(g) tying the sale of one product to that of another;

(h) exclusive purchase clauses;

(i) exclusive sale clauses.

The Court of Justice indicated in *Pronuptia de Paris* v *Schillgalis* (161/84) [1986] ECR 353 that it was prepared to consider the necessity of such clauses or, in other words, how reasonable it is that commercial agreements contain such clauses. Prior to this case, such matters had been considered but only under Article 85(3) (now 81(3)) when the Commission was deciding whether to grant an exemption to an otherwise void agreement. In *Pronuptia* the Court considered whether such clauses were economically justified in order to determine whether the agreement was prohibited by Article 85(1) (now 81(1)) at all.

The *Pronuptia* case involved a dispute concerning a distribution franchise. Mrs Schillgalis owned a shop where she had a franchise from Pronuptia to sell goods supplied by them (e.g., wedding dresses) and related services. The Court held that franchising was a business method which promoted competition and that, without certain types of protection, the franchisor would not grant a franchise that obliged him to supply know-how and training and generally to support a franchisee. Certain clauses which were prima facie restrictive of competition were fundamental to the franchisor's willingness to grant a franchise, e.g. clauses which prohibited the franchisee from competing with the franchise network or disclosing confidential information to people outside the network. In the opinion of the Court, when performing the analysis under Article 85(1) (now 81(1)) to see if these clauses had the effect of preventing, restricting or distorting competition, one had to balance any identifiable anti-competitive effects against any effects which were pro-competitive. In *Pronuptia*, such pro-competitive effects could be seen because franchising helps small businesses to start up, thus increasing consumer choice. In the past, the presence of pro-competitive effects had always been considered, but for the purpose of an exemption under Article 85(3) (now 81(3)) (see further **3.2** below). If the Commission was now to weigh such considerations under Article 81(1) (ex 85(1)), one might ask what was left to consider on the issue of exemption? Indeed, the European Commission has posed this very question itself, while at the same time acknowledging that it had 'adopted this approach to a limited extent' and that

> the current division between paragraph 1 and paragraph 3 in implementing Article 81 is artificial and runs counter to the integral nature of Article 81, which requires economic analysis of the overall impact of restrictive practices. (See *White Paper on Modernisation of the Rules implementing Articles 81 and 82 of the EC Treaty*, April 1999.)

There is no doubt that the ECJ intended, in *Pronuptia*, to alter significantly the way in which we should analyse agreements under Article 81(1) (ex 85(1)). This intention was reinforced by its subsequent judgment in *Delimitis* v *Henninger Braü AG* (see **2.4.4.6**). But the Commission remains cautious:

> if more systematic use were made under Article 81(1) of an analysis of the pro- and anti-competitive aspects of a restrictive agreement, Article 81(3) would be cast aside, whereas any such change could be made only through revision of the Treaty. (*White Paper*, 1999.)

In December 1997, the Commission issued a Notice on the 'definition of the relevant market for the purposes of Community competition law' (OJ 1997 C 372). The Notice sets out how the Commission will ascertain the relevant market, in terms of product(s) and geography. This is nothing new when analysing behaviour under Article 82 (ex 86) (see **5.2**) but the Notice is quite explicit in its relevance to Article 81 (ex 85), too:

> Market definition is a tool to identify and define the boundaries of competition between firms. It allows to establish [sic] the framework within which competition policy is applied by the Commission. The main purpose of market definition is to identify in a systematic way the competitive constraints that the undertakings involved face.

> The objective of defining a market in both its product and geographic dimensions is to identify those actual competitors of the undertakings involved that are capable of constraining their behaviour and of preventing them from behaving independently of an effective competitive pressure. [So far, this is quite standard for Article 82 (ex 86)

analysis but the Notice continues] It is from this perspective, that the market definition makes it possible, *inter alia*, to calculate market shares that would convey meaningful information regarding market power for the purposes of assessing dominance *or for the purposes of applying Article 85* [now 81]. (emphasis added)

The Notice is quite explicit on how to define the relevant market:

- the product market 'comprises all those products and/or services which are regarded as interchangeable or substitutable by the consumer, by reason of the products' characteristics, their prices and their intended use'; while

- the geographical market 'comprises the area in which the undertakings concerned are involved in the supply and demand of products or services, in which the conditions of competition are sufficiently homogenous and which can be distinguished from neighbouring areas because the conditions of competition are appreciably different in those areas'.

Once the relevant market has been ascertained, then its total size and the market shares of the relevant undertakings can be determined (either by volume or value, although the Commission prefers the latter as providing a truer picture of the 'relative position and strength' of each supplier).

The Notice states that the market needs to be defined in an Article 81(1) (ex 85(1)) analysis, to see if there is an appreciable effect on competition, as well as under Article 81(3) (ex 85(3)) to see if the criterion in (3)(b) is satisfied. If the Commission has an understanding of the relevant market, when considering if there is evidence of an infringement of Article 81(1) (ex 85(1)), it will be in a sound position to assess both the pro-competitive and anti-competitive effects of the suspect behaviour. This can only be good for the application of a rule of reason to Article 81(1) (ex 85(1)). See further **5.2**.

2.4.4 SOME EXAMPLES

It is useful to look at several types of behaviour mentioned in Article 81(1) (ex 85(1)), to see how and why such behaviour might fall foul of Article 81(1). The examples chosen are: price fixing, limiting production, controlling markets, sharing markets, ties and exclusive purchasing.

2.4.4.1 Price fixing

Price fixing is a real 'no-no', particularly when the parties operate in cartel form, i.e. in a *horizontal* arrangement. The reason for this emphasis on such horizontal cooperation is that it can remove price competition from an entire level of the market place (e.g. all manufacturers of this product) and is thus seen as against the interest of consumers. See, for example, the judgment of the ECJ in *ICI* v *Commission*, at paras 12 and 17.

Horizontal price fixing is traditionally not allowed — it is never acknowledged as 'necessary' or as setting a 'reasonable price'. A good illustration of horizontal price fixing is the case of *Vereeniging van Cementhandelaren* v *Commission* (8/72) [1972] ECR 977, which involved the Dutch Cement Dealers' Association (CDA).

CDA alleged that its system of 'target prices' was rarely adhered to in practice, and did not constitute a restraint on members (see para. 16 of judgment). The ECJ said (para. 21) that price fixing, even of a target, has an effect on competition as it enables all participants to 'predict with a reasonable degree of certainty' what their competitors' pricing policy is going to be.

A similar attitude can be seen in the more recent Commission Decision *Re Scottish Salmon Board* 1992 OJ L246/37:

there was a price-fixing agreement on farmed salmon, between the Scottish Salmon Growers' Association and the Norwegian Fish Farmers' Sales Organisation. This agreement infringed Article 85 [now 81] but there was no fine even though neither party had notified the Commission of the agreement, perhaps as this was the first infringement of Article 85 [now 81] in the economic sector of fish farming. The Commission observed that any concern about low Norwegian prices for salmon could be attacked through the anti-dumping procedure in the EC Treaty, not via an illegal arrangement.

The ban on horizontal price fixing includes indirectly fixing prices, for example, through exchange of information about prices (e.g., discussions on proposed increases; press conferences; exchange of new price lists), or through concertation on discounts (i.e., how much or even deciding not to give them).

Coming more up to date, in 1998 the Commission imposed large fines on price-fixing cartels involving, for example, stainless-steel producers (see OJ 1988 L/100, total fines ecu 27 million) and sugar producers (OJ 1998 L/284, total fines ecu 50 million).

A quote from the XXVIIIth Report of the European Commission on Competition Policy, published in 1999, is also illuminating:

> Of all restrictions of competition, restrictive practices in the form of secret agreements are undoubtedly the most destructive. Very often, these concerted practices involve a substantial number of economic operators in a given area of activity and, as such, they have a very marked impact on the relevant markets. Furthermore, these agreements almost invariably concern prices and thus severely undermine competition. The Commission is committed to an extremely tough stance against cartels ... The positive impact of the launch of the euro ... must not be countered by restrictive agreements designed to side-step market confrontation by artificially fixing prices or other trading conditions, which in the longer term could push up inflation and undermine the foundations of economic and monetary union.

The same prohibitory attitude does not exist for *vertical* agreements. This difference of approach between horizontal and vertical agreements is quite general, and does not apply just in the area of price fixing. The distinction can also be seen in the block exemptions which exclude the application of Article 81(1) (ex 85(1)): they are usually couched in the form of vertical arrangements, with agreements between competitors often specifically excluded. See, e.g., Recital 10 and Article 3(a) of Regulation 1983/83; Article 3(a) of Regulation 1984/83. See also the Green Paper produced by the Commission on Vertical Restraints in Competition Policy 1996.

2.4.4.2 Limiting production

This might involve, for example, establishing quotas for existing companies. It is likely to be linked to price increases with a corresponding fall in production. The idea is to preserve everyone's market share. The victim is the consumer: he has to pay more money to buy the product, there are fewer satisfactory goods available and he is driven to consume inferior substitutes. It should be noted that if there are *acceptable* substitutes, such a system breaks down: see *Rhône-Poulenc SA v Commission* (T-1/89) [1991] ECR II-867.

Limiting technical development is a related prohibition for reasons which are partly economic, partly social. The ban is economic in the sense of preventing wasted resources — money could be better spent in other ways; it is social in the sense of Article 2 EC — seeking to guarantee an increase in living standards.

2.4.4.3 Controlling markets

This might be done through the use of guarantees, e.g., if they are valid only in the country of manufacture, not the country of purchase or use. This would act as a disincentive to buy 'foreign' goods. Typical instances can be seen in the consumer journals for SLR cameras or computer games and equipment, which often warn consumers against the otherwise tempting offers in the 'grey' unofficial import market.

In another economic sector, see the proceedings involving *Honda*, Commission Press Release, August 1992. The Commission looked at, *inter alia*, Honda's spare parts distribution system in Europe. This had allowed Honda importers in single Member States to set up exclusive distribution networks designed to protect their distributors against parallel imports. In the light of the Commission's interest, Honda agreed to introduce a single standard form distribution and servicing agreement for the whole Community. This gave distributors an exclusive right to provide in their territory the guarantee services offered by Honda to purchasers of its motorbikes. In exchange, distributors had to service all users who had a guarantee certificate from Honda, which must accompany the motorbike until it reached the end user.

Also, consider the Commission's response to a question asked in the European Parliament, by Commissioner Van Miert (OJ 1992 C66/40). He stated that the Commission was concerned about major manufacturers who operate over a Community-wide market, offering guarantees which claim to be 'European'. They are actually valid in all Member States but their content and scope vary considerably from one Member State to another. This was seen by the Commission as very unsatisfactory and the Commission had still to investigate the explanations given.

2.4.4.4 Sharing markets

This might involve quotas as the means of restricting competition. It prevents price competition, e.g., through export bans or absolute territorial exclusion, a ban on either an active or passive 'foreign' sales policy. Isolation lessens competition (either inter- or intra-brand) because everyone has their own exclusive territory.

The Commission has often been strongly against such territorial protection but may justify it in certain circumstances, e.g., a new product or market or process. If the risks involved are such that no one would venture into the market without 'protection', it may be in the long-term interests of consumers to permit such protection for at least a short period. It is more likely to be allowed in vertical, rather than horizontal, arrangements. See, e.g., *Nungesser* v *Commission* (258/78) [1982] ECR 2015; *Pronuptia*.

Absolute territorial protection is probably the one major example of a *vertical prohibition*. In this context, we could usefully consider the proceedings involving *Fyffes/ Chiquita Europe*, Commission Press Release, IP(92) 461. C was the largest importer of bananas into the EC, selling principally under the Chiquita trade mark in continental Europe. Prior to 1986, its UK sales were made through Fyffes Group Ltd (FGL), a wholly-owned subsidiary. C also sold bananas under the Fyffes trade mark through Europe, as a secondary brand after introducing its Chiquita brand.

In 1986, C sold off FGL. In an agreement on trade marks, FGL granted C exclusive rights to use the Fyffes trade mark outside the UK and Ireland for three years and a non-use clause, stopping FGL using the Fyffes trade mark for any fresh fruit outside the UK and Ireland until 2006 (or such earlier date as C might decide). After 1989, C stopped using the Fyffes trade mark but would not allow FGL to use it in continental Europe. Following FGL's complaint, the Commission felt the non-use clause restricted competition because of loss of competitive advantage in selling under a strong trade mark. The clause could not be regarded as legitimate protection of C's continental goodwill following sale of the UK company. After agreement on the worldwide use of the trade mark between the parties, the Commission agreed to close its file.

On a similar note, see *Viho/Parker Pen* 1992 OJ L233/27. V, a Dutch company, tried to buy Parker pens in Germany and Italy for resale in The Netherlands. P's distributors in both countries refused to sell to V, alleging that a clause in their contracts with P, making them distributors for their national market, forbad them to sell outside their territory. V complained to the Commission. On investigation, P submitted that the express export ban was inserted into the distribution agreements on a marketing director's personal initiative, acting without P's authority. P immediately revoked the restrictions. The infringement had lasted over two years. P was fined ECU 700,000 (reduced to ECU 400,000 on appeal to CFI), the German distributor Herlitz was fined ECU 40,000. The Commission observed that export bans are always restrictions of competition. The director's lack of authority was irrelevant — the company was still liable, either because it had allowed him to act in that fashion or because it had failed to supervise him properly.

The Commission continues to be vigilant to promote the goals of market integration and 'opening up' markets. In 1998, the Commission concluded its investigation into the behaviour of Volkswagen AG. It had received numerous complaints about difficulties encountered by German or Austrian consumers who wished to buy Volkswagen or Audi cars in Italy. Its investigation showed that Volkswagen had pursued a policy of market-partitioning for about ten years. Volkswagen's Italian dealers were effectively forbidden from selling the cars to foreign buyers, in particular those from Germany and Austria. The Commission imposed a fine of ecu 102 million and noted, in its XXVIIIth Report on Competition Policy, that this was the largest fine ever imposed on a single company (see also OJ 1998 L/124).

2.4.4.5 Ties

This is the name given to an arrangement where you can buy the thing you want but only if you buy something else which you do not want (either at all or at that price). The more natural home for the prohibition of ties is Article 82 (ex 86), where market power would allow an undertaking to compel the acceptance of unwanted terms or products. However, it is also an example given in Article 81 (ex 85). Maybe the example is intended to regulate contractual relations with third parties?

Examples of ties can be found in *Vaessen/Moris* [1979] 1 CMLR 511. There was a patented machine to make saucissons de Boulogne; the machines were sold with a requirement to buy all sausage casings from the manufacturer too. See also *Hilti* (although this involved Article 82 (ex 86)), a Commission decision recently confirmed by the Court.

These ties can be justified — for example, if the price for the machine is paid via *use* of the machine; this can be policed through the number of casings sold (you would need to check thoroughly by stamping your mark on the casings).

Another recent example of tying might be the freezer exclusivity arrangements concluded by Langnese and Schöller, regarding retail ice cream sales in Germany. See, e.g., 1993 ECLR at R-41 and below at **2.4.4.6**. These have also been the subject of litigation in Ireland, involving the Mars Corporation.

2.4.4.6 Exclusive purchasing

The Commission has issued block exemptions dealing with exclusive distribution and exclusive purchasing (Regulations 1983/83 and 1984/83). The exclusive purchasing regulation was considered in *Delimitis* v *Henninger Braü AG* in 1991. In this case, the ECJ looked at beer supply agreements in Germany. It considered the advantages offered to both supplier and reseller by such an agreement, e.g. the supplier gets guaranteed outlets, a motivated reseller and the ability to plan production and distribution more effectively; the reseller gets access to the beer resale market under favourable conditions (favourable loans, technical installations), guaranteed supply, and help in securing product quality.

The ECJ concluded that such agreements *may not* have the *object* of restricting competition, but it is still necessary to examine their *effect*. The ECJ said that one must look at the totality of such beer supply agreements to get the full picture; in the present case it was 'necessary to analyse the effects of a beer supply agreement, taken together with other contracts of the same type, on the opportunities of national competitors or those from other Member States, to gain access to the market for beer consumption or to increase their market share and, accordingly, the effects on the range of products offered to consumers'.

First, you must define the market in terms of product and territory. Here, the market was the distribution of beer through premises for the sale and consumption of drinks (*not* retail outlets) in Germany. Secondly, see if the existence of several beer supply agreements impedes *access* to that market. You need to examine the effect of all of them, not just the one you are presently concerned with. Relevant factors are the proportion of tied outlets compared to 'free' houses, duration of agreements, quantities of beer involved and how that compares to quantities sold by free houses.

Even if there is 'a considerable effect' on chances to gain access, that is insufficient in itself to allow a finding that the market is inaccessible. It is simply one factor among several, economic and legal. For example, you should also consider opportunities for access — a competitor might take over an existing national brewery with its tied sales outlets, or build new pubs. You need to examine any laws relating to such actions and (an economic factor) find the minimum number of outlets needed to operate a distribution system economically. Then see how the market itself works, competitively, to see how easy access is. Find the number and size of producers on the market, the degree of saturation of the market and customers' brand loyalty. A saturated market with high brand loyalty to a few large producers is more difficult to break into 'than a market in full expansion in which a large number of small producers are operating without any strong brand names'.

Lastly, if this examination of the totality of such contracts shows that they do *not* have the cumulative effect of denying access to new national or foreign competitors, the individual agreements cannot restrict competition within Article 81(1) (ex 85(1)) and so are not prohibited.

If access is found to be hard to attain, it is still necessary to assess the extent to which the 'suspect' brewery's contracts contribute to the cumulative effect of all such agreements. Breweries whose beer supply agreements make an *insignificant* contribution to the cumulative effect are not prohibited by Article 81(1) (ex 85(1)).

Whether the contribution is significant or not is determined by:

(a) the brewery's market share (and that of any group it belongs to);

(b) the number of outlets tied to it (or its group) compared to the total number of such outlets in the relevant market;

(c) the duration of the agreement compared to the average for that market, e.g., a brewery with a relatively small market share but which ties up sales outlets for many years may make as significant a contribution to sealing-off the market as a brewery with a relatively strong market position which regularly releases outlets at shorter intervals.

Applying those principles to the case, the ECJ considered the economic and legal effect of an *access clause* in the beer supply agreement (this was the referring court's fourth question, shown as A(4) in the Report). Such a clause allows the reseller to buy beer from other Member States. In theory, this should reduce the scope of the prohibition on competition in a beer supply agreement. If, in practice, the effect of the access clause is hypothetical or economically insignificant, one can ignore the clause. This may be the situation where the clause only authorises the reseller directly to buy beers from other Member States, rather than allowing him to buy beers imported by other companies into his Member State. Similarly, if the agreement has a clause requiring minimum quantities to be purchased by the reseller from the brewery (especially if backed by financial penalties for failure), those minimum amounts may be high in comparison to sales normally achieved by the pub in question; any 'freeing-up' of access here would be illusory.

If the access clause allows a national/foreign supplier '*a real possibility*' of supplying the pub in question, the agreement is not in principle capable of affecting trade between Member States. It therefore falls outside the prohibition in Article 81(1) (ex 85(1)).

The *Delimitis* case has many other facets to it, but is of great importance here because it shows the ECJ going to considerable lengths to conduct more than a knee-jerk analysis under Article 81(1) (ex 85(1)). A great deal of economic and legal analysis was required by the ECJ, and the Commission was expected to follow this lead in future investigations. The Commission responded by putting out a Notice on 'beer supply agreements of minor importance', putting into practice some of the ECJ's thoughts on economic significance. See OJ 1992, C121/2, amending Regulations 1983/83 and 1984/83.

Subsequently, the Commission had to consider exclusive purchase in the context of 'impulse' ice cream sales in Germany in *Langnese-Iglo, Schöller-Lebensmittel* OJ 1993 L183/1. It said that, in *normal* market conditions, exclusivity agreements are beneficial to competition because they strengthen the position of the undertaking which concluded the agreement. But, if access to the market by other suppliers is impeded *as a result of the market structure* and other significant barriers to entry, then exclusivity is unacceptable. That appears to have been the case here. Two companies had a duopoly over wholesale ice cream sales in Germany and access to that market was difficult because of the 'freezer exclusivity' arrangements they had with retailers. Generally, there is room for one ice cream freezer in a shop selling other goods (newspapers, etc.). If that freezer is supplied to the shopkeeper by the wholesaler on condition that it is used to stock only a specific manufacturer's goods, then no other manufacturer can get access to that retail outlet. In its final Decisions in these two cases, the Commission distinguished between 'outlet exclusivity' and 'freezer exclusivity'. The former was anti-competitive because it foreclosed that outlet for other suppliers, while the latter was permissible as a *quid pro quo* for making the ice creams available.

For a cogent criticism of the Commission's Decisions in the 'ice cream' cases, based on its failure to follow or distinguish *Delimitis*, see *Korah* [1994] 3 ECLR 171. However, it should also be noted that the decision of the Commission has been upheld, in very large part, by the CFI (*Langnese-Iglo* v *Commission* (T–7/93) [1995] ECR II-1533). An appeal to the ECJ was subsequently dismissed (Case (C-279/95P) [1998] ECR I-nyr).

2.5   Negative Clearance

The negative clearance procedure allows undertakings to ascertain whether the Commission considers that their arrangement or their behaviour is or is not prohibited by Article 85(1) [now 81(1)], or Article 86 [now 82] of the EC Treaty or by Article 53(1) or Article 54 of the EEA Agreement. This procedure is governed by Article 2 of Regulation 17. The negative clearance takes the form of a decision by which the Commission certifies that, on the basis of the facts in its possession, there are no grounds pursuant to Article 85(1) [now 81(1)] or Article 86 [now 82] of the EC Treaty ... for action on its part in respect of the arrangement or behaviour. (Extract from a complementary note to Form A/B in Regulation 3385/94)

Negative clearance is not an exemption, but is a simple statement of the Commission's opinion. It is, therefore, binding on neither the European Court nor the national courts. The clearance may be withdrawn if the circumstances change or if new information is revealed.

Insofar as negative clearance represents the end of a full investigation, it is quite rare for an undertaking to achieve this result. The Commission completes only a few individual cases each year (and gives priority to those which raise important questions of interpretation). This is one reason why it introduced block exemptions. An application for negative clearance is likely to end up by being the subject of a comfort letter (see **3.4.3**). The number of investigations resolved by negative clearance is likely to increase relative to exemptions as the Commission (encouraged by the ECJ in *Pronuptia* and subsequently in *Delimitis*) adopts a rule of reason approach to its analysis under Article 81(1) (ex 85(1)), i.e., it should test the pro- and anti-competitive effects of a contract or conduct before deciding whether there is an infringement.

THREE

ARTICLE 81(3): ESCAPE FROM PROHIBITION

3.1   Introduction

Having seen that an agreement will be void if it falls within Article 81(1) (ex 85(1)), we must now consider the possibility of its resurrection! Under Article 81(3) (ex 85(3)), the Commission may exempt an agreement from the application of Article 81(1) and (2) if it satisfies certain criteria.

A person or organisation seeking exemption must apply to the Commission. This is done by *notifying* the Commission of the agreement. Alternatively, if a company is unsure whether one of its agreements falls within Article 81(1) at all, it can seek the opinion of the Commission on this point. If the Commission decides in the company's favour, it gives the agreement *negative clearance* (see **2.5**).

3.2   Qualifying for Exemption

Currently, only the Commission can grant an exemption; the burden of proof rests on the company seeking exemption to show it is merited. Under Article 81(3) (ex 85(3)) (the substantive provision on exemptions), agreements etc., will be exempted if they satisfy four conditions. They are to:

(a)   help to improve the production or distribution of goods (e.g., make available a larger amount of a product) or promote technical or economic progress (raising of living standards). They must also;

(b)   give consumers a fair share of the resulting benefit;

(c)   restrict competition only to the extent and in ways which are totally necessary to achieve these pro-competitive ends; and

(d)   not allow the companies concerned to wipe out competition to any great degree.

We must remember a caveat from the noted US writer on anti-trust law, Barry Hawk, when looking at reported decisions on exemption. To a large extent they are 'fact-specific', i.e., *ad hoc,* and give few, if any, general principles to use. As he says, 'This makes hazardous the extrapolation of general rules beyond the four express statutory conditions in Article 85(3) [now 81(3)] itself.'

Let us look at the four conditions in more detail:

(a)   *The agreement must contribute to either an improvement in production/distribution of goods or the promotion of technical/economic progress.* This harks back to Article 2 EC. This condition is the most important of the four. It is used to overcome the original anti-competitive diagnosis under Article 81(1) (ex 85(1)). The question to ask is, 'Does the agreement as presently constituted give *benefits* which would not be available in the absence of such agreement?'. Or, as asked by the Commission, do the restrictions 'bring about an improvement over the situation which would have existed in their absence?' (*GERO-fabrik* 1977 OJ L16/8, Commission Decision). Such benefits might be, for example, a reduced cost per unit because of longer production runs; the facilitation of entry into new markets (either product or geographical); an improvement in distribution through continuity of supplies, or the availability of a wider range of products. If this condition is met, we can consider the second one.

(b) *Consumers must receive a fair share of the resulting benefits* (e.g., better standard of living; wider choice of products). Remember that 'consumer' here has a broad definition — not just the ultimate user but everyone down the manufacturing-marketing chain who makes use of the goods or services affected by the agreement. Korah notes the case of *ACEC/Berliet* [1968] CMLR D35, where the 'consumers' of a bus were held to be the bus companies and tour operators, not the likely passengers; 'consumer' is a translation of the French *utilisateur* — the ultimate buyer, whether for private or business use. The 'benefit' may be given to consumers in price or other terms, e.g. the provision of qualified staff or service, a repair facility or the availability of a guarantee of quality. This condition is one of the less demanding to satisfy. Once it is met, we can turn to the third condition.

(c) *The restrictions on competition which the agreement makes must be* indispensable *to attaining the identifiable benefits.* This is a recurring EC theme — an exception to a fundamental principle (e.g. free movement of workers, or normal competition) may be permitted but will be very strictly construed. The exception must do no more than is absolutely necessary to achieve the legitimate goal. The major question must be, 'Are less restrictive alternatives available which achieve the same benefits?' For example, could we get the same advantages over a shorter timespan, or with a smaller territory? There is an obvious link with the first condition here.

A good recent example of exactly how strictly this requirement can be construed is the judgment of the CFI in *UK Publishers Association* v *Commission* (T-66/89) [1992] ECR II-1995 — general restrictions covering all Member States will not be allowed if the only benefit occurs within a single Member State. The case concerned the Net Book Agreement (NBA) between publishers in the UK. A Decision by the Commission that it was contrary to Article 85(1) (now 81(1)) and did not merit exemption under Article 85(3) (now 81(3)) was challenged. The CFI was not persuaded that the restrictions on competition did not go beyond what was strictly necessary to attain the objectives permitted by Article 85(3) (now 81(3)) so the Commission's decision was upheld.

The CFI felt that, even if one accepted that the NBA produced beneficial effects within the UK, if that occurred at the cost of trade between Member States then the benefit was irrelevant:

> . . . a price maintenance system that restricts competition within the *common market* cannot qualify for exemption on the ground that it must continue to operate in order to produce beneficial effects inside a *national market.*

However, this judgment only affects the trade between Member States, i.e. books imported into the UK, *not* domestic publications (a result similar in many respects to an earlier case on the Dutch and Flemish book industries, *VBVB/VBBB* v *Commission* [1984] 1 ECR 19). The Commission originally felt that the publishers could achieve their desired effect without recourse to the NBA (i.e. the restriction went beyond that which was necessary to attain an identifiable benefit). Christopher Bright of Linklaters and Paines, at [1992] ECLR 269, presumes that this means the imposition of resale price maintenance as a standard condition of sale. It is debatable whether or not this could be a legitimate tactic to adopt.

In a rather bizarre series of events, in January 1995, the ECJ overturned the judgment of the CFI. In the spring, it was announced that the OFT had applied to the Restrictive Practices Court for leave to apply to end the NBA. Finally, in the autumn of 1995, the NBA collapsed following the resignation from it of several large publishers.

It should be noted that this third condition probably ranks second in importance behind the first one. If it is met, we can turn finally to the fourth and least important condition.

(d) *The parties to the agreement must not have been given the chance to* eradicate *competition regarding a substantial part of the products in question.* It is sufficient to say that, if an agreement satisfies the other three conditions, it is most unlikely to lose out under this head.

3.3   Notifying the Commission

3.3.1   WHY SHOULD YOU NOTIFY?

Regulation 17/62 introduced the idea of notification — essentially, taking a pre-emptive step to forestall accusations of anti-competitive behaviour. There is no need to notify the Commission of agreements, etc., which you are sure will not infringe Article 81 (ex 85), EC Treaty, but otherwise notification is probably a good idea. It does carry potential disadvantages, e.g. it alerts the Commission to your existence — who knows what else they may find in the filing cabinet?

The main purpose of notification is to get your agreement exempted by the Commission: there can be no exemption of an agreement which has not been notified. Ancillary benefits are an immunity from fines under Article 15(5) of Regulation 17/62 (see further **7.8.5**) and the possibility that the undertaking will acquire a reputation for being 'Community-spirited' — something which may stand it in good stead should it ever need some goodwill in its dealings with the Commission.

Certain agreements do not need to be notified to the Commission as a precondition for obtaining an exemption; see Regulation 17/62, Article 4(2). These agreements (of which there were originally four categories) may be notified if the parties wish to obtain an exemption. In the absence of a notification, if the Commission happens to consider such an agreement (for example, following a complaint about it), the Commission may grant an exemption to that agreement and the exemption can be back-dated to the inception of the agreement. This situation represents quite a fundamental exception to the basic requirement of notification and, as a result, Article 4(2) has been applied quite narrowly. However, the Commission is currently trying to reduce the number of notifications. As can be seen elsewhere in this Manual, the Commission now seeks to distinguish vertical agreements from horizontal agreements, since the former are less likely to restrict competition in unacceptable ways. With effect from June 1999, Regulation 17/62, Article 4(2), has been amended so that vertical agreements which deal with the purchase, sale or resale of certain goods or services no longer need to be notified in order to be eligible for exemption (see Council Regulation 1216/1999, OJ 1999 L148/5). These agreements can involve two or more undertakings but each must be operating at different levels of the production or distribution chain. This may seem quite complicated, but the intention is made explicit in recital 8, Regulation 1216/1999:

(8)   Whereas the scope of Article 4(2) of Regulation No. 17 should ... be extended, and all vertical agreements should be dispensed from the requirement of notification prior to exemption ...

In 1995, the Commission received some 368 notifications, an increase of some 55% on the preceding year (source: the Commission's XXVth Annual *Report on Competition Policy*). Some of this increase can be attributed to cases transferred to the Commission by the EFTA Surveillance Authority, following the accession to the EU of Austria, Finland and Sweden. Over the next three years, numbers settled down to run at just over 200 annually (for example, in 1998 there were 216 notifications — XXVIIIth Annual *Report*). Nevertheless, the Commission feels that there are too many notifications still. Furthermore, the situation can only get worse when the European Union expands to 20 or more Member States. In its 1999 White Paper on Modernisation, the Commission looks back on a warning given to it in 1961 by the Economic and Social Committee:

> Although some might see the authorisation system [i.e., notification and exemption/ negative clearance] as a means of obtaining better knowledge of the existence of agreements that were harmful to competition, such a system risked diverting the Commission from its true mission by overloading it with administrative work that would prevent it from carrying out a serious, in-depth examination of agreements between undertakings and of their real effects.

In 1999, the Commission observed that this warning had turned out to be correct. The Commission saw itself as reactive, not proactive. The Commission wanted to revise the system so that it could address itself more efficiently to the implementation of Article 81, in particular taking on more 'own-initiative' procedures which currently accounted for only 13% of new cases registered. How did it propose to revise the system? One answer was to decentralise the application of the EC competition rules, to national competition authorities and national courts. The 1999 White Paper contained a proposal to that effect but the far more radical proposal was to abolish the notification system entirely! The idea is to replace it with a 'directly applicable exception system'. This means that agreements will be presumed to be valid until such time as it can be shown that they are not. National competition authorities and courts will be empowered to determine the legality of agreements, looking at Article 81 in its entirety. The White Paper notes that these changes will require far-reaching amendment of Regulation 17, as well as many other measures. It is 'intended as a point of departure of a wide-ranging debate'. The closing date for submissions is set as 30.9.1999. It will be interesting to see what conclusions are reached!

3.3.2 HOW TO NOTIFY: FORM A/B

Whether a company is applying for negative clearance or giving notification of an agreement to be exempted, the same form is used. Form A/B must be filled in and 17 copies sent to the Commission. Form A/B was originally published in Commission Regulation 27/62; the current example is reproduced in **Appendix 4**. Rather curiously, there is no actual form to fill in. An undertaking simply provides the required information, in documentary form, using the section and paragraph numbers to correlate the information.

Exemption is granted from a specific date which, generally, cannot be earlier than the date of notification. It will be granted for a limited, renewable period. It may be withdrawn; it may be granted subject to conditions (usually requiring alteration of some of the terms of the agreement).

There must be full disclosure of information in Form A/B and its Annexes. Any failure to do so, whether intentional or simply negligent, may result in the Commission imposing a fine (see Article 15(1)(a), Regulation 17). This fine can range between 100 and 5,000 units of account. If a company appeals against the fine to the Court of First Instance, the Court has the power to cancel, reduce or increase it.

3.3.3 BEING FLEXIBLE

If an undertaking considers that its agreement infringes Article 81(1) (ex 85(1)), it may notify it formally to the Commission for the purpose of getting an exemption pursuant to Article 81(3) (ex 85(3)). It is possible that the Commission may disagree with the undertaking, finding that the agreement does not infringe Article 81(1) in the first place and therefore does not need exemption. In such a case, the Commission would be minded to grant negative clearance to the agreement and will do so if the undertaking has completed Form A/B sensibly (the Form allows companies to seek negative clearance or exemption as alternatives in a single application). It used to be unlikely that the Commission would not find a notified agreement to be anti-competitive (i.e., would disagree with the undertaking's own analysis), but this seems to be more frequent since the Court's judgment in *Pronuptia de Paris* v *Schillgalis* encouraged the Commission to take a more reasonable look at the competitive pros and cons of an agreement before condemning it as anti-competitive, rather than leaving this analysis until the time when it considers the grant of an exemption.

3.4   Alternatives to Individual Exemption

3.4.1   WHY ARE ALTERNATIVES NEEDED?

After Regulation 17/62 was introduced, the Commission quickly became snowed under with notifications seeking exemption for existing agreements. By 1967, over 35,000 had accumulated in the system. The Commission is able to grant very few individual exemptions each year. In part, this is due to a relatively small number of staff (around 150 even by 1998) in DG IV. Also, the system is cumbersome — before a formal decision can be taken:

- the notified agreement must be investigated,

- a notice must be published in the Official Journal (in 11 languages) allowing interested parties to submit their views,

- the Advisory Committee must be consulted on the draft decision,

- the Commission must adopt the decision,

- lastly, the decision must be published in the Official Journal (again, in the 11 official languages).

To deal with this backlog, the Commission introduced two new procedures — the block exemption and the comfort letter.

The Commission's problems with its workload persist today. In 1998, the Commission registered 509 new cases under either Article 81 (ex 85), 82 (ex 86) or 86 (ex 90). Five hundred and eighty-one such cases were 'closed' during 1998; this figure represents a significant improvement on preceding years but less than 10% of these were formal decisions. Of cases which proceeded to a formal decision on the merits, the average length of proceedings was almost five years. The quickest resolution came in a little more than two years, while the longest case ran for eight years. The Commission has a continuing annual carry over of around 1,200 cases. Without its informal procedures (and the right to refuse to investigate complaints, see **7.2.1**), the Commission would simply have been unable to cope.

3.4.2   BLOCK EXEMPTIONS

First, the Commission enacted secondary legislation creating block exemptions. All four conditions in Article 81(3) (ex 85(3)) are applied by the Commission in the block exemption Regulations. If you look at the block exemption Regulations, you can see how the Commission has tried to demonstrate compliance with the four conditions. See, for example, Regulation 1983/83 recitals (5) to (12) in **Appendix 2** below. Block exemptions deal with specific, common types of agreement (e.g., exclusive distribution agreements) — where commonly-encountered clauses are set out in 'black lists' or 'white lists'. Both lists contain clauses which are usually seen as being anti-competitive. In the white list are clauses which, in the circumstances described in the block exemption, are deemed to be acceptable (i.e., exemptable); while the black list contains those clauses which cannot be permitted on an unseen basis.

If the subject-matter of an agreement appears to fall within a block exemption but the agreement contains black-listed clauses, the parties have three options. First, they can keep quiet and hope the Commission never finds out about it (thus running the risk of substantial fines); second, they can delete the offending clauses; or, third, they can notify the agreement to the Commission and seek individual exemption (Article 81(3) (ex 85(3)) based on the particular circumstances of their case. If an agreement contains anti-competitive clauses but they are all white-listed, the block exemption applies and there is no need to notify the Commission of the agreement. Be warned that some block exemptions also contain a 'grey list'!

Block exemptions have been enacted (in the form of Commission regulations) in various fields to date. They usually have a fixed 10-year life span but this may be extended (as in Regulation 2349/84) or abbreviated (as in Regulation 556/89). These have included:

(a)   Regulation 1983/83 on exclusive distribution agreements;

(b)   Regulation 1984/83 on exclusive purchasing agreements;

(c)   Regulation 2349/84 on patent licensing agreements;

(d)   Regulation 4087/88 on franchising;

(e)   Regulation 556/89 on know-how licences; and

(f)   Regulation 240/96 on technology transfer.

These regulations (and others) are printed in the Official Journal and most of them are in a Commission publication, *Competition Law in the EEC and the ECSC* (available from The Stationery Office). Extracts from some block exemptions are set out in **Appendix 2**. The two regulations on patent licences and know-how licences have been superseded by a single new block exemption on technology transfer (Regulation 240/96). This came into effect on 1 April 1996.

3.4.2.1   Using an opposition procedure

Some of the block exemption regulations contain a provision known as the 'opposition procedure', notably the technology transfer Regulation 240/96 (Article 4, see **4.2**). Some patent licence agreements contain clauses which restrict competition but which appear in neither the white list nor the black list. The opposition procedure indicates that such an agreement should be notified to the Commission on Form A/B, with an indication that the opposition procedure could be used. The result is that the Commission has four months to indicate its opposition to the block exemption being applied to the agreement. If it does not oppose within four months, the agreement automatically falls within the block exemption.

A problem associated with the current opposition procedure is that there is no requirement for the Commission to publicise those agreements which are notified under the opposition procedure (although Member States must be kept informed). This makes it very difficult for those who might wish to object to an exemption — they are unlikely to be able to make representations or present evidence to the Commission simply through their ignorance of what is happening.

An example of the opposition procedure in use is the case of the *Scandinavian Ferry Operators* v *Commission* IP(92) 396, Commission Press Release. Three companies each provided a ferry service between a Danish port and a Swedish port (Helsingor-Helsinborg). They decided to operate a joint ferry service and notified the agreement under block exemption Regulation 4056/86 on maritime transport, utilising the opposition procedure (see **3.4.2.1**). There was no opposition by the Commission. Its view was that, although the agreement would impose substantial restrictions *if not total elimination* of competition on *this route* (author's emphasis), the agreement would improve services on the route and promote technical and economic progress, while consumers would get a fair share of the benefits — more frequent sailings, larger new vessels and better ability to match capacity to demand so producing lower costs and prices. Also, there was still sufficient competition on the market, e.g., through direct ferry services between Sweden and Germany. In this report you can see the Commission trying to check that the four conditions for exemption are satisfied.

3.4.3　COMFORT LETTERS

3.4.3.1　Generally

The second step taken by the Commission was the introduction of comfort letters. These give neither an exemption nor a negative clearance, but were created for reasons of administrative convenience. Rather than take a formal decision in a case, the Commission will send a letter, announcing that it has closed its file, i.e., terminating proceedings against the undertaking or conduct under investigation.

A comfort letter may be sent on various grounds:

(a)　On the facts, the agreement does not seem to infringe Article 81(1) (ex 85(1)).

(b)　The agreement falls within a block exemption.

(c)　The agreement merits exemption.

The issue of a comfort letter may be preceded by negotiations between the undertakings and the Commission, intended to bring about modifications in the notified agreement. An example is *ICL/Fujitsu* 1986 OJ C210. ICL entered into several agreements providing for the transfer of know-how and industrial property rights relating to computer components. Another agreement covered sales of Fujitsu mainframe computers to ICL, to be resold under the ICL brand. The agreements were notified to the Commission. The Commission decided that the sales agreement was outside the scope of the block exemption for exclusive distribution agreements and probably did not qualify for individual exemption either. This agreement was cancelled. The remaining agreements were seen as enabling an important transfer of technology to take place; the anti-competitive restrictions in them were indispensable and thus the agreements merited individual exemption under Article 85(3) (now 81(3)). A comfort letter was issued to this effect.

A comfort letter may be taken into account by a national court in litigation concerning an agreement but it is not binding on that court: see *Guerlain* (253/73) [1980] ECR 2327; *Lancôme v Etos* (99/79) [1981] ECR 2511. This permissive language is echoed in the Commission's Notice on Cooperation between National Courts and the Commission (1993) and leaves the legal effect of any comfort letter as the subject of speculation.

This lack of legal certainty has been noted by the Commission as raising a serious concern over the utility of comfort letters. In addition, despite their obvious assistance to the Commission (some 150–200 issued yearly, with over 90% of notifications closed informally by either comfort letter or closing the file with no further action), the Commission has identified a second 'major drawback' to them (see its 1999 White Paper). Regulation 17/62 requires an intended administrative act (such as the closing of an investigation) to be published in the Official Journal, so that interested parties may make their views known on the issue (see Regulation 17/62, Article 19(3)). Comfort letters do not meet the goals of publication and transparency because they are rarely preceded by a notice in the Official Journal. For both reasons, the Commission has concluded that comfort letters, together with other measures taken to 'stem the flood of notifications', have done as much as they can and now more radical changes to the system are needed.

3.4.3.2   Changes in circumstances

It should be noted that a change in circumstances, such as the entry of new competitors into a market, or the belated discovery of previously unknown facts, can justify the Commission re-opening its file. This will have the effect of setting aside the comfort letter. If the firm which received the comfort letter claims that this new action infringes its legitimate expectations, that claim is likely to fail (see e.g., *Langnese-Iglo GmbH* v *Commission* (C-279/95P) [1998] ECR I-nyr).

3.4.3.3   Problems with the *Rovin* comfort letter

The first reported use of this type of comfort letter (see (c) above) was in *Rovin* [1984] 1 CMLR 128 (and see *ICL/Fujitsu*). It probably causes more problems than it solves because, by saying that the agreement merits exemption, it suggests that the agreement infringes Article 81(1) (ex 85(1)).

If the parties to an agreement fall out, their dispute often comes before the courts of a Member State. The party who wishes to escape from the agreement may allege it is void, being within Article 81(1) (ex 85(1)), EC Treaty. If the other party tries to rebut this allegation by producing a comfort letter from the Commission, a *Rovin* letter may provoke the following argument from the 'escapee':

(a)   The letter implies the agreement is within Article 81(1) (ex 85(1)).

(b)   It is therefore void unless exempted.

(c)   The comfort letter is not an exemption.

(d)   National courts cannot grant an exemption.

(e)   It follows that the agreement is unenforceable.

Rather than stop any litigation on this 'technical' point, it might be better to adjourn (or 'stay') the national case and seek a final ruling on the original investigation from the Commission. The Commission will prioritise such cases (see the Notice on Cooperation between national courts and the Commission, OJ 1993 C39/6, para. 37).

3.4.4   INFORMAL SETTLEMENTS

3.4.4.1   Giving an undertaking to the Commission

The Commission is sometimes prepared to accept undertakings from a company that it will modify its suspect behaviour. This may be for the duration of the investigation — this will count as a mitigating factor if the company is eventually fined (see, e.g., *Hilti* [1985] 3 CMLR 619). Alternatively, the Commission may agree to suspend its investigation indefinitely in return for the company giving appropriate undertakings as to its future conduct. Perhaps the best example of this is *IBM* [1984] 3 CMLR 147. The Commission issued a Notice, saying that its investigation of IBM under Article 86 (now 82) would be suspended in return for certain promises. The Notice made it clear that IBM's future conduct would be monitored carefully to ensure compliance.

Undertakings are effectively binding on the Commission, once accepted by someone with the authority to do so (see, e.g., *FRUBO* v *Commission* (71/74) [1975] ECR 563). This is the result of applying the general principle of legitimate expectations; it would cease to apply if new facts were discovered, or there was a change in circumstances. See generally Bourgeois, in Slot and McDonnell (eds) (1993).

3.4.4.2   Negotiated settlements

These are closely connected with undertakings given by 'suspect' companies. An investigation under Regulation 17/62 can stop at an early stage if the company being investigated agrees (maybe on a non-admission basis) to modify its behaviour. A good example is the Italian Coca-Cola case: *San Pellegrino SpA* v *Coca-Cola Export Corporation Filiale Italiana* [1989] 4 CMLR 137, Commission Settlement. San Pellegrino complained to the Commission that Filiale Italiana had a dominant position in the

Italian cola market and was excluding competitors by offering discounts to distributors who agreed to sell no one else's cola. After a preliminary investigation, the Commission told Filiale Italiana that it agreed with the complaint. Filiale Italiana amended its contracts to remove the offending clauses and the Commission simply closed its file on the investigation.

3.4.5 BLOCK EXEMPTIONS IN THE FUTURE

In very general terms, the current block exemptions cover vertical arrangements between firms but exclude from their protection agreements made between competitors (that is, horizontal agreements). Although the present system of block exemptions is really aimed at helping vertical agreements, it was felt that it might not be doing so very effectively. In 1996, the Commission issued a *Green Paper on Vertical Restraints in Competition Policy*. The move was prompted by a feeling that the block exemptions are form-based, too legalistic and constrict firms unduly. Further, the Commission was concerned that efforts to comply with a block exemption could prevent a firm from improving its competitive position in the market. The move towards a more liberal attitude towards vertical restraints is echoed elsewhere, for example, in the Notice on agreements of minor importance (OJ 1997 C 372).

In September 1998, the Commission published the results of its consultation exercise, *Communication on the application of the EC Competition Rules to vertical restraints* (issued 30 September 1998). The *Communication* reiterated that many of the suggestions that it had received would not resolve the problems inherent in the present system. What is now proposed is 'a profound change of policy'. Rather than use the current system of block exemptions, covering a specific type of business behaviour, the Commission wants to introduce a single, very wide block exemption. This will cover vertical restraints regardless of the nature of the business relationship between the parties to the contract. It should cover goods and services, and goods in their intermediate stages (where they might be integrated into other products as part of a manufacturing process) should be covered as well as those in their 'final' form. The new block exemption will concentrate on what is prohibited rather than trying to list what is exempted.

The new block exemption will use market share to determine market power. In the absence of significant market power, vertical restraints will be assumed to have no 'significant net negative effects'. There will also be a number of so-called 'hardcore' restrictions on competition which will always fall outside the safe haven of the block exemption. In essence, these will be restrictions upon resale prices and absolute territorial protection.

These proposals, and other related changes, require legislation. The Commission intends that all necessary changes will be in place by 2000. Amendments to Regulation 19/65 are now in force (from June 1999), permitting the Commission to promulgate the new, single block exemption (see Council Regulation 1215/99, OJ 1999 L 148/1).

FOUR

REGULATION 240/96: THE BLOCK EXEMPTION ON TECHNOLOGY TRANSFER

4.1   Introduction

As we saw in **3.4.1**, block exemptions were introduced (through the medium of Commission regulations) in order to lighten the workload of the Commission. They have been adopted in several common types of business arrangement, most notably perhaps in the area of exclusive dealing. Here, after an initial single regulation covering exclusive dealing in its entirety (Regulation 67/67, which ran for 15 years), the Commission issued two further measures in 1983, one for exclusive distribution and a second for exclusive purchase (Regulations 1983/83 and 1984/83, respectively). Relevant parts of these latter two regulations have been extracted and appear in **Appendix 2**. They were both due to expire in 1997 but have been extended to 31 December 1999 (see Commission Regulation 1582/97).

The Commission published a Notice to offer 'a certain amount of interpretative guidance' to the two 1983 block exemptions (OJ 1984 C101/2). This perhaps reflects a recognition that the format of the block exemptions did (and still does) not lend itself to immediate comprehension or practical application. As the Commission's Notice points out (at para. 2):

> In determining how a given provision is to be applied, one must take into account, in addition to the ordinary meaning of the words used, the intention of the provision as this emerges from the preamble. For further guidance, reference should be made to the principles that have been evolved in the case law of the Court of Justice of the European Communities and in the Commission's decisions on individual cases.

One key piece of advice is offered in that passage. When trying to apply a block exemption, and divine its meaning, the reader should always try to cross-refer between the laws (the articles in a regulation) and the explanation of purpose (the preamble or recitals in a regulation). The latter often shed light on what a provision means or how it is intended to operate; often they make reference to a specific provision in an article. The other piece of advice that is on offer in this chapter is: try to understand how the conduct or contractual clause which a provision refers to will actually operate in practice. What sort of behaviour is being described in the article? Why is the Commission prepared to exempt it on an 'unseen' basis? The block exemptions can be extremely useful analytical tools if you are prepared to invest the time in understanding them and how to use them. As well as helping you to decide whether a particular clause, for example, is protected by a block exemption, your familiarity with the Commission's attitude to a method of doing business (e.g. distribution franchising, Regulation 4087/88) will also help you when determining if a particular contract or conduct infringes Article 81(1) (ex 85(1)) or might qualify for individual exemption under Article 81(3) (ex 85(3)).

The rest of this chapter is intended to help you achieve greater familiarity with one of the block exemptions, namely Regulation 240/96 on technology transfer. In **4.2**, you will find the text of the regulation, as issued by the Commission in 1996. Then in **4.3** you will find a commentary on the regulation which, it is hoped, will help you to see one way of 'dissecting' the regulation and making it of practical application to you. It is hoped that, when reading the commentary, you will make copious cross-references to the text of the regulation itself.

4.2 Regulation 240/96: the Block Exemption

COMMISSION REGULATION (EEC) NO. 240/96 OF 31 JANUARY 1996
on the application of Article 85(3) of the Treaty to certain categories
of technology transfer agreements
(text with EEA relevance)
(OJ [1996] L 31/2)

THE COMMISSION OF THE EUROPEAN COMMUNITIES,

Having regard to the Treaty establishing the European Community,

Having regard to Council Regulation 19/65/EEC of 2 March 1965 on the application of Article 85(3) of the Treaty to certain categories of agreements and concerted practices, as last amended by the Act of Accession of Austria, Finland and Sweden, and in particular Article 1 thereof,

Having published a draft of this Regulation,

After consulting the Advisory Committee on Restrictive Practices and Dominant Positions,

Whereas:

(1) Regulation 19/65/EEC empowers the Commission to apply Article 85(3) of the Treaty by regulation to certain categories of agreements and concerted practices falling within the scope of Article 85(1) which include restrictions imposed in relation to the acquisition or use of industrial property rights — in particular of patents, utility models, designs or trademarks — or to the rights arising out of contracts for assignment of, or the right to use, a method of manufacture of knowledge relating to use or to the application of industrial processes.

(2) The Commission has made use of this power by adopting Regulation (EEC) 2349/84 of 23 July 1984 on the application of Article 85(3) of the Treaty to certain categories of patent licensing agreements, as last amended by Regulation (EC) 2131/95, and Regulation (EEC) 556/89 of 30 November 1988 on the application of Article 85(3) of the Treaty to certain categories of know-how licensing agreements, as last amended by the Act of Accession of Austria, Finland and Sweden.

(3) These two block exemptions ought to be combined into a single regulation covering technology transfer agreements, and the rules governing patent licensing agreements and agreements for the licensing of know-how ought to be harmonised and simplified as far as possible, in order to encourage the dissemination of technical knowledge in the Community and to promote the manufacture of technically more sophisticated products. In those circumstances Regulation (EEC) 556/89 should be repealed.

(4) This Regulation should apply to the licensing of Member States' own patents, Community patents and European patents ('pure' patent licensing agreements). It should also apply to agreements for the licensing of non-patented technical information such as descriptions of manufacturing processes, recipes, formulae, designs or drawings, commonly termed 'know-how' ('pure' know-how licensing agreements), and to combined patent and know-how licensing agreements ('mixed' agreements), which are playing an increasingly important role in the transfer of technology. For the purposes of this Regulation, a number of terms are defined in Article 10.

(5) Patent or know-how licensing agreements are agreements whereby one undertaking which holds a patent or know-how ('the licensor') permits another undertaking ('the licensee') to exploit the patent thereby licensed, or communicates the know-how to it, in particular for purposes of manufacture, use or putting on the market. In the light of experience acquired so far, it is possible to define a category of

licensing agreements covering all or part of the common market which are capable of falling within the scope of Article 85(1) but which can normally be regarded as satisfying the conditions laid down in Article 85(3), where patents are necessary for the achievement of the objects of the licensed technology by a mixed agreement or where know-how — whether it is ancillary to patents or independent of them — is secret, substantial and identified in any appropriate form. These criteria are intended only to ensure that the licensing of the know-how or the grant of the patent licence justifies a block exemption of obligations restricting competition. This is without prejudice to the right of the parties to include in the contract provisions regarding other obligations, such as the obligation to pay royalties, even if the block exemption no longer applies.

(6) It is appropriate to extend the scope of this Regulation to pure or mixed agreements containing the licensing of intellectual property rights other than patents (in particular, trademarks, design rights and copyrights, especially software protection), when such additional licensing contributes to the achievement of the objects of the licensed technology and contains only ancillary provisions.

(7) Where such pure or mixed licensing agreements contain not only obligations relating to territories within the common market but also obligations relating to non-member countries, the presence of the latter does not prevent this Regulation from applying to the obligations relating to territories within the common market. Where licensing agreements for non-member countries or for territories which extend beyond the frontiers of the Community have effects within the common market which may fall within the scope of Article 85(1), such agreements should be covered by this Regulation to the same extent as would agreements for territories within the common market.

(8) The objective being to facilitate the dissemination of technology and the improvement of manufacturing processes, this Regulation should apply only where the licensee himself manufactures the licensed products or has them manufactured for his account, or where the licensed product is a service, provides the service himself or has the service provided for his account, irrespective of whether or not the licensee is also entitled to use confidential information provided by the licensor for the promotion and sale of the licensed product. The scope of this Regulation should therefore exclude agreements solely for the purpose of sale. Also to be excluded from the scope of this Regulation are agreements relating to marketing know-how communicated in the context of franchising arrangements and certain licensing agreements entered into in connection with arrangements such as joint ventures or patent pools and other arrangements in which a licence is granted in exchange for other licences not related to improvements to or new applications of the licensed technology. Such agreements pose different problems which cannot at present be dealt with in a single regulation (Article 5).

(9) Given the similarity between sale and exclusive licensing, and the danger that the requirements of this Regulation might be evaded by presenting as assignments what are in fact exclusive licenses restrictive of competition, this regulation should apply to agreements concerning the assignment and acquisition of patents or know-how where the risk associated with exploitation remains with the assignor. It should also apply to licensing agreements in which the licensor is not the holder of the patent or know-how but is authorised by the holder to grant the licence (as in the case of sub-licences) and to licensing agreements in which the parties' rights or obligations are assumed by connected undertakings (Article 6).

(10) Exclusive licensing agreements, i.e., agreements in which the licensor undertakes not to exploit the licensed technology in the licensed territory himself or to grant further licences there, may not be in themselves incompatible with Article 85(1) where they are concerned with the introduction and protection of a new technology in the licensed territory, by reason of the scale of the research which has been undertaken, of the increase in the level of competition, in particular inter-brand competition, and of the competitiveness of the undertakings concerned resulting from the dissemination of innovation within the Community. In so far as agreements of this kind fall, in other circumstances, within the scope of Article 85(1), it is appropriate to include them in Article 1 in order that they may also benefit from the exemption.

(11) The exemption of export bans on the licensor and on the licensees does not prejudice any developments in the case law of the Court of Justice in relation to such

agreements, notably with respect to Articles 30 to 36 and Article 85(1). This is also the case, in particular, regarding the prohibition on the licensee from selling the licensed product in territories granted to other licensees (passive competition).

(12) The obligations listed in Article 1 generally contribute to improving the production of goods and to promoting technical progress. They make the holders of patents or know-how more willing to grant licences and licensees more inclined to undertake the investment required to manufacture, use and put on the market a new product or to use a new process. Such obligations may be permitted under this Regulation in respect of territories where the licensed product is protected by patents as long as these remain in force.

(13) Since the point at which the know-how ceases to be secret can be difficult to determine, it is appropriate, in respect of territories where the licensed technology comprises know-how only, to limit such obligations to a fixed number of years. Moreover, in order to provide sufficient periods of protection, it is appropriate to take as the starting-point for such periods the date on which the product is first put on the market in the Community by a licensee.

(14) Exemption under Article 85(3) of longer periods of territorial protection for know-how agreements, in particular in order to protect expensive and risky investment or where the parties were not competitors at the date of the grant of the licence, can be granted only by individual decision. On the other hand, parties are free to extend the term of their agreements in order to exploit any subsequent improvement and to provide for the payment of additional royalties. However, in such cases, further periods of territorial protection may be allowed only starting from the date of licensing of the secret improvements in the Community, and by individual decision. Where the research for improvements results in innovations which are distinct from the licensed technology the parties may conclude a new agreement benefitting from an exemption under this Regulation.

(15) Provision should also be made for exemption of an obligation on the licensee not to put the product on the market in the territories of other licensees, the permitted period for such an obligation (this obligation would ban not just active competition but passive competition too) should, however, be limited to a few years from the date on which the licensed product is first put on the market in the Community by a licensee, irrespective of whether the licensed technology comprises know-how, patents or both in the territories concerned.

(16) The exemption of territorial protection should apply for the whole duration of the periods thus permitted, as long as the patents remain in force or the know-how remains secret and substantial. The parties to a mixed patent and know-how licensing agreement must be able to take advantage in a particular territory of the period of protection conferred by a patent or by the know-how, whichever is the longer.

(17) The obligations listed in Article 1 also generally fulfil the other conditions for the application of Article 85(3). Consumers will, as a rule, be allowed a fair share of the benefit resulting from the improvement in the supply of goods on the market. To safeguard this effect, however, it is right to exclude from the application of Article 1 cases where the parties agree to refuse to meet demand from users or resellers within their respective territories who would resell for export, or to take other steps to impede parallel imports. The obligations referred to above thus only impose restrictions which are indispensable to the attainment of their objectives.

(18) It is desirable to list in this Regulation a number of obligations that are commonly found in licensing agreements but are normally not restrictive of competition, and to provide that in the event that because of the particular economic or legal circumstances they should fall within Article 85(1), they too will be covered by the exemption. This list, in Article 2, is not exhaustive.

(19) This Regulation must also specify what restrictions or provisions may not be included in licensing agreements if these are to benefit from the block exemption. The restrictions listed in Article 3 may fall under the prohibition of Article 85(1), but in their case there can be no general presumption that, although they relate to the transfer of technology, they will lead to the positive effects required by Article 85(3), as would be necessary for the granting of a block exemption. Such restrictions can be declared exempt only by an individual decision, taking account of the market position of the undertakings concerned and the degree of concentration on the relevant market.

(20) The obligations on the licensee to cease using the licensed technology after the termination of the agreement (Article 2(1)(3)) and to make improvements available to the licensor (Article 2(1)(4)) do not generally restrict competition. The post-term use ban may be regarded as a normal feature of licensing, as otherwise the licensor would be forced to transfer his know-how or patents in perpetuity. Undertakings by the licensee to grant back to the licensor a licence for improvements to the licensed know-how and/or patents are generally not restrictive of competition if the licensee is entitled by the contract to share in future experience and inventions made by the licensor. On the other hand, a restrictive effect on competition arises where the agreement obliges the licensee to assign to the licensor rights to improvements of the originally licensed technology that he himself has brought about (Article 3(6)).

(21) The list of clauses which do not prevent exemption also includes an obligation on the licensee to keep paying royalties until the end of the agreement independently of whether or not the licensed know-how has entered into the public domain through the action of third parties or of the licensee himself (Article 2(1)(7)). Moreover, the parties must be free, in order to facilitate payment, to spread the royalty payments for the use of the licensed technology over a period extending beyond the duration of the licensed patents, in particular by setting lower royalty rates. As a rule, parties do not need to be protected against the foreseeable financial consequences of an agreement freely entered into, and they should therefore be free to choose the appropriate means of financing the technology transfer and sharing between them the risks of such use. However, the setting of rates of royalty so as to achieve one of the restrictions listed in Article 3 renders the agreement ineligible for the block exemption.

(22) An obligation on the licensee to restrict his exploitation of the licensed technology to one or more technical fields of application ('fields of use') or to one or more product markets is not caught by Article 85(1) either, since the licensor is entitled to transfer the technology only for a limited purpose (Article 2(1)(8)).

(23) Clauses whereby the parties allocate customers within the same techno-logical field of use or the same product market, either by an actual prohibition on supplying certain classes of customer or through an obligation with an equivalent effect, would also render the agreement ineligible for the block exemption where the parties are competitors for the contract products (Article 3(4)). Such restrictions between undertakings which are not competitors remain subject to the opposition procedure. Article 3 does not apply to cases where the patent or know-how licence is granted in order to provide a single customer with a second source of supply. In such a case, a prohibition on the second licensee from supplying persons other than the customer concerned is an essential condition for the grant of a second licence, since the purpose of the transaction is not to create an independent supplier in the market. The same applies to limitations on the quantities the licensee may supply to the customer concerned (Article 2(1)(13)).

(24) Besides the clauses already mentioned, the list of restrictions which render the block exemption inapplicable also includes restrictions regarding the selling prices of the licensed product or the quantities to be manufactured or sold, since they seriously limit the extent to which the licensee can exploit the licensed technology and since quantity restrictions particularly may have the same effect as export bans (Article 3(1) and (5)). This does not apply where a licence is granted for use of the technology in specific production facilities and where both a specific technology is communicated for the setting-up, operation and maintenance of these facilities and the licensee is allowed to increase the capacity of the facilities or to set up further facilities for its own use on normal commercial terms. On the other hand, the licensee may lawfully be prevented from using the transferred technology to set up facilities for third parties, since the purpose of the agreement is not to permit the licensee to give other producers access to the licensor's technology while it remains secret or protected by patent (Article 2(1)(12)).

(25) Agreements which are not automatically covered by the exemption because they contain provisions that are not expressly exempted by this Regulation and not expressly excluded from exemption, including those listed in Article 4(2), may, in certain circumstances, nonetheless be presumed to be eligible for application of the block exemption. It will be possible for the Commission rapidly to establish whether this is the case on the basis of the information undertakings are obliged to provide

*under Commission Regulation (EC) 3385/94. The Commission may waive the require-
ment to supply specific information required in form A/B but which it does not deem
necessary. The Commission will generally be content with communication of the text
of the agreement and with an estimate, based on directly available data, of the
market structure and of the licensee's market share. Such agreements should
therefore be deemed to be covered by the exemption provided for in this Regulation
where they are notified to the Commission and the Commission does not oppose the
application of the exemption within a specified period of time.*

*(26) Where agreements exempted under this Regulation nevertheless have
effects incompatible with Article 85(3), the Commission may withdraw the block
exemption, in particular where the licensed products are not faced with real competition in the licensed territory (Article 7). This could also be the case where the licensee
has a strong position on the market. In assessing the competition the Commission will
pay special attention to cases where the licensee has more than 40% of the whole
market for the licensed products and of all the products or services which customers
consider interchangeable or substitutable on account of their characteristics, prices
and intended use.*

*(27) Agreements which come within the terms of Articles 1 and 2 which have
neither the object nor the effect of restricting competition in any other way need no
longer be notified. Nevertheless, undertakings will still have the right to apply in
individual cases for negative clearance or for exemption under Article 85(3) in
accordance with Council Regulation No 17, as last amended by the Act of Accession
of Austria, Finland and Sweden. They can in particular notify agreements obliging the
licensor not to grant other licences in the territory, where the licensee's market share
exceeds or is likely to exceed 40%.*

HAS ADOPTED THIS REGULATION:

Article 1

*1. Pursuant to Article 85(3) of the Treaty and subject to the conditions set out
below, it is hereby declared that Article 85(1) of the Treaty shall not apply to pure
patent licensing or know-how licensing agreements and to mixed patent and know-
how licensing agreements, including those agreements containing ancillary provisions relating to intellectual property rights other than patents, to which only two
undertakings are party and which include one or more of the following obligations:*

*(1) an obligation on the licensor not to license other undertakings to exploit the
licensed technology in the licensed territory;*

*(2) an obligation on the licensor not to exploit the licensed technology in the
licensed territory himself;*

*(3) an obligation on the licensee not to exploit the licensed technology in the
territory of the licensor within the common market;*

*(4) an obligation on the licensee not to manufacture or use the licensed product,
or use the licensed process, in territories within the common market which are
licensed to other licensees;*

*(5) an obligation on the licensee not to pursue an active policy of putting the
licensed product on the market in the territories within the common market which are
licensed to other licensees, and in particular not to engage in advertising specifically
aimed at those territories or to establish any branch or maintain an [sic] distribution
depot there;*

*(6) an obligation on the licensee not to put the licensed product on the market in
the territories licensed to other licensees within the common market in response to
unsolicited orders;*

*(7) an obligation on the licensee to use only the licensor's trademark or get up
to distinguish the licensed product during the term of the agreement, provided that
the licensee is not presented from identifying himself as the manufacturer of the
licensed products;*

*(8) an obligation on the licensee to limit his production of the licensed product to
the quantities he requires in manufacturing his own product and to sell the licensed
product only as an integral part of or a replacement part for his own products or
otherwise in connection with the sale of his own products, provided that such
quantities are freely determined by the licensee.*

2. Where the agreement is a pure patent licensing agreement, the exemption of the obligations referred to in paragraph 1 is granted only to the extent that and for as long as the licensed product is protected by parallel patents, in the territories respectively of the licensee (points (1), (2), (7) and (8)), the licensor (point (3)) and other licensees (points (4) and (5)). The exemption of the obligation referred to in point (6) of paragraph 1 is granted for a period not exceeding five years from the date when the licensed product is first put on the market within the common market by one of the licensees, to the extent that and for as long as, in these territories, this product is protected by parallel patents.

3. Where the agreement is a pure know-how licensing agreement, the period for which the exemption of the obligations referred to in points (1) to (5) of paragraph 1 is granted may not exceed ten years from the date when the licensed product is first put on the market within the common market by one of the licensees.

The exemption of the obligation referred to in point (6) of paragraph 1 is granted for a period not exceeding five years from the date when the licensed product is first put on the market within the common market by one of the licensees.

The obligations referred to in points (7) and (8) of paragraph 1 are exempted during the lifetime of the agreement for as long as the know-how remains secret and substantial.

However, the exemption in paragraph 1 shall apply only where the parties have identified in any appropriate form the initial know-how and any subsequent improvements to it which become available to one party and are communicated to the other party pursuant to the terms of the agreement and to the purpose thereof, and only for as long as the know-how remains secret and substantial.

4. Where the agreement is a mixed patent and know-how licensing agreement, the exemption of the obligations referred to in points (1) to (5) of paragraph 1 shall apply in Member States in which the licensed technology is protected by necessary patents for as long as the licensed product is protected in those Member States by such patents if the duration of such protection exceeds the periods specified in paragraph 3.

The duration of the exemption provided in point (6) of paragraph 1 may not exceed the five-year period provided for in paragraphs 2 and 3.

However, such agreements qualify for the exemption referred to in paragraph 1 only for as long as the patents remain in force or to the extent that the know-how is identified and for as long as it remains secret and substantial whichever period is the longer.

5. The exemption provided for in paragraph 1 shall also apply where in a particular agreement the parties undertake obligations of the types referred to in that paragraph but with a more limited scope than is permitted by that paragraph.

Article 2

1. Article 1 shall apply notwithstanding the presence in particular of any of the following clauses, which are generally not restrictive of competition:

(1) an obligation on the licensee not to divulge the know-how communicated by the licensor; the licensee may be held to this obligation after the agreement has expired;

(2) an obligation on the licensee not to grant sublicences or assign the licence;

(3) an obligation on the licensee not to exploit the licensed know-how or patents after termination of the agreement in so far and as long as the know-how is still secret or the patents are still in force;

(4) an obligation on the licensee to grant to the licensor a licence in respect of his own improvements to or his new applications of the licensed technology, provided:

—that, in the case of severable improvements, such a licence is not exclusive, so that the licensee is free to use his own improvements or to license them to third parties, in so far as that does not involve disclosure of the know-how communicated by the licensor that is still secret,

—and that the licensor undertakes to grant an exclusive or non-exclusive licence of his own improvements to the licensee;

(5) an obligation on the licensee to observe minimum quality specifications, including technical specifications, for the licensed product or to procure goods or services from the licensor or from an undertaking designated by the licensor, in so far as these quality specifications, products or services are necessary for:

(a) a technically proper exploitation of the licensed technology; or

(b) ensuring that the product of the licensee conforms to the minimum quality specifications that are applicable to the licensor and other licensees;
and to allow the licensor to carry out related checks;

(6) obligations:

(a) to inform the licensor of misappropriation of the know-how or of infringements of the licensed patents; or

(b) to take or to assist the licensor in taking legal action against such misappropriation or infringements;

(7) an obligation on the licensee to continue paying the royalties:

(a) until the end of the agreement in the amounts, for the periods and according to the methods freely determined by the parties, in the event of the know-how becoming publicly known other than by action of the licensor, without prejudice to the payment of any additional damages in the event of the know-how becoming publicly known by the action of the licensee in breach of the agreement;

(b) over a period going beyond the duration of the licensed patents, in order to facilitate payment;

(8) an obligation on the licensee to restrict his exploitation of the licensed technology to one or more technical fields of application covered by the licensed technology or to one or more product markets;

(9) an obligation on the licensee to pay a minimum royalty or to produce a minimum quantity of the licensed product or to carry out a minimum number of operations exploiting the licensed technology;

(10) an obligation on the licensor to grant the licensee any more favourable terms that the licensor may grant to another undertaking after the agreement is entered into;

(11) an obligation on the licensee to mark the licensed product with an indication of the licensor's name or of the licensed patent;

(12) an obligation on the licensee not to use the licensor's technology to construct facilities for third parties; this is without prejudice to the right of the licensee to increase the capacity of his facilities or to set up additional facilities for his own use on normal commercial terms, including the payment of additional royalties;

(13) an obligation on the licensee to supply only a limited quantity of the licensed product to a particular customer, where the licence was granted so that the customer might have a second source of supply inside the licensed territory; this provision shall also apply where the customer is the licensee, and the licence which was granted in order to provide a second source of supply provides that the customer is himself to manufacture the licensed products or to have them manufactured by a subcontractor;

(14) a reservation by the licensor of the right to exercise the rights conferred by a patent to oppose the exploitation of the technology by the licensee outside the licensed territory;

(15) a reservation by the licensor of the right to terminate the agreement if the licensee contests the secret or substantial nature of the licensed know-how or challenges the validity of licensed patents within the common market belonging to the licensor or undertakings connected with him;

(16) a reservation by the licensor of the right to terminate the licence agreement of a patent if the licensee raises the claim that such a patent is not necessary;

(17) an obligation on the licensee to use his best endeavours to manufacture and market the licensed product;

(18) a reservation by the licensor of the right to terminate the exclusivity granted to the licensee and to stop licensing improvements to him when the licensee enters into competition within the common market with the licensor, with undertakings connected with the licensor or with other undertakings in respect of research and development, production, use or distribution of competing products, and to require the licensee to prove that the licensed know-how is not being used for the production of products and the provision of services other than those licensed.

2. In the event that, because of particular circumstances, the clauses referred to in paragraph 1 fall within the scope of Article 85(1), they shall also be exempted even if they are not accompanied by any of the obligations exempted by Article 1.

3. *The exemption in paragraph 2 shall also apply where an agreement contains clauses of the types referred to in paragraph 1 but with a more limited scope than is permitted by that paragraph.*

Article 3
Article 1 and Article 2(2) shall not apply where:

(1) one party is restricted in the determination of prices, components of prices or discounts for the licensed products;

(2) one party is restricted from competing within the common market with the other party, with undertakings connected with the other party or with other undertakings in respect of research and development, production, use or distribution of competing products without prejudice to the provisions of Article 2(1)(17) and (18);

(3) one or both of the parties are required without any objectively justified reason:

(a) to refuse to meet orders from users or resellers in their respective territories who would market products in other territories within the common market;

(b) to make it difficult for users or resellers to obtain the products from other resellers within the common market, and in particular to exercise intellectual property rights or take measures so as to prevent users or resellers from obtaining outside, or from putting on the market in the licensed territory products which have been lawfully put on the market within the common market by the licensor or with his consent;
or do so as a result of a concerted practice between them;

(4) the parties were already competing manufacturers before the grant of the licence and one of them is restricted, within the same technical field of use or within the same product market, as to the customers he may serve, in particular by being prohibited from supplying certain classes of user, employing certain forms of distribution or, with the aim of sharing customers, using certain types of packaging for the products, save as provided in Article 1(1)(7) and Article 2(1)(13);

(5) the quantity of the licensed products one party may manufacture or sell or the number of operations exploiting the licensed technology he may carry out are subject to limitations, save as provided in Article (1)(8) and Article 2(1)(13);

(6) the licensee is obliged to assign in whole or in part to the licensor rights to improvements to or new applications of the licensed technology;

(7) the licensor is required, albeit in separate agreements or through automatic prolongation of the initial duration of the agreement by the inclusion of any new improvements, for a period exceeding that referred to in Article 1(2) and (3) not to license other undertakings to exploit the licensed technology in the licensed territory, or a party is required for a period exceeding that referred to in Article 1(2) and (3) or Article 1(4) not to exploit the licensed technology in the territory of the other party or of other licensees.

Article 4
1. *The exemption provided for in Articles 1 and 2 shall also apply to agreements containing obligations restrictive of competition which are not covered by those Articles and do not fall within the scope of Article 3, on condition that the agreements in question are notified to the Commission in accordance with the provisions of Articles 1, 2 and 3 of Regulation (EC) 3385/94 and that the Commission does not oppose such exemption within a period of four months.*

2. *Paragraph 1 shall apply, in particular, where:*

(a) the licensee is obliged at the time the agreement is entered into to accept quality specifications or further licences or to procure goods or services which are not necessary for a technically satisfactory exploitation of the licensed technology or for ensuring that the production of the licensee conforms to the quality standards that are respected by the licensor and other licensees;

(b) the licensee is prohibited from contesting the secrecy or the substantiality of the licensed know-how or from challenging the validity of patents licensed within the common market belonging to the licensor or undertakings connected with him.

3. *The period of four months referred to in paragraph 1 shall run from the date on which the notification takes effect in accordance with Article 4 of Regulation (EC) 3385/94.*

4. *The benefit of paragraphs 1 and 2 may be claimed for agreements notified before the entry into force of this Regulation by submitting a communication to the Commission referring expressly to this Article and to the notification. Paragraph 3 shall apply mutatis mutandis.*

5. *The Commission may oppose the exemption within a period of four months. It shall oppose exemption if it receives a request to do so from a Member State within two months of the transmission to the Member State of the notification referred to in paragraph 1 or of the communication referred to in paragraph 4. This request must be justified on the basis of considerations relating to the competition rules of the Treaty.*

6. *The Commission may withdraw the opposition to the exemption at any time. However, where the opposition was raised at the request of a Member State and this request is maintained, it may be withdrawn only after consultation of the Advisory Committee on Restrictive Practices and Dominant Positions.*

7. *If the opposition is withdrawn because the undertakings concerned have shown that the conditions of Article 85(3) are satisfied, the exemption shall apply from the date of notification.*

8. *If the opposition is withdrawn because the undertakings concerned have amended the agreement so that the conditions of Article 85(3) are satisfied, the exemption shall apply from the date on which the amendments take effect.*

9. *If the Commission opposes exemption and the opposition is not withdrawn, the effects of the notification shall be governed by the provisions of Regulation No 17.*

Article 5

1. *This Regulation shall not apply to:*

(1) *agreements between members of a patent or know-how pool which relate to the pooled technologies;*

(2) *licensing agreements between competing undertakings which hold interests in a joint venture, or between one of them and the joint venture, if the licensing agreements relate to the activities of the joint venture;*

(3) *agreements under which one party grants the other a patent and/or know-how licence and in exchange the other party, albeit in separate agreements or through connected undertakings, grants the first party a patent, trademark or know-how licence or exclusive sales rights, where the parties are competitors in relation to the products covered by those agreements;*

(4) *licensing agreements containing provisions relating to intellectual property rights other than patents which are not ancillary;*

(5) *agreements entered into solely for the purpose of sale.*

2. *This Regulation shall nevertheless apply:*

(1) *to agreements to which paragraph 1(2) applies, under which a parent undertaking grants the joint venture a patent or know-how licence, provided that the licensed products and the other goods and services of the participating undertakings which are considered by users to be interchangeable or substitutable in view of their characteristics, price and intended use represent:*

—*in case of a licence limited to production, not more than 20%, and*

—*in case of a licence covering production and distribution, not more than 10%;*
of the market for the licensed products and all interchangeable or substitutable goods and services;

(2) *to agreements to which paragraph 1(1) applies and to reciprocal licences within the meaning of paragraph 1(3), provided the parties are not subject to any territorial restriction within the common market with regard to the manufacture, use or putting on the market of the licensed products or to the use of the licensed or pooled technologies.*

3. *This Regulation shall continue to apply where, for two consecutive financial years, the market shares in paragraph 2(1) are not exceeded by more than one-tenth; where that limit is exceeded, this Regulation shall continue to apply for a period of six months from the end of the year in which the limit was exceeded.*

Article 6

This Regulation shall also apply to:

(1) agreements where the licensor is not the holder of the know-how or the patentee, but is authorised by the holder or the patentee to grant a licence;

(2) assignments of know-how, patents or both where the risk associated with exploitation remains with the assignor, in particular where the sum payable in consideration of the assignment is dependent on the turnover obtained by the assignee in respect of products made using the know-how or the patents, the quantity of such products manufactured or the number of operations carried out employing the know-how or the patents;

(3) licensing agreements in which the rights or obligations of the licensor or the licensee are assumed by undertakings connected with them.

Article 7

The Commission may withdraw the benefit of this Regulation, pursuant to Article 7 of Regulation 19/65/EEC, where it finds in a particular case that an agreement exempted by this Regulation nevertheless has certain effects which are incompatible with the conditions laid down in Article 85(3) of the Treaty, and in particular where:

(1) the effect of the agreement is to prevent the licensed products from being exposed to effective competition in the licensed territory from identical goods or services or from goods or services considered by users as interchangeable or substitutable in view of their characteristics, price and intended use, which may in particular occur where the licensee's market share exceeds 40%;

(2) without prejudice to Article 1(1)(6), the licensee refuses, without any objectively justified reason, to meet unsolicited orders from users or resellers in the territory of other licensees;

(3) the parties;

(a) without any objectively justified reason, refuse to meet orders from users or resellers in their respective territories who would market the products in other territories within the common market; or

(b) make it difficult for users or resellers to obtain the products from other resellers within the common market, and in particular where they exercise intellectual property rights or take measures so as to prevent resellers or users from obtaining outside, or from putting on the market in the licensed territory products which have been lawfully put on the market within the common market by the licensor or with his consent;

(4) the parties were competing manufacturers at the date of the grant of the licence and obligations on the licensee to produce a minimum quantity or to use his best endeavours as referred to in Article 2(1), (9) and (17) respectively have the effect of preventing the licensee from using competing technologies.

Article 8

1. For purposes of this Regulation:

(a) patent applications;

(b) utility models;

(c) applications for registration of utility models;

(d) topographies of semiconductor products;

(e) certificats d'utilité and certificats d'addition under French law;

(f) applications for certificats d'utilité and certificats d'addition under French law;

(g) supplementary protection certificates for medicinal products or other products for which such supplementary protection certificates may be obtained;

(h) plant breeder's certificates,

shall be deemed to be patents.

2. This Regulation shall also apply to agreements relating to the exploitation of an invention if an application within the meaning of paragraph 1 is made in respect of the invention for a licensed territory after the date when the agreements were entered into but within the time-limits set by the national law or the international convention to be applied.

3. This Regulation shall furthermore apply to pure patent or know-how licensing agreements or to mixed agreements whose initial duration is automatically prolonged by the inclusion of any new improvements, whether patented or not, communicated by the licensor, provided that the licensee has the right to refuse such improvements

or each party has the right to terminate the agreement at the expiry of the initial term of an agreement and at least every three years thereafter.

Article 9

1. Information acquired pursuant to Article 4 shall be used only for the purposes of this Regulation.

2. The Commission and the authorities of the Member States, their officials and other servants shall not disclose information acquired by them pursuant to this Regulation of the kind covered by the obligation of professional secrecy.

3. The provision of paragraphs 1 and 2 shall not prevent publication of general information or surveys which do not contain information relating to particular under-takings or associations of undertakings.

Article 10

For purposes of this Regulation:

(1) 'know-how' means a body of technical information that is secret, substantial and identified in any appropriate form;

(2) 'secret' means that the know-how package as a body or in the precise configuration and assembly of its components is not generally known or easily accessible, so that part of its value consists in the lead which the licensee gains when it is communicated to him; it is not limited to the narrow sense that each individual component of the know-how should be totally unknown or unobtainable outside the licensor's business;

(3) 'substantial' means that the know-how includes information which must be useful, i.e., can reasonably be expected at the date of conclusion of the agreement to be capable of improving the competitive position of the licensee, for example by helping him to enter a new market or giving him an advantage in competition with other manufacturers or providers of services who do not have access to the licensed secret know-how or other comparable secret know-how;

(4) 'identified' means that the know-how is described or recorded in such a manner as to make it possible to verify that it satisfies the criteria of secrecy and substantiality and to ensure that the licensee is not unduly restricted in his exploitation of his own technology, to be identified the know-how can either be set out in the licence agreement or in a separate document or recorded in any other appropriate form at the latest when the know-how is transferred or shortly thereafter, provided that the separate documents or other record can be made available if the need arises;

(5) 'necessary patents' are patents where a licence under the patent is necessary for the putting into effect of the licensed technology in so far as, in the absence of such a licence, the realisation of the licensed technology would not be possible or would be possible only to a lesser extent or in more difficult or costly conditions. Such patents must therefore be of technical, legal or economic interest to the licensee;

(6) 'licensing agreement' means pure patent licensing agreements and pure know-how licensing agreements as well as mixed patent and know-how licensing agreements;

(7) 'licensed technology' means the initial manufacturing know-how or the necessary product and process patents, or both, existing at the time the first licensing agreement is concluded, and improvements subsequently made to the know-how or patents, irrespective of whether and to what extent they are exploited by the parties or by other licensees;

(8) 'the licensed products' are goods or services the production or provision of which requires the use of the licensed technology;

(9) 'the licensee's market share' means the proportion which the licensed products and other goods or services provided by the licensee, which are considered by users to be interchangeable or substitutable for the licensed products in view of their characteristics, price and intended use, represent the entire market for the licensed products and all other inter-changeable or substitutable goods and services in the common market or a substantial part of it;

(10) 'exploitation' refers to any use of the licensed technology in particular in the production, active or passive sales in a territory even if not coupled with manufacture in that territory, or leasing of the licensed products;

(11)   'the licensed territory' is the territory covering all or at least part of the common market where the licensee is entitled to exploit the licensed technology;

(12)   'territory of the licensor' means territories in which the licensor has not granted any licenses for patents and/or know-how covered by the licensing agreement;

(13)   'parallel patents' means patents which, in spite of the divergences which remain in the absence of any unification of national rules concerning industrial property, protect the same invention in various Member States;

(14)   'connected undertakings' means:

(a)   undertakings in which a party to the agreement, directly or indirectly:

—owns more than half the capital or business assets, or

—has the power to exercise more than half the voting rights, or

—has the power to appoint more than half the members of the supervisory board, board of directors or bodies legally representing the undertaking, or

—has the right to manage the affairs of the undertaking;

(b)   undertakings which, directly or indirectly, have in or over a party to the agreement the rights or powers listed in (a);

(c)   undertakings in which an undertaking referred to in (b), directly or indirectly, has the rights or powers listed in (a);

(d)   undertakings in which the parties to the agreement or undertakings connected with them jointly have the rights or powers listed in (a): such jointly controlled undertakings are considered to be connected with each of the parties to the agreement;

(15)   'ancillary provisions' are provisions relating to the exploitation of intellectual property rights other than patents, which contain no obligations restrictive of competition other than those also attached to the licensed know-how or patents and exempted under this Regulation;

(16)   'obligation' means both contractual obligation and a concerted practice;

(17)   'competing manufacturers' or manufacturers of 'competing products' means manufacturers who sell products which, in view of their characteristics, price and intended use, are considered by users to be interchangeable or substitutable for the licensed products.

Article 11

1.   Regulation (EEC) 556/89 is hereby repealed with effect from 1 April 1996.

2.   Regulation (EEC) 2349/84 shall continue to apply until 31 March 1996.

3.   The prohibition in Article 85(1) of the Treaty shall not apply to agreements in force on 31 March 1996 which fulfil the exemption requirements laid down by Regulation (EEC) 2349/84 or (EEC) 556/89.

Article 12

1.   The Commission shall undertake regular assessments of the application of this Regulation, and in particular of the opposition procedure provided for in Article 4.

2.   The Commission shall draw up a report on the operation of this Regulation before the end of the fourth year following its entry into force and shall, on that basis, assess whether any adaptation of the Regulation is desirable.

Article 13

This Regulation shall enter into force on 1 April 1996.

It shall apply until 31 March 2006.

Article 11(2) of this Regulation shall, however, enter into force on 1 January 1996.

This Regulation shall be binding in its entirety and directly applicable in all Member States.

Done at Brussels, 31 January 1996.

4.3   A Commentary on the Regulation

The subject of technology transfer is largely about licensing others to exploit your technological progress. This may occur by transferring 'know-how' to the licensee or permitting them to exploit a patent that you hold, or both. Originally, there was just a block exemption on patent licensing (Regulation 2349/84). That was due to expire at the end of 1994 but its 'life' was subsequently extended three times. The Commission subsequently issued a block exemption on 'know-how' transfer agreements (Regulation 556/89). That was not due to expire until 31 December 1999 but was relatively short-lived because on 31 January 1996, the Commission promulgated a new block exemption on technology transfer agreements (see OJ 1996 L31/2).

Regulation 240/96 came into effect on 1 April 1996, with a 10-year life. It replaced both the patent licensing block exemption *and* the know-how block exemption; as recital (3) to the Regulation states, the Commission felt that the two sets of rules ought to be harmonized and simplified as far as possible, in order to encourage the dissemination of technical knowledge in the Community and to promote the manufacture of technically more sophisticated products (see also recital 8). With those objectives in mind, agreements which are solely for the purpose of sale are excluded (recital (8)). The Commission endeavoured to show why an exemption was merited for this type of agreement; as with all of the block exemptions, the four criteria in Article 85(3) (now 81(3)) had to be satisfied. Taking them in turn, the Commission said that:

(i)   the obligations ... in Article 1 generally contribute to improving the production of goods and to promoting technical progress. They make the holders of patents or know-how more willing to grant licences and licensees more inclined to undertake the investment required to manufacture, use and put on the market a new product or to use a new process;

(ii)   consumers will, as a rule, be allowed a fair share of the benefit resulting from the improvement in the supply of goods on the market but to ensure they do ...

(iii)   ... it is right to exclude from the application of Article 1 cases where the parties agree to refuse to meet demand from users or resellers within their respective territories who would sell for export, or to take other steps to impede parallel imports. The obligations referred to above [i.e. in Article 1] only impose restrictions which are indispensable to the attainment of their objectives.

(iv)   in connection with the need to ensure that the agreement does not offer the opportunity to eradicate a significant portion of the 'competition', the Commission may withdraw the benefit of the block exemption. This may happen 'in particular where the licensed products are not faced with real competition in the licensed territory' and 'could also be the case where the licensee has a strong position on the market' (defined as a market share in excess of 40%).

See recitals 12, 17 and 26.

The new block exemption is not intended to be more restrictive than its predecessors: agreements which were in force on 31 March 1996 and fulfilled the requirements of either Regulation 2349/84 or 556/89 continue to be exempt (Article 11(3), Regulation 240/96). References to articles or recitals (in the preamble) in this chapter can be assumed to refer to Regulation 240/96 unless the contrary is stated.

4.3.1   WHAT AGREEMENTS ARE COVERED BY THE BLOCK EXEMPTION?

The block exemption applies to:

- pure patent licensing agreements;

- know-how licensing agreements; and

- mixed patent and know-how licensing agreements.

See Article 1(1) and the definition of *licensing agreement* in Article 10(6).

4.3.2 WHAT IS A PATENT?

One might have thought this was quite straightforward but there is a rather broad list in Article 8 which includes 'topographies of semiconductor products' and 'plant breeder's certificates'. All of these items are described as 'industrial property rights' in recital 1. Curiously, recital 1 also includes trademarks although these really only appear as *ancillary* intellectual property rights in the rest of this block exemption. Recital 4 specifies that the exemption applies to patents granted by Member States, Community patents and European patents.

4.3.3 WHAT IS KNOW-HOW?

Know-how is defined in Article 10. One should note its component parts, it must be:

(a) Technical information.

(b) Secret, that is:

    (i) not generally known or easily accessible;

    (ii) its communication gives the licensee a 'lead' over others;

    (iii) it is not limited to situations where each element of know-how is totally unknown or unobtainable outside the licensor's business.

(c) Substantial: it must be useful, either regarding entry to new markets or gaining a competitive edge.

(d) Can be identified in any form:

    (i) which allows it to be verified as secret and substantial;

    (ii) to ensure the licensee is not unduly restricted in exploitation of his own technology (i.e. it is not a backwards step really);

    (iii) identification can be in the licence agreement or a separate document or recorded in any other appropriate form, which can be made available if the need arises.

Know-how may be found in 'descriptions of manufacturing processes, recipes, formulae, designs or drawings'; see recital (4).

4.3.4 BASIC OVERVIEW OF REGULATION 240/96

Article 1 sets out the 'white list': clauses which automatically qualify for exemption.

Article 2 sets out the 'grey list': clauses which are not generally restrictive of competition but which are exempted in case circumstances arise which make them restrictive.

Article 3 sets out the 'black list': clauses, the presence of which, will take the agreement outside the block exemption.

Article 4 contains the opposition procedure. What if you have clauses which are restrictive of competition but which are not saved by Articles 1 or 2? So long as they do not fall within Article 3, you can notify the Commission, on Form A/B, and if the Commission raises no opposition within four months, you get the exemption.

Article 5 lists categories of agreement to which the block exemption does not apply (see also recital 8). Essentially, these are agreements for pooling patents or know-how. Such agreements are likely to frustrate technological progress by the partners and certainly act as a substantial barrier to anyone outside the pool. Also excluded are patent swaps; substantial licences of other intellectual property rights; and agreements purely for the purpose of sale. However, many of these apparently prohibited agreements can still be rescued in certain circumstances: see Article 5(2).

Article 6 lists further categories of agreement to which the block exemption applies. There are three:

(a)   where the licensor is not the intellectual property holder;

(b)   assignments where the risk stays with the assignor (typically his royalties depend on the degree of successful exploitation by the licensee);

(c)   situations where the risks or obligations of either licensor or licensee are assumed by connected undertakings.

Article 7 provides for withdrawal of the exemption if the Commission finds a specific agreement should not qualify (i.e. it actually examines that agreement). See also recital 26.

Article 8, as mentioned already, allows a liberal application of the block exemption (and see recital 4). It provides a broad definition of 'patent'; covers agreements to exploit an invention where no patent exists but one is timeously applied for; and agreements for an indefinite term may be covered in certain circumstances.

Article 9 specifies the use that may be made of information that the Commission acquires through use of the opposition procedure.

Article 10 is a 'definitions' article.

Article 11 repeals the old block exemptions from 1 April 1996.

Article 12 provides for reviews by the Commission of how the block exemption is working.

4.3.5   KEY ARTICLES FROM THE REGULATION IN MORE DETAIL

4.3.5.1   Article 1: the white list
There must be only two undertakings as parties to the agreement. There is nothing unusual in this; it is typical for block exemptions to contain this limitation. The article allows a degree of exclusivity (or market protection):

(a) **For the licensee:**

    (i)   The licensor is not to *license others for exploitation* within the licensed territory (Article 1, para. 1(1)).

    (ii)   The licensor is not to *exploit* the technology himself in the licensed territory (Article 1, para. 1(2)).

(b) **For the licensor:**

    (i)   The licensee is not to *exploit* the technology within the licensor's territory (Article 1, para. 1(3)).

(c) **For other licensees:**

    (i)   The licensee is not to *manufacture or use* the licensed *product* or use the licensed *process* in other licensees' territories (Article 1, para. 1(4)).

(ii) An *active sales ban*, i.e. the licensee must not actively *put the product on the market* in territories of other licensees and must not target such areas through advertising (Article 1, para. 1(5)).

(iii) A *passive sales ban* (Article 1, para. 1(6)). Where the agreement is a *pure patent licence*, this ban applies only to territories if they are covered by parallel patents and (in any event) expires five years after the licensed product was first put on the market by a licensee (see Article 1, para. 2). If the agreement is a *pure know-how licence*, this ban expires five years after the licensed product was first put on the market by a licensee (see Article 1, para. 3). Where the agreement is a *mixed* patent and know-how licence, this ban expires *at the latest* five years after the licensed product was first put on the market by a licensee (and earlier if the patent expires *and* the know-how becomes 'worthless'; see Article 1, para. 4).

Article 1 also deals with **trade marks**. The licensee can be obliged to apply *only the licensor's trademark* or get-up, so long as the licensee can identify itself as the manufacturer (Article 1, para. 1(7)). There is nothing new here. It respects the function of a trademark, while allowing a degree of protection for the licensee against suffering a terminal drop in market share once the agreement ends.

Article 1 also contains a (sort of) **field-of-use** provision (for true field-of-use restrictions, see Article 2, para. 1(8)). The licensee may be restricted to selling the licensed product only as an integral part of (or replacement part for) his own products and not to produce any surplus (i.e. the licensor can prevent a separate market opening up). The licensee must remain free to determine the quantities he needs for this purpose. (See Article 1, para. 1(8).)

Article 1 stipulates that there are **time limits** on the exemptions. If the agreement is a *pure patent licence* agreement, the restrictions in Article 1, para. 1(1), (2), (3), (4), (5), (7) and (8) are permitted only for so long as there is a *parallel patent in force* in the protected territory (see Article 1, para. 2). If the agreement is a *pure know-how licence* agreement, the restrictions in Article 1, para. 1(1)–(5) are permitted for a *maximum of 10 years* from the date of first marketing by a licensee. The restrictions in para. 1(7) and (8) can subsist for the *lifetime* of the agreement, *so long as* the know-how stays secret and substantial (see Article 1, para. 3). If the agreement is a *mixed patent and know-how licence* agreement, then the restrictions in para. 1(1)–(5) and (7)–(8) can last for the lifetime of the patent in territories where there is patent protection, or 10 years from the date of first marketing by a licensee, whichever is the longer. If the patent expires but the know-how is still secret and substantial, the protection continues; conversely, if the know-how becomes public but the patent remains, the protection continues. If the patent expires *and* the know-how becomes public, the protection stops forthwith. (See Article 1, para. 4; recital 16.) It does not follow that longer periods of exclusivity are not allowed, but they can only be granted by *individual* exemption (see recital 14).

4.3.5.2 Article 2: the grey list

This Article contains a long list of obligations which are not normally restrictive of competition. They are included in the regulation in order to clarify that, 'in the event that because of the particular economic or legal circumstances they should fall within Article 85(1) [now 81(1)], they too will be covered by the exemption' (recital 18). These obligations include:

(a) Protection of **confidentiality** in the form of:

(i) non-disclosure (Article 2, para. 1(1) — this can continue post-termination);

(ii) non-exploitation; and

(iii) enforcement. The licensee can be obliged to tell the licensor of any 'leak' of know-how or patent infringement; and participate in taking legal action against the offender. See Article 2, para. 1(6).

There are several examples of non-exploitation given:

(i) *Simple* non-exploitation. See Article 2, para. 1(3); recital 20. This applies post-termination for the lifetime of the patent or as long as the know-how is still secret.

(ii) Article 2, para. 1(12): the licensee can be obliged not to use the licensed technology to build *facilities for third parties*. The licensee can, however, expand or build additional facilities *for himself*.

(iii) The licensor can reserve the right to pursue a *patent infringement action against the licensee*, should the licensee seek to exploit the patent/ technology *outside the licensed territory* (maybe by going somewhere without patent protection or short-life patents). See Article 2, para. 1(14).

(iv) The licensor can require the licensee to prove that the know-how is not being used in connection with non-licensed products where the licensee gets involved with *competing products*. See Article 2, para. 1(18); also see 'non-competition' below.

(b) Power to control **who holds a licence** (see Article 2, para. 1(2)).

(c) **Grant-back** licences regarding improvements or new applications discovered by the licensee. But these are approved only if the licensor agrees to grant a licence (exclusive or otherwise) to the licensee for his own improvements. Also, if the improvement is severable, the licence grant-back must not be exclusive; i.e. the licensee must remain free to use his own improvements or even licence them to third parties, if he can do so without disclosing still-secret know-how.

(d) Methods of ensuring **quality control** over the licensed product or technology. These can include observance of minimum quality specifications, technical specifications, or sourcing goods/services from nominated suppliers. See Article 2, para. 1(5). Cf. *assignment* of improvements *forbidden* by Article 3(6).

(e) Issues over **royalty** payments:

(i) **guaranteeing income** for the licensor in the form of a minimum royalty or an obligation to produce a minimum quantity of the licensed product or to use the licensed technology a minimum number of times (see Article 2, para. 1(9));

(ii) **spreading royalties** over the duration of the agreement, even if the patents have expired (because to do so may 'facilitate' payment; see Article 2, para. 1(7)(b)); and

(iii) requiring the licensee to pay royalties in accordance with the terms of the agreement throughout the life of the agreement, **even though** the **know-how** has become **public** (so long as publication has not been by action of the licensor). Clearly, if know-how has been published by action of the licensee, there may be a claim for additional damages by the licensor against the licensee. See Article 2, para. 1(7)(a); recital 21.

(f) (True) **field-of-use** restrictions on licensee. See Article 2, para. 1(8); recital 22.

(g) **'Most favoured partner'** status for the licensee. In other words, if some later licensee cuts a better deal, then the previous one(s) also get the benefit. This is useful because, as time goes by, circumstances may change; a licensee would not want to suffer by being the first in line. It is an added incentive to be first in line — it encourages and accelerates exploitation of the licensed product or technology. See Article 2, para. 1(10).

(h) Obligation to **identify** the licensor and/or the patent by a mark. Not, presumably, the licensor's trademark since that was covered by Article 1, para. 1(7). This must be a little broader. See Article 2, para. 1(11).

(i) **Limits on quantity** to be supplied to a customer. This applies only to particularised customers and where the licence was only granted to provide for possible shortfalls in the quantity that might be supplied to that customer by another licensee in that territory (i.e. the limited licensee is created as a fall-back or second-source supplier). See Article 2, para. 1(13); recital 23.

(j) **Non-challenge** clauses. This seems a very strange provision. If the licensee contests whether the know-how is secret or substantial, or challenges the validity of the patent, or claims the patent is unnecessary, the licensor may have reserved the right to terminate the agreement. One might have thought this was forbidden, since it is not in society's interests for people to pay money for unnecessary information or for monopoly profits to be earned from an unwarranted patent. The licensee is usually in the best position to raise such a claim. Is this simply a pragmatic recognition by the Commission that licensors will not licence without such 'protection'? See Article 2, para. 1(15) and (16).

(k) Limited form of **non-competition** clauses. The licensee may be required to use *best endeavours* to make and market the licensed product. See Article 2, para. 1(17). Further, the licensor may reserve the right to *terminate* the licensee's *exclusivity* and *stop licensing improvements* to him if the licensee starts to *compete* with the licensor within the common market. Such competition could be in research and development, or production, use or distribution of the product. In such circumstances, the licensor can put the licensee to proof that licensed know-how is not being misused. See Article 2, para. 1(18). Cf. Article 3(2): the agreement cannot actually prohibit competition by the licensee.

4.3.5.3 Article 3: the 'black list'

These are the 'no-no' clauses; if any of them are included in the agreement then the benefit of the block exemption is lost. As well as Article 3, see recital 19.

(a) **Price fixing** is the first entry and is still clearly forbidden. See Article 3(1); recital 24. By way of comparison, in its recent Green Paper on Vertical Restraints, the Commission noted that when an agreement exceeds the *de minimis* rules Article 81(1) (ex 85(1)) will apply 'virtually automatically to certain vertical agreements which by their very nature can only distort competition, in particular ... agreements which limit the freedom of distributors to set their resale prices (Resale Price Maintenance)'.

(b) **Non-competition** is next. Any restriction on the ability of either party to compete is forbidden (whether it applies to research and development, production, use or distribution of competing products). Clearly, the behaviour permitted by Article 2, para. 1(17) and (18) is not seen as restrictive. See Article 3(2).

(c) Hindering **parallel imports** must not occur. Where either party is required to (or does so as the result of a concerted practice)

(i) refuse orders from customers who wish to market products in other territories in the common market (this covers simple re-selling of the product and using it as a component of some new product); or

(ii) use intellectual property rights to prevent lawful marketing

then, in the absence of 'any objectively justified reason', the agreement does not benefit from the block exemption. See Article 3(3).

(d) **Restrictions on customers**. Where the parties to the agreement were competing manufacturers before the licence, there shall be no restriction on (or sharing out of) customers, except as permitted by Article 2, para. 1(13) and by Article 1, para. 1(7) (dealing with trademarks and the get-up of the product). An example of what is forbidden is the reservation of different classes of customer to the licensor. See Article 3(4); recital 23.

(e) **Maximum quantities**. Other than limiting the licensee to only making as much as he needs (Article 1, para. 1(8)) and limiting the amount that a secondary supplier can make for a particular customer (Article 2, para. 1(13)), there can be no upper limit on the quantity of the licensed product made or the number of times that a licensed technology is used. See Article 3(5); recital 24.

(f) **Obligatory assignment** of improvements or new applications should not appear. See Article 3(6); recital 20.

(g) **Prolonging territorial protection**. If there is an attempt to prolong exclusivity, whether of the licensor or licensee, beyond the periods permitted for 'pure' agreements then the benefit of the block exemption is lost. Such an attempt might include prolonging exclusivity as the result of communicating improvements. See Article 3(7); recital 14.

The other major 'no-no' that one might have expected to find in the black list is absolute territorial protection. One sees in the Commission Green Paper on Vertical Restraints, para. 21, that agreements which establish absolute territorial protection 'by their very nature can only distort competition'. However, although that point is 'central to Commission policy', it is mentioned only in the context of distribution. A different line has often been taken with technically innovative licences. An early example came with the judgment of the Court of Justice in *Nungesser and Eisele* v *Commission* (258/78) [1982] ECR 2015; this is echoed in recital (10) of Regulation 240/96:

> exclusive licensing agreements ... may not be in themselves incompatible with Article 85(1) [now 81(1)] [again, signs of a rule of reason approach] where they are concerned with the introduction and protection of a new technology in the licensed territory, by reason of the scale of the research which has been undertaken, of the increase in the level of competition, in particular inter-brand competition, and of the competitiveness of the undertakings concerned resulting from the dissemination of innovation within the Community.

4.3.5.4 Article 4: the opposition procedure

Parties to a licensing agreement are encouraged to use the opposition procedure in two specific instances:

(a) Where the licensee is obliged to accept licences, or procure goods or services, which are not necessary for a technically satisfactory exploitation of the licensed technology or for ensuring respect for quality standards. These are forms of **tie** which previously have been black-listed (cf. the patent licensing regulation 2349/84 at Article 3(4) and (9); the know-how regulation 556/89 at Article 3(3)). In the block exemptions for patent licensing and know-how, such obligations were prohibited unless they were necessary for a technically satisfactory exploitation of the licensed invention, or perhaps necessary to ensure respect for quality standards during production. See Article 4, para. 2(a).

(b) Where the licensee is prohibited from contesting the licensed know-how or challenging the validity of the licensed patent. Again, this prohibition was black-listed in the patent and know-how block exemptions (see Article 3(1) and Article 3(4), respectively). In both cases, the licensor was allowed to retain a right to terminate the licence in the event of such a challenge. See Article 4, para. 2(b); recital 25.

FIVE

ARTICLE 82: ABUSE OF A DOMINANT POSITION

5.1 The Elements of Article 82

Any abuse by one or more undertakings of a dominant position within the common market or in a substantial part of it shall be prohibited as incompatible with the common market in so far as it may affect trade between Member States. Such abuse may, in particular, consist in:

(a) directly or indirectly imposing unfair purchase or selling prices or other unfair trading conditions;

(b) limiting production, markets or technical development to the prejudice of consumers;

(c) applying dissimilar conditions to equivalent transactions with other trading parties, thereby placing them at a competitive disadvantage;

(d) making the conclusion of contracts subject to acceptance by the other parties of supplementary obligations which, by their nature or according to commercial usage, have no connection with the subject of such contracts.

Generally speaking, the competition rules are not concerned with the acquisition of monopoly power by an individual enterprise but rather with the way in which such power is used — or abused (see **5.6**). Only those businesses which are dominant within the common market or a substantial part of it are at risk of infringing Article 82 (ex 86), EC Treaty — the Community is not concerned with big fishes in insignificant pools. Article 82 (ex 86) may be broken up into several significant elements:

(a) relevant product market; (plus)

(b) relevant geographical market; (leads to)

(c) a dominant position;

(d) for one or more undertakings;

(e) in a substantial part of the Common Market;

(f) abusive behaviour;

(g) effect on trade between Member States.

We shall examine each of these in this chapter.

5.2 Dominant Position

5.2.1 FOUR QUESTIONS TO ASK

It has been said (Korah, *An Introductory Guide to EC Competition Law & Practice*, p. 80) that, in order to determine whether there is a dominant position, you must ask four questions:

(a) Which firm is accused?

(b) Which products sold by it are involved in the complaint?

(c) Who buys them?

(d) What else could be used by those customers with minimal adaptation to their business? (i.e., what substitutes are there?)

Identification of the products and the location of customers is very important because these factors will be crucial in determining the relevant market share of the suspect undertaking.

The analysis is usually described as defining the relevant product market and the relevant geographical market. The ECJ has consistently said that an undertaking can have a dominant position only if it dominates in a relevant product and geographical market. It may seem to be stating the obvious but you cannot ascertain market share (or power) unless you first ascertain what the appropriate market is.

5.2.2 RELEVANT PRODUCT MARKET

The issue here is essentially what product(s) are we interested in? To assist in defining the product market, we could try to answer Professor Korah's four questions (at **5.2.1**):

(a) Identify your suspect undertaking. It may be a corporate group or a parent and subsidiary.

(b) Identify which of its products are the subject of the investigation.

(c) Who buys them? This is important for three reasons. First, because, having identified the customers, you can start to see what alternative products would satisfy them. Then, having decided who are the customers, you can see *where* they are. It is useful to know what territory should be considered. Why do you need to know this?

   (i) To define the geographical market for the product. This will be the next step in defining the market — an undertaking's share of sales will vary according to both what is sold and over what territory. A good example is *Michelin* (see **5.2.3.2**). A company's market share of saloon car tyres will probably differ from its market share for all types of motor vehicle tyres. Again, market share will vary according to whether we look at (say) just The Netherlands or the whole common market.

   (ii) Jurisdiction. If you have a dominant position in an insubstantial part of the common market, a *de minimis* argument will apply. No matter how abusive your behaviour, if you are a big fish in a little pond the European Commission is not likely to be interested. See, e.g., *Cutsforth* v *Mansfield Inns Ltd* [1986] 1 WLR 558, *Hugin/Liptons* v *Commission* (22/78) [1979] ECR 1869 and, by analogy, the Commission's Notices on Agreements of Minor Importance.

(d) What acceptable substitutes there are (on both the supply side and demand side)? We need to know because we are concerned with the undertaking's ability to act independently of others.

5.2.2.1 Substitution

The way(s) in which the Commission and ECJ define 'market' has (have) been criticised by economists. They complain that the notion of a single, compartmentalised market is usually unattainable because there will often be substitutes. Further, as Barry Hawk, has observed, 'market definition more often than not reflects a legal conclusion, not an economic fact'.

As a general rule, the broader the definition of the relevant product market (and the same applies for the geographical market), the less likely you are to find a dominant position. Why? Because of *substitutes*, basically.

For the product market, let us return to the example of *Michelin* v *Commission* (322/81) [1983] ECR 3461. If we define the relevant product as 'tyres', the company faces competition from all other sources of tyre; every other tyre is a potential substitute and so the company's market share is likely to be low. We may wish to define the product more narrowly: not simply 'tyres', but 'new tyres'. At least we now remove second-hand tyres from our analysis. We could go further and define the product ever more narrowly: new tyres; new tyres for vehicles other than saloon cars; new tyres for commercial goods vehicles; new tyres for heavy goods vehicles; new replacement tyres for HGVs. As we continue down this road, the number of potential substitutes drops and thus our company's market share rises. If we then look at the geographical market we could find that over different areas tastes may change; transport costs may inhibit long-range shipment of goods so that market share drops: so, the larger the territory, the smaller the market share is likely to be. It may be concluded that if the product is defined very narrowly and the chosen geographical market is small, substitution becomes less likely and market share will rise.

Reference was made above to substitutes being either supply-side (who else could step into your shoes?) or demand-side (what else could customers use to replace your product?) An example of a case where the Commission looked at *supply-side* substitutes is *Europemballage Corp. and Continental Can Co.* (6/72) [1973] ECR 215. The product was found to be light metal containers for meat and fish, and lids for jars. The Commission cast around for other manufacturers who could step into the shoes of Continental Can but seemed unable to conclude that companies who make light metal containers for fruit and vegetables (for example) might be able to supply Continental Can's customers. However, the Commission was criticised for its confused thinking by the ECJ on appeal (see paras 33–36 of ECJ judgment). This may explain why the Commission does not undertake this supply-side analysis very often.

A case where the Commission looked at *demand-side* substitutes is *United Brands* v *Commission* (27/76) [1978] ECR 207. The Commission found the product market was limited to fresh bananas (as opposed to fresh fruit generally, or non-citrus fruits). The Commission's decision was upheld by the ECJ, rather surprisingly given the apparent fluctuations in the price of bananas during the year coinciding with the availability of other fruits (see, e.g., paras 15 and 16 of the judgment). Apparently, the banana has particular qualities of softness and seedlessness and is good for the young, the old and the sick (described by Barry Hawk as a Clint Eastwood classification). The ECJ described the banana as a 'privileged fruit' (see paras 23-25 of the judgment). The Commission's Notice on the definition of the relevant market (OJ 1997 C 372) states that demand substitution:

> constitutes the most immediate and effective disciplinary force on the suppliers of a given product, in particular in relation to their pricing decisions.

The Commission appears to favour a test known as the SSNIP test. In this test, one looks at the consequences of a firm imposing a small but significant non-transitory increase in the price of its product. If a permanent price rise, of the order of 5–10%, would be unprofitable because customers would switch to other, substitute, products, then those products should be included in the definition of the relevant product market. However, this is only one possible measure for defining the product market, amongst many. Product characteristics and intended use are, by themselves, seen as inadequate guides to demand substitution. The Commission has identified several sources of evidence:

- actual substitution in the recent past;

- quantitative economic and statistical tests;

- the views of customers and competitors, expressed directly and through market research studies;

- barriers and other costs involved in switching demand to substitute products;

- the existence of different categories of customers (the presence of whom might indicate specific niche markets).

A consideration of product definition and substitutability outside the European Community came in the Full Federal Court of Australia (see *Singapore Airlines Ltd* v *Taprobane Tours WA Pty Ltd* (1992) ATPR 41-159). T was a wholesale travel agent. One of its products was package tours to the Maldives from Australia, with the flights provided by Singapore Airlines (SA). After three years, SA reduced the number of flights between Australia and the Maldives, limited them to departures from one State in Australia and raised the prices it charged to T but not to other wholesalers. T sued, alleging an abuse of market power (analogous to Article 82 (ex 86), EC Treaty). The Full Federal Court held that the relevant product market was 'airline services to destinations outside mainland Australia' and package tours to such places, *not* return air flights to the Maldives. SA was dominant in such flights but there were many other holiday destinations and many other package tours to them, i.e. plenty of substitutes, so the court held that SA had insufficient market power for the case to succeed.

Time is also important when considering the possibility of substitution. When the Commission looks at supply-side substitutes, it usually does so in the short term (who could step in and meet demand *now*?), while a longer-term view might result in more substitutes being able to come forward (e.g. other companies could re-tool their plant, retrain staff, end existing contracts). A good illustration of the Commission's use of this short time-span is found in the 'Vitamins' case, see **5.2.4.5**. The Commission has stated, in its Notice on the definition of the relevant market (OJ 1997 C 372), that:

> When supply side substitutability would imply the need to adjust significantly existing tangible and intangible assets, additional investments, strategic decisions or time delays, it will not be considered at the stage of market definition.

5.2.3 RELEVANT GEOGRAPHICAL MARKET

As mentioned earlier, we need to consider this for three reasons:

(a) it helps to define the market (and, indirectly, dominance);

(b) it determines whether a substantial part of the common market is involved;

(c) it helps to see if there is any effect on trade between Member States.

5.2.3.1 Defining the geographical market

The geographical market may be delimited by, for example, consumer tastes and transport costs — those matters which establish a separate market. In fact, we also need to see where goods sold in the market come from. If 'local' prices are high, this may encourage some suppliers, who are geographically remote, to transport their product from there to here. This may suggest that the geographical market is to include here and there too.

Barry Hawk has stated that in most decisions of the Commission, there is little or no analysis of the relevant geographical market. He says that this may be because it was obvious in the particular case — he gives the example of *Commercial Solvents* (the company was found to possess a worldwide monopoly and thus a dominant position in the common market).

Often an abstract formulation is offered by either Court or Commission but this is of little practical assistance in forecasting the way a decision will go (or advising one's clients).

The ECJ has insisted that different territories must present homogenous conditions for trade to form a comparable basis for analysis of market power. The ECJ and Commission seem very keen to use single Member States as the geographical market — where they go beyond this, similarity of trading conditions is important.

5.2.3.2   Three examples

(a) A simple example is *Alsatel Société Alsacienne et Lorraine de Télécommunications et d'Eléctronique* v *Novasam SA* (247/86) [1988] ECR 5987. A was found by the Regional Court, Strasbourg, to have a major share of the regional market in the relevant product (telephone installations) but the ECJ held, on a preliminary reference, that 'the relevant context within which the conditions of competition are sufficiently uniform to enable the economic strength of the undertaking in question to be assessed is the market in telephone installations for *the whole of France'*. Since A was dominant only in the Alsace-Lorraine area and had no dominant position in the relevant product market for the whole of France, the ECJ found that Article 86 (now 82) did not apply.

(b) *United Brands* (see paras 36-53 of the judgment). The Commission was right to consider Germany, Denmark, Ireland, The Netherlands and Belgium/Luxembourg as the geographical market because all six had free competition in bananas (whilst not necessarily being the same in trading conditions, e.g. transport costs), while in the other three Member States (i.e., France, Italy, the United Kingdom) there was State interference in the market (see, e.g., paras 36, 38, 44, 46, 51-53 of the judgment).

(c) *Michelin.* The Commission took The Netherlands as the relevant geographical market for heavy truck tyres. Michelin NV (which was the undertaking under investigation) complained to the ECJ that this was too narrow (see para 23 of the judgment). Michelin NV relied on the fact that the Commission had considered factors pertaining to the whole Michelin group when looking at market power, e.g. its technological lead over rivals and group financial strength. Michelin said that this suggested 'a much wider market' or even the world market. Its main competitors are worldwide. The Commission's response was that tyre makers have chosen to sell tyres through national subsidiaries in the national markets; thus, Michelin NV faces competition on The Netherlands market. The ECJ upheld the Commission's decision — tyre dealers who are established in The Netherlands in practice obtain their supplies only from suppliers operating in The Netherlands. So, Michelin NV's competition is 'mainly' on The Netherlands market and it is at that level that the objective conditions of competition are the same for traders.

5.2.3.3   Conclusion

It may be concluded that both the Commission and the European Court are often prepared to limit the relevant geographical market to the territory of a single Member State. They may be unlikely to consider a larger territory even where there is (apparently) clear evidence of competition from outside the Member State or cross-elasticity of supply.

Remember, we must also determine the geographical market in order to establish whether the area under consideration is at least a *'substantial part of the common market'* (the fourth element of Article 82 (ex 86)). This is related to the jurisdictional point referred to earlier (i.e., whether there is any effect on inter-State trade). See **5.7**.

5.2.4   MARKET POWER

5.2.4.1   The ability to act independently

Once you have defined the market, you can then try to assess the undertaking's market power. Barry Hawk says that 'Neither the definition nor the determination of dominant position under Article [82] bears much resemblance to the economic analysis of market power'.

We must remember that we are looking at the ways in which people who are basically lawyers have interpreted and applied Article 82 (ex 86). Bearing that in mind, what are the symbols of such power in a market that enable us to say the undertaking has a dominant position? According to decided cases, they are:

(a) the power to prevent effective competition; and/or

(b) the power to behave independently of competitors, suppliers and customers, to an appreciable extent.

We can see this test in the following extract from the Court's judgment in *Hoffmann-La Roche* v *Commission* (85/76) [1979] ECR 461 (the 'Vitamins' case):

[D]ominant position relates to a position of economic strength enjoyed by an undertaking which enables it to prevent effective competition being maintained on the relevant market by affording it the power to behave to an appreciable extent independently of its competitors, its customers and ultimately of the consumers.

In *Michelin* v *Commission* (322/81) [1983] ECR 3461 the Court stated:

[I]t is not a precondition for finding that a dominant position exists in the case of a given product that there should be a complete absence of competition from other partially interchangeable products so long as such competition does not affect the undertaking's ability to influence appreciably the conditions in which that competition may be exerted or at any rate to conduct itself to a large extent without having to take account of that competition and without suffering any adverse effects as a result of its attitude.

It should be noted that although most of the reported cases on 'dominant position' refer to an independence of action over one's competitors, this 'horizontal' form of dominance is not the only way to achieve a dominant position. One may be 'vertically' dominant — that is, a company may dominate its supplier (or its customers). An example of supplier-dominance may be seen in the *Volvo* v *Veng* case (see **5.3** and **8.6**), while customer-dominance could be illustrated by the purchasing power of the National Health Service in the United Kingdom (or British Telecom or the Ministry of Defence) regarding appropriate products.

5.2.4.2 Absolute domination is unnecessary

Although the ECJ said in *Hoffmann-La Roche* v *Commission* that the possession of a very large share of the market was a highly important element in establishing a dominant position, it is clear that absolute domination of the market is not needed. This is best illustrated by *United Brands* v *Commission*, where the 'dominant' enterprise was engaged in losing a price war with its main competitor (Chiquita against Dole bananas). What you have to do is analyse the market share of the suspect undertaking.

5.2.4.3 Diagnosing market power

We have seen the criteria set out by the Court for a dominant position, but how are we to determine whether those criteria have been satisfied in any particular case? It seems that the existence of a dominant position may derive from several factors which, taken separately, are not necessarily determinative; but among these factors a highly important one is the existence of very large market shares. See *Hoffmann-La Roche* v *Commission*.

An economist might assert that market power can be directly measured by examining (for example):

(a) whether the company's customers can buy the product from someone else;

(b) whether the company is charging an excessively high price compared to its marginal cost;

(c) whether the company is making monopoly profits;

(d) whether the company is engaging in price discrimination.

5.2.4.4   Market share

In practice, all of these four measurements are difficult to determine with certainty. The most simple symptom to spot (and therefore the one most relied on) is *market share*. This gives a 'rough and ready' diagnosis and may affirm the presence of a dominant position where a more sophisticated analysis would reject it; but often such sophisticated analysis is very difficult to do. Barry Hawk describes the use of market share as a benchmark as 'a necessary evil'.

So, how has this worked in practice? We can use *Hoffmann-La Roche* to illustrate the situation. In this case the Commission relied on Hoffmann-La Roche's market share in seven vitamins to demonstrate its dominance, especially when compared to the market shares of its competitors (see p. 504 of the judgment).

The ECJ reiterated its 'test' of whether an undertaking can prevent effective competition and act, to an appreciable extent, independently. It then went on (para. 41):

> . . . the view may legitimately be taken that very large shares are *in themselves*, and save in exceptional circumstances, evidence of the existence of a dominant position.

We can see the same analysis in the later case of *AKZO Chemie BV* v *Commission* (C-62/86) [1991] ECR I-3359, where market share of over 50% appears to show a dominant position in the absence of exceptional circumstances and the onus of proof shifts to the suspect undertaking to disprove its dominance (see further **5.2.4.7**).

The same approach has been used by the Court of First Instance, in *Hilti AG* v *Commission* (T-30/89) [1991] ECR II-1439 where market shares between 70 and 80% were, in themselves, clear indications of a dominant position. Hilti disputed these figures before the CFI, saying they were unreliable. Hilti's credibility was rather stretched by the fact that it had supplied the figures in response to a request from the Commission (pursuant to Article 11, Regulation 17).

The Court of First Instance also observed that the several patents which Hilti possessed went towards strengthening its position on the market. This leads on to a consideration of the secondary symptoms which may support the initial diagnosis of a dominant position.

5.2.4.5   Ancillary factors

In *Hoffmann-La Roche*, the significant factors for the Commission were (see para. 42 of judgment):

   (a)   the size of Hoffmann's market share;

   (b)   the size of the disparity between its market share and that of its rivals;

 *(c)   the fact that it produces a much wider range of vitamins than its competitors;

 *(d)   the fact that Hoffmann is the largest manufacturer of vitamins in the world with a turnover exceeding that of all the other producers;

   (e)   its technological advantages over the others, originally given by patent but now achieved by its 'leading role' in the field;

   (f)   its very extensive and highly specialised sales network;

   (g)   the absence of potential competition.

In addition to market share, heads (b), (e), (f) and (g) were all relevant factors according to the ECJ. Head (b) enables an undertaking's competitive strength to be assessed; (e) and (f) represent technical and commercial advantages; (g) is the result of having obstacles which prevent entry to the market by potential competitors.

*Conversely, head (c) was rejected by the ECJ as immaterial — there are separate markets for each vitamin. Head (d) was also rejected by the ECJ — other companies who make vitamins play on the world market with other products and enjoy the freedom to set off one market against another.

The ECJ then applied each of these factors to the seven different product markets under consideration.

Looking at the *Michelin* case, we can see the Court attaching significance to the relative economic strengths of Michelin and its Dutch competitors. Michelin is part of a group of undertakings operating throughout Europe and the world. This gives it an advantage in investment and research. It also has an unusually large product range — for certain types of tyre, Michelin is the only supplier in The Netherlands. Michelin has a larger network of sales representatives than its competitors, offering an excellent service. (The French Government intervened, alleging that Michelin was being penalised for providing a good product and service — the argument was rejected by the ECJ.)

A similar analysis can be clearly seen in the *United Brands* case. The Commission found United Brands' market share to be 45%. United Brands pointed out that in 1975 this dropped to 41%. The ECJ observed that a trader can only be in a dominant position with a product if it has 'succeeded in winning a large part' of the market. The Court said the evidence showed that United Brands' market share was always more than 40% and nearly 45%. 'This percentage does NOT permit the conclusion that the company automatically controls the market.' So the Court had to look at other factors — for example, it must take into consideration the strength and number of United Brands' competitors. United Brands' market share was several times greater than its nearest competitor, with the rest far behind. This situation can indicate its preponderant strength in the market.

5.2.4.6 The time factor

The timescale which is used when measuring the possibility of other companies entering the market is an important consideration in determining if there are potential supply-side substitutes for the relevant product. The Commission and ECJ have both relied on a very short-term look at the possible competitors. In *Hoffmann-La Roche*, the test was, if Hoffmann-La Roche pushed prices up (or decreased production), would those companies with smaller market shares 'be able to meet *rapidly* the demand from those who would like to break away from the undertaking which has the largest market share?'. This short timespan for potential competitors to become actual competition can be criticised.

Again, in *Commercial Solvents*, the ECJ said that if there was a raw material on the market which could be substituted without difficulty for nitropropane or aminobutanol when making ethambutol, this could mean that Commercial Solvents did not have a dominant position, but no such raw material then existed.

In *Michelin*, you might be forgiven for thinking that as the relevant product was a specific type of tyre, it would be quite easy for other tyre manufacturers to switch production over to that type and so provide a substitute for Michelin's product. The ECJ took a different view (at para. 41):

> ... there is no elasticity of supply between tyres for heavy vehicles and car tyres owing to significant differences in production techniques and in the plant and tools needed for their manufacture. The fact that time and considerable investment are required in order to modify production plant for the manufacture of light-vehicle tyres instead of heavy-vehicle tyres or vice versa means that there is no discernible relationship between the two categories of tyre, enabling production to be adapted to demand on the market.

5.2.4.7 Disproving dominance

As noted above, in the *Akzo Chemie* case, the ECJ held that mere possession of a market share in excess of 50% would, in the absence of exceptional circumstances, shift the onus of proof onto the company to disprove dominance. How might a company discharge that onus?

In *Hoffmann-La Roche*, the company argued that it faced 'lively competition'. The ECJ said that this does not preclude a dominant position. A dominant position means that such competition goes on without the dominant undertaking having to modify its behaviour or suffering any detrimental effects from not modifying its behaviour. But if a competitor's price reductions compelled an undertaking to cut its own prices, this behaviour would be incompatible with the independence which marks out a dominant position. (See paras 69-71 of the judgment.)

Again, turning to *Michelin*, the company argued that over recent years it had made a loss. The ECJ observed that 'temporary unprofitability or even losses are not inconsistent with the existence of a dominant position'. (See para. 59 of the judgment.)

Similar arguments had been tried and found wanting in *United Brands*. The company complained that it had suffered 'fierce competition'. The ECJ said that it is unnecessary to have eliminated all competition in order to be in a dominant position: United Brands always held out successfully against the attacks of its competitors. Also, United Brands pointed out that it had made losses for five years while its competitors made profits; if a dominant position gave a company the power to fix prices, then making a loss did not show a dominant position. The ECJ rejected this — over the five years customers continued to buy more bananas from United Brands even though it was the dearest vendor: this was a more significant factor. It is a particular feature of a dominant position and was determinative in this particular case.

5.3 Legal Monopolies and a Dominant Position

It might seem that to hold a legal monopoly in a product — e.g. through a patent, copyright or registered design — might lead to the relevant company having a dominant position with regard to that product. Of course, whether this was the situation in fact should depend on the availability of substitute products to satisfy customer demand. The Court of Justice has not said that mere possession of a legal monopoly over a product is enough to create a dominant position in the market for that product: e.g., *Deutsche Grammophon* v *Metro-SB Grossmarkte* (78/70) [1971] ECR 487.

In *Volvo AB* v *Erik Veng (UK) Ltd* (238/87) [1988] ECR 6211 the ECJ was specifically asked by the High Court, on a preliminary reference, whether the possession of exclusive rights to manufacture and import certain car body panels gave Volvo a dominant position. (Volvo had the exclusive rights because they held the UK registered designs for those parts.) The ECJ was also asked a second question — whether a refusal to license others to import the panels constituted an abuse under Article 86 (now 82). The ECJ answered the second question, saying that there was no proof of abuse, and therefore it found it unnecessary to answer the first question.

The topic was raised again in 1988 in an Italian case involving Renault car parts (*Consorzio Italiano della Componentistica di Ricambio per Autoveicoli and SpA Maxicar* v *Regie Nationale des Usines Renault* (53/87) [1988] ECR 6039). One question posed by the Italian court was whether the obtaining of protective rights in respect of ornamental models for car bodywork components and the exercise of the resultant exclusive rights constituted an abuse of a dominant position within Article 86 (now 82)? With respect to the drafter of the preliminary reference, this seems to roll up two questions into one, and the ECJ gave a straightforward answer: 'the mere fact of obtaining protective rights in respect of ornamental designs for car bodywork components does not constitute an abuse of a dominant position within the meaning of Article 86 [now 82] of the Treaty.' It does appear, though, from the subsequent text of the judgment that the ECJ still thought that the mere possession of an exclusive right did not constitute a dominant position. (See, in particular, para. 18 of the judgment.)

This straightforward view may be in the process of changing, though. In the case of *Radio Telefis Eireann et al* v *Commission* (T-69-70/89, 76/89) [1991] ECR II-485, the Commission initially found that various broadcasting organisations had a factual monopoly over television listings. This meant that any third parties who were interested in publishing a weekly guide to such listings were in a position of economic dependence on those organisations. (Such dependence is often owed to those who are in a dominant position.) The Commission found that this factual monopoly was strengthened into a legal monopoly by the use of copyright. The Commission found that the organisations did not permit third-party competition and inferred that they each held a dominant position.

The decision was challenged in the Court of First Instance. The Court decided that the relevant product was 'weekly television guides with comprehensive listings for the week'. Because of their copyright, the organisations had a monopoly over publication of such listings and a dominant position on the market for the listings. They also had a dominant position in the secondary market for magazines in which such listings are published. This has subsequently been upheld by the ECJ (1995).

We can see that the nub of the judgment may be the decision to extend the copyright monopoly over listings into a different market — that of printed weekly television guides. We can apply this argument to the *Volvo* situation and see that Volvo are likely to have a dominant position in the market for new spare parts for Volvo vehicles. This could be regarded as a secondary market (the primary one being the market for new, factory-fresh Volvos) and we would then have the answer to the question that the ECJ dodged answering in *Volvo* itself. However, the ECJ stated explicitly in the *RTE* appeal (1995) that the mere ownership of an intellectual property right does *not* confer a dominant position.

Before leaving this topic, we should note also the assertion by Claus-Dieter Ehlermann, in 1993 14 ECLR 61, that it is the 'well-established case-law of the [ECJ] that an undertaking which holds *an exclusive right* in a substantial part of the Common Market can be considered to be in a dominant position within Article 86 [now 82]'. He cites *CBEM/CLT* (311/84) [1985] ECR 3261 as authority for this (the 'Telemarketing' case). However, these exclusive rights appear to be basically those permitting public utilities to have a form of monopoly (e.g., BT, British Gas, etc.). The position there may be much clearer than it is in the 'pure' private sector. Lastly, on a national note, we should be aware of a more recent judgment in the English Patents Court — *Chiron Corporation and others* v *Organon Teknika Ltd and others* [1992] 3 CMLR 813.

5.4   One or More Undertakings

This element of Article 82 (ex 86) does not require a great deal of elaboration. The Article clearly envisages a situation where two or more undertakings abuse a dominant position. This seems to be aimed at corporate groups which act as a single unit, e.g. parent and subsidiary, as in *Commercial Solvents Corp.* v *Commission* (6-7/73) [1974] ECR 223.

An alternative meaning is that one can take a number of separate undertakings, add together their market shares, and see if they have a dominant position between them. The ECJ seems to have accepted this in situations where several companies have agreed to act in concert but, as this behaviour will usually fall within Article 81(1) (ex 85(1)), the additional infringement of Article 82 (ex 86) adds little. The ECJ seems to avoid suggesting that independent companies, against whom there is no evidence of collusion, should be examined to see if they have joint dominance even though no individual has a dominant position. The ECJ concept of dominance relies on a *unilateral* exercise of power: see the decision of the Court in *Zuchner* v *Bayerische Vereinsbank* [1981] ECR 2021 and the opinion of (then) Advocate-General Slynn who said:

[O]ne of the hallmarks of a dominant position covered by Article 86 [now 82] is its unilateral nature. As a result... it is right to point out that only [Article 81 (ex 85)] applies if the facts establish the existence of a concerted practice.

The concept of 'one or more undertakings' has been the subject of attention from the Court of First Instance. In the 'Italian Flat Glass' case (*Società Italiana Vetro SpA et al v Commission* (T-68, 77 and 78/89) [1992] ECR II-1403 three companies each made flat glass in Italy. They allegedly operated a cartel. The Commission alleged that this cartel (clearly a breach of Article 85 (now 81)) also contravened Article 86 (now 82) as, taken together, the three companies held a dominant position on the Italian market for flat glass. The Court rejected the suggestion that the same factors which showed a breach of Article 85 (now 81) could also be used to demonstrate a breach of Article 86 (now 82). However, the Court accepted the argument that circumstances could arise where several undertakings together abuse a dominant position, although that was only likely to be the case where they were united by 'economic links' of some form. It remains to be seen whether this represents any real advance beyond the position noted above in *Commercial Solvents*.

5.5 Within the Common Market or a Substantial Part of It

The relevant territory was considered as an element within 'dominant position' because we need to establish the relevant geographical market before we can begin to ascertain the market share of a company. The phrase 'within the Common Market or a substantial part of it' appears in Article 82 (ex 86) to shift attention to jurisdiction. If the dominant position is not held over the whole of the Community or an economically significant part of it, there is no 'Community interest' in how the dominant company behaves. That is not to say that national authorities will be similarly uninterested in the behaviour; it just means that the Commission, as Community watchdog, will not need to get involved.

Examples of geographical areas which have fulfilled this requirement are:

(a) The entire common market: *Hoffmann-La Roche* v *Commission* ('Vitamins').

(b) The United Kingdom: *Hugin/Liptons* v *Commission*.

(c) The Netherlands: *Michelin* v *Commission*; *BP* v *Commission* (77/77) [1978] ECR 1511 (oil traders).

(d) South-western Germany: *Suiker Unie* v *Commission* (40/73 et al.) [1975] ECR 1663 (the sugar cartel).

(e) Italian ports: *Merci Convenzionali Porto di Genova* v *Siderurgica Gabrielli SPA* (C-179/90) [1991] ECR I-5889.

It remains open to question whether the smallest Member States (in terms of numbers of consumers) — Denmark, Ireland and Luxembourg — are substantial parts of the common market. In *BAT and Reynolds* v *Commission* (142 and 156/84) [1978] ECR 4487 the Commission found Rothmans International was dominant in Belgium *and* Luxembourg with 47.8% of that market. This territory was a substantial part of the EEC. It is likely that political expediency, if nothing else, will dictate that the smaller states are all found to be substantial parts of the common market.

We can see an example of such expediency, perhaps, in the *Radio Telefis Eireann* case. RTE alleged that the geographical area under consideration (Eire and Northern Ireland) did not constitute a substantial part of the common market. This allegation was based on the number of households in the territory (i.e. 1 million; or less than 1% of the Community total). This type of test had been used before by the ECJ — see, for example, the *Suiker Unie* case — but the Court of First Instance held that the island of Ireland was 'undeniably a substantial part of the common market'.

The notion of 'a substantial part' has also entered the domestic law of the United Kingdom. The Monopolies and Mergers Commission was required to have a 'reference area' when it conducted a merger investigation under the Fair Trading Act. This area should be 'a substantial part of the United Kingdom'. A recommendation of the MMC, relating to activities of South Yorkshire Transport Limited (a bus company) was quashed by the High Court as the reference area was not a substantial part of the UK. This judgment was upheld by the Court of Appeal: see *The Times*, 9 December 1991, *R v MMC, ex parte South Yorkshire Transport Ltd*.

5.6 Abusive Behaviour

In the French language version of the EC Treaty this is rendered as 'abusive exploitation', which may make its scope clearer. Unlike Article 81 (ex 85), which caught behaviour that was *intended* to restrict competition or had that effect, Article 82 (ex 86) is concerned with *conduct*. Article 82 gives several examples of behaviour that will constitute an abuse. You should note that there is no possibility of getting an exemption from prohibition if the abuse in question in fact has some beneficial effects for consumers (unlike Article 81(3) (ex 85(3)).

The Court of Justice considered the meaning of 'abuse' in *Europembellage Corp. and Continental Can Co. v Commission*: it said that Article 86 (now 82) aimed at stopping not just behaviour which was directly detrimental to consumers (e.g. selling at unfair prices or deliberately cutting back on production in order to obtain a higher price for the product), but also behaviour which could harm consumers indirectly, usually by terminating effective competition in the market (i.e. wiping out the existing competition or making it more difficult for others to enter the market and compete).

In *Hoffmann-La Roche v Commission* the Court returned to the notion of 'abuse' and this time noted that an abuse was abnormal behaviour (that which would not occur in conditions of normal competition) which had the effect of either causing existing competition to wither or remain (stagnant) at present levels.

'Abuse' requires a company to engage in an activity; merely possessing a dominant position is not an abuse in itself. This was made clear by the ECJ in *Michelin*:

> A finding that an undertaking has a dominant position is not in itself a recrimination but simply means that, irrespective of the reasons for which it has such a dominant position, the undertaking concerned has a *special responsibility* not to allow its conduct to impair genuine undistorted competition on the common market.

None of this really helps us to determine what specific types of behaviour might be found to be an abuse. Article 82 itself offers some assistance in heads (a)–(d) (see **5.1**). These are not intended to be exhaustive; see *Continental Can* at para. 26: 'The list merely gives examples, not an exhaustive enumeration....'

Article 82, heads (a) and (b) are indicative of attempts to regulate performance directly: unfair prices (price increases) or restrictions on output have a direct effect on the customer/consumer (although price *cuts* may benefit consumers; but not perhaps in the long term?). By looking at Article 82 heads (c) and (d), one sees that the provision aims not only at 'practices which may cause damage to consumers directly, but also at those which are detrimental to them [i.e. consumers] through their impact on an effective competition structure' (*Continental Can*, para. 26).

Examples (c) and (d) show that unfair or discriminatory conduct is covered by Article 82 (e.g. price discrimination and tie-ins). We should remember that *Continental Can* was a merger case (in a time before the Merger Regulation). This may explain the bold statement in the judgment that simply strengthening a dominant position may be an abuse within Article 82, *regardless of the means and procedure by which it is achieved*, if it has the effect of substantially fettering the competition.

Is it useful to try to *classify* the types of abuse that fall within Article 82? Arguably, this is what the Article itself does with the four examples. However, the Commission and Court often fail to refer to heads (a)–(d) specifically; or else they refer to more than one of them; or, if they do use just one, they fail to state how it is that the example is demonstrated by the facts in the particular case. We may need to create a classification for ourselves.

5.6.1 THREE CLASSES OF ABUSE?

It has been suggested (by John Temple Lang) that there are three basic classes of abuse:

(a) exploitative abuses, e.g., excessive prices;

(b) anti-competitive abuses, e.g., tie-ins, mergers and discriminatory pricing;

(c) reprisal abuses, e.g., refusals to deal, predatory pricing.

It should be noted that these provide a basic framework but are not necessarily mutually exclusive: e.g., tie-ins are anti-competitive but also allow exploitation; predatory pricing is anti-competitive but may be used as a reprisal weapon. The United Kingdom Government's Green Paper on 'Abuse of Market Power' (November 1992) uses 'anti-competitive' and 'exploitative' abuses as a system to underpin several practical examples of abusive behaviour (see p. 19 of the Green Paper).

Examples of abuse were found in the following cases:

(a) *Commercial Solvents Corp.* v *Commission*: refusal to supply a competitor.

(b) *United Brands* v *Commission*: discriminatory pricing — different prices applied to sales of bananas brought by ship from the Caribbean. Also refusal to deal — termination of dealer in Denmark after it became an exclusive for another brand of bananas.

(c) *AKZO* (C-62/86) [1991] ECR I-3359: threats to enter the victim's market, coupled with a predatory pricing policy.

An alternative to classification is to look at *particular types of conduct* and see what is indicated by precedent. We can examine three types:

(a) discounts (**5.6.2**);

(b) refusals to deal (**5.6.3**);

(c) unfair pricing (**5.6.4**).

5.6.2 DISCOUNTS

This activity had been tried by Hoffmann-La Roche and was considered by the Court of Justice in what is sometimes called the 'Vitamins' case. The company had a variety of exclusive or preferential supply contracts with several bulk vitamin 'users'. The customers were required either to buy *only* from Hoffmann-La Roche, or to buy most of their requirements from the company. In return, they got a *fidelity rebate*, i.e. a discount based on past purchases. The customers had to get past a threshold percentage of their previous requirements. The principle behind the rebate was said to be — the more you buy the cheaper it gets. The rebate also applied to more than one vitamin, so if a customer bought more of any Hoffmann-La Roche vitamin, this increased their discount on purchases of any other Hoffmann-La Roche vitamin.

These fidelity rebates were rejected by the ECJ as abusive, even if they were entered into willingly by the customer. They were not based on an economic transaction which justified this burden but were designed to *deprive or restrict* the customer's *choice* in sources of supply. This rebate system also hindered other vitamin producers from getting *access* to the market. The rebates were wrong because they were based on loyalty (i.e., Hoffmann tied up an outlet against its competitors) rather than simple *quantity of purchase*. One *can* discount on quantity usually because of economies of scale — these can be passed on to the customer. Here, customers qualified on a percentage of their *need,* whether great or small.

Incidentally, Hoffmann-La Roche also had so-called 'English' clauses in their rebate agreements. These allowed the customer to buy the product elsewhere if they had a better offer from another supplier but they were obliged to tell Hoffmann about the better offer. The ECJ held that 'English' clauses were unacceptable — although superficially they *prevented foreclosure* by allowing the customer to shop elsewhere, the fact of an obligation to inform Hoffmann-La Roche of its competitors' moves helped it to identify competitors and deal with them.

Discounts were also considered in *Michelin*: the ECJ observed that discounts *per se* are not abusive (para. 71 of its judgment) but loyalty rebates are. The problem is that discounts, especially for quantity, can be offered on a one-off basis but loyalty rebates operate on a rolling basis and require continuity of purchase. This results in competitors being denied access to one's customers. Discounts must be justified by some economic service. Here, discount periods were measured over a one-year qualifying period. Customers came under heavy pressure to buy Michelin tyres over the whole period. Also, Michelin kept changing the qualifying rules and not telling customers, so uncertainty prevailed and customers were less likely to switch to another supplier. This stopped free selection by customers and was not competitively-justified behaviour.

5.6.3   REFUSAL TO DEAL

A useful article has been written by Romano Subiotto, 'The right to deal with whom one pleases under EC competition law: a small contribution to a necessary debate' 1992 ECLR 234.

Refusals to deal occur in various ways, e.g. as a response to shortages; as a threat of punishment for misconduct; as a result of forward vertical integration. Refusals can be competitively justified: for example, in *United Brands*, the company argued that its ban on resale was to protect both its brand name and consumers by guaranteeing the quality of the product. The ECJ said it was permissible if it did not raise obstacles, the effect of which went beyond the (legitimate) objective to be achieved.

Examples of legitimate refusal might be:

(a)   in a selective distribution system where a distributor fails to meet (proper) requirements;

(b)   genuine shortages, if properly dealt with (cf. the 'Dutch Oil' case, *ABG/BP* [1977] 2 CMLR D1);

(c)   when a customer transfers its central activity to promoting a rival brand. The supplier could review its relationship with the customer and legitimately terminate that relationship, giving adequate notice (taken from the Subiotto article, citing the Commission decision in *Brass Band Instruments/Boosey & Hawkes* OJ 1987 286/36, Commission Decision). But this must be compared with *United Brands*: United Brands terminated supplies to a long-standing customer (Olesen) after Olesen gave priority to a competing brand of bananas. This was held to be a 'penalty' used to discourage others from following Olesen's example of independent action. It was designed to have a serious adverse effect on competition. (See paras 169-178, 182-196 of the judgment.)

If a company engages in forward vertical integration, the desire of the Commission to protect its *competitors* seems overwhelming. See, for example, *Commercial Solvents*, where the refusal to supply is condemned even though one can see it as the simple replacement of one company by another. The case is often seen thus by its critics, *but* we should note that *potential* competition was eliminated — the situation changed from one actual supplier plus one potential supplier to just one actual supplier. A very strict test was applied in *Commercial Solvents* — intention seemed to be irrelevant — the Court noted that the company's objective had been to reserve the raw materials it produced for its own in-house fabrication of the finished product.

This approach finds an echo in a more recent decision, that of the French *Conseil de la Concurrence* (or Competition Board): *Re Supply of Metallic Calcium* [1992] BOCCRF 185. Here, a dominant supplier of standard industrial calcium supplied the product to a smaller company producing high-grade calcium granules. The dominant company was slow in making deliveries and failed to provide necessary technical information about the product. So the customer went to other, more expensive, sources and had to raise its own prices. According to the *Conseil*, the requests for supply were normal and it found that the delays were due to the supplier's wish to develop its own in-house production of the high-grade product.

The urgency of the customer's need for supplies seems to be irrelevant, as may be seen from para. 26 of the judgment in *Commercial Solvents*.

The Subiotto article (above) refers to the American 'doctrine of *essential facilities*'. This idea, that an undertaking which possesses such a facility is under some obligation to its competitors in a 'downstream' market, seems to be assuming significance in Europe. A good example is *B & I/Sealink Harbours and Stena Sealink* [1992] 5 CMLR 255.

Sealink is both a British ferry operator and the port authority at Holyhead, Wales. Both Sealink and B & I use berths at Holyhead. The B & I berth is at the harbour mouth and, when Sealink's ferries pass, the water level rises so that B & I have to interrupt loading or unloading of their ferry. Only one such incident occurred per B & I ferry until October 1991 when Sealink announced new sailing times which would involve two ships passing each docked B & I ferry. B & I sought interim measures, prohibiting the new sailings, which the Commission granted.

The Commission said that a dominant undertaking which owns or controls an essential facility and which uses that facility will be guilty of an abuse within Article 82 (ex 86) if it either:

(a)   refuses to grant access to competitors; or

(b)   grants access on terms less favourable than those which it gives to its own services.

An essential facility is one to which competitors must have access in order to provide a service to customers. One might easily draw parallels between such a (typically physical) situation and that where access to information protected by an intellectual property right in one market is necessary to enable a separate market to be developed (cf. *Volvo* v *Veng* and *Radio Telefis Eireann* v *Commission* (C-241-242/91) [1995] ECR I-743. The ECJ said that a refusal to grant a licence for an intellectual property right would only constitute abusive behaviour in 'exceptional circumstances'.

5.6.4   UNFAIR PRICING

A basic problem in proving unfair or predatory pricing lies in the assessment of the cost structure of the suspect. Various theories exist on how costs are to be assessed but there is no real consensus. The task is easiest where a bald threat exists but a 'guilty' verdict in such a situation seeks to punish behaviour (intent) with little consideration of the effect. A good example of this is the *ECS/AKZO* litigation, where there was a 'smoking gun' letter and the issue of intent seems to have been accorded great significance.

The fact that behaviour, rather than effect, is caught by the notion of predatory pricing can be shown by the words of the ECJ in *Sirena* v *Eda* (40/70) [1971] ECR 69:

> ... as regards the abuse of a dominant position, although the price level of the product may not of itself necessarily suffice to disclose such an abuse, it may, however, if unjustified by any objective criteria, and if it is particularly high, be a determining factor.

So, price increases may be caught, as well as price reductions!

In *United Brands* (1976), the ECJ said that 'charging a price which is excessive because it has no reasonable relation to the economic value of the product supplied is ... an abuse' (see p. 252 of the judgment). When calculating the economic value of a product, we must take into consideration the production costs.

The formula set out by the ECJ for establishing whether predatory pricing has occurred looks like this:

First, find   £ x (i.e. price actually charged for a unit of product)
then deduct   £ y (i.e. costs actually incurred on making it)
Result?   £ z

We should then determine whether £ z is excessive or not. Assuming that someone (usually the Commission) can answer 'Yes' to the question 'Is £ z excessive?', we should next see if £ x is unfair, either in itself or in comparison with competing products. If this can be answered affirmatively, we have a case of unfair or predatory pricing.

The formula is useless to apply in practice for two reasons. First, no one can agree on the method of costs analysis which should be used. Secondly, the notion that '£ z is excessive' implies a comparison with something else but it is not clear what we should use for the comparison. The ECJ has appreciated the difficulties involved in an analysis of production costs but has suggested (correctly) that some tests exist for determining excessive prices and that the Commission should use them when alleging excessive pricing. A problem remains, in that there is a plurality of such tests.

Let us take the *AKZO* case as an illustration. The Court said that prices which are lower than the average variable cost (AVC) and which are used as a tool to lever out a rival *must* be regarded as an abuse; a dominant undertaking has no interest in such action except to eliminate rivals in order to then raise prices. The reason it has no interest other than this is that every one of its sales represents a *loss*, i.e. all the fixed costs plus at least part of the variable costs for each unit sold.

Where an undertaking charges prices above AVC but below average total cost (i.e., the sum of its fixed costs plus variable costs — ATC), these prices must be an abuse where they form part of an elimination plan. The dominant undertaking is able to remove undertakings who are as effective as the dominant undertaking but who cannot resist the competition due to their inferior financial capacity.

The ECJ defines variable costs as only those which vary according to the level of output. The Court says that labour costs fail to do this and so they are fixed costs. On the facts, AKZO's prices were below AVC only once. Other pricing abuses fell in the range between AVC and ATC. These were still abusive as they could not be explained away as reactions to offers made by AKZO's competitors and they continued over a long period. No abuse was proved by the Commission regarding the alleged selectivity of offers to AKZO's customers. The variation in availability of offers properly reflected the differences in the types of customer. For a cogent argument showing the limitations of the *AKZO* formula for predatory pricing, see Soames and Ryan [1994] 3 ECLR 157.

National courts seem quite willing to detect predatory pricing. See, e.g., the French 'Competition Council' in *Béton de France* [1995] 2 ECLR R-45, and the Italian Antitrust Authority in *Tekal/Italcementi* [1995] 5 ECLR R-130.

5.7 Effect on Trade between Member States

The same element occurs in Article 81 (ex 85), and there is little else to say beyond that which was said earlier (see **2.3**) except for two points. First, occasionally the European Court has interpreted this requirement quite strictly. In *Hugin/Liptons* v *Commission*, a Swedish parent company with a UK subsidiary terminated supplies of spare parts for its cash tills to the 'victim', Liptons. Liptons was a small company which operated in the Greater London area, providing a cash till repair service. The ECJ said that Liptons would normally have bought the spares from Hugin's subsidiary in the UK; the volume of trade was so small as to be insignificant and not attractive enough for other companies to want to import spares and satisfy Liptons' demand; finally there was no evidence that Liptons was likely to expand its business into another Member State. Thus there was no effect on trade between Member States and therefore no breach of Article 82 (ex 86).

Secondly, under Article 82 (ex 86) the Court and the Commission are more likely to consider the harm done to one's competitors as affecting inter-State trade, even where this does no immediate harm to the ultimate consumer. The most typical example is the actual or threatened elimination of a rival (e.g. *AKZO* (Commission Decision); *Commercial Solvents Corp.* v *Commission*) or someone in a rival 'camp' (e.g., *United Brands* v *Commission* — trade buyer deciding to promote a rival brand). This is a rather broader test than that used for Article 81 (ex 85), so conduct which distorts the structure of the market may be regarded as affecting the inter-State trade.

5.8 Negative Clearance and Article 82

Can you notify the Commission of your own abuse of a dominant position? Naturally, an undertaking is unlikely to want to volunteer information about its abusive conduct to the Commission, but companies may want to alert the Commission to certain agreements or practices so that it can put the company's mind at rest. It can do this by giving the agreement etc. negative clearance, i.e., stating that, on the facts then known to the Commission, the agreement etc. does not infringe Article 82 (ex 86). (See Article 2, Regulation 17/62.) What a company cannot do is notify its agreements or practices and hope to have those which infringe Article 82 (ex 86) exempted from prohibition. Exemption is only possible for breaches of Article 81 (ex 85).

5.8.1 THE RELATIONSHIP BETWEEN ARTICLE 82 AND EXEMPTION UNDER ARTICLE 81(3)

In the first *Tetra Pak* case (*Tetra Pak Rausing* v *Commission* (T-51/89) [1990] ECR II-309) the Court of First Instance considered the relationship between Article 82 (ex 86) and exemption under Article 81 (ex 85), when the same behaviour is under examination.

The Court concluded that if behaviour is illegal under Article 82 (ex 86), then that is conclusive of the matter. The fact of exemption under Article 81(3) (ex 85(3)) (in this case via the patent licensing block exemption, Regulation 2349/84) is irrelevant. If conduct was exempt under Article 81(3) (ex 85(3)), the usual consequences would follow but undertakings in a dominant position still had a separate obligation to comply with Article 82 (ex 86). Tetra Pak's complaint about being left in a position of legal uncertainty was dismissed. Tetra Pak was subsequently fined a record sum by the European Commission for these activities — see **7.8.2.2**.

For further reading on Article 82 (ex 86), see chapter 4 in Korah; chapter 12 in Hawk; or chapter 14 in Steiner — all works cited in **Appendix 9**. See also the European Economic Area Agreement, Article 54, which replicates Article 82 (ex 86) *mutatis mutandis* (text in [1993] 14 ECLR supplement).

SIX

COMPLIANCE

6.1 Who Cares about Compliance?

6.1.1 THE COMPANY THAT MAY BE GUILTY OF AN INFRINGEMENT

A company may well be concerned about possible infringement of Article 81(1) (ex 85(1)), through its contracts with suppliers or distributors perhaps, or if it is in a dominant position it may be concerned to ensure that its actions are not perceived as an abuse of a dominant position and contrary to Article 82 (ex 86). Many large companies now have compliance departments in order to cope with the large volume of regulatory material by which businesses have to abide. A company may infringe one of the EC competition rules without intending to but that would be no defence to a Commission decision imposing a fine (though it might lead to a reduction). Companies have the opportunity to apply to the Commission for negative clearance and thus get a clean bill of health for the agreement or conduct that they were concerned about; they can do this in respect of either Article 81(1) (ex 85(1)) or 82 (ex 86) or both (using Form A/B). In practice, they are unlikely to get a formal decision from the Commission but they may get a comfort letter indicating that, on what the Commission currently knows about their situation, there seems to be no infringement. That letter will not stop the Commission from investigating the company if the circumstances change or new information is sent to the Commission (and it is not binding on national courts) but usually the comfort letter works as its name suggests.

Alternatively, a company may have a good idea that its agreement infringes Article 81(1) (ex 85(1)) but it may also think that there are sound, pro-competitive reasons for it to act in this way. It should first check whether a block exemption may apply: generally, these protect contracts between undertakings in a vertical relationship (i.e. between companies operating at different economic levels). If that is of no help, the company should look at the current criteria for agreements of minor importance: they may be too weak on the relevant market to attract the Commission's attention. That does not mean, though, that they will necessarily escape the attention of national competition authorities. If none of this helps, the company should consider making a notification to the Commission (on Form A/B) and applying for an individual exemption under Article 81(3) (ex 85(3)). Again, a comfort letter is the most likely outcome of benefit to the company. If the company suspects it may be infringing Article 82 (ex 86), its advisers should remind it that no exemption is possible.

6.1.2 THE COMPETITORS OF A COMPANY THAT MAY BE GUILTY OF AN INFRINGEMENT

Companies in competition with a 'suspect' firm are unlikely to have any contractual dealings with that firm, although it is not impossible. It is more likely that these competitors feel they are being excluded from a profitable market by the actions of the suspect firm, or that they are being hit by an unfair pricing policy operated by that firm. There are many ways in which competitors can be damaged by breaches of Article 81(1) (ex 85(1)) or 82 (ex 86) by a suspect firm. Indeed, an English judge recently declared that Article 81(1) (ex 85(1)) was intended solely to regulate the relationships between competitors operating in the same market (see *Scottish & Newcastle plc* v *Bond*, 25 March 1997, unreported). Such companies may wish to alert the Commission to the existence of an infringement: they should do so by means of a complaint. This should comply with the headings in Form C. The Commission is not obliged to investigate complaints, though, and a complainant company may find its complaint being referred down to the appropriate national competition authorities for further action. This is likely to be the case where the anti-competitive effects of an agreement or conduct are felt within the territory of a single Member State of the EU.

6.1.3 THE SUPPLIERS OF A COMPANY THAT MAY BE GUILTY OF AN INFRINGEMENT

Whether a supplier feels aggrieved will, no doubt, depend entirely upon whether the supply contract suits it or not. It may be that the supplier is in a weak bargaining position, compared to the other party to the contract, and has been obliged to accept certain anti-competitive clauses or to sell at an uncompetitive price, or to accept other restrictions (perhaps upon who or where else it can supply the contract goods). Sometimes a change in the market (or a related market) may make the present contract less advantageous than it seemed at first: so complaints can be used as tactical weapons in an essentially commercial struggle. It is likely that a supplier will complain about its contract with another party only where it wishes either to amend the contract and make it less onerous (or restrictive) or to escape from the contract altogether (since infringing Article 81(1) (ex 85(1)) or 82 (ex 86) will render the relevant provisions void). A complaint may bring about the termination of the relationship, whether desired or not: once a company is being investigated by the Commission, its own interests often take priority over the particular wishes of the complainant. It will often be the case that a supplier is better advised to use the *threat* of a complaint as a lever in re-negotiating the terms of the contract, rather than actually going to the Commission. If it did so, the complaint would follow the headings in Form C.

6.1.4 THE CUSTOMERS OF A COMPANY THAT MAY BE GUILTY OF AN INFRINGEMENT

The end user may well be a private citizen, in which case a complaint to the Commission is unlikely. It may be that if enough people are affected by the allegedly infringing behaviour (maybe excessively high prices charged by a dominant supplier), some sort of collective complaint may be possible. An unusual complaint can be seen in the OJ 1992 C2/32. Scottish MEPs were asking questions in the European Parliament, in the course of which it emerged that the Commission had received a formal complaint in 1990 from a 'pressure group'. This group was the Scottish Steel Campaign Trust and its complaint was about the alleged anti-competitive behaviour of British Steel in closing down the hot strip mill at Ravenscraig. Sir Leon Brittan, for the Commission, replied that the Commission had investigated the complaint and taken a decision. Also, it is not impossible to envisage complaints coming from trade unions, concerned about a company's decisions and their effect on the workforce.

Where customers have entered into a contract, which they now allege is anti-competitive, they may also be guilty of the infringement if Article 81(1) (ex 85(1)) is involved. It is much better for them if their partner is in a dominant position and they can try to lay any blame at the door of the dominant firm. If a customer wishes to complain to the Commission about a supposed infringement, it will do so in a document adopting the headings in Form C.

6.2 Using Form A/B

There is no actual Form A/B but companies that wish to apply for negative clearance or an individual exemption (or utilise an opposition procedure in a block exemption) should notify the Commission in a document which adopts the relevant headings from those set out in the 'operational part' of Regulation 3385/94 (see **Appendix 4**). Any undertaking which is party to an agreement (or to a decision of associations of undertakings, or to a concerted practice) can apply for negative clearance or exemption. The Commission encourages joint applications from the several parties to an agreement 'since it is helpful to have the views of all the parties directly concerned at the same time' but it is not compulsory (suspicious minds might feel that the phrase 'cut throat defence' springs to mind). If the application comes in from a single party, then the other(s) should be informed by the applicant (see Article 1(1)(b), Regulation 3385/94). Although the application is made through a document, the applicant must send in 17 copies of it, plus multiple copies of any relevant documents (particularly copy agreements).

The section headings in Form A/B, insofar as they are relevant to the scope of this book, are as follows.

Section 1   Identity of the undertakings or persons submitting the notification

Under this head, one would identify the applicant's undertaking(s), state whether any non-notifiers have been informed of the application and provide contact names, addresses and telephone and fax numbers.

Section 2   Information on the parties to the agreement and the groups to which they belong

This heading does not seem to lend itself to concerns about Article 82 (ex 86), since there need not be 'an agreement' involved. However, the regulation encourages under-takings to adopt the headings in Form A/B, when applying for negative clearance under Article 82 (ex 86) even though use of the Form is not compulsory (unlike the position under Article 81 (ex 85).

Each party to the agreement should be identified, with addresses and contact names and numbers. The nature of the undertakings' business should be explained (a previous version of the Form suggested 'motor vehicle manufacturer' was the level of description required; its absence now may indicate a desire for full information). If a party has more than one 'business', it would be helpful to set them all down now; one does not know where the Commission will draw the line in defining the relevant market. If a party is in a corporate group, that should be stated, with a summary of the industries the group is involved with, plus the world-wide turnover of the group (useful when looking at market shares and when deciding the level of any fine).

Section 3   Procedural matters

Under this head, a company indicates if any other competition authority is examining the situation. Also, if the company needs an urgent resolution of the application, this is the place to say so. Lastly, the applicant should indicate if it will be content with a comfort letter as a result and, if not, explain why. A company might take the initiative and detail precisely what type(s) of comfort letter it would be prepared to accept and those it would not.

Section 4   Full details of the arrangements

This really requires the applicant to set out the terms of any agreement. This can be done by annexing copies of the contract to the application document; similarly, copy correspondence might be attached. Those clauses, or conduct, which are the catalyst for the application should be identified clearly; it might be helpful to use some of the labels listed in Section 4 to describe each relevant clause or to classify them under the labels as headings.

Section 5   Non-confidential summary

The Commission may want to publicise the application swiftly, in order to stimulate comments from third parties. So that it can act without further reference to the applicant, this section requires the applicant to provide certain information at a non-confidential level of detail. This non-confidential summary can then be included in the published preliminary notice.

Chapter II   Section concerning the relevant market

Sections 6–10 seek detailed information about the relevant market, both in terms of product and geographical extent, and the structure of that market (e.g. identify the five main competitors of the parties and supply contact details for each; again with the five main customers of the parties). The information sought is quite specific but locating it may entail some delay in submitting the Form, especially if a party to the contract is in a corporate group or has associated companies which are also active in the market.

(Chapter III is concerned with structural joint ventures.)

Chapter IV   Final sections

This chapter is quite important. In **Section 16**, the applicant sets out the reasons why, if it is the case, it is applying for negative clearance. To do so, it must first identify the provisions or effects which have led it to apply for negative clearance and then argue why Article 81(1) (ex 85(1)) or 82 (ex 86) does not apply to them. There may be some tortuous logic to these arguments! Similarly, **Section 17** demands reasons why an individual exemption should be granted, if sought. In particular, the applicant should show evidence of how the criteria for individual exemption are satisfied on the facts. Chapter IV concludes with details of the supporting documents required and a declaration to be signed to the effect that the information supplied in the application document is true to the best of the signatories' knowledge and belief.

6.3   Using Form C

A special form (Form C) exists for complainants to use. Its use is not mandatory but complainants should always ensure that their reasons for alleging a breach of Article 81 (ex 85) and/or 82 (ex 86) are clearly set out in writing for the Commission. In 1997, the Commission registered 177 complaints and 101 cases were opened on the Commission's own initiative (source: XXVIIth Report on Competition Policy).

Like Form A/B, Form C is merely a guide to help an undertaking to satisfy the requirements of the Commission. There are six heads to use in the complaint document, as follows:

1.   Identify the parties

It is probably a good idea to give a brief indication of the relationship (if any) between them, with a description of the nature of their business.

2.   Give details of the alleged infringements

The complainant should set out exactly what has gone on, perhaps with reference to specific contract clauses or the content of letters, faxes or telephone calls.

3.   Demonstrate a legitimate interest

This may be quite easy to do, especially if the complainant can be seen as a victim of the other company's anti-competitive acts. Any damage which has been or may be suffered by the complainant as a result of the anti-competitive acts should be particularised.

4.   Produce documents and refer to the evidence relied on

Usually a job for solicitors, working closely with the lay client, but clear instructions must come from counsel or whoever is in charge of organising the complaint document as to what is wanted (i.e. specific documents, types of invoices, relevant periods of time).

5.   Termination

The complainant should set out any steps taken to alert the suspect company to its breach of the competition rules. This is of a similar nature to a letter before action in English civil proceedings.

6.   Declaration

That the previous information is correct, signed by a properly mandated officer of the complainant undertaking.

6.4 National Competition Authorities and the Commission

Although this chapter has been largely concerned with the Commission, it should not be forgotten that national authorities also supervise the behaviour of undertakings. By 1998, eight Member States had incorporated Articles 81 (ex 85) and 82 (ex 86) into their national laws — Belgium, France, Germany, Greece, Italy, The Netherlands, Portugal and Spain. National competition authorities in those countries applied those Articles directly to undertakings. The UK now has provisions in its national law which are based upon the Articles in the Competition Act 1998. The Act is expected to come into force on 1 March 2000.

In the Competition Act 1998, ss. 2, 9 and 18 reproduce, almost word for word, Articles 81 (ex 85)(1), (2) and (3) and 82 (ex 86). This new national system is intended to work in 'a consistent manner' with the EU regime (see the Explanatory and Financial Memorandum which was attached to the Competition Bill during its passage through Parliament). For example, s. 60 of the Competition Act 1998 requires the UK courts, when interpreting the national rules, to

> *act ... with a view to securing that there is no inconsistency between ... the principles applied ... by the court ... and the principles laid down by the Treaty and the European Court. The court must, in addition, have regard to any relevant decision or statement of the Commission.* (Competition Act 1998, s. 60(2))

In a similar fashion, an agreement will be exempt (a 'parallel exemption') from prohibition under the Competition Act 1998, s. 2, if the agreement is already exempted from Article 81(2) (ex 85(2)) by reason of Article 81(3) (ex 85(3)). The Community exemption may arise either by means of a regulation (i.e. a block exemption), an individual decision or through application of an opposition procedure.

There are still differences between the UK competition regime and that established by the EC Treaty. Both of the UK prohibitory rules apply only where the anti-competitive behaviour *may affect trade within the United Kingdom.* Under s. 2, agreements and concerted practices are prohibited only if they have (or are intended to have) an effect on competition *within the United Kingdom.* Under s. 18, undertakings must possess a dominant position *within the United Kingdom.*

The UK authorities will be:

(a) the Director General of Fair Trading, who will be responsible for the enforcement of the Competition Act 1998, ss. 2 and 18; and

(b) the Competition Commission, which will hear appeals from decisions of the Director General. It will also take on the work of the current Monopolies and Mergers Commission.

The idea behind the Act is that competition matters of significance at EU level will continue to be examined by the European Commission while 'domestic' matters are dealt with by the UK authorities.

This position is possibly different to the one the Commission would like to see in place. The Commission issued a Notice in 1997, setting out details of the relationship between itself and the various national competition authorities; see OJ 1997 C313/3. This Notice is similar in nature to the one issued in 1993 dealing with cooperation between the Commission and national courts. The 1997 Notice was intended 'to reduce the number of complaints addressed to the Commission if they can be dealt with effectively by the national authorities' (Commission White Paper, 1999). The fact remains that the Competition Act 1998 focuses on internal matters, within the United Kingdom. The emphasis in s. 2 is upon agreements which may affect trade within the UK. That concept may be interpreted liberally by the UK courts so that an agreement which may affect trade between Member States, one of which is the UK, will fall under both Article 81 (ex 85) and the Competition Act 1998, s. 2. It may be that the Act's emphasis on trade within the UK is intended to mark out a 'horizontal' boundary between its competence to oversee agreements and the competencies of other Member States, rather than having any impact upon the 'vertical' jurisdictional divide between the UK and the European Commission. All of that remains to be seen. Perhaps the national courts remain the appropriate route for enforcement of Articles 81 (ex 85) and 82 (ex 86) within the UK? Articles 81(1) and (2) (ex 85(1) and (2)) are directly effective and have been used by litigants in English courts for several years. The Commission has recognised the different roles of the national courts on the one hand, and itself and national competition authorities on the other:

> It is the task of national courts to safeguard the individual rights of private persons in their relations with one another . . . [B]oth the Commission and national competition authorities act in the public interest in performing their general task of monitoring and enforcing the competition rules.

Whether one should try to interest the national competition authority in a complaint or instead sue in a national court remains unclear. What is clear is the fact that:

> Complainants remain reluctant to apply to the national courts or competition authorities when they consider they have been harmed by an infringement of Community law . . . [T]he mechanisms for cooperation with national authorities have not to date encountered the success expected, owing to the Commission's monopoly for the application of Article 81(3) of the Treaty. (Commission White Paper, 1999)

One major reason for this reluctance to turn to national courts or authorities is identified by the Commission in that passage — its monopoly over the grant of exemptions. Once a company notifies an agreement to the Commission, and seeks exemption, the effect is to thwart the proceedings of the national authority. National authorities automatically lose jurisdiction once the Commission initiates proceedings (see Regulation 17/62, Article 9(3)). National courts are likely to adjourn a case until the Commission takes its decision on exemption.

Until recently, there had been no proposal that national authorities should be given the power to grant exemptions under Article 81(3) (ex 85(3)). The closest that we have come to such derogation is the ability of national courts to assert that Article 81(3) (ex 85(3)) does not apply to an agreement — that is, the agreement does not qualify for exemption. If a court thinks that the agreement merits exemption, it has no power to go on and grant that exemption.

In 1999, the Commission issued a White Paper on Modernisation of the Rules implementing Articles 81 and 82. One of its central suggestions is that the Commission's 'monopoly of exemption' be removed and the national competition authorities be able to determine if the criteria in Article 81(3) (ex 85(3)) are met. Similarly, undertakings in national courts would be able to rely on the direct applicability of Article 81(3) (ex 85(3)), using it as a defence to allegations that an agreement is prohibited and void. This fundamental shift in control would be noteworthy for at least two reasons. First, it would require amendment of Council Regulation 17/62, since Article 9(1) currently states unambiguously that 'the Commission shall have sole power to declare Article 85(1) inapplicable pursuant to Article 85(3) of the Treaty'. Secondly, the Commission is prepared to cede its monopoly over Article 81(3) (ex 85(3)) for pragmatic reasons, largely to help reduce its workload and speed up its turnover of cases. The shift is justified on the basis that the Articles have been in operation for a considerable length of time. Over this period, there have been many Commission decisions and judgments of the European Court. Interpretation, scope and application of the Articles are all much clearer now than they were in 1962. National authorities and courts are better informed and so are more able to be trusted to apply the Treaty Articles correctly and uniformly. However, as the Commission's White Paper states: '. . . if this reform is really to improve the application of the [EC] competition rules, the seven Member States that have not yet done so will have to empower their competition authorities to apply Community law.'

SEVEN

INVESTIGATIONS

7.1 Investigations

This chapter looks at the procedures used by the European Commission when it investigates cases of suspected infringement of the EC competition rules. The main body of procedural rules is found in Council Regulation 17/62; throughout this chapter the Regulation will be referred to as 'Regulation 17'.

7.1.1 NON-INVESTIGATIONS

This chapter does not look at the work done by the Commission following:

- an application for negative clearance by an undertaking (see Article 2, Regulation 17);

- a notification by an undertaking seeking an exemption under Article 81(3) (ex 85(3)) (see Article 4, Regulation 17);

- a notification by an undertaking seeking to use the opposition procedure in a block exemption (see e.g. Article 4, Regulation 240/96).

Undertakings which want the Commission to give them the benefit of any of the above procedures will make a written application on Form A/B (see **Chapter 6**). It is unlikely, although not impossible, that any of the Commission's more severe investigative powers would be brought to bear in the process of resolving any of these applications.

7.2 Starting an Investigation

The Commission may act either on its own initiative or on application by a Member State (see Article 85 (ex 89), EC Treaty). In practice, these have not produced many investigations. Regulation 17 adds a third category to those who may initiate an investigation: applications may be made by 'natural or legal persons who claim a legitimate interest (Article 3(2)(b), Regulation 17; they may use Form C to complain, see **Chapter 6**). This addition has enabled many companies, firms, associations and individuals to alert the Commission to alleged infringements (comparison might be made to the practice in the anti-trust system of the USA, where the prospect of considerable awards of damages has encouraged many alleged victims of anti-competitive behaviour to take the malefactor to court themselves, thus relieving the pressure on central enforcement agencies). This category of applicants are typically referred to as 'complainants'. Complainants, by definition, have a particular interest in the outcome of any investigation but there are limits on what they may do.

7.2.1 RIGHTS OF COMPLAINANTS

A complainant is entitled to be kept informed of the acceptance (or otherwise) of the complaint, to be told of the Commission's preliminary findings, to apply to be heard by the Commission (in writing or orally) in the course of any investigation, and to challenge the final decision of the Commission at the Court of First Instance (see Article 230 (ex 173), EC Treaty and *Metro SB-Grossmarkte* v *Commission* (26/76) [1977] ECR 1875). However, the complainant does not have the same degree of access to the Commission's file on the investigation as does the undertaking being investigated (see e.g. *ICI* v *Commission* (T-36/91) [1995] ECR II-1847). Even more importantly, a complainant cannot force the Commission to investigate a complaint. While it is inconceivable that the Commission would refuse to investigate, following an application to do so from a Member State, a complaint by a natural or legal person does not carry the same weight with the Commission. The Commission is entitled to prioritise complaints and the Court of First Instance has decided (in *Automec srl* v *Commission* (T-24/90) [1992] ECR II-2223) that the Commission is not bound to conduct an investigation, nor to take a formal decision on the existence of any alleged infringement (with one exception — where the complaint raises an issue that the Commission alone can deal with). So, there is no right for a complainant to obtain a formal decision on the existence, or otherwise, of an infringement *even if the Commission has become persuaded that such an infringement has occurred* (*Bureau European des Medias de l'Industrie Musicale* v *Commission* (T-114/92) [1995] ECR II-147). It should be noted that, other than in very exceptional cases, where an agreement is of minor importance the Commission will not institute proceedings against it, neither on its own initiative nor following an application. Going further, the Commission has said it will not institute proceedings against an agreement, even where the parties to it exceed the relevant *de minimis* thresholds for market share, if they are small or medium-sized undertakings (see Commission Notice relating to the revision of the Notice on agreements of minor importance, 1996).

The Commission is entitled to reject a complaint either before embarking upon an investigation, or after the preliminary stages of an investigation. It can do so if it finds that the case shows 'insufficient Community interest' to warrant any (or further) investigation (see e.g. *Bureau European des Medias*). The idea of referring many complaints to national competition authorities accords with the concept of *subsidiarity*, which was accelerated by the Maastricht conference. It also eases the work-load of the Commission and it has been suggested (by Dr Claus-Dieter Ehlermann) that if the Court had not decided *Automec* in the way it did, the Commission might have had to seek amendment of Regulation 17 to achieve a similar result. This was because the number of complaints being received by the Commission was too great. It seems that the Commission gets about 100 complaints annually, although 'exact figures are hard to come by and tend to be contradictory' (see Bo Vesterdorf, a judge of the Court of First Instance, in 1994 CMLR 31:77, 'Complaints concerning infringements of competition law within the context of European Community law'). It is not possible to determine whether this apparent popularity confirms the real value of the procedure to complainants. What else could they do?

The obvious 'next-best' alternatives for the would-be complainant are:

- to start litigation in the legal system of an appropriate Member State against the alleged infringer; or

- to re-submit the complaint to the appropriate competition authority in a Member State.

A person or firm considering making a complaint to the Commission may also seek advice on bringing a private legal claim against the alleged infringer. The advisers should be clear that the advantages and disadvantages of both courses are considered. Whilst there is no legal bar on running the two procedures simultaneously, the commencement of proceedings on a 'private' level may help to persuade the Commission that the matter is one that is better dealt with at the national level.

7.2.2 THE COMPLAINANT AS A PRIVATE 'ENFORCER' OF THE COMPETITION RULES

An alleged victim of anti-competitive behaviour which contravenes either Article 81(1) (ex 85(1)) or Article 82 (ex 86) may bring a claim in the appropriate national court. Both

Articles are directly effective in the courts of the Member States, giving rights to, and imposing obligations on, individuals (see *BRT* v *SV SABAM* (127/73) [1974] ECR 51). The procedural rules which apply and the remedies which are available vary from one State to another (for England and Wales, see **Chapter 9**). The effectiveness of enforcement will correspondingly shift, according to the ease with which a claim can be brought and whether the national legal system offers meaningful remedies to the complainant (who may, for example, be seeking modifications to behaviour instead of or as well as financial compensation). The US anti-trust legislation can offer 'treble' damages to a successful litigant (i.e. the proven damage is simply multiplied by three to arrive at the total award), while EU Member States show a great reluctance to award damages at all in anti-competition suits. The availability and scope of interim remedies will be another factor in determining whether a complainant would be well-advised to launch a private claim against an alleged infringer.

There is an additional consideration for complainants, where anti-competitive behaviour crosses national boundaries: in which legal system should they sue? If a product market embraces two or more Member States, and the complainant alleges that it has sustained damage across the market, should separate claims be brought in each Member State, and the damages claim broken down so that the losses are shown for each national territory? If so, there is the danger of different outcomes to the claims, for example, different limitation periods may apply, or there may be different rules on proving the amount of loss or remoteness of damage (note a call for the Member States to develop common procedural rules when making damages claims based upon Community law ([1995] 1 ECLR 49)). Such variations will do little to encourage private enforcement of the competition rules. In these situations, it is desirable that the Commission is willing to take charge of the complaint and investigate it.

7.2.3   FURTHER ACTION BY A COMPLAINANT

If the Commission refuses to investigate, a complainant is not bound to seek an alternative source of succour. The refusal itself may be challenged in the Court of First Instance, using the procedure in Article 230 (ex 173), EC Treaty (see **9.3**). The Court envisages three stages, leading up to a refusal by the Commission:

- First, the Commission examines a complaint to see what action it will take. This may include informal correspondence between the Commission and complainant, to clarify and expand the issues of concern.

- Secondly, the Commission sends a letter to the complainant setting out the reasons (if any) why it considers there are insufficient grounds to proceed with the complaint. The letter will invite further comments from the complainant.

- Finally, the Commission may reject the complaint. This third stage is a decision (see Article 249 (ex 189), EC Treaty) and may be challenged by an action for annulment using Article 230 (ex 173), EC Treaty. See e.g. *Guérin Automobiles* v *Commission* (T-186/94) [1995] ECR II-1753.

Frustrated complainants should note that, if the Commission is engaged in the second stage of this procedure, the complaint may enter a state of limbo. If the Commission sends a letter, telling a complainant that its complaint cannot be dealt with individually at present, this will not be subject to an action for annulment under Article 230 (ex 173), EC Treaty. Conversely, the letter will be a sufficient definition of the Commission's position, and will defeat an action for failure to act under Article 232 (ex 175), EC Treaty (see *Guérin Automobiles*).

7.2.4   THE IMPORTANCE OF COMPLAINTS

Although the exact number of complaints remains somewhat mysterious (see **7.2.2**), the Commission has observed that the number of complaints 'continues to be high' (XXVIIIth Annual Report on Competition Policy). Also, its 1999 White Paper states that formal complaints make up nearly a third of new cases taken to the Commission, while most of the investigations begun on its own initiative start with information being sent to the Commission informally. The Commission wants to encourage firms, or others with a legitimate interest, to continue to complain to the Commission since information 'supplied in this way is a very valuable means of detecting infringements of the competition rules'.

In order to facilitate the lodging of complaints, the Commission proposes a number of new measures:

- the introduction of a time limit for deciding whether or not to reject a complaint (probably four months);

- simplifying the procedure for rejecting a complaint;

- the incorporation into Regulation 17/62 of a straightforward restatement of the situation regarding interim relief for a complainant (see **7.5**);

- publication of an explanatory notice about complaints, including advice to help the would-be complainant decide whether the complaint would be better brought to the Commission or a national authority.

7.3 Conducting the Investigation

An official of DG IV will be appointed as *rapporteur* for the case. The initial task will be to gather information in order to understand the context of the complaint. This will usually include early attempts to define the relevant market in terms of product and territory (see e.g. the current draft Commission Notice on the *definition of the relevant market for the purposes of Community competition law*).

7.3.1 REQUESTS FOR INFORMATION

The Commission is empowered to get information from governments and authorities of the Member States and undertakings. Under Article 11, Regulation 17, the Commission can send a request for information which sets out:

- the purpose of the request;

- its legal basis;

- a time-limit for compliance; and

- the possibility of fines for supplying incorrect information, either intentionally or negligently (see Article 15, Regulation 17; **8.8** below).

An undertaking's owners (or the officers of the undertaking if it has a separate legal personality) must supply the information requested. If either no information is supplied, or it is incomplete, the Commission may then take a formal decision which:

- requires the information to be supplied;

- specifies what information is wanted;

- gives a new time-limit for compliance; and

- contains a reminder about possible fines (either one-off or incremental) if information is incorrect or not supplied (see Article 11(5)).

This is a two-stage process and the Commission cannot proceed to the second stage (of taking a formal decision) unless a simple request has already been made which proved unsuccessful. There is no need to demonstrate manifest obstruction on the part of an undertaking in order to take a formal decision, an undertaking is under a duty to 'cooperate actively' and failure to do so will suffice: *Scottish FA* v *Commission* (T-46/92) [1994] ECR II-1039.

7.3.2   NECESSARY INVESTIGATIONS

Under Article 14, Regulation 17, the Commission can undertake all 'necessary investigations' when looking into possible infringements. This differs from Article 11 in that an Article 14 investigation typically involves Commission officials physically attending the premises of an undertaking, where they can examine the records of the business (and take copies of documents), ask for 'oral explanations on the spot' from employees and generally go anywhere on the premises of an undertaking. As with Article 11, there are two types of visit:

- one where the officials arrive and simply ask to come in; there is no obligation on the undertaking to comply and, if denied access, the officials will leave (Article 14(2)); and

- one where the Commission has taken a decision to order the investigation; when its officials arrive, usually without prior warning, and demand entry, access cannot be denied (Article 14(3).

In order to avoid confusion, the Commission officials will provide the undertaking with a certified copy of the decision (in addition to their written authorisation and proof of identity; see the XIIIth Report on Competition Policy).

The rights of the undertaking under investigation are rather confined. In both types of visit, the undertaking may be allowed to consult a legal adviser but not if this will cause a delay and prejudice the effectiveness of the investigation. While the second type of visit may seem quite draconian, there is no two-stage process that has to be followed, unlike Article 11 (see *National Panasonic* v *Commission* (136/79) [1980] ECR 2033). The essence of this type of visit (sometimes known as a 'dawn raid') is precisely that it takes place without warning, thus allowing undertakings minimal time to dispose of any incriminating evidence before it can be discovered. Any need for a previous, unsuccessful visit pursuant to Article 14(2) would simply alert an undertaking to the need to plug in its paper shredder. As the Court stated in *National Panasonic*:

> [Article 14(3)] does not . . . prevent the Commission from carrying out an investigation solely pursuant to a written authorisation given to its officials without adopting a decision, but in other respects it contains nothing to indicate that it may only adopt a decision within the meaning of Article 14(3) if it has previously attempted to carry out an investigation by mere authorisation. Whereas Article 11(5) expressly makes the adoption of a Commission decision subject to the condition that the latter has previously asked for the necessary information by means of a request addressed to those concerned and specifies in Article 11(3) the essentials which such a request must contain, Article 14 makes the investigating procedure by means of a decision subject to no preliminary of this kind.

And the point is acknowledged by the Commission too:

> If the Commission has reason to believe that the competition rules of the [EC] Treaty may have been seriously infringed, it obliges the companies in question to submit to verifications at all of their premises. These verifications are normally not announced in advance, in order to ensure that evidentiary documents are not hidden or even destroyed.

(Commission Press release IP/93/893, concerning a penalty payment imposed on Akzo Chemicals B.V.)

7.3.2.1   Use of 'dawn raids'

While one can appreciate the need, in certain circumstances, to avoid alerting the suspect undertaking to the fact of an impending visit to company premises, this power should be strictly limited in its use. One might say that this limitation is in-built due to the requirement for a decision to have been taken by the Commission, prior to a dawn raid. However, several of those who have been investigated have complained about the absence of any independent third party which could have a role in the Commission's use of its power under Article 14(3). A comparison might be made with the procedures in England for searching a premises in criminal and civil proceedings and parallels could be drawn with search warrants and search orders; in both situations, application must be made to a court for grant of the warrant or order.

Article 14 itself provides that:

- the Commission must consult with 'the competent authority of the Member State in whose territory the investigation is to be made' before taking the formal decision (Article 14(4)); and

- the formal decision is subject to the suspect's right to have it reviewed (post-execution) by the European Court (Article 14(3)).

Neither of these requirements really addresses the problem, though. It should be a simple matter to legislate so that the Commission must seek approval from a judge of the Court of First Instance (or even a national judge) before executing a formal decision to raid a company.

7.3.2.2 The scope of an investigation

When investigating under Article 14, officials of the Commission are entitled to enter all of the suspect's premises and seek out information which is not already known about or fully identified (*Hoechst* v *Commission* (46/87, 227/88) [1989] ECR 2919). The Commission is under no obligation to identify in advance those files or documents which it wishes to see, although the written authorisation should indicate clearly the subject-matter and purpose of the investigation. It has been said that the Commission cannot use its powers under Article 14(3) to justify a 'fishing expedition' (see *National Panasonic*), but it still has a broad area to trawl through once it has decided to launch its boats. The investigation (or 'verification' as the Commission sometimes describes it) may have the character of enabling the Commission officials to verify existing information, gleaned from other sources, or to obtain further details on a topic or event.

In its 1999 White Paper on Modernisation, the Commission expressed concerns about its enquiries under Article 14. These were two-fold. First, before conducting a visit under Article 14(3), it is necessary to apply to a judge of the relevant Member State for authorisation (see, for example, the Competition Act 1998, s. 61, in the United Kingdom). If the Commission's investigation involves two or more Member States, it becomes a difficult task to coordinate these applications and to ensure that the outcomes are the same. This problem could be overcome by removing the task of judicial oversight to the European Court for a single decision. An alternative solution would be to 'harmonise and simplify the procedural law in the Member States' but, as the White Paper recognises, this is a much more complex option which would almost certainly require amendments to procedural law in most Member States.

The second concern was that some doubt has arisen over exactly what the Commission officials can ask about during an investigation. The White Paper proposes the amendment of Regulation 17/62 to make it clear that the authorised officials of the Commission can ask a company's staff or representatives 'any questions that are justified by and related to the purpose of the investigation, and to demand a full and precise answer'. Official minutes of the answers could be drawn up and those minutes placed in the Commission's file, for possible use later in the investigation.

7.3.2.3 Fines and further attempts

Although there is no obligation to allow officials of the Commission to enter an undertaking's premises, where the visit takes place pursuant to Article 14(2), if the undertaking does permit entry and provides information (whether written, oral or otherwise) it must be careful. If the undertaking supplies incomplete information (in the form of its books or other business records), whether deliberately or through negligence, it may be fined pursuant to Article 15(1)(c) (see further **7.8.1.1** and **7.8.2.1** below).

When the visit takes place pursuant to Article 14(3), there is the additional possibility that, if entry is denied by the undertaking, it may face a fine for that denial and penalty payments (increasing on a daily basis) for continued denial (see Article 15(1)(c); Article 16(1)(d)). Also, if an undertaking is delaying or denying entry to properly-authorised Commission officials, Member States are required to afford any assistance necessary to enable the officials to do their job.

In the UK at present, this might mean seeking an injunction, similar to a search order under the Civil Procedure Rules, from the Commercial Court. The Attorney-General has also had the power to apply, without notice, to the High Court for an order (see further *Hoechst* v *Commission* (46/87, 227/88) [1989] ECR 2919; *Ukwal* (1992) OJ L 121/45). When the Competition Act 1998 comes into force (expected to be 1 March 2000), specific provision is made for application to a High Court judge. The judge may issue a warrant authorising entry to named premises, for the purposes of searching for books and records, using reasonable force where necessary. Such a warrant may only be issued where the judge is satisfied that a Commission investigation is being, or is likely to be, obstructed. Intentional obstruction of any person exercising powers under such a warrant is to be a criminal offence, punishable in the Crown Court by two years' imprisonment and an unlimited fine. See further the Competition Act 1998, ss. 62 and 65.

7.3.3 WITHHOLDING INFORMATION FROM THE COMMISSION

Given the fact that fines may be imposed for supplying incorrect or incomplete information to the Commission and the incentive to volunteer information (see **8.8.1.3**), it may seem odd for an undertaking to even think about withholding information. However, attempts have been made to do this on a variety of grounds:

- confidentiality;

- privilege against self-incrimination;

- legal professional privilege.

The topics of confidentiality and disclosure are the subject of an article by Julian M. Joshua at [1994] 2 ECLR 68.

7.3.3.1 Confidentiality

Whether information is obtained under Article 11 or Article 14, it can only be used for the purpose of the relevant investigation (see Article 20(1), Regulation 17). The Commission may pass this information onto the competition authorities of Member States (see Article 10, Regulation 17) but it cannot then be used in evidence against its supplier in national proceedings (*Dirección General de Defensa de la Competencia* v *AEB* (C-67/91) [1992] ECR I-4785). The information can be used as the catalyst for national proceedings, however. Thus, some semblance of a balance is maintained between the desire for confidentiality and the public interest in competition authorities being able to take effective action. The situation becomes clouded, though, where the supplier of information is in competition with an undertaking which is owned or controlled by the State: receipt of confidential information by the national competition authority may place it in a difficult position.

That is what happened in *SEP* v *Commission* (C-36/92P) [1994] ECR I-1911. The Commission requested information from an undertaking: specifically a copy of a contract for the supply of gas between SEP and Statoil. Statoil was in competition with the Dutch state-owned gas supplier, Gasunie. SEP refused to disclose the contract to the Commission on the ground that:

- it contained commercially sensitive information, and

- the Commission would disclose it to the Dutch competition authority.

The Court of Justice vindicated SEP's concern, stating that there could be no 'Chinese wall' erected between officials in the Dutch competition authority dealing with Statoil matters and those looking at the commercial policy of Gasunie. Article 20, Regulation 17, did not provide an effective barrier against possible misuse of confidential information. It might be thought that the Court of Justice then upheld SEP's claim to withhold the contract from the Commission but that was not so. The Court decided that the Commission had no duty to pass the information on to the Dutch (cf. Article 10, Regulation 17) and so the possible conflict of interest might never come about. Disclosure was ordered.

A further problem has arisen since then, with the notice on cooperation between the Commission and national competition authorities (see the draft in OJ 1996 C262/7). The notice indicates that, in cases where the Commission rejects a complaint as having insufficient Community interest (see **8.1.1**), it will refer the matter to the appropriate national competition authority and put the relevant documents in its possession at the authority's disposal. It seems that in some cases at least, the concern about information 'leaking' between government officials may become of greater significance than was envisaged by the Court of Justice in 1992. See also **8.7.5**.

7.3.3.2 Privilege against self-incrimination

For many years, it seemed that there was no general right to remain silent in the face of a Commission investigation (note, e.g., the power to 'ask for oral explanations on the spot' in Article 14(1)). In 1989, the Court of Justice acknowledged a privilege against self-incrimination: where questions are asked which effectively require an undertaking to admit its guilt, they are likely to be ruled void (see *Orkem SA* v *Commission* (374/87) [1989] ECR 3283, involving questions asked in a request for information under Article 11). Things have moved on since then: in 1993, the European Court of Human Rights decided that there is a right (under Article 6 of the European Convention on Human Rights and Fundamental Freedoms (ECHR)) to remain silent and not incriminate oneself (see *Funke* v *France* [1993] 1 CMLR 897). Thus, *if* this judgment was applied to competition investigations within the European Community, Commission officials would probably have to caution undertakings (or individual employees) in a manner analogous to a criminal investigation.

One step back from this was taken in Norway (an adherent to the ECHR, although not within the EC); the Norwegian Supreme Court ruled that the reasoning in *Funke* was too brief to be relied upon for the purpose of overturning 'long-established procedures under Norwegian competition law concerning the duty to render information to investigating officers' (see *Norway* v *Rieber & Son AS* [1995] 2 ECLR R-51). Another retreat came with the decision of the Court of Justice that a national court, when considering the application of Article 81 (ex 85) or 82 (ex 86), is not required to recognise the privilege against self-incrimination as established in Community law (see *Otto* v *Postbank* (C-60/92) [1993] ECR I-5683). So it seems that the privilege may be used in response to requests for information from (or direct questions asked by) the Commission, but it will be of little or no use when proceedings are taken in Member States based on the competition rules of the EC.

7.3.3.3 Legal professional privilege

Not all documents have to be shown to the Commission. An undertaking which is undergoing an investigation is entitled to withhold documents which are protected by legal professional privilege (see *AM & S Europe Ltd* v *Commission* (155/79) [1982] ECR 1575). The privilege attaches to written advice from independent (i.e. not in-house) lawyers who are registered and practising in the EC. Protection extends to all written communications exchanged between lawyer and client after the start of the administrative procedure under Regulation 17 and it will also cover earlier written communications which relate to the subject-matter of that procedure.

The onus of proof rests with the undertaking. If unsatisfied, the Commission can then take a decision requiring the undertaking to produce the relevant document(s). The undertaking may then seek annulment of the decision under Article 173, EC Treaty, before the Court of First Instance.

7.4 After the Investigation: the Statement of Objections

Having concluded its initial look into the allegations, a decision will be taken whether to initiate a procedure against the undertaking(s) involved (this is not a decision within Article 249 (ex 189), EC Treaty and cannot usually be challenged on appeal). A statement of objections will then be issued and served on each undertaking. In many respects, the statement of objections resembles the particulars of claim familiar to English lawyers. The relevant facts will be set out, together with the conclusions that the Commission avers can be drawn from those facts. Copies of documents and other evidence which support the factual picture constructed by the Commission, and its conclusions, must be supplied to the undertaking(s). The factual assertions must be set out in sufficient detail that an effective response can be made; a time limit will usually be set for an undertaking to pass its observations onto the Commission. The statement of objections essentially crystallises the Commission's case against the undertaking(s). Any subsequent decision finding an infringement of Article 81(1) (ex 85(1)) or 82 (ex 86) must be based upon the allegations of fact as set down in the statement of objections. A little further refinement of the Commission's case may be permitted, as the undertaking submits its comments or evidence, but the Commission must be careful to allow the undertaking sufficient time to make a proper response to any further developments. The right of a 'defendant' undertaking to be heard is considered in **7.6.5**.

7.5 Interim Measures

It will be cold comfort to a complainant that the Commission's investigation has resulted in the termination of an infringement, or the modification of another undertaking's behaviour, if the complainant has suffered serious or irreparable damage whilst awaiting an outcome to the investigation. Articles 242 and 243 (ex 185 and 186), EC Treaty expressly allow the European Court to grant temporary relief. Such power will be exercised initially by the Court of First Instance, but in order to have jurisdiction an action must be proceeding before the Court. During the investigative stages prior to a decision, therefore, a victim may seek relief only from the Commission. The Commission has no such express power, under the terms of the EC Treaty or Regulation 17, but the European Court of Justice has ruled that the Commission has *implicit* power to grant interim relief during an investigation (see *Camera Care* v *Commission* (792/79R) [1980] ECR 119). The rationale is that decisions of the Commission should not become 'ineffectual or illusory', which might happen if the complainant ceased trading as a result of the infringement.

The power to grant interim measures can be exercised only if certain criteria are satisfied by the applicant who seeks them. The applicant must prove that:

- the measures are *temporary, conservatory* and are the minimum needed in the present situation (i.e. *proportionate*);

- such measures are needed *urgently* in order to avoid a situation which is either

- likely to cause *serious and irreparable damage* to the applicant, or

- which is *intolerable* for the *public interest*.

Although the purpose of the implied powers is to allow the final outcome to have a meaningful effect, there is not *carte blanche* to prop up a failing applicant by any means within the suspect's powers. Any interim measures must fall within the scope of the final decision which the Commission could reach on finding an infringement (see *Ford* v *Commission* (228/82) [1984] 2 ECR 1129; *Brass Band Instruments/Boosey & Hawkes* OJ 1987 L286/36, [1988] 4 CMLR 67).

In a sense, this type of application mirrors the English interim injunction (or Scottish interdict), but one significant difference is that no undertaking in damages is demanded from the applicant to compensate the suspect undertaking if it should turn out that there was no infringement (see *American Cyanamid Co.* v *Ethicon Ltd* [1975] AC 396). It might be thought that an alternative way to protect a 'suspect' undertaking from compliance with unjustified requirements would be to impose a high standard of proof on the applicant to show why the interim measures being sought is justified. That has not been done: the applicant need only show a *prima facie* case that Article 81(1) (ex 85(1)) or 82 (ex 86) has been broken; there is no need to demonstrate a clear and flagrant breach (cf. the English position — show a 'serious question to be tried'). Further, the standard of proof used by the Commission should not be too high regarding 'serious and irreparable damage' (see *La Cinq SA* v *Commission* (T-44/90) [1992] ECR II-1). Damage is 'irreparable' if it cannot be made good by the final decision on the merits (see *La Cinq*) but the Commission has no power to order an infringer to pay financial compensation to a victim. If it transpires that no infringement is finally found proved by the Commission, or the procedure is settled informally, no compensation is payable by the complainant. Whilst one cannot fault the European Court for attempting to maximise the effectiveness of Commission investigations, the position does seem a little unbalanced, with the rights of the suspect undertaking not perhaps being protected as one would wish (the criterion that the measures be 'proportionate' does not really address this). This is, no doubt, the result of the procedure under Article 3, Regulation 17 being inquisitorial, rather than adversarial (see *BAT and Reynolds* v *Commission* (142 and 156/84) [1978] ECR 4487).

In the circumstances, it might seem good advice to give a client who is being harmed by the activities of another undertaking to complain to the Commission and seek interim measures; even better if someone else has already complained since there is no apparent requirement that the applicant for interim measures be the original complainant. However, the Commission does not grant many applications for interim measures (since *Camera Care* in 1980, we are still in single figures). While it may be that such applications are more often resolved with the 'suspect' informally agreeing to modify its behaviour on a temporary basis, it is still likely to be quicker and simpler to seek interim measures from a national court (or competition authority, perhaps); this is certainly likely to be the case in England and Wales. The Commission has recognised this fact:

> national courts can usually adopt interim measures and order the ending of infringements more quickly than the Commission is able to do.

(*Notice on Cooperation between national courts and the Commission in applying Articles 85 and 86*, OJ 1993 C39/6, para. 16.)

The only additional requirements for the 'victim' undertaking in going to an English court are:

- the likely need to give an undertaking in damages; and

- the need to have a civil claim running or about to start against the 'suspect'.

Disadvantages for the 'victim' in turning to an English court for help are:

- the possible payout to the 'suspect' on the undertaking in damages, at the end of proceedings;

- the requirement to satisfy national rules on the grant of interim measures (e.g. a claim on the basis that damage might otherwise be sustained which would be 'intolerable for the public interest' may not succeed in an English court; if the alleged future harm can be compensated by money, an English court is likely to deny the application);

- launching proceedings in a national court may carry some weight in persuading the Commission to reject any subsequent complaint by the victim under Article

3, Regulation 17, on the basis that the complaint lacks sufficient Community interest.

In principle, there is no reason why the two avenues should not be explored simultaneously. Overall, the advice to the client is likely to be to apply to a national court, certainly in the UK, in preference to seeking relief from the Commission.

7.6   Hearings

7.6.1   INTRODUCTION

Before taking certain decisions under Regulation 17, the Commission is required to give the undertaking(s) concerned the chance to be heard on matters relevant to the potential decision. These decisions are:

- The decision to grant negative clearance pursuant to Article 2, Regulation 17.

- The decision to order termination of an infringement of Article 85(1) or Article 86 pursuant to Article 3, Regulation 17.

- The decision to grant an exemption under Article 85(3) pursuant to Articles 6, 7 and 8, Regulation 17.

- The decision to impose a fine pursuant to Article 15, Regulation 17.

- The decision to impose periodic penalty payments pursuant to Article 16, Regulation 17.

In 1963, the Commission enacted Regulation 99/63 to regulate such hearings. Subsequently, it published decisions setting out the terms of reference for hearing officers (the latest of these is Decision 94/810, OJ 1994 L330/67). Most recently, the Commission issued Regulation 2842/98 in December 1998. This Regulation replaces 99/63, and several similar measures governing hearings in other fields. Regulation 2842/98 contains various procedural improvements, in the light of experience gleaned from using 99/63 over so many years, and is intended to make the whole procedure of hearings much clearer. It came into force on 1 February 1999.

Undertakings against whom objections are raised by the Commission, shall have the chance to express their views in writing, as shall natural or legal persons who show a sufficient interest. A time limit for receipt of views will be imposed. When it takes its decision, the Commission can only rely on those matters which were notified to the undertaking(s) and thus upon which they were able to express their views. The Court of Justice has said that Regulation 17:

> ... applies the general rule that a person whose interests are perceptibly affected by a decision taken by a public authority must be given the opportunity to make his point of view known.

See, e.g., *Musique Diffusion Française* v *Commission* (100-103/80) [1983] ECR 1825.

7.6.2   HEARINGS FOR COMPLAINANTS

Specific provision is made for complainants (under Article 3(2), Regulation 17) to be informed if the Commission proposes to dismiss their complaint; the complainant must be told the reasoning behind the proposal and allowed to submit any further written comments before any decision is taken to grant negative clearance or an exemption (see Article 6, Regulation 2842/98). This communication to the complainant is not a decision (within the meaning given by Article 249 (ex 189), EC Treaty) capable of judicial review under Article 230 (ex 173), EC Treaty: see *Automec* v *Commission I* (T-64/89) [1990] ECR II-367. On the other hand, it is a definition of the

Commission's position, sufficient to defeat an application to the European Court under Article 232 (ex 175), EC Treaty, alleging failure to act: see *Guérin Automobiles* v *Commission* (T-186/94) [1995] ECR II-1753. Ultimately though, there must a formal decision on the merits, taken by the Commission, which is susceptible of judicial review: see *Automec* v *Commission II* (T-24 and 28/90) [1992] ECR II-2223.

7.6.3 ORAL HEARINGS

As part of its proceedings under Regulation 17, the Commission may send one of several letters to an undertaking or other natural or legal person. These include:

- a statement of objections (as part of infringement proceedings against that undertaking);

- an invitation to a natural or legal person, having shown sufficient interest to be heard as a third party, to submit written comments;

- a letter to a complainant, explaining that in the Commission's view there are insufficient grounds to find an infringement and inviting the submission of any further written comments;

- a letter to a natural or legal person, explaining that in the Commission's view that person has not shown sufficient interest to be heard as a third party.

A recipient of any of the foregoing letters may submit written comments in reply. These written comments may contain an application to be heard at an oral hearing. Regulation 2842/98 distinguishes between three categories of applicant in this context:

(a) parties against whom objections have been laid by the Commission (i.e., suspect undertakings). If they request an oral hearing, they shall be given one in order to develop their arguments;

(b) complainants, whether the Commission has taken up the complaint or is disposed to dismiss it. If they request an oral hearing, the Commission may afford them the opportunity of expressing their views, where appropriate;

(c) 'other third parties' who have applied to be heard and have shown a sufficient interest in the subject-matter. Where the Commission has issued objections against an undertaking, it may invite other third parties to develop their arguments at the oral hearing. Generally, the Commission may afford to any other third party the opportunity to express their views orally.

See, respectively, Articles 5, 8 and 9 of Regulation 2842/98.

The oral hearing will take place in private and be conducted by the Hearing Officer. Those summoned to attend may be assisted or represented by lawyers. Those who attend to be heard may be heard separately or in the presence of others so summoned; this is a decision for the Hearing Officer to take but he or she must bear in mind the need to observe the desire of undertakings to protect their business secrets. A useful article on oral hearings, by C.S. Kerse, may be found at [1994] ECLR 40.

7.6.4 THE HEARING OFFICER'S REPORT

The Hearing Officer is administratively a part of DG IV but is intended to be independent of the investigation. This independence is said to be demonstrated by the Officer's right to present an opinion, on the case under investigation, directly to the Commissioner for Competition Affairs. In any case, after a hearing, the Hearing Officer will report to the director-general for competition about the hearing and the conclusions he or she draws from it. The Hearing Officer's opinion is not normally disclosed to anyone outside the Commission itself. It is characterised as an internal working document of the Commission; as such, it should not be disclosed to an undertaking under investigation unless an allegation of serious misuse of power has been made against the Commission and it is thought the Hearing Officer's report may be relevant (see e.g. *BAT and Reynolds* v *Commission* (142 and 156/84) [1987] ECR 4487).

7.6.5 AN EFFECTIVE RIGHT TO BE HEARD?

7.6.5.1 Access to the Commission's file

Whether making comments in writing or addressing the Hearing Officer orally, an undertaking is entitled to do so effectively. In the case of an undertaking under investigation, the proper exercise of the right to be heard may be hampered if the Commission is in possession of material which has not been disclosed to the undertaking. If the material is incriminatory (maybe comments from third parties), then in one sense we could say that the undertaking benefits from non-disclosure. This would be because the Commission is not permitted to take account of any undisclosed material or arguments when reaching its decision on whether there has been an infringement or not (see Article 2(2), Regulation 2842/98). However, such material may colour the Commission's (or DG IV's) thinking and it may be that, if the undertaking was informed of the incriminatory material, it could provide a satisfactory explanation, consistent with innocence.

What may be worse is if the Commission is in possession of material which could positively assist the defence of the undertaking. Non-disclosure here could result in a serious injustice. As the Court of First Instance observed in *ICI plc* v *Commission* (T-36/91) [1995] ECR II-1847:

> The purpose of providing access to the file in competition cases is to enable the addressee of a statement of objections [i.e. the suspect undertaking] to examine evidence in the Commission's file so that on the basis of that evidence it may effectively express its views on the conclusions reached by the Commission in its statement of objections.

> That access is one of the procedural safeguards intended to protect the rights of the defence, which is a general principle, the proper observance of which requires that the undertaking concerned be afforded the opportunity . . . effectively to make known its views on the truth and relevance of the facts, charges and circumstances relied on by the Commission . . . In the defended proceedings for which Regulation 17/62 provides, it cannot be for the Commission alone to decide which documents are of use for the defence. Where difficult and complex economic appraisals are to be made [the case involved parallel conduct alleged to demonstrate a concerted practice], the Commission must give the advisers of the undertaking concerned the opportunity to examine documents which may be relevant so that their probative value for the defence can be assessed.

To an extent, the Commission had already sought to do the bidding of the Court of First Instance. In its decision on the terms of reference for Hearing Officers (Decision 94/810, OJ 1994 L330/67), the Commission introduced a new provision on disclosure. Article 5 of that decision states that if an undertaking, or natural or legal person, has received one of the letters listed in Article 4(3) (see **8.7.3**), and it has reason to believe

(a) that the Commission has not disclosed all of its documents, and

(b) that those documents are necessary for the proper exercise of the right to be heard,

then it may make a reasoned request for disclosure. A reasoned decision, either for or against disclosure, will be communicated to the undertaking which made the request and to any other undertaking or person concerned by the procedure.

In its XXVth Report on Competition Policy (1995), the Commission recorded that it was examining the impact of *ICI* and related cases (involving a soda-ash cartel) on its current practice. The result came in January 1997, when the Commission published a Notice on its internal rules of procedure for processing requests for access to the file in competition cases (see OJ 1997 C23/03; **Appendix 3**). This Notice attempted to ensure compatibility between the Commission's current practice on access to the file and the judgments of the European Court in the 'soda-ash' cases (e.g. the *ICI* case mentioned above). The Notice recognised that, in principle, the addressee of a statement of objections must have access to all documents in the Commission's file. This is subject to three exceptions:

- business secrets of other undertakings;

- internal Commission documents;

- other confidential information.

'Business secrets' are not fully defined yet (see e.g. *BAT and Reynolds v Commission* (142 and 156/84) [1987] ECR 4487). The Notice suggests that they include 'strategic information on [an undertaking's] essential interests and on the operation or development of [it's] business' which is not known outside the undertaking.

7.6.5.2 Procedure for implementing access to the Commission's file

When supplying information to the Commission, undertakings are asked to indicate which documents (or parts of documents) are claimed to contain business secrets or are otherwise confidential. Any claim for confidentiality should be substantiated and a non-confidential version of such document(s) supplied. Any claim for confidentiality will be determined swiftly on a provisional basis. Subsequently, there will be a 'final assessment' of the accessibility of the document(s). The Commission reserves the right to allow suspect undertakings to have access to documents, overriding the supplier's objection, where the document 'serves as a basis for the decision' (on infringement) or may assist the suspect undertaking. An exception exists in cases of alleged infringement of Article 82 (ex 86): the Commission acknowledges that an undertaking in a dominant position may be able to take retaliatory steps against its customers, suppliers or competitors if it learns they have been in communication with the Commission. Thus, communications with such third parties, even though of value in giving the Commission a better understanding of the relevant market, are unlikely to be disclosed in order to minimise the risk of retaliation by a dominant undertaking.

The Commission will draw up a list of documents in its file, giving each one an access code. This code will show the document to be either

- accessible;

- partially accessible;

- non-accessible.

Non-accessible documents will be those containing business secrets, other confidential information and the Commission's internal working documents. The list will have a summary, so that the content and subject of such documents may be identified. This should enable undertakings to determine whether to request access to a document, notwithstanding its present classification. A reasoned request for such access should be made to the Hearing Officer. Inevitably, a balancing exercise is involved; where a document is alleged to contain business secrets, the Commission must assess:

- the relevance of the information to the determination of whether an infringement has occurred;

- the probative value of the information;

- whether the information is indispensable;

- the potential harm that disclosure might cause;

- how serious the infringement is.

Every document containing business secrets must be considered individually to assess if the need for access outweighs the possible harm in granting access. It should be noted that the Court of Justice has previously said that access should *not* be given to documents containing business secrets (see *BAT and Reynolds* v *Commission* (142 and 156/84) [1987] ECR 4487; *Akzo* v *Commission* (53/85) [1986] ECR 1965). It seems that the Notice takes a less principled, more pragmatic approach. Other confidential information may be disclosed if the Commission needs to rely on it to establish an infringement or if it may assist the defence (a non-confidential version will be used, where possible).

Access to documents will usually be given on the premises of the Commission, although undertakings can choose to have all outstanding accessible documents sent to them.

7.6.5.3 Access to the file for complainants

The Commission is quite explicit in its Notice that the degree of disclosure given to undertakings which are the subject of investigations does not extend to those who are complainants, still less to third parties. The Notice states:

> ... there are no grounds for treating the rights of the complainant as equivalent to those of the firms [which are the addressees of a statement of objections].

When a complainant is informed that the Commission intends to reject the complaint, it may ask to see those documents which the Commission has considered. The Notice explicitly states that a complainant will not be given access to any confidential information or business secrets, either of the suspect undertaking or of third parties. This contrasts with the position previously examined by the Court of Justice in the *BAT* case (142 and 156/84) and *Akzo* (53/85) where the Commission could disclose documents to a complainant, although they contained confidential information, in order to obtain the complainant's opinion on them, if to do so was necessary for the proper conduct of the investigation. See also *Matra Hachette* v *Commission* (T-17/93) [1994] ECR I-595.

7.6.5.4 Challenging a denial of access

The appropriate action to take is to seek judicial review of the denial, using Article 230 (ex 173), EC Treaty, in the Court of First Instance. An applicant may rely on either the infringement of an essential procedural requirement (e.g. Article 2(2), Regulation 2842/98) or the infringement of a rule of law relating to the application of the EC Treaty (e.g. 'hear both sides'; see e.g. *ICI* v *Commission* (T-36/91) [1995] ECR II-1847). Complainants may face obstacles in mounting a challenge based on their right to be heard. Complainants must have an opportunity to defend their legitimate interests which means, in practice, that the Commission must consider all legal and factual material which the complainant draws to its attention. The rights of a complainant are not co-extensive with those of the suspect company and the investigation is not adversarial in nature. A complainant's rights expire when they start to conflict with the right of a suspect to a fair hearing. See *BAT and Reynolds* v *Commission* (142 and 156/84) [1987] ECR 4487.

When should the challenge be made? The moment of denial would seem appropriate but that is wrong in the opinion of the Court of First Instance. Access to files may underpin the right to be heard but there is no legal effect on a suspect undertaking until such time as the Commission finds there has been an infringement of Article 81(1) (ex 85(1)) or Article 82 (ex 86) and, perhaps, imposes a fine (or when it finds there has not been an infringement, if a complainant has been denied access to the file). The Court of First Instance has said, in an action to challenge the denial of access under Article 230 (ex 173), EC Treaty, that such an action is premature and inadmissible if it precedes a formal decision on the substantive merits of the case. See *Cimenteries CBR SA and others* v *Commission* (T-10-12/92 and 15/92) [1993] 4 CMLR 259. While a 'wait-and-see' approach may satisfy the pragmatist (and most undertakings may be used to looking at the end rather than worrying about the means too much), it does little for principles and it may be hard to conclude that justice has been served if the full picture has not emerged.

7.7 The Decision of the Commission on Infringement

7.7.1 THE PROCEDURE

After allowing the undertakings, and other interested parties, to be heard, the Commission will consult with the Advisory Committee on Restrictive Practices and Monopolies (the UK is usually represented on the Advisory Committee by an official from the Office of Fair Trading). A copy of the draft decision will be before the Committee, together with the most important evidence. The Committee may deliver an opinion to the Commission but this is not published and does not bind the Commission. The decision itself must be taken by the full Commission, it is not within the scope of the delegated powers of the Commissioner for Competition. The procedural rules for taking a decision must be strictly complied with: failure to do so is likely to lead to the measure being annulled by the Court of First Instance (see e.g. *Commission v BASF and others* (C-137/92P) [1994] ECR I-2555). The decision must be published, although the obligation to respect business secrets often results in much of the substance being removed from the published version of the decision. The undertakings to whom the decision is addressed will receive the full version.

Finally, an undertaking which is aggrieved by the decision may challenge it, either on procedural or substantive grounds, before the Court of First Instance, using Article 230 (ex 173), EC Treaty to seek its annulment. It should be noted that the right of challenge is not limited to the suspect undertaking(s). In particular, a complainant will normally have the standing to challenge the Commission's finding. An illustration of this can be found in *BAT and Reynolds v Commission* (142 and 156/84) [1987] ECR 4487.

BAT complained to the Commission about a joint venture company which was established by two of its rivals in the European cigarette industry, Philip Morris and Rembrandt. The Commission began an investigation but then decided there were no longer any grounds for investigating, after the two suspect companies modified their agreement. The Commission wrote to BAT, telling them it was closing its file. BAT challenged this in the Court of Justice (there was no Court of First Instance then), using Article 230 (ex 173). On the question of its ability to use this procedure, the Court of Justice said that BAT had received the letter from the Commission. All it needed to do was show that the letter was a reviewable act, i.e. it produced legal effects for BAT. This had been done by asserting that the change in the market structure which the Commission had, in effect, approved meant it was likely that BAT would suffer financial losses in the future.

7.7.2 THE CONTENT OF A DECISION

Having investigated under Article 3, Regulation 17, where the Commission finds an infringement of Article 81(1) (ex 85(1)) or 82 (ex 86) has been proven, it is empowered to 'require the undertakings . . . concerned to bring such infringement to an end'. There may be a variety of ways in which a specific infringement could be brought to an end: while the Commission should give a reasonable indication of the infringement, it should usually leave decisions on how best to comply with that finding to the undertaking (see e.g. *Automec v Commission* (T-24/90) [1992] ECR II-2223). Occasionally, though, the Commission has been permitted to impose quite specific requirements as part of the obligation to terminate an infringement. A typical example can be found in a series of cases where a supplier (or small number of suppliers) comprised the sole source of a product or service: if the Commission finds that a refusal to supply or maintain supplies (or give access to a service) constitutes an infringement (of Article 81(1) (ex 85(1)) or 82 (ex 86)), it may order a resumption of supplies (or the commencement thereof). Such cases include *Commercial Solvents v Commission* (6 and 7/73)

[1974] ECR 223; *Radio Telefis Eireann* v *Commission* (C-241 and 242/91P) [1995] ECR I-743. This is rather an exceptional situation and the Commission can probably order an undertaking to take such positive steps (rather than stop an act or end a contract) only where that is the sole effective way to terminate the infringement.

It seems that other, minor, forms of positive action that an undertaking can be required to take are:

- filing regular reports with the Commission, to confirm that problems are not recurring; and

- taking steps to inform others with an interest in the termination of the infringement that termination has occurred, and the consequences thereof for them (for example, the opportunity or need to renegotiate a contract).

7.7.3   ALTERNATIVES TO A DECISION

The Commission does not reach formal decisions very often in competition investigations. In recent years, the number of formal decisions on the merits has typically been in the 'teens, although in 1994 some 33 decisions were taken. As the number of complaints is around 100 annually, one can see that a large backlog would build up in the absence of another way to resolve complaints. One way, which may gain increasing numbers over the next few years, is to farm complaints out to national competition authorities. Another is to reach an informal conclusion to the investigation. Thus, without perhaps having the quality of evidence needed to prove the existence or duration of an infringement, the Commission may be content to close its file where the suspect undertaking agrees to modify its behaviour (see e.g. the history in *Metro SB-Grossmarkte* v *Commission* (26/76) [1977] ECR 1875).

7.8   Fines

7.8.1   FINES AND PERIODIC PENALTY PAYMENTS

Regulation 17/62 provides for the imposition of fines and periodic penalty payments upon undertakings. Under Article 15 (fines) and Article 16 (periodic penalty payments) of Regulation 17, the Commission is empowered to take a decision (see Article 249 (ex 189), EC Treaty) to impose financial penalties on undertakings or associations of undertakings. Fines take the form of a one-off penalty, while periodic penalty payments will be applied on a daily basis and the total will increase until the undertaking complies with the decision of the Commission.

7.8.1.1   The range of fines

Fines imposed under Article 15(1) may range from 100 to 5,000 units of account. Units of account (ECUs) basically means the euro now, and the Commission typically specifies only an amount in terms of euros when taking a decision to fine an undertaking. The value of the euro rate can be found in broadsheet newspapers; it is usually in the range of 1 euro: 60-70p. Fines imposed under Article 15(2) run from a minimum of 1,000 units of account to a maximum of 1 million. That ceiling may be exceeded, subject to an overall limit on the fine of not more than 10% of the turnover of the undertaking in the preceding business year ('turnover' here refers to the global turnover of the undertaking, across its entire product range: see e.g. *Pioneer* (C 100-103/80) [1983] ECR 1825).

Examples of fines imposed by the Commission are:

(a)   *Re Konica UK Ltd* [1988] 4 CMLR 848— ECU 75,000.

(b)   *Re Quaker Oats UK Ltd* [1989] 4 CMLR 553— ECU 300,000.

(c) *Hilti* [1989] 4 CMLR 677 — ECU 6 million for a very serious breach of Article 81 (ex 86), EC Treaty, even taking into account mitigating factors like:

    (i)   Hilti's cooperation;

    (ii)   its voluntary offer of a remedial undertaking prior to the outcome of the investigation; and

    (iii)   its introduction of a compliance programme governing its future conduct.

The fine was upheld through appeals to the Court of First Instance and then the Court of Justice (see (C-53/2P) [1994] ECR I-667).

(d) *Re Polypropylene Cartel* [1988] 4 CMLR 347 — a cartel among the major producers of polypropylene in the EC infringed Article 81(1) (ex 85(1)). It led to fines totalling nearly ECU 58 million being imposed on some 15 firms, e.g. Hoechst (ECU 9 million), ICI (ECU 10 million), and Shell (ECU 9 million). The producers appealed. Several had their appeals rejected (e.g. Hoechst) while others had their fines reduced, usually on the basis that the Commission had insufficient evidence to establish that their membership of the cartel covered the full period alleged.

(e) *Akzo Chemie BV*, OJ 1985 L374/1, [1986] 3 CMLR 273. The original fine of ECU 10 million was reduced by 25% on appeal to the Court of Justice. Two reasons for the reduction were:

    (i)   that the Community policy on predatory pricing was largely unknown when Akzo embarked on its conduct; and

    (ii)   that the market shares of Akzo and its rival, ECS, had not been significantly affected by the conduct.

(f) *Tetra Pak* (C-333/94) [1997] 4 CMLR 662. A fine of ECU 75 million was imposed by the Commission for abuse of a dominant position. Tetra Pak, a Swiss company owned by Swedes, was found guilty of carrying out a 'deliberate policy aiming to eliminate actual or potential competitors'. The fine was a record amount and the subject of unsuccessful appeals to the Court of First Instance and Court of Justice. The absence of precedent did not result in any reduction in this case (cf. *Akzo*).

(g) *Re Cartonboard Cartel*, OJ 1994 L243/1. A cartel of cartonboard producers was fined in excess of ECU 130 million, with several individual members fined more than ECU 15 million each. On appeal to the CFI, the total amount was reduced to some ECU 120 million (*Cartonboard* (T–295/94)).

A table of fines imposed on undertakings by the Commission can be found in Bellamy & Child, *Common Market Law of Competition*, at 12-064.

7.8.1.2   The range of periodic penalty payments

According to Article 16(1), Regulation 17, periodic penalty payments start at 50 units of account (now 'euros') per day, and may be as high as 1,000 units of account.

7.8.1.3   Calculating the amount of a fine or periodic penalty payment

Periodic penalty payments should be a simple matter of taking the daily rate, as specified in the decision, and multiplying that by the number of days it took the undertaking to comply with the requirement. In fact, after compliance has occurred, the Commission has to take a second decision to fix the total amount of the periodic penalty payment. It is allowed to fix this at a lower figure than the original calculation would produce (Article 16(2)); if the Commission does not take a second decision to set a total amount, then nothing will be due.

Fines may be imposed where an undertaking has acted either negligently or intentionally. One may expect fines to be higher where the undertaking has deliberately set out to act in a way that infringes the rules; that seems to be the situation in practice. Conversely, if an undertaking is found to have infringed the rules in a novel way, maybe where it could not have known that its actions would be assessed as infringements, the unprecedented nature of the infringement may result in a reduction in the fine; the novelty will not excuse the act from being condemned as an infringement (cf. *Akzo Chemie BV* v *Commission* (C-62/86) [1991] ECR I-3359; *Tetra Pak International SA* v *Commission* (C-333/94) [1997] 4 CMLR 662). The Commission has to take account of the duration as well as the gravity of the infringement. It will need to have clear evidence of the relevant period(s) to avoid the possibility of a legal challenge and should specify the period(s) to the undertaking concerned.

What should the Commission take as its starting point? In its XXIst Annual Report on Competition Policy (1991), the Commission stated that:

> The financial benefit which companies infringing the competition rules have derived from their infringements will become an increasingly important consideration. Wherever the Commission can ascertain the level of this ill-gotten gain, even if it cannot do so precisely, the calculation of the fine may have this as its starting-point. When appropriate the amount could then be increased or decreased in the light of the other circumstances of the case, including the need to introduce an element of deterrence or penalty in the sanction imposed on the participating companies.

A fine may be mitigated if the undertaking takes prompt action to terminate the infringement, or comply with a requirement, once the Commission's view has been drawn to their attention. So, a quick acceptance of 'guilt' (coupled with remedial action) after notification that the Commission is to investigate an undertaking may save money, at least compared to the position where the undertaking refuses to cooperate through a full investigation. In 1996, the Commission took a more active approach to encourage 'whistle-blowers'. The Commission recognised that companies involved in a cartel may wish to end their participation and tell the Commission about the cartel but could be deterred from doing so by the possibility of facing a high fine. It therefore issued a Notice (Commission Notice on the non-imposition or reduction of fines in cartel cases, OJ 1996 C207/4) setting out the conditions on which 'informer' undertakings may be exempted from fines or be granted a reduction in the amount of fine imposed on them. This Notice breaks down the amount of incentive, according to the degree of cooperation, so, in essence:

- an undertaking which cooperates fully may receive a reduction of at least 75%, and maybe total exemption, from the fine that would otherwise have been imposed;

- an undertaking which cooperates fully, after the Commission has undertaken an unsuccessful investigation on the premises of the cartel members, can expect a reduction of 50–75%;

- less substantial forms of cooperation may result in reductions of 10–50% of the fine.

An undertaking may only take advantage of this Notice when it informs the Commission through a properly-mandated officer of the undertaking. So, if an individual employee 'blows the whistle' on his or her employer to the Commission, the company concerned cannot subsequently claim any reduction on the basis of this Notice.

Participants may receive quite different fines depending upon their level of responsibility for the infringement. So, ringleaders should be identified, along with those who were just 'making up the numbers'. The undertakings who were central to the activity can expect to be hit hardest, while those on the margins, or who participated under duress, may be treated more leniently.

The Commission reduced fines for 'cooperative' firms, for the first time, when dealing with the *Cartonboard* cartel members in 1994. Although this predates the Commission Notice, it does offer some insight into how the Commission will 'reward' firms. Depending upon the degree of cooperation, fines were reduced under this heading by either ⅓ or ⅔. In 1998, the Commission concluded its investigation into the British sugar industry and fined four producers a total of ECU 50.2 million. One of the four producers was Tate & Lyle plc. The Commission's decision is explicit in working through the reduction in fine that it accorded to Tate & Lyle in application of the 1996 'informer' notice. Starting with a basic sum of ECU 10 million for the gravity of the infringement, the Commission then increased that to ECU 14 million to take account of the duration of the infringement. However, Tate & Lyle alerted the Commission to the existence of the cartel before the Commission was aware of it and before any investigation had begun. Tate & Lyle also supplied two self-incriminatory letters to the Commission; these constituted the first hard evidence that the Commission had of the existence of the cartel. Lastly, Tate & Lyle ended its involvement in the cartel (sensibly, you may think) shortly before it informed the Commission of the cartel's existence. Strangely, the Commission's decision states that, thereafter, Tate & Lyle 'did not maintain continuous and complete cooperation with the Commission throughout the investigation'. Thus, it was not entitled to a full discount. Nevertheless, its early actions resulted in Tate & Lyle having its fine reduced by 50%, or ECU 7 million.

Before deciding to impose a fine, the Commission must allow the undertaking a chance to express its views, both written and oral. Officials within DG IV will advise the Commissioner for Competition on the amount of any fine; the Commissioner will then make a recommendation to the College of Commissioners who make the final, formal, decision. There have been calls from outside DG IV for the methodology of quantifying fines to be made more transparent, with some curtailment on the Commission's current wide discretion. See e.g. Ivo van Bael, 'Fining à la carte: the lottery of EU Competition law' [1995] 4 ECLR 237; and compare Luc Gyselen, *The Commission's Fining Policy in Competition Cases*, Slot & McDonnell ed., 1993.

In December 1997, the Commissioner responsible for competition affairs, Karel van Miert, published guidelines for the calculation of fines under Articles 81 (ex 85) and 82 (ex 86). This represented an attempt to provide the transparency that had been sought by those outside the Commission. The gravity and duration of an infringement provide the starting points for calculation. One begins with *gravity* and considers:

- the nature of the infringement;

- the size of the relevant geographic market; and

- the impact of the infringement upon the market, where this can be determined.

The information thus gathered should enable the Commission to put the infringement into one of three categories:

- *minor* — these would normally involve only vertical restraints, having only limited impact on the market and not covering a wide territory. Likely range of fine 1,000–1 million ECU;

- *serious* — these are more likely to involve horizontal restraints, and will have a greater impact on the market, over a more extensive territory. Less significant abuses of a dominant position would fall to be considered in this category. Likely range of fine 1 million–20 million ECU;

- *very serious* — the worst types of horizontal restraint, such as sharing markets through quotas, other forms of market partitioning, and price cartels, will appear here. The worst abuses of a dominant position will also be regarded as *very serious*. Likely range of fine — in excess of 20 million ECU.

Within these ranges, the nature of the infringement will indicate whether the fine should fall towards the bottom, middle or top of the range. Deterrence will also play a part here, as will the size of the undertaking (that is, bigger firms usually have the resources to know what acts will infringe the competition rules). Completing the calculation will give a base figure.

Having got this basic idea of the fine to be imposed on an undertaking, one then turns to consider the *duration* of the infringement. Again, there are three categories and which one applies to the infringement determines whether the base figure will stay the same or may be increased:

- short duration (less than one year) will result in no change;

- medium duration (one to five years) allows an increase of up to 50% on the base figure;

- long duration (over five years) allows an increase of up to 10% for each year on the base figure.

The possibility of significant increases in the fine where the infringement is of long duration, coupled with the reductions for 'whistle-blowers', is intended to stimulate firms to turn 'informer' and deal with the Commission.

Having calculated the new basic figure, one looks for any aggravating or mitigating factors. Amongst these are:

- ringleader (aggravating factor);

- ancillary role (mitigating factor);

- repeating the infringement (aggravating factor);

- negligent or unintentional infringement (mitigating factor);

- cooperation with the Commission — refusal to do so (aggravating factor) or enthusiasm for doing so (mitigating factor);

- swift termination of the infringement following intervention by the Commission (mitigating factor);

- the need to 'claw back' ill-gotten gains, earned because of the infringement (aggravating factor).

The next step is to apply the 1996 Notice on the reduction or non-imposition of fines, and redetermine the definitive amount of the fine (which may be nil by now). At this point, one should take into account the ceiling for fines (set out in Article 15(2), Regulation 17), namely that the fine must not exceed 10% of the firm's world-wide turnover in the previous financial year (so the fine should be reduced if it exceeds that sum). Lastly, adjustments to the amount are made to comply with 'certain objective factors'. These will include:

- 'a specific economic context';

- any economic or financial benefit derived (although this seemed also to appear earlier in the calculation);

- the 'specific characteristics' of the firm(s); and the firm's 'real ability to pay in a specific social context'.

Whatever figure you now have on your piece of paper is the amount of the fine! As an attempt to increase transparency, these guidelines do a reasonable job until that final step. It remains to be seen if those people who had previously criticised the Commission for its opaqueness will be mollified by the publication of these guidelines.

Calculation of the fine in seven easy stages:

Stage 1   Decide on the gravity of the infringement in broad terms. Is it (a) minor, (b) serious, or (c) very serious?

Stage 2   Decide, more specifically, where it falls within the appropriate range. Is it towards the top, middle or bottom? (a) Minor range is 1,000 to 1 million ECU; (b) serious range is 1 million to 20 million ECU; (c) very serious range is more than 20 million ECU. You should now have a figure to work with.

Stage 3   Move onto consider duration. Was it of (a) short, (b) medium, or (c) long duration? Depending upon the answer, your figure will either stay the same or increase.

Stage 4   Increase or reduce the figure to take account of aggravating or mitigting factors.

Stage 5   Make any reductions necessary to 'reward' firms who cooperate or are whistle-blowers.

Stage 6   Determine the ceiling for the fine, set at 10% of global turnover for the firm in its last financial year. Make any necessary adjustment to your figure.

Stage 7   Make final adjustments, up or down, but no more than 10% of turnover, to take account of 'certain objective factors'.

An extremely thorough and clear example of the Commission working its way through the application of both the 1997 'calculation' guidelines and the 1996 'informer' notice can be found in its decision on the British sugar producers' cartel — *British Sugar, Tate & Lyle, Napier Brown and James Budgett*, OJ 1999 L76, 22 March 1999.

7.8.2   WHEN A FINE CAN BE IMPOSED

7.8.2.1   'Procedural' fines
When an undertaking applies to the Commission for negative clearance (under Article 2) or notifies an agreement to the Commission (under Articles 4 or 5), it will have to supply information to the Commission, typically on Form A/B. When looking into possible infringements, the Commission can request information from an undertaking, pursuant to Article 11; it may set a deadline for compliance. The Commission may conduct an investigation and require an undertaking to produce business records, under Article 14. Under Article 15(1), Regulation 17, fines can be imposed on an undertaking which:

- supplies incorrect, incomplete or misleading information to the Commission; or

- fails to supply requested information within the deadline; or

- refuses to submit to an investigation.

7.8.2.2   'Substantive' fines
Under Article 15(2)(a), Regulation 17, if the Commission finds an undertaking to have infringed Article 81(1) (ex 85(1)) or 82 (ex 86), a fine may be imposed. Also, when the Commission grants an individual exemption to an undertaking, pursuant to Article 81(3) (ex 85(3)), it may attach conditions and obligations to the exemption (see Article 8(1), Regulation 17). If the undertaking subsequently is found to be in breach of any such obligation, it may be fined (Article 15(2)(b)). If the Commission finds an agreement infringes Article 81(1) (ex 85(1)) but the parties did not notify it to the Commission because they assumed, in good faith, that it satisfied the criteria to be an agreement

of minor importance (see **2.3.2**), then the Commission 'will not consider imposing fines' (Commission Notice relating to the revision of the 1986 Notice on agreements of minor importance, 1996).

In many notifications, the file will not be closed with a formal decision to grant an individual exemption. Instead, the file will be closed by using one of the 'informal procedures' (see **Chapter 3**). This may involve the undertaking agreeing to do (or not do) specific acts (so that, for example, it is to modify its behaviour, or delete a contractual clause). It does not seem that an undertaking has any liability to a fine under Article 15(2)(b) in such a case if it subsequently fails to comply with the terms of its settlement with the Commission. There remains the possibility that the Commission will re-open the file and resume proceedings against the undertaking.

7.8.3 WHEN A PERIODIC PENALTY PAYMENT CAN BE IMPOSED

The situation is governed by Article 16, Regulation 17. Again, it may be divided into 'procedural' and 'substantive' payments. The objective of imposing a daily penalty is to maximise the probability of swift and full compliance with whatever demands are imposed on an undertaking.

7.8.3.1 'Procedural' periodic penalty payments

When seeking information from an undertaking, pursuant to Article 11, Regulation 17, the Commission follows a two-stage process (see **7.3.1**). When taking a decision under Article 11(5) to require information to be supplied, the Commission is to indicate the penalty for non-compliance and set a deadline. This penalty may be a one-off fine (see Article 15(1)(b)) or it may be a periodic penalty payment (see Article 16(1)(c)). Similarly, if the Commission takes a formal decision, requiring an undertaking to submit to an investigation, pursuant to Article 14(3), Regulation 17, it may also attach a periodic penalty payment (or fine, see Article 15(1)(c)) to the decision (see Article 16(1)(d)).

7.8.3.2 'Substantive' periodic penalty payments

If the Commission takes a decision that an undertaking is infringing either Article 81(1) (ex 85(1)) or 82 (ex 86), it may impose a periodic penalty payment in order to compel the undertaking to put an end to the infringement (Article 16(1)(a), Regulation 17). Likewise, if the Commission grants an individual exemption and requires an undertaking to refrain from any specific acts, it may attach a periodic penalty payment to compel such restraint (see Article 16(1)(b)). In practice, it seems that this last power could only be used where the prohibited act is in existence at the time the decision to exempt is taken and is likely to continue thereafter.

7.8.4 LIMITATION PERIODS

7.8.4.1 Council Regulation 2988/74

Regulation 17 is silent on the topic of limitation periods for lump sum fines and periodic penalty payments. According to the Court of Justice, this meant that there was no limitation period (see *Boehringer Mannheim* v *Commission* (45/69) [1970] ECR 769). By Regulation 2988/74, the Council required the Commission to observe limitation periods when imposing a fine on an undertaking. The period varies, depending upon whether the fine is imposed for a procedural infringement, or is imposed for a substantive infringement of either Article 81(1) (ex 85(1)) or 82 (ex 86).

The periods are:

(a) Three years for infringements of provisions concerning:

   (i)   applications or notifications of undertakings;

   (ii) requests for information (Article 11, Regulation 17);

   (iii) carrying out investigations (Article 14, Regulation 17).

(b) Five years for any other infringement, i.e.:

(i) being in breach of Article 81(1) (ex 85(1)) or 82 (ex 86); or

(ii) failing to comply with a requirement imposed as part of the grant of an exemption pursuant to Article 81(3) (ex 85(3)).

Time starts to run from the day the infringement occurs. If the infringement is repeated, or is in the nature of a continuing infringement, then time runs from the date the infringement ceases. This may enable the Commission to establish a long-running infringement going back over many years; this may have serious repercussions for the undertaking(s) involved since duration is an important factor in determining the amount of any fine.

7.8.4.2 Limitation period for enforcement

What is the Commission to do if it takes a decision to impose a fine, but the fine is not then paid? Further, what happens if the Commission takes a decision fixing the total amount due from an undertaking, as the result of a periodic penalty payment order, and that amount is unpaid? Article 4, Regulation 2988/74, establishes a five-year period within which the Commission is empowered to enforce the decision. Time starts to run on the day the decision became final.

7.8.4.3 Interrupting the limitation period

The limitation period 'clock' may be reset in certain circumstances. Typically, this *interruption* (sic) occurs when the Commission notifies at least one undertaking which has participated in an infringement that it has commenced proceedings for infringement; alternatively, issuing a written request for information would interrupt the limitation period, as would notification of a decision by the Commission to investigate pursuant to Article 14, Regulation 17. Interruption against any one undertaking constitutes interruption against all concerned undertakings (Article 2(2), Regulation 2988/74).

If an undertaking decides to challenge the decision of the Commission, then the limitation period is *suspended* (sic) for the duration of proceedings before the European Court (see Article 3, Regulation 2988/74).

Every interruption starts the clock afresh (Article 2(3), Regulation 2988/74). This is subject to a ceiling of double the relevant limitation period (i.e. six or ten years), plus any period of suspension. If the Commission has not imposed a fine or penalty by the expiry of this time, it is now too late for it to do so.

7.8.4.4 Example

Let us suppose that company A and company B agree to divide up a certain product market between themselves, and in so doing they act contrary to Article 81(1) (ex 85(1)). If the agreement comes to an end on, say, 31 December 1996 (or, subsequently, the Commission cannot prove that it continued beyond that date) then the limitation period commences on that date. If it is to impose a fine for the breach of Article 81(1) (ex 85(1)), the Commission must do so within five years — that is, by 30 December 2001. If the Commission sends a request for information to company A, which is received by A on 31 December 1999, then the clock is reset for both A and B. The Commission need not worry about running out of time now until 30 December 2004. If the Commission subsequently serves a Statement of Objections on company B on 31 December 2002, again the clock returns to zero. However, the Commission does not have until 30 December 2007 to impose a fine for infringement of Article 81(1) (ex 85(1)) because the ceiling of double the limitation period will expire on 30 December 2006 (i.e. ten years from the date of cessation of the infringement).

7.8.5 IMMUNITY FROM FINES

The parties to an agreement usually notify the Commission if they want either a negative clearance or an exemption from the Commission. An undertaking may claim immunity from fines for infringement of Article 81(1) (ex 85(1)) for the period following notification to the Commission (pursuant to Article 3, Regulation 17), up to the date when the Commission takes a decision on exemption, pursuant to Article 81(3) (ex 85(3)). However, that immunity will be lost if the Commission informs the undertaking that, after its preliminary examination, it considers that Article 81(1) (ex 85(1)) has been infringed and that exemption is not justified. See Article 15(5) and (6), Regulation 17.

7.8.6 DOUBLE JEOPARDY

In some circumstances, a company may face liability for the same anti-competitive behaviour before both the Commission and (one or more) national competition authorities. Ideally, with the spirit of cooperation between the Commission and such authorities, there should not be two sets of investigations and therefore the possibility of two punishments would not arise. However, this cannot be guaranteed and so the principle is observed that, if the Commission and national authorities both proceed to use their separate powers, a company should not be fined twice for the same behaviour. What should occur is a kind of set-off, whereby the 'sentencer' who is later in time takes into account the punishment which has been imposed already. See *Boehringer Mannheim GmbH* v *Commission* (45/69) [1970] ECR 769.

7.8.7 CHALLENGING A DECISION TO IMPOSE A FINANCIAL PENALTY

As the Commission's decision (whether to impose a fine or settling the total amount due under a periodic penalty payment order) will be addressed to the undertaking concerned, there should be no problem in the undertaking possessing the standing to mount a legal challenge to the decision. Article 229 (ex 172), EC Treaty and Article 17, Regulation 17, give unlimited jurisdiction to the Court of Justice to review decisions of the Commission to fix a fine or periodic penalty payment. The Court can review matters of fact as well as law; it has the power to cancel, reduce or raise the amount involved. In 1988, the jurisdiction was transferred to the Court of First Instance.

7.8.8 FUTURE INCREASES IN FIANANCIAL PENALTIES

According to the White Paper on Modernisation of the Rules implementing Articles 81 and 82 (1999), while the 10% ceiling on substantive fines has proved to be appropriate, the same cannot be said of procedural fines (see Article 15(1), Regulation 17; **7.8.1.1**). The minimum and maximum figures were established in 1962 and are not thought to be sufficiently tough today to ensure compliance. The Commission proposes to increase the ceiling for procedural fines from the current range of euro 100–5,000 up to a new range of euro 1,000–50,000. This would also have the effect of aligning the range with that in the Merger Regulation. Similarly, periodic penalty payments are thought to need increasing (see Article 16(1), Regulation 17; **7.8.1.2**). The suggestion here is that they rise from the current maximum of euro 1,000 to a new maximum of euro 25,000 per day.

Lastly, the White Paper notes that the Commission has had trouble enforcing fines against associations of undertakings. Although the ceiling is determined by the total turnover of all members of the association, Regulation 17/62 is silent on whether the members are jointly and severally liable. The White Paper has a proposal that Regulation 17 be amended to stipulate that when an association of undertakings has committed an infringement, its members at the time of that infringement are to be liable for payment of the fine jointly and severally.

EIGHT

USING THE COMPETITION RULES IN NATIONAL COURTS

8.1 Introduction

There are two preliminary points to note briefly here. First, the supremacy of EC law over national law. Secondly, the possibility of using EC laws (whether Treaty Articles or secondary measures) in the legal systems of the 15 Member States of the European Union. These topics are of general relevance to the application of EC laws in the legal systems of the Member States and are covered in more detail in **Appendix 6**.

8.2 Supremacy of EC Law

That EC law prevails over contradictory national law has been established at least since 1964, when the European Court of Justice delivered its judgment in *Costa* v *ENEL* (6/64) [1964] ECR 585. The consequence is that if conduct is legal in national law but illegal under EC rules, both the national courts and the European Court must treat it as illegal (both Articles 81(1) (ex 85(1)) and 82 (ex 86), EC Treaty refer to the conduct as 'prohibited'). This helps to ensure that similar conduct is treated in a similar fashion throughout the European Union. However, if conduct is legal under EC rules, it may still appear to be illegal under national rules. The European Court of Justice seems to think that national courts cannot contradict a decision by the Commission to exempt an agreement under Article 81(3) (ex 85(3)) (see *Anne Marty* v *Esteé Lauder SA* (37/78) [1981] ECR 2481). The then Director General of the United Kingdom Office of Fair Trading, Sir Bryan Carsberg, stated his opinion that there is 'no clear indication' whether UK rules may prohibit an agreement which has been exempted by the Commission. More recently, the current Director General of the OFT, John Bridgeman, observed that a draft Bill introducing a prohibitory system 'along the lines of Article 85 [now 81] of the Treaty of Rome' had been published in the UK. He went on to point out that the Bill was explicitly designed to ensure its provisions are interpreted in a manner that would 'avoid inconsistency and potential conflict with Article 85 [now 81]'. Nevertheless, he concluded by declaring that:

> ... the UK prohibitory provisions ... should enable me to impose more stringent conditions than required for exemption under Article 85(3) [now 81(3)] where I consider it necessary in order to take specific UK circumstances properly into account.

(Speech to the International Bar Association, Berlin, 22 October 1996; and see now the Competition Act 1998.)

Mr Bridgeman's thoughts may be contrasted with those of Advocate General Tesauro. In the Opinions that he delivered in two cases in the mid-1990s (*BMW* v *ALD* (C-70/93) [1995] ECR I-3439; *Bundeskartellamt* v *Volkswagen and VAG Leasing* (C-266/93)

[1995] ECR I-3477), the Advocate General stated clearly that agreements which had been exempted by the Commission could not be prohibited by the national competition authorities, using more restrictive provisions, other than in very exceptional circumstances. The Court of Justice did not resolve the issue in either case.

To state the position clearly for our purposes, if a clause in a contract or some sort of behaviour infringes either Article 81 (ex 85) or 82 (ex 86), EC Treaty and is thus prohibited by them, then any national laws in the UK will not save that clause or behaviour from prohibition, nor will national laws save the undertaking(s) concerned from any penalty that might be imposed for such infringement.

8.3 Direct Effect of EC Law

Both Articles 81 (ex 85) and 82 (ex 86) have been held to be directly effective and therefore capable of use in the national courts of Member States (see *BRT* v *SV SABAM* (127/73) [1974] ECR 51, paras 14–16, 21 and 22):

It must ... be examined whether the national courts, before which the prohibitions contained in Articles 85 [now 81] and 86 [now 82] are invoked in a dispute governed by private law, must be considered as 'authorities of the Member States'.

The competence of those courts to apply the provisions of Community law, particularly in the case of such disputes, derives from the direct effect of those provisions.

As the prohibitions of Articles 85(1) [now 81(1)] and 86 [now 82] tend by their very nature to produce direct effects in relations between individuals, these Articles create direct rights in respect of the individuals concerned, which the national courts must safeguard.

[I]f the Commission initiates a procedure in application of Article 3 of Regulation No.17 such a court may, if it considers it necessary for reasons of legal certainty, stay the proceedings before it while awaiting the outcome of the Commission's action.

On the other hand, the national court should generally allow proceedings before it to continue when it decides either that the behaviour in dispute is clearly not capable of having any appreciable effect on competition or on trade between Member States, or that there is no doubt of the incompatibility of that behaviour with Article 86 [now 82].

8.4 Which Court?

With the introduction of the Civil Procedure Rules in 1998, a decision which previously faced any claimant — whether to sue in the High Court or county court — has been removed from them. A claimant will request a court (either High Court or county court) to issue a claim form. It is now for the Procedural Judge (either a District Judge or a Master) to determine into which management track the case will fall — the small claims track, the fast track or the multi-track. As with every other civil case launched in England from April 1999 onwards, the parties will usually have to fill in an allocation questionnaire (see CPR, r. 26). While the financial value of any claim is clearly very significant to the question of allocation (any claim for less than £15,000 is likely to be allocated to either the small claims track or the fast track, in the county court), other significant factors include:

(a)   the likely complexity of the facts, law or evidence;

(b)   the importance of the claim to persons who are not parties to the proceedings.

Also of possible relevance is CPR, r. 26.6(5), which indicates that even if a claim is worth less than £15,000, the fast track (county court) is unlikely to be appropriate if the trial is expected to last for longer than one day and there is likely to be oral evidence from several experts. Conversely, the Practice Direction that supports CPR, r. 29, suggests that claims with an estimated value of under £50,000 will generally be transferred to a county court unless, for example, they fall within a specialist list. Reference should also be made to the *Civil Litigation Manual*.

Where, then, should a claim involving Article 81 (ex 85) or 82 (ex 86) be tried? The initial choice is between fast track (county court) and multi-track (High Court or county court). Thereafter, if the case goes for trial in the High Court, a choice must be made (by the court) about whether it should be tried in the Queen's Bench Division (QBD) or the Chancery Division. Most claims which raise issues of EC competition law will be best described as claims in contract or tort. The QBD is usually the most appropriate division of the High Court for such claims if the remedy sought includes damages. However, in the past (pre-CPR) there was no bar on starting claims involving contract or tort in the Chancery Division, and a swift glance at reported English cases involving the EC competition rules shows that at least half of them were dealt with in the Chancery Division. One reason for that is that the judges in the Chancery Division handle most of the commercial litigation and, over many years, have probably built up greater collective expertise in handling points of EC and EU law.

Where a High Court claim will be heard will depend upon the list in which it is placed. Under the CPR, cases are allocated to different lists according to their subject-matter. According to the editors of 'The Civil Procedure Rules', issued by the publishers of the *White Book*, one specialist list covers what the CPR refer to as 'specialist proceedings'. Under CPR, r. 49, 'specialist proceedings' include 'commercial and mercantile actions and Patent Court business'. It is likely that some claims involving the EC competition rules will thus be specialist proceedings and continue to be dealt with by judges who are knowledgeable about EC and EU law. If a claimant decides to issue a claim form in the High Court, seeking money from the defendant, the claim form should state that the claimant expects to recover in excess of £15,000 and/or state that the claim is in one of the specialist High Court lists, specifying which one.

8.5 Causes of Action

8.5.1 A BREACH OF STATUTORY DUTY?

As a sword, certainly within the United Kingdom, attempts to rely on the EC competition rules have met with a varied reaction. Several years ago Lord Denning suggested that Articles 85 and 86 (now 81 and 82) represented 'new economic torts' — see, e.g., his speech in *Application des Gaz SA* v *Falks Veritas* [1974] 3 All ER 51 — and could be used as causes of action in order to sue someone. This idea was not enthusiastically received by his judicial brethren.

The way forward seems to be indicated by cases like *Cutsforth* v *Mansfield Inns Ltd*, *Argyll* v *Distillers and Guinness* [1986] 1 CMLR 764, and, particularly, *Garden Cottage Foods* v *Milk Marketing Board* [1984] AC 130. The plaintiffs [now claimants] in these cases have not sought to put forward the EC rules as creating some new cause(s) of action, but instead have sought (or strained) to fit them into existing categories. The most acceptable, in judicial terms, seems to be the tort of breach of statutory duty, with its attendant remedies — namely, damages and interim measures.

In *Cutsforth* the plaintiffs owned coin-operated machines such as juke boxes and game machines which were placed in public houses. As a result of a take-over of Northern Breweries by Mansfield Brewery plc, the brewery told the plaintiffs to take their machines out of some 160 tenanted pubs under brewery control. The tenants were told that they could have such machines in the pubs but that they must come from a nominated supplier. Mansfield Brewery refused to put the plaintiffs on their list of approved suppliers.

The plaintiffs issued a writ, then applied for an *ex parte* injunction. The application was successful and was followed subsequently by an *inter partes* hearing. The High Court judge (Sir Neil Lawson) accepted that, if the plaintiffs could raise a serious question as to whether or not the defendants were guilty of infringing either Article 85 (now 81) or Article 86 (now 82), EC Treaty, they should get their injunction. He said (at p. 563) that such conduct would be unlawful; the plaintiffs would be entitled to seek its prohibition in the High Court:

> . . . as it is clear on the authorities that breaches of the relevant provisions of the EEC Treaty give rise to a cause of action in the domestic courts by a plaintiff who contends that he is the victim of such breaches.

The judge also considered whether the brewery's modified agreement with its tenants fell within the block exemption for exclusive purchase agreements (Regulation 1984/83), but decided it did not. He concluded that there was a serious question to be tried in relation to Article 85 (now 81) and that damages would not be an adequate remedy for the plaintiffs, whereas they would for the defendant.

Conversely, the plaintiffs lost their argument under Article 86 (now 82). Sir Neil Lawson held that:

(a)   there was no evidence that the brewery held a dominant position;

(b)   the area in which the brewery operated was not a 'substantial part of the common market' (although there is nothing in the judgment to indicate their area of operations, as distinct from that of the plaintiffs whose territory was 'Humberside and the surrounding district'); and

(c)   no effect on inter-state trade had been shown.

The take-over battle for Distillers plc was the subject of (at least) two court cases between Argyll Group plc and Guinness plc — one in England and one in Scotland. In Scotland, when a revised bid by Guinness was not referred to the Monopolies and Mergers Commission, Argyll applied to the Court of Session for an interim interdict, to prevent the merger on the basis that it would contravene Article 86 (now 82), EC Treaty.

The court accepted the proposition (from *Garden Cottage Foods* v *Milk Marketing Board*, apparently, rather than *BRT* v *SV SABAM*) that Article 86 (now 82) was directly effective. It said that it was entitled to consider breaches of Article 86 (now 82) on an application for interim relief and noted that, taking *Europembellage and Continental Can Co.* v *Commission* into account, it was possible for a merger to infringe that Article.

All three parties argued about the effect of *Continental Can Co.* on the merits of the case (all with contradictory opinions), but the judge concluded that, on the available evidence, there was no prima facie case that a dominant position existed (or would exist); nor that the proposed merger would be an abuse. (The judge considered the relevant market in terms of geography and product.)

In *Garden Cottage Foods* the House of Lords considered the uses of Article 86 (now 82) in English courts. The defendants had cut off supplies of butter which the plaintiffs needed to carry on their business. They sought an interlocutory injunction, restraining the defendants from withdrawing supplies.

The House (Lord Wilberforce dissenting) held that it was clearly arguable that a breach of Article 86 (now 82) would give rise to a cause of action in English law at the behest of an individual who has suffered pecuniary loss by reason of the infringement; and that the remedy of damages would be available to compensate for such loss. Lord Diplock noted that Article 86 (now 82) had been held to be directly effective, citing *BRT* v *SV SABAM*, and that this was binding on English courts. A breach of the Article:

... can thus be categorised in English law as a breach of statutory duty that is imposed ... for the benefit of private individuals to whom loss or damage is caused by a breach of that duty.

According to Lord Diplock, whilst it was barely arguable that a breach of Article 86 (now 82) was not actionable as a breach of statutory duty in English courts, it could not be disputed that, if the cause of action existed, a remedy in damages must be available. In a dissenting speech, Lord Wilberforce thought that an open mind should be kept on whether or not a breach of Article 86 (now 82) simply gave rise to the remedy of an injunction; furthermore, it was still debatable what the nature of the cause of action was — it need not be defined as a tort or a 'breach of statutory duty'. The remaining three Law Lords agreed with Lord Diplock.

By way of completeness, we must also take note of *Bourgoin* v *Ministry of Agriculture, Fisheries and Food* [1986] QB 716. The case involved decisions of MAFF to keep French turkeys out of the UK. These decisions were subsequently declared to be illegal by the ECJ (under Article 30 (now 28), EC Treaty — free movement of goods). The plaintiffs were French turkey producers and distributors. They claimed damages from MAFF, alleging substantial loss. The causes of action were stated to be:

(a) breach of statutory duty under Article 30 (now 28), EC Treaty;

(b) the commission of an 'innominate tort' by so breaching Article 30 (now 28); and

(c) misfeasance in a public office (i.e. deliberate abuse of power).

The Court of Appeal held (by a two to one majority) that, although Article 30 (now 28) gave rights to individuals and imposed obligations on Member States, it said nothing about procedures or remedies. National courts had to offer the same remedies as are available for breach of a similar right in national law. A breach of Article 30 (now 28) was akin to an ultra vires act under an English statute. It would give rise to judicial review, a declaration on the invalidity of the measure containing the illegality, and possibly an order of mandamus, but *not* a claim for damages.

The majority in the Court of Appeal held that a prima facie cause of action existed for misfeasance in public office, but there was no cause of action under the 'innominate tort' or breach of statutory duty (cf. Oliver LJ). The distinction between this case and *Garden Cottage Foods (supra)* was that the latter dealt with 'private law rights'. The present case involved breach of negative obligations by a Member State and 'public law rights', which were only susceptible to judicial review. Even Lord Justice Oliver (who dissented in the result) pointed to the decisions of the Court of Justice in cases like *Bayerische HNL Vermehrungsbetriebe GmbH & Co. KG* v *Council and Commission of the EC* (83 and 94/76, 4, 15 and 40/77) [1978] ECR 1209 (the skimmed milk powder case), which limit the rights of individuals to claim damages for the legislative acts of the Community under Article 288(2) (ex 215(2)), EC Treaty.

For another examination of the impact of EC Article 28 (ex 30) on our national law (this time by the Court of Justice, although note in the law reports the acceptance of it by the House of Lords), see the judgment in *Allen & Hanburys Ltd* v *Generics (UK) Ltd* (434/85) [1988] ECR 1245.

Lastly, it should be noted that, however you dress up your claim, it needs to persuade the judge that it can apply to the factual situation that confronts the court. An apparent failure to do so can be found in one of several cases involving breweries (or companies running chains of pubs) and their tenants: *Scottish & Newcastle plc* v *Bond*, 25 March 1997, unreported. The tenant of a S & N pub stopped paying rent and got his supplies of beer elsewhere. S & N sued for the rent arrears and mesne profits. The tenant claimed that the beer tie provisions contravened Article 85(1) (now 81(1) and so were void. According to the report, the judge found there was no arguable defence to S & N's claim, observing that Article 85 (now 81) is intended to regulate the position between competitors who operate in the same market but not between a particular supplier and customer. It is unclear how this decision could be reconciled with earlier English cases like *Cutsforth v Mansfield Inns Ltd* [1986] 1 WLR 558 and *Holleran v Daniel Thwaites* [1988] 2 CMLR 817, let alone *Delimitis v Henninger Braü AG* (C-234/ 88) [1991] ECR I-935, all three of which set Article 85 (now 81) in the context of the relationship of pub or bar tenants with their landlords and suppliers. See also **8.11**.

8.5.2 EQUAL AND EFFECTIVE PROTECTION

In *Bourgoin*, Lord Justice Oliver stated that the English courts are under a twofold obligation. First, to protect the rights of any individual infringed by a breach of a directly effective Article of the Treaty, in a manner not inferior to the protection given for similar rights in domestic law (equal protection). Secondly, to do so effectively (effective protection). To withhold a remedy of damages from a claim against the Crown would deny equal and effective protection to the individual. It would not be equal and effective because the infringement should be classified as the tort of breach of statutory duty and attract the same remedies. Although this was a dissenting judgment, it was by far the longest in the case and very well argued. The Court gave leave to appeal to the House of Lords but the case was subsequently settled. The EC points raised in this case have not subsequently been aired in an appellate court in England and remain, at least temporarily, unresolved. (See also *R v Pharmaceutical Society of Great Britain, ex parte Association of Pharmaceutical Importers* [1987] 3 CMLR 951 and (266 and 267/87) [1989] ECR 1321, [1990] 2 WLR 445 — a preliminary reference to the ECJ by the Queen's Bench Divisional Court.)

English courts may now be required to accord better than equal protection to claimants who rely on Community law — see the *ex parte Factortame* cases (C-213/89 etc.). The Court of Justice ruled (on a preliminary reference from the House of Lords) that interim relief could be granted to a litigant in a case concerning Community law if the 'sole obstacle' to such relief was a rule of national law. The relief in that case was the temporary suspension of an Act of Parliament in respect of the applicants.

The judgment of the ECJ in *Francovich and others v Italian Republic* (C-6/90 and C-9/90) [1991] ECR I-5357 may prove to be a landmark in the development of national remedies for breaches of EC laws. In essence, the ECJ held that a Member State may become liable in damages for failure to implement an EC directive. There are clear limits on how far one may infer from this judgment some broader right to damages, in particular between private individuals (as distinct from 'vertically' where an individual sues the State) but the case offers a way forward. It is, of course, binding on English courts and has been clarified by the judgment of the Court of Justice in *Brasserie de Pêcheur SA v Federal Republic of Germany* (C-46 and 48/93) [1996] 2 WLR 506; *R v Secretary of State for Transport, ex parte Factortame Ltd (No. 4)*. On a preliminary reference, the ECJ said that Member States could be liable in damages where individuals had suffered harm as the result of a breach of Community law which was attributable to the acts or omissions of the national legislature. In *Factortame*, Spanish fishermen alleged that they had suffered financial harm as a result of their exclusion from fishing in British waters, by virtue of provisions of the Merchant Shipping Act 1988. This statute had previously been held to be contrary to Community law (see *Factortame (No. 3)* [1992] QB 680) and, at the time of writing, the Spanish fishermen have just succeeded with a claim in the High Court, seeking damages in excess of £50 million against the United Kingdom.

8.6 Defensive Use of the Rules

8.6.1 INTRODUCTION

As a shield, one finds the competition rules used in cases like *British Leyland Motor Corporation v Armstrong Patents Co. Ltd* [1986] AC 577, *Volvo AB v Erik Veng (UK)* (238/87) [1988] ECR 6211, and *R v Henn and Darby* (34/79) [1979] ECR 3795. Where people are sued in national courts for infringement of intellectual property rights (patents, copyright, trademarks, etc.), they may allege that the litigation is an abuse of a dominant position or that the grant of the property right is the fruit of an anti-competitive agreement between undertakings. A recent example is the lengthy litigation over an alleged patent infringement, *Chiron* v *Murex*. The defendant company tried to raise in its defence an allegation of breach of Article 86 (now 82). However, its defence was struck out at first instance (upheld by the Court of Appeal) as it had apparently not pleaded its Community law defence properly. Given the absence of Euro-defences from major works on drafting precedents, one can perhaps sympathise with the defendant here.

One should note in passing that ancillary arguments, made by way of 'Euro-defences', can include reliance on the rules providing for free movement of goods within the Community (see **Chapter 10**). This has occurred both in the field of infringement of intellectual property rights and in criminal prosecution for importation of obscene material where the offending subject-matter had come, quite lawfully, from another member state. (See, e.g., *R* v *Henn and Darby*, and cases on free movement of goods such as *Hoffman-La Roche* v *Commission* and *Centrafarm* v *Sterling*.)

8.6.2 A DEFENCE OF BREACH OF STATUTORY DUTY?

Despite the advice of the House of Lords in *Garden Cottage*, it seems unusual to find that one should rely on a defence that the claimant is in breach of a statutory duty. This is not unknown in the form of a counterclaim perhaps (one could imagine, in a claim for trespass to property, finding a counterclaim for damage suffered by the defendant contrary to the occupier's liability legislation) but that would not normally excuse the defendant from liability in the original claim.

What happens in practice is that the defence alleges, first, that the claimant has infringed either Article 81 (ex 85(1)) or 82 (ex 86) (or both) and gives full particulars of the allegation. The defence then goes on to argue that the effect of such infringement is to deprive the claimant of his cause of action. The argument may be that the claimant is suing on a contract or licence which the defendant argues is void and thus unenforceable. Or it may be that the claimant is alleged to be in a dominant position, and his abuse of that position is argued to excuse the defendant from liability (as may be the case in a patent infringement claim where the patentee sues a parallel importer). In these situations, it makes little sense on the facts to defend oneself simply with an allegation that the claimant is guilty of a breach of statutory duty; after all, such duty may not be intended to prevent the type of damage that the defendant relies on (cf. *Gorris* v *Scott* (1874) LR 8 Ex 125). In using Article 81 (ex 85) or 82 (ex 86) defensively, then, you will usually find it makes sense to set out the material facts in a manner which appears consistent with the allegations made in the particulars of claim. This should also help to persuade any judge that there is a sufficient nexus between your EC defence and the cause of claim (see **8.6.3**). Any reference in the Defence to the claimant being in breach of statutory duty will usually appear as a very short 'further or alternative' paragraph, after the substance of the alleged infringement has been dealt with.

8.6.3 THE NEED FOR A NEXUS

It almost goes without saying, but there does need to be a connection between the cause of claim of the claimant (and the remedies sought in the claim) and the EC point relied on by the defendant. The point was well made by Megarry V-C in *ICI* v *Berk Pharmaceuticals* [1981] 2 CMLR 81:

> If the plaintiffs [now claimants] are imposing unfair selling prices in that they charge too much for their product, I cannot see why this breach of the prohibitions of Article 86 [now 82] means that the defendants are thereby set free from any liability to the plaintiffs if they, the defendants, commit the tort of passing off (or, indeed, any other tort) against them.

In a similar vein, there has been a spate of cases involving public house licensees and their landlords (in particular, Inntrepreneur Estates). In these cases, typically the property company sues the pub licensee for rent arrears; the licensee then defends the claim arguing that the 'tie' relating to the purchase of beer contravenes Article 81(1) (ex 85(1)) — thus the tie is void and so is the lease itself. This argument has failed on two bases. First, assuming the tie is void as claimed, there is no suggestion that the obligation to pay rent under the lease is itself void by virtue of Article 81(2) (ex 85(2)); secondly, even if the tie is void, it can be severed from the rest of the lease leaving the rent payable as claimed by the claimant. See e.g. *Inntrepreneur Estates* v *Boyes* (1983) 47 EG 140. See also *IBM* v *Phoenix International* [1984] RPC 251; also, *Chiron Corp.* v *Murex Diagnostics Ltd* [1992] 3 CMLR 813.

8.6.4 DECLARATIONS AND SEVERANCE

If a defendant has to rely on Article 81 (ex 85) to argue that a contract clause is void, it would be best to seek a declaration to that effect. Further, if the defendant really wants out of the contract altogether, it may be necessary to seek a declaration that the entire contract is void (in a counterclaim). A claimant who is confronted by a defendant counterclaiming for a declaration that the whole contract is void may attempt to overcome that claim by seeking severance of any offending clause (see *Inntrepreneur Estates* above).

These days it is settled law that just because a specific clause in a contract is anti-competitive, it does not follow that the whole contract is void by virtue of Article 81(2) (ex 85(2)). If the offending clause can be severed from the contract, and leave the rest, then that is what will happen. Issues of severance are for the national courts to decide in accordance with their usual rules on the topic. In England, the rule might be simply described as a 'blue pencil' test: if, after deletion of the offending clause(s), one is left with no meaningful contract or one which is so changed in character that the parties would not have entered into it in the first place, then severance is not possible. See *Société Technique Minière* v *Maschinenbau Ulm GmbH* (56/65) [1966] ECR 235 and *Société de Vente de Ciments et Bétons* v *Kerpen & Kerpen* (319/82) [1983] ECR 4173 for the view of the Court of Justice; and *Chemidus Wavin* v *TERI* [1978] 3 CMLR 514 for the leading Court of Appeal case in England. Per Buckley LJ in *Chemidus Wavin*:

> [I]n applying Article 85 [now 81] to an English contract, one may well have to consider whether, after the excisions required by the Article . . . have been made from the contract, the contract could be said to fail for lack of consideration or on any other ground, or whether the contract would be so changed in its character as not to be the sort of contract that the parties intended to enter into at all.

The series of 'pub' cases mentioned in **8.6.3** seemed to indicate that severance was a rather remote possibility: beer ties were being excised, leaving enforceable leases, but it may be significant that the lessor in those cases was not usually a brewery so maybe the supply of beer was not paramount to it. Anyway, they might be contrasted with a case involving the supply of cars to a dealer (*Richard Cound Ltd* v *BMW (G.B.) Ltd*, 10 May 1985, Court of Appeal, unreported). Here, various clauses were severed from a car distribution agreement whereby the buyer (the car dealer) had agreed to resell the new cars he bought from BMW, and to resell the spare parts he bought from them and to provide a service facility for BMW cars, regardless of their place of purchase. The Court of Appeal thought that, by severing these requirements, what was left would be a simple contract for the sale of new BMW cars and spares. This would be (per Balcombe LJ):

> an agreement so different that . . . it is apt to regard the effect of severance as 'altering entirely the scope and intention of the agreement' or as removing the heart and soul of the agreement . . .

8.7 To Sue or be Sued?

An undertaking which considers that another is infringing either Article 81(1) (ex 85(1)) or Article 82 (ex 86) has a choice. Apart from making a complaint to the Commission, the undertaking may:

- start a claim against the alleged infringer, seeking various remedies;

- carry on as normal and wait until the alleged infringer sues it (the cause of claim is not important here).

There are several factors which an undertaking should consider when confronted with this choice. It may be relatively easier to get a declaration that an infringement has occurred; relatively harder to get damages to compensate for any losses. Thus, it is important to minimise one's financial claim: carrying on as normal might achieve that. Also important is timing: it may be that there is insufficient evidence of an infringement available to your client at present. The best evidence of an infringement may be provided by the very act of the infringer launching a legal claim against your client (cf. e.g. *Consten and Grundig* v *Commission* (56 and 58/64) [1966] ECR 299).

Of course, you should always consider what the client's objectives are. If there is a contract or licence agreement of some sort between your client and the alleged infringer then the first question is: does the client want to escape from the contract? If not, then it might be best not to initiate a claim as any reliance on Article 81(1) (ex 85(1)) or 82 (ex 86) may result in the contract being declared void despite your best endeavours. There is also the problem that, even if your client does want out of the contract, the judge may not agree that there is a cause of claim; it may be simpler to act as if the contract is at an end (e.g. send the other party a letter terminating the contract or find a replacement for the other party and stop dealing with them).

Expense is unlikely to be an issue in deciding whether to sue or be sued. In particular, the cost of the evidence needed to substantiate your allegations of anti-competitive behaviour will not vary according to whether your client is claimant or defendant. This is because it is rather unusual to find a claim where both parties allege breaches of EC competition rules have occurred. Clearly, a claimant bears a heavy financial burden in acquiring the evidence needed to discharge the burden of proof; equally, since the use of an EC competition point in a Defence is likely to raise entirely different issues to those in the Particulars of Claim, the defendant will bear the burden of proof on the competition issues and the accompanying cost of acquiring the evidence.

8.7.1   EXAMPLE

This example tries to show some of the questions that you should consider, and their possible outcomes. When confronted by a problem which might involve an issue of EC competition law, it is important not to focus too heavily on that, especially when advising the client. Nevertheless, the possible uses of the competition law rules, and the information needed to advise thereon, should be borne in mind when considering advice on strategy.

Your client is Folio Ltd, an undertaking which is acting in possible breach of another's intellectual property rights (e.g. manufacturing patented goods without a licence). Folio is warned by the patentee of a possible claim for patent infringement if manufacturing continues. The options for Folio are:

- stop manufacturing forthwith (and maybe pay compensation for past infringement);

- start proceedings to overturn the grant of the patent (simple possession of a patent is not going to ground a claim alleging abuse of a dominant position, using Article 82 (ex 86); there may be grounds to challenge the validity of the patent, though);

- ask the patentee to grant Folio a licence to manufacture the goods (which, if granted, is very likely to result in Folio paying royalties);

- just carry on manufacturing.

The first option might be the easiest one to take, but if Folio has been manufacturing in the knowledge that they were infringing a patent it seems an unlikely option for them to take now. Assuming the patent to be valid, Folio has no ground to sue the patentee, which rules out the second option. Folio could try the third option, if it is prepared to pay royalties. If it approaches the patentee for a licence and is refused, or considers the royalties demanded to be too high, then *if* the patentee is in a dominant position, Folio might start a claim alleging breach of Article 82 (ex 86) (the objective being to compel the patentee to grant a licence; cf. *Volvo AB* v *Erik Veng* (UK) (238/87) [1988] ECR 6211). At first glance, the last option seems a poor one to take. Your client is asking to be sued for infringement and ordered to pay damages. The fourth option makes more sense if the patentee is in a dominant position because, if the patentee then sues your client, you can make the claim in Folio's defence that the patent claim constitutes an abuse of that dominant position. An alternative question would be to ask if the patentee is in fact an assignee of the patent. If so, it might be worth considering if there has been an attempt by the original patentee and its assignee(s) to divide up the single, common market by the use of national intellectual property rights.

8.8 Using the Competition Rules in English Civil Claims

8.8.1 REMEMBER THE RULES

As we have seen, a civil claim may involve either Article 81 (ex 85) (1), (3), or Article 82 (ex 86), EC Treaty. A litigant may use the competition rules offensively or defensively, and at an interim stage as well as at trial. The main 'engines' for all of these purposes are really the statements of case, and we can concentrate on:

(a)   the particulars of claim; and

(b)   the defence and Part 20 claim (previously a 'counterclaim').

This section is not intended to replicate the excellent books on precedent and procedure for the practitioner (the *White Book*; Bullen, Leake and Jacobs, *Precedents of Pleadings* (Sweet & Maxwell); *A Practical Approach to Civil Procedure*, Stuart Sime (Blackstone Press); *A Practical Approach to Legal Advice and Drafting*, Susan Blake (Blackstone Press); *Pleadings Without Tears*, William Rose (Blackstone Press)); all are extremely helpful in their different ways. What they tend to omit is any guidance on how to draft issues of EC competition law (often the only help one finds is assistance on drafting a question for preliminary reference to the Court of Justice, under Article 234 (ex 177), EC Treaty). (An attempt to fill this gap has been made recently: see *European Courts Practice and Precedents* (Sweet & Maxwell, 1996).) So what help can we offer to anyone who has to draft a statement of case involving issues of EC competition law?

Of course, your statement of case here is inherently no different from that which you are already familiar with; only the substantive law is different. The primary obligation is to comply with the Civil Procedure Rules, Part 16, on statements of case. Your statement of case must set out the necessary particulars of any claim, defence or other matter intended to be advanced at trial. Further, the statement of case should contain a concise statement of the facts which are material to the claim or defence advanced. Prior to the CPR, the old rules of civil procedure specified that one should not plead the evidence by which the material facts were to be proved. That never sat very easily with the practices developed by practitioners in the EC/EU field and CPR, PD 16 specifies, for example, that where a claim is based upon a written agreement, a copy should be attached to the particulars of claim; similarly, where a claim is based upon an oral agreement, the particulars of claim should state the actual words used, by who, to whom and when and where they were spoken (see PD 16, para. 9). Furthermore, in the past statements of case involving the EC competition rules have contained more points of law than was usual in more 'domestic' claims.

That practice now seems set to become legitimate, since PD 16 permits a claimant to refer in his or her particulars of claim to any point of law on which his claim is based.

As you can see, the rules for statements of case now seem to reflect existing practice for drafters in many respects. It is nevertheless important to consider in detail how these rules will apply to cases using Articles 81 (ex 85) and 82 (ex 86), EC Treaty.

8.8.2   WHAT TO INCLUDE

Typically, when relying on Article 81(1) (ex 85(1)) in one's statement of case, the novice's mistake is to focus the allegations of infringement on the relationship between the claimant and the defendant in the particular case. This happens because the drafter is representing one party to the claim, has received instructions from that party and seeks remedies (of whatever sort) which are intended to benefit that party. In other words, the drafter's focus is on the individual. This can cause a problem in that Article 81(1) (ex 85(1)) looks at matters on a bigger scale. Clearly, the statement of case must show how the client has been harmed and how their damage might be quantified; but of equal importance is the need to demonstrate the infringement of the competition rules. The economic analysis required to do so means that the statement of case may deal with matters somewhat divorced from the obvious subject-matter of the litigation. What is needed is that:

the factual allegations regarding effect on competition should be pleaded in such terms that it can be seen how the effect complained of flows from the agreement or concerted practice ...

(per Ferris J in *Intergraph Corp.* v *Solid Systems CAD Services Ltd*, 7 December 1983, Chancery Division, unreported).

There may be less conceptual difficulty with Article 82 (ex 86). Here the abusive exploitation which is alleged against one party typically has the other party as its victim. Obvious examples occur when there is:

- a refusal to supply *your client* (cf. *Hugin/Liptons*; *Boosey & Hawkes/Brass Band Instruments*);

- denial of access to essential services for *your client* (for example, *B & I/Stena*);

- predatory pricing directed against *your client* (see *ECS/Akzo*).

Nevertheless, these situations may fall outside the common grasp of how tortious liability is established in England. The harm envisaged by Article 82 (ex 86) may be seen as harm to the 'market' or to the interests of consumers. In the last of the three examples above, the effect of the anti-competitive act (predatory pricing) is directed against the competitors of the dominant undertaking. Where there are several competitors, can they all sue for infringement of Article 82 (ex 86)? Might there be a 'floodgates' problem here? This is perhaps the difficulty in relying upon individual undertakings taking action to 'protect' the 'normal' competitive working of the (collective) market. At the least, we should note that the drafter of a statement of case who relies upon Article 82 (ex 86) will need to show a causal connection between the alleged infringement and the loss or damage borne by the client.

We have seen (in **Chapters 2** and **6**) that the proper analysis of whether there has been an infringement of Article 81(1) (ex 85(1)) or 82 (ex 86), EC Treaty demands a meaningful economic analysis of the relevant market (see e.g., *Delimitis* v *Henninger Braü AG* (C-234/89) [1991] ECR I-935; *Hoffmann La-Roche* v *Commission* (85/76) [1979] ECR 461). It cannot be denied sensibly that such a definition of the market is an essential part of one's analysis under these Articles, but should it appear in the statement of case? The material facts have to be in the statement of case and that means those facts which are necessary for the formulation of a complete cause of action (see Scott LJ in *Bruce* v *Odhams Press Ltd* [1936] 3 All ER 287). So, it seems that some attempt must be made in your statement of case to define the relevant market. This does not mean that the full details of an expert's report should be included (although this will be fundamental *evidence* to persuade the trial court of the nature and operation of the relevant market) but it does mean that you should assert what are the relevant products and what territory is involved. Are we concerned with the effects on others as well as, or instead of, just our client? Both Articles 81(1) (ex 85(1)) and 82 (ex 86) require an effect (actual or potential) on inter-State trade: the evidence to show that may come from the effect of the anti-competitive behaviour on other undertakings, not on the client; whilst we should avoid, or at least minimise, the incorporation of evidence into our statement of case, the allegation has to be made.

What about the relief sought? This must be set out in the body of your statement of case, and you must check that the nature of your claim facilitates your chosen remedy(ies). *Garden Cottage* said that the proper cause of action was breach of statutory duty, but suppose that the most appropriate remedy for your client is not one commonly (or ever) awarded to parties in statutory duty cases? It is quite usual to set your statement of case out in a manner which gives the 'best fit' for the material facts and the optimal remedies *and* then to allege, as being further or alternative to the initial allegations, that the 'matters aforesaid' also constitute a breach of statutory duty (really as a sort of insurance policy for your drafting).

In essence, when relying upon Article 81(1) (ex 85(1)) or 82 (ex 86), each and every element of the relevant Article should appear on your checklist and when you have finished a draft you should be able to read through it and tick off each element as your statement of case deals with it. Adopting a 'belt-and-braces' approach, you might even want to assert the direct effect of the relevant competition rule, thus entitling your client to rely on it in the course of a private civil claim in the national legal system (see **8.3**).

8.8.3   EXAMPLE FOR PARTICULARS OF CLAIM

Facts

Two undertakings, All Ice plc and Barry Jones, enter a contract. All Ice agrees to supply Barry Jones with ice cream products. All Ice is a large-volume manufacturing company, specialising in ice creams but with interests in other frozen food products too. Barry Jones is a sole trader, operating newsagent/general stores in three villages. While the contract is still operating, Barry Jones is approached by a rival ice cream maker, Polar Glaces SA. Polar offers to supply its ice cream products to Barry Jones. Polar's range of products is similar to All Ice's but Polar is a foreign-based company, now seeking to establish itself in the UK. Polar currently has a low degree of brand recognition for its products in the UK and is willing to price its supplies to Barry Jones to reflect this. Barry Jones would like to take some of his requirement for ice cream from Polar but is unwilling to terminate his contract with All Ice as All Ice is the biggest supplier in the market, an established manufacturer who is well-known and has a wide range of the most popular brand names and products. Barry Jones' shop has space for only one ice cream freezer cabinet; currently that is supplied at a very low rental by All Ice, with a requirement that only All Ice products be stored there. Barry Jones has asked All Ice for permission to stock Polar's products and been turned down; in fact, All Ice threatened to take Barry Jones to court to enforce the exclusivity clause in the supply contract. Polar has encountered this situation in many locations across the UK and is having great difficulty in finding a viable number of retail outlets for its products.

Choices

Should Barry Jones sue All Ice, alleging that his contract with All Ice infringes Article 81(1) (ex 85(1))? Should Polar sue All Ice, alleging that the contract All Ice has with Barry Jones and/or many others infringes Article 81(1) (ex 85(1))? Would Polar be better advised to sue All Ice using Article 82 (ex 86), to allege that All Ice is abusing a dominant position (if All Ice in fact has a dominant position)? Should Barry Jones simply accept supplies from Polar and wait to see what action, if any, All Ice takes? These are all relevant questions but for our purposes we shall assume that Barry Jones has decided to sue All Ice, alleging an infringement of Article 81(1). We shall further assume that Barry Jones is quite happy to keep the All Ice contract going and keep the freezer, with its low rental cost — he just wants the freedom to store anyone's ice cream products in it.

IN THE HIGH COURT OF JUSTICE   Claim No. 1999 HC 1234

CHANCERY DIVISION

BETWEEN:

BARRY JONES   <u>Claimant</u>
(a sole trader)

and

ALL ICE PLC   <u>Defendants</u>

PARTICULARS OF CLAIM

---

1.   The Claimant owns 3 newsagent and general shops in and around Hadley, Hertfordshire, where he sells a variety of goods including ice creams. On the 4th March 1995, the Claimant entered into a written contract with the Defendants, whereby the Defendants would supply the Claimant with a range of their ice creams for sale in his shops. Such products would be for consumption either immediately ('impulse purchase') or away from the premises ('home consumption'). The Defendants are a public company engaged in the manufacture and distribution of various frozen food products, including industrially-produced ice cream products.

2.   The following were material terms of the contract:

(a)   Clause 1.1   The Company [namely, the Defendants] will supply an extensive range of their ice cream products (hereafter 'products') to the Customer [namely, the Claimant]. Such supplies shall take place in quantities that the Company, in its experience, judges sufficient for the demand of the Customer.

(b)   Clause 1.2   The Company shall supply such of its range of ice cream products to the Customer as the Company considers appropriate. The Company retains complete discretion as to the brands and sizes of such products to be supplied.

(c)   Clause 2.3   The Customer shall observe all proper standards of hygiene and cleanliness in the storing and display of the products supplied to him by the Company, from time to time.

(d)   Clause 2.7   The Customer shall store and display the products in a freezer; such freezer to be of appropriate size and dimensions for the efficient resale of the products. The Company shall offer to supply to the Customer such a freezer, at a rental price of five pounds per month.

(e)   Clause 3.6   On agreeing to use a freezer supplied by the Company, the Customer will receive a 2.5% discount on every one hundred pounds of the Company's products that he buys.

(f)   Clause 3.7   When using a freezer supplied by the Company, the Customer agrees to keep only ice cream products therein; in particular, the Customer agrees to use the freezer exclusively for the purpose of storing and displaying the products of the Company.

3.   The Claimant agreed to rent 3 freezers from the Defendants. Upon receipt of the freezers, the Claimant was obliged to re-order the shop fittings to accommodate the freezers. There is room for only one freezer and no other in each of the Claimant's shops.

4.   On the 3rd February 1999, the Claimant approached the Defendants, seeking permission to store and display ice cream products manufactured in France by another company, Polar Glaces SA (hereafter 'Polar'). The Claimant had been offered supplies of ice creams by Polar in a range comparable to that of the Defendants but at prices which, on average, were 20% less than those charged to the Claimant for the Defendants' products. The Defendants refused permission and threatened to take legal action to enforce their exclusive access to the freezers.

5.   The Claimant expected to sell Polar ice cream products in a ratio of 1:4 to those supplied by the Defendants.

6.   The Claimant and the Defendants are and have been undertakings to which Article 81(1) of the European Community Treaty applies. The contract is an agreement between undertakings which has as its object or effect the restriction, distortion or prevention of trade between Member States of the European Community and which thereby infringes Article 81(1).

Particulars of Infringement

(1)   *The market*   The Defendants manufacture and sell ice cream products through-out the United Kingdom. Their share of industrial impulse and home consump-tion ice cream sales, of the type as are made through the Claimant's shops, was 35% in 1997.

(2)   The contract entered into by the Claimant with the Defendants was in the standard form of contract used by the Defendants for the sale and supply of their ice cream products. The Defendants have placed their freezers in many shops and other retail outlets throughout the United Kingdom.

(3)   *Restriction on trade*   The operation of clauses 2.7 and 3.6 were such that the Claimant was induced to rent freezers from the Defendants. By virtue of his rental of freezers from the Defendants, together with the Defendants' insistence on applying clause 3.7, the Claimant is prevented from selling ice cream products from other manufacturers, in particular Polar. Further, such manu-facturers and other suppliers are thereby denied access to the market, namely sales of industrial impulse and home consumption ice cream products to retail outlets.

(4)   *Effect on trade between Member States*   Polar is, and other manufacturers and suppliers may be, based in Member States of the Community other than the United Kingdom.

7.   In the premises, clause 3.7 of the contract between the Claimant and the Defend-ant is prohibited and void, by the operation of Article 81(1) and 81(2) of the European Community Treaty.

8.   The infringement of Article 81(1) has caused the Claimant loss and damage. The Claimant contends that he would have been able to obtain cheaper supplies of ice cream products from other sources, in the absence of the infringement, in particular from Polar.

Particulars of Loss and Damage

From 3rd February 1999 to date
30 weeks at an estimated loss of profits of £ a per week   £ [30 × a = current total]
and continuing.

[We need to get a figure for £ a from Barry Jones to insert into the Particulars]

9.   Further the Claimant claims interest on the sums found due to him pursuant to section 35A of the Supreme Court Act 1981 at such rate and for such period as this Court shall think fit.

AND the Claimant claims:

(1)   A declaration that clause 3.7 of the contract between the Claimant and the Defendants is prohibited and void as contrary to Article 81(1) of the European Community Treaty, and that the Claimant is no longer bound by it.

(2)   Damages for the infringement of Article 81(1).

(3)   Interest pursuant to section 35A of the Supreme Court Act 1981.

[Statement of truth]
The Claimant believes that the facts stated in these particulars of claim are true. I am duly authorised by the Claimant to sign this statement.

Denise Smith
Of Sime, Blake and Rose

[signed by counsel]

SERVED this 5th day of September 1999 by Sime, Blake & Rose of 600 Gray's Inn Road, London, Solicitors for the Claimant.

8.8.4   EXAMPLE FOR AN OPINION

8.8.4.1   Introduction

What follows (in **8.8.4.2**) is a set of instructions to Counsel, to advise a client and then draft a Defence and Counterclaim. Preliminary work on an Opinion is set out after the Particulars of Claim (in **8.8.4.3**); this Opinion is necessarily in draft form because one would never be able to give definite advice on many topics until after a full interview with, in this case, the Managing Director of the client company.

The set of instructions is of a simple nature, which could easily be given to someone new to practice on. If you are a newcomer to this area, you may want to use the instructions in this case to practice your analytical skills. If so, don't immediately read the draft Opinion that follows the Instructions to Counsel, try to jot down your own conclusions and questions. Think about how you might structure an Opinion for the client company. Try to spot and address all the issues raised by the Instructions, both explicit and implicit. Then read the draft Opinion in **8.8.4.3** and see how it compares with your work: it is not intended to be some sort of perfect model but rather a work in progress. Some paragraphs are not set out in any detail as a basic knowledge of opinion writing is assumed. The Instructions, and specifically the Particulars of Claim contained in them, have been used again as the basis for a 'first draft' Defence and Counterclaim; this is set out in **8.8.5**.

8.8.4.2   Instructions to Counsel

DEEPDIN UK LIMITED

and

ARNOLD'S WORLD OF SOUND LIMITED

INSTRUCTIONS TO COUNSEL

With these Instructions, Counsel has:

(1)   copy agreement

(2)   statement of Terry Arnold

(3)   copies of correspondence

(4)   particulars of claim.

Instructing Solicitors represent Arnold's World of Sound Ltd ('AWS'). On the 2 January 1997, AWS entered an exclusive purchase agreement with Deepdin UK, manufacturer of the well-known Deepdin range of hi-fi equipment. Prior to the agreement, and for a time thereafter, the business of AWS was conducted exclusively within the United Kingdom. Until earlier this year, Instructing Solicitors are informed, the agreement operated to the apparent satisfaction of both parties. Over the last few months, however, there has been a breakdown in the relationship. This has arisen over the refusal of Deepdin to permit AWS to export its products outside the United Kingdom; the correspondence refers. To summarise, a company selling Deepdin products in France, HappiSound SA, wrote to AWS placing an order for the sale and delivery to them of 100 Deepdin CD Triple X hi-fi systems. Subsequently, on the 23 May 1999, AWS contacted Deepdin seeking permission to fulfil the order. Permission was denied by letter. Thereafter Mr Arnold rang Deepdin and told them he was determined to go ahead and fulfil the order from HappiSound.

The result is that Deepdin have started proceedings against AWS in the High Court. Counsel will find enclosed Particulars of Claim, seeking an injunction forcing AWS to comply with the terms of the agreement, in particular clause 2(11). We have been informed by Browning Lloyd, Deepdin's solicitors, that they will be applying for an interim injunction quite soon.

We have advised AWS that they may have a defence, and possibly a claim too, based on Article 81 of the EC Treaty. Counsel is asked to advise on the status of the export clause (2(11)). In fact, Mr Arnold is emphatic that he wants to end the entire agreement. He now feels that AWS would be more profitable if it was free to sell hi-fi equipment from several different manufacturers.

Instructing Solicitors have done some preliminary work, looking into the nature of the hi-fi market in the United Kingdom. Through perusing the trade journals, it appears that there are the following manufacturers:

Rebound	12%
Whatmore	25%
Goodsound	27%
Deepdin	8%
Other makes	28%

According to AWS the wholesale price of Deepdin hi-fi equipment is higher in other Member States of the European Union than in the United Kingdom. This explains the purchase order from HappiSound in France.

Counsel is requested to draft a Defence and Counterclaim in this matter. Counsel is further requested to advise:

— generally

— in particular, whether or not a complaint should be made to the European Commission

— on the steps to be taken in relation to (i) a complaint, if so advised, and (ii) the High Court proceedings.

[Copy agreement]

This PURCHASE AGREEMENT dated 2 January 1997 between DEEPDIN UK LIMITED Deepdin House Swaledale Estate Barnsley Yorkshire and ARNOLD'S WORLD OF SOUND LIMITED Tottenham Court Road London WC2

WHEREBY: DEEPDIN UK LIMITED ('the Company') and ARNOLD'S WORLD OF SOUND LIMITED ('the Exclusive Purchaser') have agreed that the Company will supply Deepdin hi-fi equipment to the Exclusive Purchaser upon the terms and conditions set out herein

INTRODUCTION

(a) The Company produces high quality and technically complex consumer hi-fi products. They are subject to continuous technological development.

(b) Consumers of the Company's products require informed and expert advice prior to making their purchase decision. They also require installation services and a full after sales service, including warranty service.

(c) The Company has established a network of exclusive purchasers for Deepdin products in order to provide all the services required by consumers.

AGREED TERMS:

1. The Company undertakes and agrees with the Exclusive Purchaser that the Company will

(i) supply the Exclusive Purchaser with all hi-fi products for sale in the exclusive Purchaser's business

(ii) not sell Deepdin products by way of retail to the Exclusive Purchaser's customers, except with the prior consent of the Exclusive Purchaser

(iii) use all reasonable endeavours to ensure that other exclusive purchasers do not sell Deepdin products by way of retail to the Exclusive Purchaser's customers.

2. In consideration of the above undertakings and obligations on the part of the Company, the Exclusive Purchaser hereby undertakes and agrees with the Company:

(1) For a period of five years from the date hereof to purchase from the Company all hi-fi products to be sold in its business;

(2) To pay the Company for all Deepdin products purchased by the exclusive Purchaser from the Company not later than the Saturday of the week following delivery thereof to the Exclusive Purchaser;

(3) To use its best endeavours to increase the sale of Deepdin products in its business;

(4) To give the Company at least one month's written notice of the exclusive Purchaser's wish to dispose of all or any part of the goodwill of its business or any interest therein;

(5) Upon any sale by the Exclusive Purchaser of the whole or a substantial part of its business to apply the proceeds of such sale in the discharge of any sums due to the Company from the Exclusive Purchaser;

(6) Not to manufacture or distribute hi-fi products which compete with Deepdin products;

(7) To purchase hi-fi products from across the Company's complete range;

(8) To purchase from the Company Deepdin products to the value of at least £100,000 within the period of five years;

(9) Not to tamper with or obliterate the trademark 'Deepdin';

(10) To provide installation services and a full after sales service including a warranty service to the Exclusive Purchaser's customers;

(11) Not to export any Deepdin products outside the territory of the United Kingdom without the prior written consent of the Company. Any enquiries for orders from outside the United Kingdom should be forwarded to the Company at its registered address.

3. The Company will provide training, information, guidance and promotional material relating to the sale and servicing of Deepdin products.

4. Either party may terminate this agreement forthwith if the other party commits an irremediable breach of any of its provisions.

5. Upon termination the Exclusive Purchaser will return or dispose of, in accordance with the Company's instructions, all promotional materials, specifications, and other documents and offer for sale back to the Company all Deepdin products belonging to the Exclusive Purchaser at a price equal to that which the Exclusive Purchaser paid for them.

THIS AGREEMENT constitutes the entire contract between the parties and may not be varied except by written agreement between them.

Deepdin products are the consumer electronic products sold under the Deepdin Trademark or Deepdin brand name which include Colour Televisions, Video Cassette Recorders, Camcorders, Hi-Fi Systems.

In witness whereof

STATEMENT OF TERRY ARNOLD

I am the Managing Director of Arnold's World of Sound. Two years ago we agreed with Deepdin UK that we would buy all our hi-fi requirements from them. They make hi-fi equipment at the quality end of the market, with basic equipment starting at about £1,000 wholesale. For their very top range, prices can be about ten times that. How much we paid for orders from Deepdin was dependent on the particular range we ordered from. As examples, a complete Deepdin Mashup sound system has a current cost price to us of £800 per unit, a Deepdin CD Triple X system costs £850 and the Deepdin Quality Airtime costs £2,385 each. To start with, the arrangement with Deepdin worked well. In the first trading year we bought in excess of £350,000 worth of Deepdin product.

At the start of this year, I attended the Paris Audio Vision Fair. This attracts manufacturers and dealers from all over Europe, as well as other major brand names. Whilst there, I learnt from other Deepdin dealers that the cost of Deepdin products varied considerably. Generally, they were higher than I was paying in the UK — for example, in France wholesale prices were on average 6–8% higher and in Germany they could be higher still. I spoke informally with several foreign Deepdin dealers in Paris and then in April this year I received a letter from M. Happi of HappiSound SA. He wanted to place an order with AWS for Deepdin products, to be supplied to him in July this year. Given the price differentials, it seemed to make sense for both of us, so I wrote to Deepdin asking for permission to supply the equipment. Deepdin turned me down pretty abruptly. I didn't like their response so I rang their MD, Oliver Din, and told him I was going to fulfil the order regardless. I could not see how he could stop HappiSound getting their stock. A week or so later I got their Particulars of Claim in the post.

I don't want to carry on with this agreement now, it seems too restrictive. AWS would be better off financially if we could sell hi-fi equipment across several brands and manufacturers. If needed, I can confirm that from some research we've done. I have written to M. Happi asking him to supply details of sales of Deepdin in France.

HappiSound SA

Avenue Coeur de Lion
Paris
France

30 April 1999

Arnold's World of Sound Ltd
1193 Tottenham Court Road
London
WC2

Dear Mr Arnold

We would be grateful if you would supply to us at HappiSound in July 1999, 100 CD Deepdin Triple X stereo sound systems at your quoted price of £1,100 per unit.

Yours sincerely,

Maurice Happi

Arnold's World of Sound Limited

Tottenham Court Road
London
WC2

23 May 1999

Mr O. Din
Deepdin UK Limited
Deepdin House
Swaledale Estate
Barnsley
Yorkshire

Dear Oliver,

Please find enclosed a request which we have received from HappiSound SA, a French dealer. We would be grateful to have your permission to fulfil this order.

Best wishes,

Terry Arnold

Deepdin UK Limited

Deepdin House
Swaledale Estate
Barnsley
Yorkshire

28 May 1999

Mr Terry Arnold
Arnold's World of Sound Ltd
1193 Tottenham Court Road
London
WC2

Dear Sir

Thank you for your letter of 23 May. In the circumstances, I am afraid that we cannot agree to your company fulfilling this order. We shall be instructing our French distributor to enquire of HappiSound SA whether they wish to purchase from our French agents.

Yours faithfully

Oliver Din

IN THE HIGH COURT OF JUSTICE   Claim No. 1999 HC 3217

QUEEN'S BENCH DIVISION

BETWEEN:

DEEPDIN UK LIMITED   Claimants

and

ARNOLD'S WORLD OF SOUND LIMITED   Defendants

PARTICULARS OF CLAIM

---

1.   At all material times the Claimants have carried on business as suppliers of hi-fi equipment. The Defendants have carried on a hi-fi distribution business.

2.   By an agreement in writing dated 2nd January 1997 made between the Claimants and the Defendants, it was agreed that the Defendants would purchase for a period of five years Deepdin hi-fi products only from the Claimants.

3.   It was an express term of the agreement that the Defendants would not sell Deepdin hi-fi equipment outside the United Kingdom without the prior written consent of the Claimants.

4.   Notwithstanding that written term, the Defendants have threatened to act in breach of contract by selling a quantity of Deepdin hi-fi equipment to a French company, HappiSound SA.

PARTICULARS OF BREACH OF CONTRACT

(a)   On 30th April 1999 a French company HappiSound SA requested the Defendants to provide it with 100 CD Deepdin Triple X sound systems.

(b)   By letter dated 23rd May 1999, the Defendants requested permission from the Claimants to fulfil the order. By letter dated 28th May 1999, permission was refused.

(c)   By telephone conversation Mr Arnold, the Managing Director of the Defendants, informed Mr Oliver Din of the Claimants that he would nevertheless satisfy the order from HappiSound.

5.   In the premises, the Defendants threaten and intend unless restrained by injunction to sell Deepdin hi-fi equipment to HappiSound SA in breach of contract.

6.   In the alternative, the Claimants will suffer loss and damage.

PARTICULARS

Full particulars will be provided in due course.

7.   Further the Claimants claim interest on the amount found due to them pursuant to section 35A of the Supreme Court Act 1981 and/or the inherent jurisdiction of the Court.

AND the Claimants claim:

(1) An Order that the Defendants be restrained from exporting Deepdin hi-fi products.

(2) Alternatively, damages.

(3) Interest.

LOUDON PROWD

[statement of truth omitted]

SERVED this 5th day of June 1999 by BROWNING LLOYD of Lincoln's Inn, Solicitors for the Claimants.

8.8.4.3   Suggested Opinion

This is a draft Opinion, very much in the style of a first draft. It is intended to start you thinking about the structure of such an Opinion (not very different from those on many other, more familiar, areas of law). Also, it should show some of the issues that a client will need advice on, together with the identification of some gaps or ambiguities that will need to be resolved through a conference with the client.

DEEPDIN UK LIMITED v ARNOLD'S WORLD OF SOUND LIMITED

DRAFT OPINION

---

1.   [Introductory paragraph, setting out who is represented, the contract and the basic allegations made by Deepdin in its S/C.]

2.   [Again, probably just setting out the issues on which advice is being sought/given]

- generally

- whether a complaint should be made to the EC Commission

- steps to take re (i) any complaint and (ii) the H/C proceedings.

3.   [Perhaps a <u>summary</u> of the advice and/or steps to be taken]

- Deepdin should get NO injunction and NO damages because there has been no breach of a contract term. Cl. 2(11) is void as an export ban, prohibited by Article 81(1).

- Counterclaim for a declaration that the contract is void, by virtue of Article 81(1) and (2). Severance of the offending clause is not being sought [although query whether it might be so sought by Deepdin in any Reply]. Damages might be counterclaimed for the lost deal with HappiSound SA but we would need to check if the deal had actually fallen through. There is also a possible problem about *ex turpi causa* re the damages — if we are a willing party to a prohibited contract.

- A complaint to the EC Commission is unnecessary. The High Court has the power to declare Article 81(1) applicable and thus a contract clause void. In cases of doubt, reference should be made to the Notice on Cooperation between national courts and the Commission. The High Court proceedings may be stayed while advice is sought from the Commission.

- The block exemption 1984/83 on exclusive purchasing is inapplicable. Reason — [state very briefly, cross-refer to paragraph 5 for full detail].

- *De minimis* is not a problem [again, state why briefly, cross-refer to paragraph 8].

- The action brought by Deepdin may also be an abuse of a dominant position because we suggest the relevant product market is top-range, premium hi-fi equipment and they are one of the two biggest players in that market in the UK. However, much more information is needed on market structure (including the geographical market) before anything definite can be decided on Article 82.

- Steps to be taken are — [concise list, drawn from the body of the Opinion].

4. Article 81 [Good idea to use headings — helps to focus reader's attention; provides easy access later.] [Tick off the elements and evidence for an Article 81(1) allegation]

- Agreement between undertakings — as pleaded in the Particulars of Claim.

- Effect on trade between Member States — the deal between AWS and HappiSound SA in particular, and other price differentials disclosed by Terry Arnold's statement; this raises issues about intra-brand competition being stifled. We might also want to advance an argument over the foreclosure of AWS as a distributor of hi-fi equipment from other manufacturers and suppliers to make a point about inter-brand competition (taking our cue from the *Delimitis* v *Henninger Braü* case).

- Object or effect — export ban in Cl. 2(11) probably qualifies under both now. Would have been *object* initially but now, in light of the refusal by Deepdin to allow AWS to export, it is also *effect*.

- Restriction, etc. of competition — maintaining price differentials between Member States, thwarting creation of single market, reference to French distributor in Deepdin's letter is a naked attempt to maintain a price structure for resales and prevent parallel imports.

  Price differentials between Member States *might* be explicable as the result of different national tastes or just higher transport costs to distant markets but the way Cl. 2(11) is set up (coupled with the reaction of Deepdin to such a request) shows that price-fixing and market protection is the objective.

  Cl. 2(11) operates in a similar fashion to so-called 'English' clauses, whereby a company (under the guise of offering a better deal to its customers) optimises its information about demand and is able to stifle intra-brand competition.

  Note that Cl. 1(iii) seeks to limit competition between the exclusive purchase network at the retail level but is silent on intra-network competition at the distribution/wholesale level. See also guideline 37 in the Commission's Notice on Regulations 1983/83 and 1984/83. This suggests that even to only use *reasonable endeavours* may fall foul of permitted restrictions in Article 2 of the Block Exemption.

  The Block Exemption is silent on export bans. They are not expressly prohibited by Article 3 but see Recital (8) — further restrictions, especially those limiting reseller's choice of customers or freedom to determine prices and conditions of sale, cannot be exempted.

- Some analysis of the rest of the contract might be expected. This is not necessary for the purpose of defending the action but may be very relevant if we try to persuade a judge at trial that the entire contract is void (because AWS want to get out of it). For example:

- Cl. 2(1) — the *term* of the agreement is 5 years (probably OK, cf. Block Exemption 1984/83, Article 3(d)) and sets up the exclusive purchase which is *prima facie* anti-competitive, hence the need for a Block Exemption (and see Article 1 thereof).

- Cl. 2(6) — a non-competition clause. AWS may be unlikely to go into manufacturing but distribution is obviously its business. Likely to be OK as to do otherwise would defeat the purpose of the contract; likewise, Cl. 2(3) re use of *best endeavours*. Both seem limited to the life of the contract. See Block Exemption, Article 2(2).

- Cl. 2(7) — full-range forcing. May be seen as restrictive of competition but obviously serves the needs of the consumer. Condemnation depends on whether the rule of reason applies at the stage of Article 81(1) or only comes in at Article 81(3). Would be exempted by the Block Exemption, Article 2(3)(a).

- Cl. 2(8) is a minimum quantity requirement. Would be exempt under the Block Exemption, Article 2(3)(b). Allows Deepdin to predict future demands with greater certainty and make more efficient use of resources (thus keeping prices lower).

- Cl. 2(8) — displaying supplier's trademark is probably not anti-competitive but see Block Exemption, Article 2(3)(c). Query silence of the clause regarding identification of AWS on the products. Cf. the Block Exemption on technology transfer (240/96).

- Cl. 2(10) — probably not anti-competitive. Smacks of selective distribution but no problem regarding 'tying' as customers are not obligated to enter a service/installation agreement or necessarily make use of such services from AWS after purchase. See Block Exemption, Article 2(3)(d).

5. The Block Exemption on Exclusive Purchasing — Regulation 1984/83
[In dealing with the application of the relevant block exemption in your Opinion, you should show a thorough knowledge of the regulation and how to use it. Reference has already been made above and will not be repeated here. You may want to show a similar structure. It is important to remember, though, that you cannot base an argument for infringement solely on the ground that an agreement does not come within the protection of a block exemption. No agreement was ever prohibited by Article 81(1) just because it was outside a block exemption; the argument for infringement has still to be made out.]

In essence, the Block Exemption does NOT apply to this contract, by virtue of Cl. 2(11). Thus, the contract as a whole is unprotected.

6. Individual exemption
[You should consider whether Deepdin has an individual exemption already; or would get one if it applied now. Both seem unlikely but it might be wise to ask AWS what they know of this; also, perhaps, approach the Commission. Deepdin may have gone through a notification before AWS entered this contract (which appears to be a standard form agreement).]

7. Article 82
[You may want to say something about abusive behaviour in this Opinion. I don't think it would be prudent to just skip over it and say nothing, based on what you currently know. It may be one of the implicit points that the instructions raise, so make a note to ask questions (in interview or in writing) in terms of seeking any further information which may be relevant. Initially, you would want to determine whether you could run an argument that Deepdin holds a dominant position. So the information you seek might include definition of the relevant product market, the structure of the market (e.g. does Deepdin's 8% of the whole UK hi-fi market translate into something more like a dominating market share if we use a more refined definition?).]

8. Remedies

[You should deal with the application of Article 81(1); also the fact that application of Article 81(3) to this contract is unlikely. It is void, subject to any severance. Severance should be dealt with because Deepdin are almost certainly going to raise it in any Reply and Defence to Counterclaim. I think severance is a possibility here. It might be worth pointing out to AWS that, if everything goes according to plan and Deepdin's attempt to compartmentalise the market and discriminate on prices is prohibited, the export market may lose the value that it currently has for AWS because the price differentials may fall or even disappear.]

The fact that the contract is void constitutes a defence to the action. A declaration to this effect in a counterclaim would allow AWS to walk away from it, as they wish, subject to severance. In any event, the fact that Cl. 2(11) is void also provides a good defence to the action.

Damages may be sought, if any have been sustained, probably via the lost HappiSound SA deal, but AWS should be asked for details of other export deals that have not been taken. Also, any projections or estimates about future earnings from developing an export market. A note of caution should be sounded on the likelihood of actually getting an award of damages.

9. *De minimis*

[You should consider this but I don't think there is a definite answer available on the information you have. Market share looks to be above the 5% threshold in the Notice on Agreements of Minor Importance, although the Green Paper on Vertical Restraints (such as we have here) suggests a 10% threshold. If the market is defined as expensive, top-quality hi-fis, then market share is probably in excess of 10% anyway. There is a lack of information on turnover — this gap needs to be filled. You can show a practical approach in your Opinion through suggestions as to how this information may be acquired.]

Tentatively, if market definition goes the way we want, then Deepdin's market share will prevent this agreement falling through the net. Figures for Deepdin's turnover should be sought — through company reports, surveys by merchant banks, MMC reports on the industry, etc. We also want to know the turnover figures for AWS: ask Mr Arnold.

10. Complaint to the Commission

[You should decide whether this offers any benefits to AWS. One benefit might be the investigative powers of the Commission and its expertise. Also, the low cost to AWS of making a complaint. However, the information which the Commission gets will not be available to the parties in *Deepdin* v *AWS* (see case-law of the ECJ), any fine will not go to AWS and no damages will be awarded by the Commission. In any event, the High Court claim needs to be defended. I can't see any great benefit to be got from complaining but it wouldn't hurt AWS. It may be that any findings of fact which the Commission made against Deepdin would be treated as conclusive evidence in the High Court proceedings but that would be a long time coming (see *Iberian UK* v *BPB Industries*). A complaint (or the threat thereof) may be a bargaining chip to use in the High Court action, against Deepdin.]

11. Steps to be taken regarding the High Court action

[Serve the enclosed Defence and Counterclaim. Seek information re lost deals from AWS. Seek information re market share of Deepdin from AWS and other sources. Advise AWS of the need to commission a report from an expert on the relevant market, unless one exists already that you can use. Any other questions that you want answers to? If so, specify what they are and, if you can, who to ask.]

Signed by counsel

8.8.5   EXAMPLE FOR A DEFENCE AND COUNTERCLAIM

What follows is a first draft for this pleading, based purely on the information supplied in the instructions to counsel in **8.8.4.2**. It simply shows one way in which the material averments might be set out. It is quite acceptable (although not used here) for sub-headings to be used, within the heading of 'Particulars of infringement', to divide up the allegations into the following categories:

- restrictive clauses in the exclusive purchase agreement;

- restriction of competition within the common market;

- effect on trade between Member States.

Comments have been added in square brackets to explain why certain things have been said or appear where they do. Obviously, these would not appear on the real thing.

IN THE HIGH COURT OF JUSTICE   Claim No. 1999 HC 3217

QUEEN'S BENCH DIVISION

BETWEEN:

DEEPDIN UK LIMITED   Claimants/Part 20
                                                            Defendants

and

ARNOLD'S WORLD OF SOUND LIMITED   Defendants/Part 20
                                                               Claimants

---

DEFENCE AND COUNTERCLAIM

DEFENCE

---

1.   Paragraphs 1 and 2 of the Particulars of Claim are admitted. In particular, the Claimants have carried on business as manufacturers and suppliers of high quality hi-fi equipment which retails in the premium price ranges. At all material times, the Claimants maintained a network of such exclusive purchasers in the Member States of the European Union, in particular in France. The agreement was in the standard form used by the Claimants in all such agreements for the exclusive purchase of their products.

[*This is important to put in as we need to persuade the judge of a 'network effect' regarding any restriction on competition. It cannot be just Deepdin and AWS as this will be economically insignificant. Cf. the Delimitis case. We will need to try and check that this is a standard form contract. We also need to make a start on defining the relevant market with more precision.*]

2.   Paragraph 3 of the Particulars of Claim is admitted, save that the said term, namely Clause 2(11), is prohibited and void by virtue of Article 81(1) and (2) of the Treaty of Rome.

PARTICULARS OF BREACH OF ARTICLE 81, EC TREATY

(a)   the contract between the Claimants and the Defendants is an agreement between undertakings;

(b)   clause 2(11) has as its object the restriction, prevention or distortion of competition within the common market in that its aim is to prevent the Defendants from fulfilling orders placed by customers in other Member States, at prices lower than those offered by the Claimants to such customers;

(c)   clause 2(11) has the effect of preventing, restricting or distorting competition within the common market since the Claimants have relied on this clause to stop the Defendants from fulfilling an order from an undertaking situated in another Member State, without good reason;

(d)   in the absence of clause 2(11), the Defendants would seek to export the goods which are the subject-matter of the contract to customers situated in other Member States.

[I think it is important to set out the particulars which rebut the cause of action here, in the Defence; however, some people would simply cross-refer to the salient paragraph in the Counterclaim.]

3.   Clause 2(11) of the contract restricts competition in a manner which is not exempted by the Block Exemption for exclusive purchase agreements, Regulation 1984/83 of the European Commission. In consequence thereof, the contract does not benefit from the Block Exemption at all.

[Strictly speaking, we don't need to mention the Block Exemption in the Defence, we could wait and see if the Claimant tries to rely on it in any Reply. But I think it may help to make the defence seem stronger, at least in the mind of the Claimant.]

4.   Paragraphs 4 and 5 of the Particulars of Claim are admitted, save that it is denied that the actions of the Defendants were, are or will be in breach of the said contract for the reasons aforesaid.

[Basically, we agree that the Particulars of Claim accurately represent what we want(ed) to do but it is not a breach of contract to do so.]

5.   Paragraph 6 of the Particulars of Claim is not admitted.

[What else can be said here? We have no details of the alleged loss. In any event, what loss could Deepdin suffer? Either it sells 100 units of the Triple X system to HappiSound SA through its French distributor or through AWS.]

6.   *[Plead counterclaim as a set-off. Standard form paragraph.]*

_____

COUNTERCLAIM

_____

7.   The Defendants repeat paragraphs 1–5 of the Defence to this action.

[These paragraphs are equally relevant to the claim we want to make for AWS against Deepdin.]

8. Further or in the alternative, the following clauses of the contract are prohibited and void, by virtue of the operation of Article 81(1) and (2).

PARTICULARS OF BREACH OF ARTICLE 81, EC TREATY

(a) clause 2(1) obliges the Defendants for the duration of the contract, namely five years, to purchase all hi-fi products to be sold in their business from the Claimants;

(b) clause 2(6) obliges the Defendants not to compete with the Claimants through the manufacture or distribution of hi-fi products;

(c) clause 2(7) obliges the Defendants to purchase hi-fi products from across the Claimants' complete range;

(d) clause 2(8) obliges the Defendants to purchase a minimum quantity of the Claimants' products, namely to the value £100,000, within the term of the contract;

(e) the specified clauses had as their object, the prevention, restriction or distortion of competition within the common market;

(f) in all the circumstances, other manufacturers and distributors of branded, high quality hi-fi equipment were prevented from selling their products to the Defendants and to all such dealers within the Claimants' network. Such manufacturers and distributors are based both in the United Kingdom and elsewhere within the common market.

[Here, we are specifying the other anti-competitive clauses, in the hope that the number of them will help us to make out the argument that the whole contract is void and severance is impractical. The consequences of such clauses, which are largely concerned with denying access to the market to Deepdin's competitors, are also alluded to, as is the possible effect on inter-State trade.]

8. In the premises, the contract between the Claimants and the Defendants is prohibited and void in its entirety.

9. By reason of the unlawful actions of the Claimants, namely the insertion of clause 2(11) into the contract and the subsequent refusal of the Claimants to consent to the sale by the Defendants of hi-fi products to a French company, HappiSound SA, the Defendants have suffered loss and damage.

PARTICULARS OF LOSS AND DAMAGE

(a) sale of 100 units of the CD Deepdin Triple X system to HappiSound SA

Cost per unit to the Defendants	£ 850
Sale price per unit	£ 1,100
Total Profit	£15,000

(b) [maybe details of any other potential sales lost in consequence of C's attitude?]

[Particulars need to be given of any loss for which we seek damages. We could get away with 'Full particulars will be supplied in due course' but as we have some specific information now, we may as well provide it.]

10. Further the Defendants claim interest on the amounts found due to them pursuant to section 35A of the Supreme Court Act 1981 and/or the inherent jurisdiction of the Court.

AND the Defendants counterclaim:

(1)   A Declaration that the contract between the Defendants and the Claimants is prohibited and void, and that the Defendants are no longer bound by it.

(2)   Damages.

(3)   Interest.

WATSON EARDRUM

[statement of truth omitted]

DATED etc.

8.9   Remedies

8.9.1   DAMAGES

Damages are often a remedy desired by clients. That they should be available to compensate those harmed by an infringement of the EC competition rules seems almost beyond doubt. Regarding English courts, you can rely on the speech of Lord Diplock in *Garden Cottage Foods*; this dealt explicitly with the notion that damages were a remedy available for the 'victim' of an abuse of a dominant position, pursuant to Article 82 (ex 86). As for the European Court, cases such as *Brasserie du Pêcheur* v *Germany* (C-46/93) [1996] ECR I-1029 can clearly be read as recognising the right of individuals to recover damages against other individuals (and not just Member States) for breaches of Community law. The matter has been explicitly dealt with by the Advocates General in two cases, *Banks (H.J.) and Co. Ltd* v *British Coal Corporation* (C-128/82) [1994] ECR I-120 and *R* v *Minister of Agriculture Fisheries and Food, ex parte Hedley Lomas (Ireland) Ltd* (C-5/94) [1996] ECR I-2553. It must be recognised, though, that the absence of a clear and simple statement from the European Court on the matter is not helpful. The view of the Commission is set out in the Notice it issued in 1993 on cooperation between itself and the national courts:

> [I]t is the right of parties subject to Community law that national courts should take provisional measures, that an effective end should be brought, by injunction, to the infringement of Community competition rules of which they are victims, and that *compensation should be awarded for the damage suffered as a result of infringements, where such remedies are available in proceedings relating to similar national law.*

(Paragraph 11 of the Notice, OJ 1993 C38/6)

One further possible obstacle to an award of damages arises in Article 81 (ex 85) cases: namely, where both claimant and defendant are parties to the agreement which, it is alleged, infringes Article 81(1) (ex 85(1)). When one party alleges that the contract is prohibited and void, it can be a little difficult to see why one party to a void contract should have to compensate the other and, indeed, why one of them should be seen as the victim of the other's infringement; after all, Article 81 (ex 85) hits at collusive anti-competitive behaviour.

8.9.2   INJUNCTIONS

English courts can grant injunctions, both interim and final, in cases concerning breaches of EC law. In *Garden Cottage Foods* v *Milk Marketing Board* [1984] AC 130, the House of Lords refused to grant an interlocutory injunction to the plaintiff (now 'claimant'), who alleged a breach of Article 86 (now 82) by the defendant. The reason for the refusal was not that there was no jurisdiction to grant the order but that damages were available as a remedy for the plaintiff at trial and would be an adequate remedy for the plaintiff. Therefore, on straightforward principles (see *American Cyanamid Co. v Ethicon Ltd* [1975] AC 386), the application was rejected. Conversely, in *Cutsforth v Mansfield Inns Ltd* [1986] 1 WLR 558, an interlocutory injunction was sought by a firm which supplied fruit machines to several pubs, ultimately owned by the defendant brewery. The brewery, on recently taking over the pubs, had told its tenants that they must take fruit machines only from a list of specified suppliers, which did not include the plaintiffs. The judge was explicit in stating that the question of whether to grant the application had to be considered in the light of the principles laid down in *American Cyanamid*. Recognising that damages were available as a remedy, and that the defendant brewery could afford to pay them, the judge nevertheless found that 'damages would not be an adequate remedy for the plaintiffs because the denial of interim relief would virtually put an end to [their] business' and granted the application.

It must be remembered that if the applicant fails to demonstrate a 'serious question to be tried' (namely, some sort of prima facie case that the respondent has infringed the EC competition rules), no interim injunction will be granted. Thus, the plaintiffs failed in *Cutsforth* under Article 86 (now 82) when the judge held that the area of the North of England covered by the defendant's pubs was not a 'substantial part of the common market'; fortunately for the plaintiffs, the judge was persuaded that there was a serious question to be tried under Article 85 (now 81).

Lastly, on the subject, we should note the ground-breaking impact of the *Factortame* litigation. In particular, the ruling of the Court of Justice that the enforcement of a British Act of Parliament could be suspended by means of an interim injunction notwithstanding the long-settled British rule which prohibited such relief. See *R v Secretary of State for Transport, ex parte Factortame* (C-213/89) [1990] ECR I-2433.

8.9.3   DECLARATIONS

A declaration is perhaps of most use where the party relying upon EC competition law is a party to a contract, and wishes that contract to continue, notwithstanding that one or more clauses in the contract are void for infringement of Article 81(1) (ex 85(1)) or 82 (ex 86). An application for severance will normally accompany a declaration in such circumstances. If the claimant and defendant are in a customer-supplier relationship, it may be that the claimant/customer does not want a complete termination of dealings. An award of damages might antagonise the defendant/supplier, who may have considerably more bargaining power than the claimant; whereas a simple declaration is merely 'an authoritative statement of the relevant legal position on which the parties can base their future actions' (D. Harris, *Remedies in Contract and Tort*, Weidenfeld Nicolson, 1988).

8.10   Cooperation between National Courts and the Commission

Some English courts have taken to the notion of cooperation with some enthusiasm. It has been held, albeit at first instance in the Chancery Division, that where the Commission has made findings of fact in a procedure in which the claimant and defendant participated, then those findings are conclusive evidence (and not merely admissible) in subsequent proceedings before the English court. See Laddie J in *Iberian UK Ltd v BPB Industries plc* [1996] 2 CMLR 601. The reason for this is given as the need for legal certainty and the desire to avoid reaching decisions which conflict; the same principle applied to findings by the Court of First Instance and the Court of Justice in competition proceedings. Certainly, one can see the sense in this, as both parties will have had a right to be heard during the Commission procedure under Regulation 17 and, if dissatisfied with the outcome, could (and perhaps did) appeal to the European Court. As Laddie J said:

> [I]t would be contrary to public policy to allow persons who have been involved in competition proceedings in Europe to deny here the correctness of the conclusions reached there.

This was only a decision at first instance, though, and one should be a little cautious before relying too heavily on it. It does seem safe to regard the Commission's findings of fact as *admissible* evidence but beyond that, one must bear in mind other, earlier, first instance decisions which appear to contradict Laddie J. One example is *Merson* v *Rover Group*, 22 May 1992, unreported (distinguished by Laddie J), where the judge held he was not bound by findings of fact from the European Court of Justice that the defendant company had infringed Article 86 (now 82). The defendant denied there had been an Article 86 (now 82) abuse and the judge refused an application for summary judgment, finding the defendant's present position did not constitute an abuse of the process of the court. One could assume that this judge would have been equally dismissive of any decision from the Commission.

The Commission takes a rather humble position on the subject. It issued a Notice on Cooperation in 1993 (OJ 1993 C39/6) in which it declared that, before a national court decides the question of whether there is an infringement of Article 81(1) (ex 85(1)) or 82 (ex 86), it should first find out if the alleged infringement has been considered already by the Commission. It may be that the Commission has already issued:

> a decision, opinion or other official statement ... Such statements provide national courts with significant information for reaching a judgment, even if they are not formally bound by them (paragraph 20).

It is worth noting that the Notice goes on to distinguish cases which have been closed with a formal decision and those where a comfort letter is used. Recognising that such letters do not bind national courts, the Commission continued:

> the Court of Justice has ... stated that the opinion expressed by the Commission constitutes a factor which the national courts may take into account in examining whether the agreements or conduct in question are in accordance with the provisions of Article 85 [now 81].

There seems no reason why this should not apply also to comfort letters dealing with Article 82 (ex 86).

More generally, the Notice observes that, while the power to grant an exemption under Article 81(3) (ex 85(3)) is exclusively within the competence of the Commission, with that exception the Commission and national courts have concurrent powers to apply Article 81(1) (ex 85(1)) and Article 82 (ex 86). The Commission is keen to encourage national courts to deal with such matters themselves, invoking the notion of subsidiarity and encouraging would-be complainants to turn instead to the appropriate national court:

> The Commission intends ... to concentrate on notifications, complaints and own-initiative proceedings [which have] particular political, economic or legal significance for the Community. Where these features are absent in a particular case, notifications will normally be dealt with by means of a comfort letter and complaints should, as a rule, be handled by national courts or authorities.

> The Commission considers that there is not normally a sufficient Community interest in examining a case when the [complainant] is able to secure adequate protection of his rights before the national courts. In these circumstances the complaint will normally be filed (paragraphs 14, 15 of the Notice).

It is important to avoid the possibility of conflicting decisions being reached by the national court and the Commission on the same facts. One way to this has been mentioned already — checking whether the Commission has already reached a decision (formal or informal) on the subject-matter (paragraph 20 of the Notice). If no such decision has been reached but the Commission has started a procedure under Regulation 17/62, the court can choose to go ahead and rule on the existence of an infringement itself or stay the proceedings to await the decision of the Commission. Where a case is stayed for this reason, the Commission will try to 'fast-track' it (see Commission Notice, paragraph 37).

An example of a situation where a court might decide to stay proceedings is where:

- it felt that Article 81(1) (ex 85(1)) was infringed; but that

- an exemption was probably merited under Article 81(3) (ex 85(3)); and

- the agreement has been properly notified to the Commission.

In the absence of proper notification to the Commission, no exemption would be possible in this example and the national court should simply rule the agreement void, pursuant to Article 81(2) (ex 85(2)). Similarly, if the court felt that the agreement could not be granted an exemption, a stay would be unnecessary.

If the agreement was one which fell within the scope of a block exemption, then that could be applied by the national court (regardless of any notification) and a stay would be unnecessary. In cases of complexity, where the application of Article 81(1) (ex 85(1)) or Article 82 (ex 86) 'gives rise to legal or economic difficulties', a court can make a preliminary reference to the Court of Justice, seeking its opinion, or seek assistance from the Commission. The latter possibility represents a novel opportunity for English courts (which has been taken on at least one occasion already; see the Commission's XXIVth Report on Competition Policy 1994). Assistance is offered, initially, through the block exemptions and notices issued by the Commission; also, a court could refer to previous published decisions of the Commission and its annual reports on competition policy. If these are inadequate then a court can, 'within the limits of [its] national procedural law', seek information from the Commission. Three types of information are offered:

- Procedural information about the case, e.g. has there been a notification? Has the Commission sent a comfort letter? How long will it take the Commission to decide on an exemption?

- Legal advice, e.g. what are the criteria for determining whether a restriction on competition is appreciable or not? In such cases, the Commission is not concerned with the facts, or merits, of the particular case but the court may also ask for an interim opinion on whether an agreement is likely to get exemption under Article 81(3) (ex 85(3)). In that situation, the Commission will look at the circumstances of the case in question. The national court retains the right to seek a preliminary ruling from the European Court under Article 234 (ex 177), EC Treaty.

- Factual information, specifically 'statistics, market studies and economic analyses'. This is subject to the Commission actually having the information in its possession and compliance with the rules on confidentiality (see Article 287 (ex 214), EC Treaty; Article 20, Regulation 17/62).

8.11 The Way Forward in English Courts

Having achieved a pragmatic solution to the problem of how the competition rules were to be integrated into the English legal system, as directly-effective supra-national rules, one might have thought that nothing too radical was likely to happen. That thought has been proved wrong in a series of cases in 1998. On the one hand, the cases show English judges becoming more familiar with Community law; on the other hand, it looks as though the competition rules might cease to be of much significance in domestic litigation. The most significant judgment is that of the Court of Appeal, to be found in *Gibbs Mew* v *Gemmell* [1999] 1 EG 117.

Gibbs Mew was a case about a pub. The brewer sued for possession and damages when the tenant fell into arrears with his rent. The tenant defended the claim and counter-claimed with allegations that the beer tie in the lease offended against Article 81(1) (ex 85(1)). The tenant argued that he was entitled to claim damages and set them off against the unpaid rent. The Court of Appeal found against the tenant — the claimant brewing company had such a small market share as to exclude the agreement from the operation of Article 81(1) (ex 85(1)) on the ground of *de minimis*. That much was uncontentious. Three further points were contained in the Court's judgment, though.

First, the Court of Appeal held that the block exemption regulation on beer ties, Regulation 1984/83, should be interpreted in a manner contrary to that set out by the Commission in its guidance on the regulation, issued in 1984. The Court of Appeal justified this on the (correct) basis that the notice was only persuasive and not binding upon national courts. In law, this analysis cannot be argued with, but it does fly in the face of the purposive interpretation of EC law which has long been the hallmark of the European Court. The relevant issue in the case is relatively insignificant (whether specifying tied beers by type rather than by brand or denomination prevented application of the block exemption) but this seemed to be an uncontentious issue, accepted by those who had to work with the block exemption, and the decision of this Court of Appeal is perhaps unlikely to accord with decisions of other national courts on the point. The Court refused leave to appeal to the House of Lords and also refused to make a preliminary reference to the European Court. Leave to appeal was subsequently also refused by the House of Lords.

Secondly, the Court of Appeal determined the point raised as a query in **8.9.1**, namely, whether a party to a contract can argue successfully that the contract (or clause within it) is prohibited and void and yet claim damages upon it. The Court of Appeal decided that breach of statutory duty did not apply on the facts; the tenant was simply claiming for damages or restitution, arising from an illegal agreement to which he was a party. English law did not permit damages to be recovered in such circumstances. Like the first point mentioned above, this decision could have been foreseen. It is important to note that the case did not turn upon Article 82 (ex 86), which does not necessarily rely upon collusive behaviour. One might object that the decision does not reflect the spirit behind Article 81(1) (ex 85(1)) and does little to encourage enforcement of the Article at a national level. However, most noteworthy is the final decision of the Court of Appeal in the case.

Thirdly, the Court held that it was inappropriate for the tenant to rely upon Article 81 (ex 85) to claim any remedy from the courts. The Article was intended to protect one's competitors, either actual or potential. All the parties to a prohibited agreement were 'the cause not the victims' of the anti-competitive behaviour and its consequences. This decision has huge significance for the ability of English courts to enforce the EC competition rules. Certainly, it seems to have put a stop to undertakings using Article 81 (ex 85) as the basis of a claim against their contract partners. Arguably, it still allows defensive use of Article 81 (ex 85), if one simply denies liability by relying on the unenforceability of the contract and does not seek any remedy as such. Most intriguingly, the judgment could be interpreted as an encouragement to competing undertakings to sue their fellows, alleging that an arrangement that the defendant company has with another, or others, is prohibited by Article 81(1) (ex 85(1)). This suggests a whole new cause of action, different from statutory duty, but it also raises some familiar obstacles to a successful claim. For example, opening the floodgates — how many of your competitors could sue your company? Also, how would the court quantify the losses? Would there be problems over issues such as remoteness and causation? It would be optimistic to think that the Court of Appeal was encouraging a new area of enforcement to open up, but it seems more likely that the effect of this judgment will be to diminish the chances of effective enforcement of Article 81 (ex 85) (at least) in England for some time to come.

One possible way around this problem has already been closed off — namely, that the three decisions taken in *Gibbs Mew* might come to be regarded as *obiter dicta*. That hope was dashed by a subsequent decision of the Court, in *Trent Taverns Ltd* v *Sykes*.

This case was decided on 22 January 1999, with similar facts to the *Gibbs Mew* case. A differently constituted Court held that the observations in *Gibbs Mew* were not *obiter*. The Court in *Trent Taverns* did consider that a preliminary reference might be helpful but declined to order one as the *Gibbs Mew* case was still pending before the House of Lords who might order a reference. In fact, as noted above, the House of Lords did not order a preliminary reference when they rejected an application for leave to appeal (on 15 July 1999).

It was stated above that 1998 saw a series of important cases involving EC rules in English courts. The other line of cases of real significance involved yet more pub tenants and their landlords. In *Passmore v Morland plc* [1998] 4 All ER 468, Laddie J held that an agreement could move into and out of nullity, as it fell within Article 81(1) (ex 85(1)) and then without it. He based this decision on the need to undertake an economic assessment of the circumstances prior to deciding whether the agreement was anti-competitive or not. If the circumstances changed, then so might the enforceability of the agreement.

On the facts of *Passmore*, the original lessor of the pub was Inntrepreneur Beer Supply Ltd. Its share of the UK retail beer market was such in 1991 that the exclusive beer purchase obligation in the lease might have contributed to a foreclosure of the market, i.e., be anti-competitive. This point was conceded by the defence, for the purposes only of the hearing. However, in 1992 Inntrepreneur assigned its interests in the lease to Morland plc. Morland is a small company and again it was conceded, for the purpose of the hearing, that an agreement between the tenant and Morland would not infringe Article 81(1) (ex 85(1)) because the size of Morland's tied estate is such that it does not contribute significantly to foreclosure of the market. The pub tenant argued that, if the lease was prohibited by Article 81 (ex 85) in the hands of Inntrepreneur, it was void *ab initio* and could not be assigned to anyone. In 1998, the tenant sued Morland and Inntrepreneur, seeking damages, restitution and a declaration that the beer tie was ineffective.

It should be noted that this was not an agreement whose 'object' was anti-competitive. It was alleged only that it had anti-competitive effects. The main argument for the tenant was that once an agreement fell foul of Article 81 (ex 85), it could have no further 'life' and would be void, unenforceable. For an agreement with an anti-competitive 'object', it would be null from its inception but other agreements would become void only once their 'effects' became anti-competitive (which would be a question of fact in each case). The tenant argued that once an agreement has anti-competitive effects, it becomes void 'as if a guillotine comes down and it does not revive subsequently'.

Counsel for the tenant relied upon a quote from the European Court of Justice (in *Société de Vente de Ciments et Bétons de l'Est SA v Kerpen & Kerpen GmbH & Co. KG* (319/82) [1983] ECR 4173), where the Court said that an agreement which is prohibited under Article 81(1) (ex 85(1)) is void and 'the nullity is absolute'. On the other hand, Morland plc argued that 'the statutory prohibition in Article [81] operates periodically, i.e., it can be turned on and off depending on the surrounding facts'. This argument was the one favoured by Laddie J. The agreement may have been void in the hands of Inntrepreneur but that ceased to be so once Inntrepreneur assigned the lease to Morland plc; thus, the beer tie was not currently unenforceable. The tenant's claim against Morland was struck out. *Passmore* was applied subsequently, in another pub case heard in the Chancery Division, in *Inntrepreneur Pub Co. (CPC) Ltd v Price, The Times*, 4 December 1998.

This issue clearly calls for an interpretation of Article 81(2) (ex 85(2)), but no preliminary reference was made in either *Passmore* or *Price*; nor was any advice sought from the Commission under the 1993 cooperation guidelines. In passing, one might note the view of the Commission on the matter, expressed most recently in its White Paper on Modernisation, published in April 1999. When introducing the notion of 'restrictive practices', the Commission ventured that 'such practices are void *ab initio*', that is, from the start. In the same White Paper, the Commission is concerned about what might happen to consistency of interpretation, if and when the application of Articles 81 (ex 85) and 82 (ex 86) is 'decentralised' (i.e., the burden of enforcement is transferred to the national bodies from the Commission). It notes that to achieve consistency and to lend support, mechanisms would need to be set up for cooperation between the courts and the Commission. For example, national courts could be obliged to inform the Commission of any cases involving Articles 81 (ex 85) and 82 (ex 86):

so that it is made aware of any problems of textual interpretation or lacunae in the legislative framework ... The Commission should also be allowed, subject to the leave of the court, to intervene in judicial proceedings that come to its attention as a result ... Allowing it intervene as *amicus curiae* would be an effective way of helping to maintain consistency in the application of the law.

8.12 Actions against a Member State

Private litigants have brought actions against Member States on several occasions. Sometimes the individual is a national of that State (e.g. *Francovich and others* v *Italian Republic* (C-6/90 and 9/90) [1991] ECR I-5357), on other occasions the claimant is a foreign national (e.g. the *Factortame* cases in the UK, e.g. *R* v *Secretary of State for Transport, ex parte Factortame Ltd (No. 4)* [1986] 2 WLR 506). All Member States of the European Union are under an enforceable obligation to abide by the EC Treaty and implement such measures, as they are required to, as part of their national laws (cf. Article 226 (ex 169), EC Treaty which empowers the Commission to take enforcement action in the European Court). Failure to act on the part of the Member State may result in liability; similarly, acting in contradiction of EC law may result in liability. In addition to the remedies of a declaration of the correct legal position, or the implementation of amending legislation, the successful private claimant may also claim damages from the Member State to compensate for losses suffered.

NINE

CASES INVOLVING THE COMPETITION RULES IN THE EUROPEAN COURT

9.1   Introduction to Direct and Indirect Actions

There are several different procedures which can be used in order to seek some form of redress from the European Court. Some are 'direct' actions, others are 'indirect'. Usually, the initial venue for EC-level litigation will be the Court of First Instance (which has been in existence only since 1989). From there, appeal lies to the European Court of Justice but only on matters of law and only insofar as the Court of First Instance has erred; the Court of Justice is not concerned with examining factual arguments which have already had two airings, once before the Commission and again in the Court of First Instance. A private litigant (a natural or legal person) will by-pass the Court of First Instance and go straight to the Court of Justice in only one situation — on a preliminary reference under Article 234 (ex 177), EC Treaty. This might make it seem that the Article 234 (ex 177) reference is the 'direct' action referred to earlier but this is not correct. The Article 234 (ex 177) reference is an interlocutory step in other litigation; that litigation is a proceeding in a court or tribunal of a Member State and will continue after the preliminary ruling of the Court of Justice. So, it is the preliminary reference under Article 234 (ex 177) by a national court or tribunal which is the 'indirect' action; the other forms of procedure dealt with in this chapter are 'direct' actions, so-called because they start and end in the European Court.

Chapter 8 looked at the ways in which private litigants might use the EC competition rules in the courts of the Member States. Such litigation may be brought against a fellow private individual or against a Member State. No doubt, there have been many cases where a dissatisfied litigant has left the court, feeling that the judge did not understand the law as it applied to their case. If their lawyer could have persuaded the judge that he or she did not understand the EC law point argued in the case, then the court might have made a preliminary reference so that the Court of Justice could give its ruling on the interpretation of the Treaty or the validity or interpretation of the acts of the EC institutions. Such a ruling might have helped to resolve the national litigation with a different outcome; on the other hand, it may not have changed the result even if it changed the way the result was arrived at. What the Court of Justice does on a preliminary ruling does not dispose of the issues in the domestic action, it merely clarifies them; the Court of Justice is not functioning as an appeal court in Article 234 (ex 177) proceedings.

What happens if an undertaking feels aggrieved at something which the Commission has done, or not done, in connection with these same rules? In other words, the target of the displeasure is not a fellow private individual, nor a Member State but is the European Commission. The European Court is given a supervisory role by Article 220 (ex 164), EC Treaty:

> The Court of Justice shall ensure that in the interpretation and application of this Treaty the law is observed.

The two main procedures which are created by the Treaty to enable this supervisory role to be fulfilled are the action to annul (under Article 230 (ex 173), EC Treaty; **9.3**) and the action for a failure to act (under Article 232 (ex 175), EC Treaty; **9.4**).

All of these procedures will be examined briefly in the following sections of this chapter. Further detail should be sought in works such as Schermers and Waelbroeck, *Judicial Protection in the European Communities*, Kluwer, 1991; there are also many useful insights to be found in *Procedure and Enforcement in EC and US Competition Law*, edited by Slot and McDonnell, Sweet & Maxwell, 1993.

9.2 Preliminary References

A preliminary reference is sought at the instigation of a court or tribunal of a Member State. The reference may be sought by one or both parties to domestic litigation, or on the national court's own initiative, but only a judicial body can make the reference. The reference may be made prior to trial of the domestic claim, or afterwards as part of an appeal within the national legal system. An English lawyer will find rules governing preliminary references in RSC O. 114 (which can still be found, in Sch. 1 of the Civil Procedure Rules) and in the Criminal Appeal (References to the European Court) Rules 1972. The procedure has three stages:

(a)   the national court makes the reference;

(b)   the national proceedings are 'stayed', or suspended, until such time as the preliminary ruling is received from the Court of Justice;

(c)   the national court applies EC law, as interpreted by the preliminary ruling, to the facts in the case and continues to judgment.

Important issues when considering asking a court to make a preliminary reference are:

• Is the national forum a court or tribunal of a Member State? This has been interpreted quite broadly so there should not usually be a problem.

• Does the national court have a discretion to refer or can it be compelled to do so? Only courts against whose decisions there is no judicial remedy must make a reference, all others have a discretion.

• Is a preliminary ruling on the EC point necessary to enable the national court to give a judgment in the case? If not, then no reference should be made. This issue is one that tends to deter first instance courts from making references, as they will not usually have found the material facts in the case by the time they must decide if the EC point is 'necessary' or not.

When a preliminary ruling is received by a national court, it is binding in those proceedings. It is not binding in other litigation but the judgment of the Court of Justice in the case will usually have several points of general application. Private individuals and Member States are usually well-advised to heed such rulings even though they were not parties to the original action.

See also Chapter 32 of the **Advocacy Manual**.

9.3 Action to Annul

There are two basic hurdles which must be cleared by an applicant if the action to annul is to succeed. First, is the act or measure which the applicant seeks to have annulled one which is susceptible to annulment? Fortunately in competition matters, measures which directly affect individuals or undertakings usually emanate from the Commission (see e.g. Regulation 17/62, **Appendix 1**); acts of the Commission are reviewable. Further, does the act have any legal effect? If it is merely a preliminary or administrative measure which is simply advisory (like a report of the Hearing Officer, see **7.6.4**) then it cannot be annulled.

The second hurdle is to establish a sufficient interest in the applicant to mount a challenge to the measure. Privileged parties (the Council, Commission and Member States) are assumed to have sufficient interest. Private applicants (natural or legal persons) must demonstrate an interest in the measure. In competition cases, they can usually do so as being the addressee of the measure (a decision finding an infringement of Article 81(1) (ex 85(1)), say, and imposing a fine) or as the complainant. Complainants have an almost automatic sufficient interest in the case generated by their complaint and should have no trouble showing that a decision (perhaps to close the Commission's file in a case) is of 'direct and individual concern' to them (cf. *Metro SB-Grossmarkte* v *Commission* (26/76) [1977] ECR 1901).

There is a limitation period of two months, which usually runs from the date of publication of the measure. The safest course is to start proceedings as soon as the adverse decision is discovered by the applicant. The four grounds on which the act may be annulled are:

(a) Lack of competence (similar to *ultra vires* in English administrative law).

(b) Infringement of an essential procedural requirement (whether any particular procedural requirement will be seen as 'essential' is determined on a case-by-case approach; case-law precedent is a good guide but one example would be the suspect undertaking's right to be heard in a competition investigation).

(c) Infringement of the EC Treaty itself or a rule of law relating to its application (this might include a challenge to a Commission decision finding an infringement of Article 81(1) (ex 85(1)) on its merits, for example; or a general principle of law may be used, such as *proportionality*, to attack the amount of a fine in a competition case).

(d) Misuse of power (the motives of the institution or official responsible for the measure will be examined).

As the comments perhaps indicate, grounds (b) and (c) are those most often used by aggrieved parties in competition cases. In the event of success, the measure is annulled. That does not prevent the institution from having another go. So if an 'improved' repetition of the relevant procedure can cure the previous infringement of an essential procedural requirement, the same measure may be promulgated for a second time and the applicant has won the battle but still lost the war (cf. the *Polypropylene Cartel* cases where decisions involving millions of ECU were annulled but then re-appeared with the complaint cured and the fines still as high as they had been in the first decision; see *Commission* v *BASF AG* (C-137/92P) [1994] ECR I-2555).

9.4 Failure to Act

This procedure is used to try to compel an EC institution (in competition cases, usually the Commission) to act. The applicant must therefore show the absence of an act, that the institution was under a duty to act and that this duty was to address an act to the applicant. The duty may be imposed on the institution either by the Treaty or under secondary legislation. Natural or legal persons may use Article 232 (ex 175). The applicant should write to the institution, requiring it to 'define its position' and giving it two months to do so. The court procedure under Article 232 (ex 175) can be launched in the absence of satisfactory action by the end of that two-month period. It should be noted that, in competition cases, a complainant cannot oblige the Commission to launch an investigation into their complaint. See *Automec srl* v *Commission* (T-24/90) [1992] ECR II-2223:

Where a complaint has been submitted to the Commission under Article 3 of Regulation No. 17, it is not bound either to give a decision on the existence of the alleged infringement unless the subject-matter of the complaint falls within its exclusive purview, as in the case of the withdrawal of an exemption granted under Article 85(3) [now 81(3)] of the Treaty, or to conduct an investigation.

9.5   Action for Damages

This procedure can be found in Article 288(2) (ex 215(2)), EC Treaty and is used to determine the non-contractual liability of the EC. The EC is required to 'make good any damage caused by its institutions or by its servants in the performance of their duties'. To succeed in a claim, an applicant must satisfy four criteria.

(a)   damage must have been suffered, usually by the applicant;

(b)   a Community institution or its servants must have acted, or omitted to act, in the performance of its duties;

(c)   there must be a causal connection between the act (or omission) and the damage;

(d)   the act or omission must be 'wrongful', i.e. there must be an element of 'fault' involved.

See e.g., *Campagnia Italiana Alcool SAS Di Mario Mariano & Co.* v *Commission* (C-358/90) [1992] 2 CMLR 876. To date, this action has not been of particular use in connection with acts or omissions of the Commission in its application of the competition rules; it is rarely used and even more rarely successful.

9.6   Compelling Member States to Act

Member States are often under an obligation to act, pursuant to the EC Treaty. This may be in the context of implementing directives into national law, for example. An action may be brought against a Member State for its failure to act as required. The action is brought either by the Commission (under Article 226 (ex 169), EC Treaty) or another Member State (under Article 227 (ex 170), EC Treaty). Due to political sensitivities, the Commission invokes proceedings under Article 226 rarely and, perhaps to avoid casting the first stone, Article 227 is hardly ever used by Member States. These procedures are not open to natural or legal persons. However, such individuals may still obtain redress for damage suffered as the result of a Member State's failure to act. This has been established clearly by the preliminary rulings of the Court of Justice in *Francovich* v *Italy* and *Brasserie du Pêcheur*. If a Member State is under a duty to implement an EC measure into its national legal system and fails to do so by the appointed date, then anyone who suffers damage as the result of such non-implementation may bring an action against the State and the State will effectively be estopped from denying liability. This type of direct redress may prove to be more efficacious than the procedures provided in the Treaty for ensuring that the Member States fulfil their obligations.

9.7   Appeals from the Court of First Instance to the Court of Justice

As mentioned earlier, private litigants who use Articles 230 (ex 173) or 232 (ex 175) in competition cases will begin their claims in the Court of First Instance (CFI). An unsuccessful litigant may appeal to the Court of Justice. Such appeal is to be made within two months of the appellant being notified of the final decision of the CFI. One may also appeal against a decision of the CFI on preliminary issues, such as lack of competence or inadmissibility (see Article 49, Protocol on the Statute of the Court of Justice of the EEC). It must be noted that appeals to the Court of Justice are limited to points of law only. The Court of Justice is vigilant to dismiss appeals on the ground that they ask the Court to re-try issues of fact.

TEN

THE RELATIONSHIP BETWEEN THE COMPETITION RULES, RULES ON FREE MOVEMENT OF GOODS AND INTELLECTUAL PROPERTY RIGHTS

10.1 The Rules on Free Movement

The Treaty rules on the free movement of goods are often understood to be those contained in Articles 28–31 (ex 30–37) of the Treaty. However, these Articles are simply 'Chapter 2' of a larger body of Articles which begins with Article 23 (ex 9). Article 23 appears under the heading 'Title I Free Movement of Goods'; the Articles with which we are concerned appear under the rather daunting heading of 'Prohibition of Quantitative Restrictions between Member States'.

The basic principle relates to the concept of a 'common market', and in Article 3(a) of the Treaty, the Community is set the task of ensuring the elimination (as between Member States) of quantitative restrictions on the import and export of goods, and of all other measures having equivalent effect (see **1.2.2** above). In essence, this elimination is carried into effect by Article 28 (ex 30) of the Treaty. Although some of the terminology may seem prolix, we are really concerned with one of the two main ways in which countries seek to protect their domestic economy. One way is to impose tariffs on imports from other countries: the removal of such tariffs (or customs duties) is the aim of Articles 23–25 (ex 9–17) of the Treaty. Articles 28–31 (ex 30–37) deal with the other basic way to stop imports: the use of quotas.

10.2 Article 28: No Quantitative Restrictions

It seems that Article 28 (ex 30) has been used by litigants in national courts with much greater frequency than the EC competition rules. Partly this is no doubt due to expediency: there is no enforcement mechanism equivalent to Regulation 17/62 in this field; so if firms want to have the benefit of the principle of free movement, they must invoke it for themselves in the courts of the Member States. This is possible since, from the end of the transitional period (1 January 1962), Article 28 (ex 30) has been directly effective in the national legal systems of the Member States.

Use of Article 28 (ex 30) by individuals in national courts tends to be defensive: often the owner of, say, a patent will start an action alleging infringement of the patent by a rival who is importing the offending product into the country from another Member State. The defendant may rely on Article 28 to try and overcome the (national) right to exclusivity held by the patentee. See, for example, *Allen & Hanburys Ltd* v *Generics (UK) Ltd* [1989] 1 WLR 414. In such a situation, the litigation is a purely private matter (albeit that the challenge to the exercise of the patent right involves a challenge to the

State through its law on patents). An alternative, still using Article 30 defensively, is where an individual or firm faces prosecution by either central or local government for commission of a regulatory offence.

Examples of such use occurring in the United Kingdom include *R* v *Henn and Darby* (34/79) [1979] ECR 3795. This case turned on the conflict between the basic EC freedom to import into a Member State goods which have been legally put onto the market in another Member State and the UK rules on the importation of obscene material. A highly-publicised use of Article 28 (ex 30) came in the spate of prosecutions of shops for trading on Sundays, in contravention of the Shops Act 1950. The basic defence in most of these cases was Article 30 (now 28): the suggestion being that the inability to trade on Sundays meant fewer sales and therefore fewer imports (i.e. an indirect quota). See *Torfaen Borough Council* v *B & Q plc* (145/88) [1990] 2 QB 19; *WH Smith Do-It-All Ltd* v *Peterborough City Council* [1990] 3 WLR 1131; *Stoke-on-Trent City Council* v *B & Q plc* [1991] 2 WLR 42.

As may be seen above, the use of Article 28 (ex 30) has grown over the years, and sometimes in rather unexpected ways. This has been the result of imaginative use of a typically broad interpretation of Article 30 (now 28) by the ECJ several years ago in *Cassis de Dijon* (*Rewe-Zentral AG* v *Bundesmonopolverwaltung für Branntwein* (120/78) [1979] ECR 649). A later judgment of the ECJ seemed to mark a watering-down of the impact of Article 28 (ex 30) on the circulation of goods around the Community: see *Keck and Mithouard* (C-267 and 268/91) [1993] ECR I-6097. This case, which turned on French legislation prohibiting the use of 'loss leaders' in retailing, found the ECJ in retreat from *Cassis*. In *Keck*, the ECJ held that rules governing selling arrangements and which applied to all traders alike in the territory were not caught by Article 30 (now 28).

A more recent preliminary ruling by the Court of Justice perhaps shows that Article 28 (ex 30) still has quite a broad application. A French law allowed for the denomination *montagne* to be applied to food products. This was intended to denote that the product in question originated in a mountain region, thus making it perhaps more attractive to a consumer. The French law went on to restrict the use of this denomination to products made in France from domestic raw materials. Imported products could not benefit from this denomination and so:

> the measure in question facilitates the marketing of goods of domestic [i.e. French] origin to the detriment of imported goods. In such circumstances, the application of the measure, even if restricted to domestic producers, in itself creates and maintains a difference of treatment between those two categories of goods, hindering, at least potentially, intra-Community trade.

The Article was held to preclude the application of the French law, even though the defendants in the proceedings in question were French nationals being prosecuted in France for misapplication of the denomination, a breach of French law. Interestingly, the Advocate General (Francis Jacobs) had previously proposed in his Opinion that Article 30 (now 28) 'has no application to a national law in so far as that law applies to national products'. See *Criminal proceedings* v *Jacques Pistre and others* (C-321 to 324/94), [1997] ECR I-2343.

Useful article: Anthony Arnull, 'What shall we do on Sunday?', (1991) ELR 112.

10.3   Free Movement and Intellectual Property Rights

As stated above, Article 28 (ex 30) aims to stop quotas: that is, the ability of a Member State to limit the volume of imports into the country. The same effect as a quota can be achieved in a much more absolute fashion by reliance on intellectual property rights. These are held (usually) in the hands of natural or legal persons rather than the State, and are much more specific than State-imposed quotas. For example, AB plc may hold a UK patent for a baby buggy. They can then stop imports into the UK of buggies which infringe their patent, but not of other buggies. The State may (in theory) impose a quota limit on imports of *all* baby buggies if it chooses; or, to alter the illustration, the State may impose a blanket ban on the import of French baby buggies only: no individual intellectual property right holder could (or would) do this.

The main difference which usually exists between State action and that taken by individuals using intellectual property rights, is that the State will impose a quota (e.g. no more than 100,000 Korean-built cars will be imported into the UK in 2001), whereas the holder of an intellectual property right wants an absolute ban on all infringing goods. This total prohibition can in principle be attained, because intellectual property rights commonly give their owner a monopoly over the item protected by the right.

10.4 Intellectual Property Rights

When referring above to intellectual property rights, a universal approach was intended, covering all such rights. It is useful to explain, very briefly, what was meant by such an all-embracing term.

10.4.1 PATENTS

The relevant statute is the Patents Act 1977. A patent is the grant of a monopoly right to (usually) the inventor of a product or process for a definite length of time. The invention must be clearly defined in the application for a patent and, to quote from WR Cornish (in *Patents, Copyright, Trademarks and Allied Rights*, Sweet and Maxwell), the invention must be 'patentable, i.e. (i) it must be novel, (ii) it must involve an inventive step, (iii) it must be capable of industrial application, and (iv) it must not belong to one of the categories of excluded subject-matter' (see Patents Act 1977, s. 1(1)).

Perhaps the most important consideration for us is the protection given by a patent to its owner. According to s. 60 of the Patents Act 1977, the patent in a product is infringed if (without the patentee's consent) someone 'makes it; disposes of it; offers to dispose of it; uses it; imports it; or keeps it whether for disposal or otherwise'.

The duration of a United Kingdom patent is from the date of publication of its grant (in the Patent Comptroller's journal) until 20 years after the patent was applied for (s. 25).

10.4.2 COPYRIGHT

The relevant statute is the Copyright, Designs and Patents Act 1988. Basically, copyright is an exclusive right to do certain specific acts in relation to specified types of work. For example, one may have the copyright in 'original literary, dramatic, musical or artistic works' (Copyright, Designs and Patents Act 1988, s. 1(1)(a)). The copyright owner then has the exclusive right to do the following acts in the United Kingdom:

(a) to copy the work;

(b) to issue copies of the work to the public;

(c) to perform, show or play the work in public;

(d) to broadcast the work or include it in a cable programme service;

(e) to make an adaptation of the work or do any of the above in relation to an adaptation (s. 16(1)).

For anyone else to do these acts without the licence of the copyright owner is an infringement of copyright, which may give rise to a claim for damages, an injunction and an account (see s. 16(2) and s. 96).

Copyright in a literary, dramatic, musical or artistic work expires at the end of 70 years after the death of the author (s. 12, as amended pursuant to EC Council Directive 93/98).

10.4.3   TRADEMARK

'Trademark' has a statutory definition in the Trademarks Act 1938. This can be summarised as:

a mark ... used ... in relation to goods for the purpose of indicating a connection in the course of trade between the goods and some person having the right either as proprietor or as registered user to use the mark, whether with or without any identification of the identity of that person.

A mark includes 'a device, brand, heading, label, ticket, name, signature, word, letter, numeral, or any combination thereof'.

Marks applied to services are also protected (see Trade Marks (Amendment) Act 1984, s. 1; Patents, Designs and Marks Act 1986, s. 2). Trade marks are of unlimited duration.

10.4.4   REGISTERED DESIGNS

The relevant statutes are the Registered Designs Act 1949 and the Copyright, Designs and Patents Act 1988. Often used to protect engineering drawings and the plans used when making a product (e.g. the 'blueprint' for an exhaust pipe on a particular model of car). A 'design right' (the 1988 Act, s. 213) lasts for a maximum of 15 years from the first recording of the design or its first use, whichever was earlier (s. 216). A 'registered design' lasts for five years from the date of registration (1949 Act, s. 8). The problem with both types of design is that they may be used to make the product without permission. An alternative problem is 'reverse engineering': a 'pirate' manufacturer obtains the product, determines its precise dimensions and composition, etc. and then makes it. The design owner could argue that this infringes the right in the design: see, for example, *British Leyland Motor Corp.* v *Armstrong Patents Co. Ltd* [1986] AC 577.

10.4.5   FOREIGN INTELLECTUAL PROPERTY LAW

Lastly, it should be noted that the above explanation is concerned with the position in English law. Definitions and the extent of protection given may vary from one country to another. It may be necessary in an individual case to have a knowledge of the particular intellectual property law of the country most closely connected with the proceedings (usually the country which granted the right under consideration). See, for example, the judgment of the ECJ in *Keurkoop* v *Nancy Kean Gifts* (144/81) [1982] ECR 2853 on the protection of designs and models in the Member States:

in the present state of Community law and in the absence of Community standard-ization or harmonization of laws the determination of the conditions and procedures under which such protection is granted is a matter for national rules. It is for the national legislature to determine which products qualify for protection, even if they form part of a unit already protected as such.

That was the position in 1982. There have been developments since then in terms of Community rights in intellectual property, in particular regarding harmonization of national rights. On 1 April 1996, the Office for Harmonization in the Internal Market ('OHIM') was opened in Alicante, Spain. This office deals with trademarks and is not part of the administrative structure based in Brussels. It aims to become self-financing through charging fees to register trade marks. The Community trademark was estab-lished in 1994 (see Regulation 40/94) and this is seen as most important in supporting the single internal market as it offers a single trademark for an EU market of 350 million consumers. The Community trademark gives its holder 'a uniform right applicable in all EU Member States on the strength of a single procedure which simplifies trademark policies at national level'. Noting that there are already more than three million trademarks in existence through the EU Member States, the OHIM is to take care that applications to register a sign do not duplicate signs already taken by prior rights. The OHIM also sees a role for itself in sharing 'with the courts in Member States the task of deciding on requests for invalidation of registered titles'. This carries echoes of the Notice issued by the Commission in 1993, on cooperation with national courts in enforcement of the competition rules. The OHIM's introductory document states that its activities are subject to Community law and the European Court is responsible for supervising the legality of OHIM decisions. The OHIM expects to apply existing Community jurisprudence in its decisions, including that on the exhaustion of rights. This can be seen in the OHIM declaration that:

> Where the proprietor of the trademark has proceeded or agreed to market goods under this trademark in a Member State of the European Union, he cannot prohibit their free movement in the European Union. This limitation on the rights conferred by the Community trademark is derived from the rule of exhaustion of those rights within the Community ... Parallel imports of products covered by the Community trademark from countries which are not members of the European Union are not subject to this rule and to this limitation ...

The OHIM may be accessed through the *europa* site on the Internet at http://europa.eu.int/agencies/ohim/english. This is an informative and helpful location for those interested in trademarks.

By comparison with the progress made on the Community trademark, the Community patent has stalled. There was a Convention on the Community Patent in 1975 and an Agreement relating to Community patents in 1989: neither was fully ratified. A Green Paper was published in 1997, by DGXV which is responsible for the single market, asking whether the Community Patent Convention of 1975 should be replaced by legislation which would allow innovators to obtain patent protection throughout the common market via a single application for a patent. As the (then) Commissioner for the single market has observed:

> The present system of patents in the Union is complex and expensive, and does not provide a unitary patent for all the member States. (Mario Monti.)

There is already a European patent, which is granted by the European Patent Office in Munich. In practice, this operates rather like a national patent. It does not give jurisdiction to the European Court to adjudicate on patent disputes; these continue to be justiciable in the national courts with all of the consequent problems of different procedures, limitation periods, etc. The single EU patent, suggested in the 1997 Green Paper, would sweep away such difficulties but it still does not exist. In February 1999, DGXV recorded that the need for a unitary patent, covering the entire territory of the EU, was expressed clearly during consultations on the Green Paper. A proposal to establish such a patent was published in February 1999. Then-Commissioner for the Single Market, Mario Monti, stated that 'We have made the introduction of a unitary patent valid throughout the Single Market a political priority'. Until such time as the proposal becomes law, the observation of the European Court in *Nancy Kean Gifts* remains pertinent.

10.5 Infringement of Intellectual Property Rights

It is important to note that, in order to make their grant effective, intellectual property rights give their holder the ability to stop others from abusing the monopoly. This abuse could occur in a variety of ways: making a patented product or using a patented process, presenting someone else's copyright work as your own, placing someone else's trademark on your goods, or using another's registered design to make a product. All of these acts can occur without infringing an intellectual property right if the holder of the right has given permission for the act, usually on payment of a royalty. Problems occur when such acts take place without proper permission. The nature of intellectual property law is that the right holder can stop any infringing activity — e.g., making, distributing or selling the offending articles — usually by getting a court injunction. This will forbid repetition, order the destruction of any remaining articles and require the infringer to account to the intellectual property right holder for the profits of the infringement.

10.6   Territorial Scope of Intellectual Property Rights

These rights are granted by the State and are usually good for the whole territory of that country. This results in the possibility that different firms or individuals will hold the same or very similar rights in different countries. There is also the possibility that, in a particular country, no one owns the intellectual property rights, or that no such right can be granted under the law of that country. Two examples may clarify the point:

(a) In the early years of the EC, Italy did not grant patent protection to pharmaceutical products. So, anyone could make a drug in Italy and sell it there without breaking Italian patent law. If company A imported the pharmaceutical product from Italy into the United Kingdom, where it was protected by a patent granted to company B, could B use its patent to stop the import?

(b) In Spain, it was not possible to obtain a patent for a new process, as distinct from a new product. If a Spanish firm used such a process to make product x, could the UK holder of a patent covering that process stop imports into the UK of the product from Spain?

The theory of a common market is that once goods are put into circulation legitimately in one Member State, they should be allowed to circulate through all other Member States. But to do so in these two examples would deprive the intellectual property right holder of the legitimate profits of his right. See, for example, the observation of the ECJ in the Italian *Renault* case (*Consorzio Italiano della Componentistica di Ricambio per Autoveicoli and SpA Maxicar* v *Regie Nationale des usines Renault* (53/87) [1988] ECR 6039):

It should be noted . . . that the authority of a proprietor of a protective right in respect of [a design] to oppose the manufacture by third parties, for the purposes of sale on the internal market or export, of products incorporating the design or to prevent the import of such products manufactured without its consent in other Member States constitutes the substance of his exclusive right. To prevent the application of the national legislation in such circumstances would therefore be tantamount to challenging the very existence of that right.

The history of Article 28 (ex 30) and its interpretation by the ECJ has largely revolved around the attempt to resolve the conflict between 'national' intellectual property rights and the 'supranational' Article 28 (ex 30). Those involved with intellectual property rights have tried to solve the problem by creating new intellectual property rights which have a Community-wide scope: e.g., the single Community patent and the Community trademark which would apply across national boundaries. These steps should achieve greater harmonization in the protection of intellectual property rights.

10.7   Abuse of an Intellectual Property Right

As well as 'gaps' in the protection of intellectual property, as indicated in **10.6**, there is also the possibility of intellectual property right holders abusing the protection the law gives them. Abuse is used subjectively here, to cover what might be seen as unjustifiable extensions of the exclusivity given by an intellectual property right. Examples of such behaviour can include the refusal without good reason to supply spare parts (where the design of the part is protected by an intellectual property right); charging an unfairly high price; or the deliberate splitting up of intellectual property rights held by the same firm in different countries in order to prevent parallel imports. A typical example of such market partitioning involved the German firm, Grundig.

Grundig had registered the trademark 'Gint' in several countries, including France. When it appointed an exclusive distributor of its products in France — Consten — it assigned its French trademark 'Gint' to Consten. In theory, this enabled Consten to stop any 'Gint'-marked goods being imported into France without its permission. If 'Gint' products were cheaper in Germany than in France, say, it might be profitable for someone outside the Grundig-Consten system to bulk buy the goods in Germany, then transport them into France and resell them there. This might result in Consten's prices being undercut *but* if Consten could bring a trademark infringement action to stop the unauthorised (parallel) imports, all would be well again for Consten. This was precisely what Consten attempted to do, with the result that the European Commission investigated and found that the two firms, Consten and Grundig, had infringed Article 85 (now 81) by having an agreement to stop parallel imports.

The ECJ has drawn a firm line between what it calls the *existence* and the *exhaustion* of intellectual property rights. Essentially, once a product has been put on the market in a Member State with the consent of (or by) the intellectual property right owner, the right is exhausted. That item is now in free circulation throughout the common market. The intellectual property right owner cannot use nationally-defined monopolies to stop parallel imports of the item. *But* whenever the product is marketed *without* the intellectual property owner's consent (e.g. pirate copies), the right has not been exhausted: any infringement may be stopped, using the appropriate national laws and remedies. As well as the *Consten and Grundig* v *Commission* (56 & 58/64) [1966] ECR 299 mentioned above, see also the '*Cassis de Dijon*' case: *Rewe-Zentral AG* v *Bundes-monopolverwaltung für Branntwein* (120/78) [1979] ECR 649.

The strict application of the doctrine of exhaustion of rights can be seen in the preliminary ruling of the Court of Justice in *Merck & Co. Inc and others* v *Primecrown and others*; *Beecham Group plc* v *Europharm of Worthing Ltd* (C-267/95 and 268/95), 5 December 1996, unreported. The plaintiffs in the English proceedings, Merck and Beecham, had marketed their pharmaceutical products in Spain and Portugal at a time when drugs could not be patented in those countries (no longer the position). The defendants had bought up quantities of the drugs in Spain and Portugal, at prices lower than those charged in the UK. The defendants then sought to import them into the UK and the plaintiffs brought proceedings for patent infringement. The Court of Justice ruled that, by putting their products on the market in Spain and Portugal, the plaintiffs had exhausted their rights in those goods. The drugs could circulate freely within the single market. If they had been under a *legal* obligation to market the products in Spain and Portugal, the position would be different:

> he cannot be deemed to have given his consent to the marketing of the products concerned and he is therefore entitled to oppose importation and marketing of those products in the State where they are protected.

But it has to be a *legal* obligation. The drugs involved in the cases were for the treatment of:

- hypertension;

- prostate problems;

- glaucoma;

and an antibiotic.

The Court of Justice ruled that:

> *ethical* obligations to provide supplies of drugs in Member States where they are needed, even though they are not patentable there, cannot provide a basis for derogating from the rule on free movement of goods.

APPENDICES

The EC legislation contained in Appendices 1, 2, 3 and 4 appears in its original form (as intended by the Treaty of Amsterdam, Article 12(3)). When reading those four Appendices you should note that, for example, references to Articles 85, 86 and 87 of the EC Treaty should be understood as references to Articles 81, 82 and 83 respectively, as renumbered by the Treaty of Amsterdam. References to other Articles, Titles and Sections of the EC Treaty have similarly been left unamended in these four Appendices.

APPENDIX ONE

REGULATION 17/62

Regulation No. 17 of the Council of 6 February 1962
First Regulation Implementing Articles 85 and 86 of the Treaty amended by
Regulation No. 59, by Regulation No. 118/63 EEC and by Regulation No.
2822/71/EEC

THE COUNCIL OF THE EUROPEAN ECONOMIC COMMUNITY,

Having regard to the Treaty establishing the European Economic Community, and in particular Article 87 thereof,

Having regard to the proposal from the Commission,

Having regard to the Opinion of the Economic and Social Committee,

Having regard to the Opinion of the European Parliament,

Whereas, in order to establish a system ensuring that competition shall not be distorted in the common market, it is necessary to provide for balanced application of Articles 85 and 86 in a uniform manner in the Member States;

Whereas in establishing the rules for applying Article 85(3) account must be taken of the need to ensure effective supervision and to simplify administration to the greatest possible extent;

Whereas it is accordingly necessary to make it obligatory, as a general principle, for undertakings which seek application of Article 85(3) to notify to the Commission their agreements, decisions and concerted practices;

Whereas, on the one hand, such agreements, decisions and concerted practices are probably very numerous and cannot therefore all be examined at the same time and, on the other hand, some of them have special features which may make them less prejudicial to the development of the common market;

Whereas there is consequently a need to make more flexible arrangements for the time being in respect of certain categories of agreement, decisions and concerted practices without prejudging their validity under Article 85;

Whereas it may be in the interest of undertakings to know whether any agreements, decisions or practices to which they are party, or propose to become party, may lead to action on the part of the Commission pursuant to Article 85(1) or Article 86;

Whereas, in order to secure uniform application of Articles 85 and 86 in the common market, rules must be made under which the Commission, acting in close and constant liaison with the competent authorities of the Member States, may take the requisite measures for applying those Articles;

Whereas for this purpose the Commission must have the cooperation of the competent authorities of the Member States and be empowered, throughout the common market, to require such information to be supplied and to undertake such investigations as are necessary to bring to light any agreement, decision or concerted practice prohibited by Article 85(1) or any abuse of a dominant position prohibited by Article 86;

Whereas in order to carry out its duty of ensuring that the provisions of the Treaty are applied the Commission must be empowered to address to undertakings or associations of undertakings recommendations and decisions for the purpose of bringing to an end infringements of Articles 85 and 86;

Whereas compliance with Articles 85 and 86 and the fulfilment of obligations imposed on undertakings and associations of undertakings under this Regulation must be enforceable by means of fines and periodic penalty payments;

Whereas undertakings concerned must be accorded the right to be heard by the Commission, third parties whose interests may be affected by a decision must be given the opportunity of submitting their comments beforehand, and it must be ensured that wide publicity is given to decisions taken;

Whereas all decisions taken by the Commission under this Regulation are subject to review by the Court of Justice under the conditions specified in the Treaty; whereas it is moreover desirable to confer upon the Court of Justice, pursuant to Article 172, unlimited jurisdiction in respect of decisions under which the Commission imposes fines or periodic penalty payments;

Whereas this Regulation may enter into force without prejudice to any other provisions that may hereafter be adopted pursuant to Article 87,

HAS ADOPTED THIS REGULATION:

Article 1   Basic provision

Without prejudice to Articles 6, 7 and 23 of this Regulation, agreements, decisions and concerted practices of the kind described in Article 85(1) of the Treaty and the abuse of a dominant position in the market, within the meaning of Article 86 of the Treaty, shall be prohibited, no prior decision to that effect being required.

Article 2   Negative clearance

Upon application by the undertakings or associations of undertakings concerned, the Commission may certify that, on the basis of the facts in its possession, there are no grounds under Article 85(1) or Article 86 of the Treaty for action on its part in respect of an agreement, decision or practice.

Article 3   Termination of infringements

1.   Where the Commission, upon application or upon its own initiative, finds that there is infringement of Article 85 or Article 86 of the Treaty, it may by decision require the undertakings or associations of undertakings concerned to bring such infringement to an end.

2.   Those entitled to make application are:
   (a)   Member States;
   (b)   natural or legal persons who claim a legitimate interest.

3.   Without prejudice to the other provisions of this Regulation, the Commission may, before taking a decision under paragraph 1, address to the undertakings or associations of undertakings concerned recommendations for termination of the infringement.

Article 4   Notification of new agreements, decisions and practices

1.   Agreements, decisions and concerted practices of the kind described in Article 85(1) of the Treaty which come into existence after the entry into force of this Regulation and in respect of which the parties seek application of Article 85(3) must be notified to the Commission. Until they have been notified, no decision in application of Article 85(3) may be taken.

2.   Paragraph 1 shall not apply to agreements, decisions and concerted practices where:

(1)   the only parties thereto are undertakings from one Member State and the agreements, decisions or practices do not relate either to imports or to exports between Member States;

(2)   not more than two undertakings are party thereto, and the agreements only:

(a)   restrict the freedom of one party to the contract in determining the prices or conditions of business upon which the goods which he has obtained from the other party to the contract may be resold; or

(b)   impose restrictions on the exercise of the rights of the assignee or user of industrial property rights — in particular patents, utility models, designs or trade marks — or of the person entitled under a contract to the assignment, or grant, of the right to use a method of manufacture or knowledge relating to the use and to the application of industrial processes;

(3) they have as their sole object:
    (a) the development or uniform application of standards or types; or
    (b) joint research and development;
    (c) specialization in the manufacture of products, including agreements necessary for achieving this,
—where the products which are the subject of specialization do not, in a substantial part of the common market, represent more than 15% of the volume of business done in identical products or those considered by consumers to be similar by reason of their characteristics, price and use, and
—where the total annual turnover of the participating undertakings does not exceed 200 million units of account.
These agreements, decisions and practices may be notified to the Commission.

Article 5   Notification of existing agreements, decisions and practices

1. Agreements, decisions and concerted practices of the kind described in Article 85(1) of the Treaty which are in existence at the date of entry into force of this Regulation and in respect of which the parties seek application of Article 85(3) shall be notified to the Commission before 1 November 1962. However notwithstanding the foregoing provisions any agreements, decisions and concerted practice to which not more than two undertakings are party shall be notified before 1 February 1963.

2. Paragraph 1 shall not apply to agreements, decisions or concerted practices falling within Article 4(2); these may be notified to the Commission.

Article 6   Decisions pursuant to Article 85(3)

1. Whenever the Commission takes a decision pursuant to Article 85(3) of the Treaty, it shall specify therein the date from which the decision shall take effect. Such date shall not be earlier than the date of notification.

2. The second sentence of paragraph 1 shall not apply to agreements, decisions or concerted practices falling within Article 4(2) and Article 5(2), nor to those falling within Article 5(1) which have been notified within the time limit specified in Article 5(1).

Article 7   Special provisions for existing agreements, decisions and practices

1. Where agreements, decisions and concerted practices in existence at the date of entry into force of this Regulation and notified within the time limits specified in Article 5(1) do not satisfy the requirements of Article 85(3) of the Treaty and the undertakings or associations of undertakings concerned cease to give effect to them or modify them in such a manner that they no longer fall within the prohibition contained in Article 85(1) or that they satisfy the requirements of Article 85(3), the prohibition contained in Article 85(1) shall apply only for a period fixed by the Commission. A decision by the Commission pursuant to the foregoing sentence shall not apply as against undertakings and associations of undertakings which did not expressly consent to the notification.

2. Paragraph 1 shall apply to agreements, decisions and concerted practices falling within Article 4(2) which are in existence at the date of entry into force of this Regulation if they are notified before 1 January 1967.

Article 8   Duration and revocation of decisions under Article 85(3)

1. A decision in application of Article 85(3) of the Treaty shall be issued for a specified period and conditions and obligations may be attached thereto.

2. A decision may on application be renewed if the requirements of Article 85(3) of the Treaty continue to be satisfied.

3. The Commission may revoke or amend its decision or prohibit specified acts by the parties:
    (a) where there has been a change in any of the facts which were basic to the making of the decision;
    (b) where the parties commit a breach of any obligation attached to the decision;
    (c) where the decision is based on incorrect information or was induced by deceit;
    (d) where the parties abuse the exemption from the provisions of Article 85(1) of the Treaty granted to them by the decision.

In cases to which subparagraphs (b), (c) or (d) apply, the decision may be revoked with retroactive effect.

Article 9   Powers

1.   Subject to review of its decision by the Court of Justice, the Commission shall have sole power to declare Article 85(1) inapplicable pursuant to Article 85(3) of the Treaty.

2.   The Commission shall have power to apply Article 85(1) and Article 86 of the Treaty; this power may be exercised notwithstanding that the time limits specified in Article 5(1) and in Article 7(2) relating to notification have not expired.

3.   As long as the Commission has not initiated any procedure under Articles 2, 3, or 6, the authorities of the Member States shall remain competent to apply Article 85(1) and Article 86 in accordance with Article 88 of the Treaty; they shall remain competent in this respect notwithstanding that the time limits specified in Article 5(1) and in Article 7(2) relating to notification have not expired.

Article 10   Liaison with the authorities of the Member States

1.   The Commission shall forthwith transmit to the competent authorities of the Member States a copy of the applications and notifications together with copies of the most important documents lodged with the Commission for the purpose of establishing the existence of infringements of Articles 85 or 86 of the Treaty or of obtaining negative clearance or a decision in application of Article 85(3).

2.   The Commission shall carry out the procedure set out in paragraph 1 in close and constant liaison with the competent authorities of the Member States; such authorities shall have the right to express their views upon that procedure.

3.   An Advisory Committee on Restrictive Practices and Monopolies shall be consulted prior to the taking of any decision following upon a procedure under paragraph 1, and of any decision concerning the renewal, amendment or revocation of a decision pursuant to Article 85(3) of the Treaty.

4.   The Advisory Committee shall be composed of officials competent in the matter of restrictive practices and monopolies. Each Member State shall appoint an official to represent it who, if prevented from attending, may be replaced by another official.

5.   The consultation shall take place at a joint meeting convened by the Commission; such meeting shall be held not earlier than fourteen days after dispatch of the notice convening it. The notice shall, in respect of each case to be examined, be accompanied by a summary of the case together with an indication of the most important documents, and a preliminary draft decision.

6.   The Advisory Committee may deliver an opinion notwithstanding that some of its members or their alternates are not present. A report of the outcome of the consultative proceedings shall be annexed to the draft decision. It shall not be made public.

Article 11   Requests for information

1.   In carrying out the duties assigned to it by Article 89 and by provisions adopted under Article 87 of the Treaty, the Commission may obtain all necessary information from the Governments and competent authorities of the Member States and from undertakings and associations of undertakings.

2.   When sending a request for information to an undertaking or association of undertakings, the Commission shall at the same time forward a copy of the request to the competent authority of the Member State in whose territory the seat of the undertaking or association of undertakings is situated.

3.   In its request the Commission shall state the legal basis and the purpose of the request and also the penalties provided for in Article 15(1)(b) for supplying incorrect information.

4.   The owners of the undertakings or their representatives and, in the case of legal persons, companies or firms, or of associations having no legal personality, the persons authorized to represent them by law or by their constitution, shall supply the information requested.

5.   Where an undertaking or association of undertakings does not supply the information requested within the time limit fixed by the Commission, or supplies incomplete information, the Commission shall by decision require the information to be supplied. The decision shall specify what information is required, fix an appropriate time limit within which it is to be supplied and indicate the penalties provided for in Article 15(1)(b) and Article 16(1)(c) and the right to have the decision reviewed by the Court of Justice.

6.   The Commission shall at the same time forward a copy of its decision to the competent authority of the Member State in whose territory the seat of the undertaking or association of undertakings is situated.

Article 12   Inquiry into sectors of the economy

1.   If in any sector of the economy the trend of trade between Member States, price movements, inflexibility of prices or other circumstances suggest that in the economic sector concerned competition is being restricted or distorted within the common market, the Commission may decide to conduct a general inquiry into that economic sector and in the course thereof may request undertakings in the sector concerned to supply the information necessary for giving effect to the principles formulated in Articles 85 and 86 of the Treaty and for carrying out the duties entrusted to the Commission.

2.   The Commission may in particular request every undertaking or association of undertakings in the economic sector concerned to communicate to it all agreements, decisions and concerted practices which are exempt from notification by virtue of Article 4(2) and Article 5(2).

3.   When making inquiries pursuant to paragraph 2, the Commission shall also request undertakings or groups of undertakings whose size suggests that they occupy a dominant position within the common market or a substantial part thereof to supply to the Commission such particulars of the structure of the undertakings and of their behaviour as are requisite to an appraisal of their position in the light of Article 86 of the Treaty.

4.   Article 10(3) to (6) and Articles 11, 13 and 14 shall apply correspondingly.

Article 13   Investigations by the authorities of the Member States

1.   At the request of the Commission, the competent authorities of the Member States shall undertake the investigations which the Commission considers to be necessary under Article 14(1), or which it has ordered by decision pursuant to Article 14(3). The officials of the competent authorities of the Member States responsible for conducting these investigations shall exercise their powers upon production of an authorization in writing issued by the competent authority of the Member State in whose territory the investigation is to be made. Such authorization shall specify the subject matter and purpose of the investigation.

2.   If so requested by the Commission or by the competent authority of the Member State in whose territory the investigation is to be made, the officials of the Commission may assist the officials of such authority in carrying out their duties.

Article 14   Investigating powers of the Commission

1.   In carrying out the duties assigned to it by Article 89 and by provisions adopted under Article 87 of the Treaty, the Commission may undertake all necessary investigations into undertakings and associations of undertakings. To this end the officials authorized by the Commission are empowered:

    (a)   to examine the books and other business records;

    (b)   to take copies of or extracts from the books and business records;

    (c)   to ask for oral explanations on the spot;

    (d)   to enter any premises, land and means of transport of undertakings.

2.   The officials of the Commission authorized for the purpose of these investigations shall exercise their powers upon production of an authorization in writing specifying the subject matter and purpose of the investigation and the penalties provided for in Article 15(1)(c) in cases where production of the required books or other business records is incomplete. In good time before the investigation, the Commission shall inform the competent authority of the Member State in whose territory the same is to be made of the investigation and of the identity of the authorized officials.

3.   Undertakings and associations of undertakings shall submit to investigations ordered by decision of the Commission. The decision shall specify the subject matter and purpose of the investigation, appoint the date on which it is to begin and indicate

the penalties provided for in Article 15(1)(c) and Article 16(1)(d) and the right to have the decision reviewed by the Court of Justice.

4. The Commission shall take decisions referred to in paragraph 3 after consultation with the competent authority of the Member State in whose territory the investigation is to be made.

5. Officials of the competent authority of the Member State in whose territory the investigation is to be made may, at the request of such authority or of the Commission, assist the officials of the Commission in carrying out their duties.

6. Where an undertaking opposes an investigation ordered pursuant to this Article, the Member State concerned shall afford the necessary assistance to the officials authorized by the Commission to enable them to make their investigation. Member States shall, after consultation with the Commission, take the necessary measures to this end before 1 October 1962.

Article 15   Fines

1. The Commission may by decision impose on undertakings or associations of undertakings fines of from 100 to 5,000 units of account where, intentionally or negligently:

(a)   they supply incorrect or misleading information in an application pursuant to Article 2 or in a notification pursuant to Article 4 or 5; or

(b)   they supply incorrect information in response to a request made pursuant to Article 11(3) or (5) or to Article 12, or do not supply information within the time limit fixed by a decision taken under Article 11(5); or

(c)   they produce the required books or other business records in incomplete form during investigations under Article 13 or 14, or refuse to submit to an investigation ordered by decision issued in implementation of Article 14(3).

2. The Commission may by decision impose on undertakings or associations of undertakings fines of from 1,000 to 1,000,000 units of account, or a sum in excess thereof but not exceeding 10% of the turnover in the preceding business year of each of the undertakings participating in the infringement where, either intentionally or negligently:

(a)   they infringe Article 85(1) or Article 86 of the Treaty; or

(b)   they commit a breach of any obligation imposed pursuant to Article 8(1).

In fixing the amount of the fine, regard shall be had both to the gravity and to the duration of the infringement.

3. Article 10(3) to (6) shall apply.

4. Decisions taken pursuant to paragraphs 1 and 2 shall not be of a criminal law nature.

5. The fines provided for in paragraph 2 (a) shall not be imposed in respect of acts taking place:

(a)   after notification to the Commission and before its decision in application of Article 85(3) of the Treaty, provided they fall within the limits of the activity described in the notification;

(b)   before notification and in the course of agreements, decisions or concerted practices in existence at the date of entry into force of this Regulation, provided that notification was effected within the time limits specified in Article 5(1) and Article 7(2).

6. Paragraph 5 shall not have effect where the Commission has informed the undertakings concerned that after preliminary examination it is of the opinion that Article 85(1) of the Treaty applies and that application of Article 85(3) is not justified.

Article 16   Periodic penalty payments

1. The Commission may by decision impose on undertakings or associations of undertakings periodic penalty payments of from 50 to 1,000 units of account per day, calculated from the date appointed by the decision, in order to compel them:

(a)   to put an end to an infringement of Article 85 or 86 of the Treaty, in accordance with a decision taken pursuant to Article 3 of this Regulation;

(b)   to refrain from any act prohibited under Article 8(3);

(c)   to supply complete and correct information which it has requested by decision taken pursuant to Article 11(5);

(d)   to submit to an investigation which it has ordered by decision taken pursuant to Article 14(3).

2.   *Where the undertakings or associations of undertakings have satisfied the obligation which it was the purpose of the periodic penalty payment to enforce, the Commission may fix the total amount of the periodic penalty payment at a lower figure than that which would arise under the original decision.*
3.   *Article 10(3) to (6) shall apply.*

Article 17   Review by the Court of Justice

The Court of Justice shall have unlimited jurisdiction within the meaning of Article 17 of the Treaty to review decisions whereby the Commission has fixed a fine or periodic penalty payment; it may cancel, reduce or increase the fine or periodic penalty payment imposed.

Article 18   Unit of account

For the purposes of applying Articles 15 to 17 the unit of account shall be that adopted in drawing up the budget of the Community in accordance with Articles 207 and 209 of the Treaty.

Article 19   Hearing of the parties and of third persons

1.   *Before taking decisions as provided for in Articles 2, 3, 6, 7, 8, 15 and 16, the Commission shall give the undertakings or associations of undertakings concerned the opportunity of being heard on the matters to which the Commission has taken objection.*
2.   *If the Commission or the competent authorities of the Member States consider it necessary, they may also hear other natural or legal persons. Applications to be heard on the part of such persons shall, where they show a sufficient interest, be granted.*
3.   *Where the Commission intends to give negative clearance pursuant to Article 2 or take a decision in application of Article 85(3) of the Treaty, it shall publish a summary of the relevant application or notification and invite all interested third parties to submit their observations within a time limit which it shall fix being not less than one month. Publication shall have regard to the legitimate interest of undertakings in the protection of their business secrets.*

Article 20   Professional secrecy

1.   *Information acquired as a result of the application of Articles 11, 12, 13 and 14 shall be used only for the purpose of the relevant request or investigation.*
2.   *Without prejudice to the provisions of Articles 19 and 21, the Commission and the competent authorities of the Member States, their officials and other servants shall not disclose information acquired by them as a result of the application of this Regulation and of the kind covered by the obligation of professional secrecy.*
3.   *The provisions of paragraphs 1 and 2 shall not prevent publication of general information or surveys which do not contain information relating to particular undertakings or associations of undertakings.*

Article 21   Publication of decisions

1.   *The Commission shall publish the decisions which it takes pursuant to Articles 2, 3, 6, 7 and 8.*
2.   *The publication shall state the names of the parties and the main content of the decision; it shall have regard to the legitimate interest of undertakings in the protection of their business secrets.*

Article 22   Special provisions

1.   *The Commission shall submit to the Council proposals for making certain categories of agreement, decision and concerted practice falling within Article 4(2) or Article 5(2) compulsorily notifiable under Article 4 or 5.*
2.   *Within one year from the date of entry into force of this Regulation, the Council shall examine, on a proposal from the Commission, what special provisions might be made for exempting from the provisions of this Regulation agreements, decisions and concerted practices falling within Article 4(2) or Article 5(2).*

Article 23   Transitional provisions applicable to decisions of authorities of the Member States

1.   *Agreements, decisions and concerted practices of the kind described in Article 85(1) of the Treaty to which, before the entry into force of this Regulation, the competent authority of a Member State has declared Article 85(1) to be inapplicable pursuant to Article 85(3) shall not be subject to compulsory notification under Article 5. The decision of the competent authority of the Member State shall be deemed to be a decision within the meaning of Article 6; it shall cease to be valid upon expiration of the period fixed by such authority but in any event not more than three years after the entry into force of this Regulation. Article 8(3) shall apply.*

2.   *Applications for renewal of decisions of the kind described in paragraph 1 shall be decided upon by the Commission in accordance with Article 8(2).*

Article 24   Implementing provisions

The Commission shall have power to adopt implementing provisions concerning the form, content and other details of applications pursuant to Articles 2 and 3, and of notifications pursuant to Articles 4 and 5, and concerning hearings pursuant to Article 19(1) and (2).

This Regulation shall be binding in its entirety and directly applicable in all Member States.[1, 2]

---

[1] **Documents concerning the Accession**
Article 25
1.   As regards agreements, decisions and concerted practices to which Article 85 of the Treaty applies by virtue of accession, the date of accession shall be substituted for the date of entry into force of this Regulation in every place where reference is made in this Regulation to this latter date.
2.   Agreements, decisions and concerted practices existing at the date of accession to which Article 85 of the Treaty applies by virtue of accession shall be notified pursuant to Article 5(1) or Article 7(1) and (2) within six months from the date of accession.
3.   Fines under Article 15(2)(a) shall not be imposed in respect of any act prior to notification of the agreements, decisions and practices to which paragraph 2 applies and which have been notified within the period therein specified.
4.   New Member States shall take the measures referred to in Article 14(6) within six months from the date of accession after consulting the Commission.
(OJ L 173, 27.3.1972, p. 92).
[2] **Documents concerning the accession of the Hellenic Republic, the Kingdom of Spain and the Portuguese Republic**
The following paragraph is added to Article 25:
'5.   The provisions of paragraphs 1-4 above still apply in the same way in the case of the accession of the Hellenic Republic, the Kingdom of Spain and of the Portuguese Republic.'
(OJ L 302, 15.11.1985, p. 165).

EXTRACTS FROM BLOCK EXEMPTIONS 1983/83 AND 1984/83

A2.1 Extracts from Regulation 1983/83 — the Block Exemption for Exclusive Distribution Agreements

COMMISSION REGULATION (EEC) No. 1983/83 OF 22 JUNE 1983 on the application of Article 85(3) of the Treaty to categories of exclusive distribution agreements

THE COMMISSION OF THE EUROPEAN COMMUNITIES,

Having regard to the Treaty establishing the European Economic Community,

Having regard to Council Regulation No. 19/65/EEC of 2 March 1965 on the application of Article 85(3) of the Treaty to certain categories of agreements and concerted practices as last amended by the Act of Accession of Greece, and in particular Article 1 thereof,

Having published a draft of this Regulation,

Having consulted the Advisory Committee on Restrictive Practices and Dominant Positions,

(1) Whereas Regulation No. 19/65/EEC empowers the Commission to apply Article 85(3) of the Treaty by regulation to certain categories of bilateral exclusive distribution agreements and analogous concerted practices falling within Article 85(1);

(2) Whereas experience to date makes it possible to define a category of agreements and concerted practices which can be regarded as normally satisfying the conditions laid down in Article 85(3);

(3) Whereas exclusive distribution agreements of the category defined in Article 1 of this Regulation may fall within the prohibition contained in Article 85(1) of the Treaty; whereas this will apply only in exceptional cases to exclusive agreements of this kind to which only undertakings from one Member State are party and which concern the resale of goods within that Member State; whereas, however, to the extent that such agreements may affect trade between Member States and also satisfy all the requirements set out in this Regulation there is no reason to withhold from them the benefit of the exemption by category;

(4) Whereas it is not necessary expressly to exclude from the defined category those agreements which do not fulfil the conditions of Article 85(1) of the Treaty;

(5) Whereas exclusive distribution agreements lead in general to an improvement in distribution because the undertaking is able to concentrate its sales activities, does not need to maintain numerous business relations with a larger number of dealers and is able, by dealing with only one dealer, to overcome more easily distribution difficulties in international trade resulting from linguistic, legal and other differences;

(6)   Whereas exclusive distribution agreements facilitate the promotion of sales of a product and lead to intensive marketing and to continuity of supplies while at the same time rationalizing distribution; whereas they stimulate competition between the products of different manufacturers; whereas the appointment of an exclusive distributor who will take over sales promotion, customer services and carrying of stocks is often the most effective way, and sometimes indeed the only way, for the manufacturer to enter a market and compete with other manufacturers already present; whereas this is particularly so in the case of small and medium-sized undertakings; whereas it must be left to the contracting parties to decide whether and to what extent they consider it desirable to incorporate in the agreements terms providing for the promotion of sales;

(7)   Whereas, as a rule, such exclusive distribution agreements also allow consumers a fair share of the resulting benefit as they gain directly from the improvement in distribution, and their economic and supply position is improved as they can obtain products manufactured in particular in other countries more quickly and more easily;

(8)   Whereas this Regulation must define the obligations restricting competition which may be included in exclusive distribution agreements; whereas the other restrictions on competition allowed under this Regulation in addition to the exclusive supply obligation produce a clear division of functions between the parties and compel the exclusive distributor to concentrate his sales efforts on the contract goods and the contract territory; whereas they are, where they are agreed only for the duration of the agreement, generally necessary in order to attain the improvement in the distribution of goods sought through exclusive distribution; whereas it may be left to the contracting parties to decide which of these obligations they include in their agreements; whereas further restrictive obligations and in particular those which limit the exclusive distributor's choice of customers or his freedom to determine his prices and conditions of sale cannot be exempted under this Regulation;

(9)   Whereas the exemption by category should be reserved for agreements for which it can be assumed with sufficient certainty that they satisfy the conditions of Article 85(3) of the Treaty;

(10)   Whereas it is not possible, in the absence of a case-by-case examination, to consider that adequate improvements in distribution occur where a manufacturer entrusts the distribution of his goods to another manufacturer with whom he is in competition; whereas such agreements should, therefore, be excluded from the exemption by category; whereas certain derogations from this rule in favour of small and medium-sized undertakings can be allowed;

(11)   Whereas consumers will be assured of a fair share of the benefits resulting from exclusive distribution only if parallel imports remain possible; whereas agreements relating to goods which the user can obtain only from the exclusive distributor should therefore be excluded from the exemption by category; whereas the parties cannot be allowed to abuse industrial property rights or other rights in order to create absolute territorial protection; whereas this does not prejudice the relationship between competition law and industrial property rights, since the sole object here is to determine the conditions for exemption by category;

(12)   Whereas, since competition at the distribution stage is ensured by the possibility of parallel imports, the exclusive distribution agreements covered by this Regulation will not normally afford any possibility of eliminating competition in respect of a substantial part of the products in question; whereas this is also true of agreements that allot to the exclusive distributor a contract territory covering the whole of the common market;

(13)   Whereas, in particular cases in which agreements or concerted practices satisfying the requirements of this Regulation nevertheless have effects incompatible with Article 85(3) of the Treaty, the Commission may withdraw the benefit of the exemption by category from the undertakings party to them;

(14)   Whereas agreements and concerted practices which satisfy the conditions set out in this Regulation need not be notified; whereas an undertaking may none the less in a particular case where real doubt exists, request the Commission to declare whether its agreements comply with this Regulation;

(15)   Whereas this Regulation does not affect the applicability of Commission Regulation (EEC) No. 3604/82 of 23 December 1982 on the application of Article 85(3) of the Treaty to categories of specialization agreements; whereas it does not exclude the application of Article 86 of the Treaty,

HAS ADOPTED THIS REGULATION:

Article 1
Pursuant to Article 85(3) of the Treaty and subject to the provisions of this Regulation, it is hereby declared that Article 85(1) of the Treaty shall not apply to agreements to which only two undertakings are party and whereby one party agrees with the other to supply certain goods for resale within the whole or a defined area of the common market only to that other.

Article 2
1. Apart from the obligation referred to in Article 1 no restriction on competition shall be imposed on the supplier other than the obligation not to supply the contract goods to users in the contract territory.

2. No restriction on competition shall be imposed on the exclusive distributor other than:

(a)   the obligation not to manufacture or distribute goods which compete with the contract goods;

(b)   the obligation to obtain the contract goods for resale only from the other party;

(c)   the obligation to refrain, outside the contract territory and in relation to the contract goods,

from seeking customers, from establishing any branch and from maintaining any distribution depot.

3. Article 1 shall apply notwithstanding that the exclusive distributor undertakes all or any of the following obligations:

(a)   to purchase complete ranges of goods or minimum quantities;

(b)   to sell the contract goods under trademarks, or packed and presented as specified by the other party;

(c)   to take measures for promotion of sales in particular:

— to advertise,

— to maintain a sales network or stock of goods,

— to provide customer and guarantee services,

— to employ staff having specialized or technical training.

Article 3
Article 1 shall not apply where:

(a)   manufacturers of identical goods or of goods which are considered by users as equivalent in view of their characteristics, price and intended use enter into reciprocal exclusive distribution agreements between themselves in respect of such goods;

(b)   manufacturers of identical goods or of goods which are considered by users as equivalent in view of their characteristics, price and intended use enter into a non-reciprocal exclusive distribution agreement between themselves in respect of such goods; unless at least one of them has a total annual turnover of no more than 100 million ECU;

(c)   users can obtain the contract goods in the contract territory only from the exclusive distributor and have no alternative source of supply outside the contract territory;

(d)   one or both of the parties makes it difficult for intermediaries or users to obtain the contract goods from other dealers inside the common market or, in so far as no alternative source of supply is available there, from outside the common market, in particular where one or both of them:

(1)   exercises industrial property rights so as to prevent dealers or users from obtaining outside, or from selling in, the contract territory properly marked or otherwise properly marketed contract goods;

(2)   exercises other rights or takes other measures so as to prevent dealers or users from obtaining outside, or from selling in, the contract territory contract goods.

Article 6
The Commission may withdraw the benefit of this Regulation, pursuant to Article 7 of Regulation No. 19/65/EEC, when it finds in a particular case that an agreement

which is exempted by this Regulation nevertheless has certain effects which are incompatible with the conditions set out in Article 85(3) of the Treaty, and in particular where:

    (a) the contract goods are not subject, in the contract territory, to effective competition from identical goods or goods considered by users as equivalent in view of their characteristics, price and intended use;

    (b) access by other suppliers to the different stages of distribution within the contract territory is made difficult to a significant extent;

    (c) for reasons other than those referred to in Article 3(c) and (d) it is not possible for intermediaries or users to obtain supplies of the contract goods from dealers outside the contract territory on the terms there customary;

    (d) the exclusive distributor:

    (1) without any objectively justified reason refuses to supply in the contract territory categories of purchasers who cannot obtain contract goods elsewhere on suitable terms or applies to them differing prices or conditions of sale;

    (2) sells the contract goods at excessively high prices.

A2.2   Extracts from Regulation 1984/83 — the Block Exemption for Exclusive Purchasing Agreements

**COMMISSION REGULATION (EEC) No. 1984/83 OF 22 JUNE 1983
on the application of Article 85(3) of the Treaty to categories of
exclusive purchasing agreements**

[Recitals omitted]

*THE COMMISSION OF THE EUROPEAN COMMUNITIES
HAS ADOPTED THIS REGULATION:*

TITLE 1

General provisions

Article 1

Pursuant to Article 85(3) of the Treaty, and subject to the conditions set out in Articles 2 to 5 of this Regulation, it is hereby declared that Article 85(1) of the Treaty shall not apply to agreements to which only two undertakings are party and whereby one party, the reseller, agrees with the other, the supplier, to purchase certain goods specified in the agreement for resale only from the supplier or from a connected undertaking or from another undertaking which the supplier has entrusted with the sale of his goods.

Article 2

    1. No other restriction of competition shall be imposed on the supplier than the obligation not to distribute the contract goods or goods which compete with the contract goods in the reseller's principal sales area and at the reseller's level of distribution.

    2. Apart from the obligation described in Article 1, no other restriction of competition shall be imposed on the reseller than the obligation not to manufacture or distribute goods which compete with the contract goods.

    3. Article 1 shall apply notwithstanding that the reseller undertakes any or all of the following obligations;

    (a) to purchase complete ranges of goods;

    (b) to purchase minimum quantities of goods which are subject to the exclusive purchasing obligation;

    (c) to sell the contract goods under trademarks, or packed and presented as specified by the supplier;

    (d) to take measures for the promotion of sales, in particular:
—to advertise,

— to maintain a sales network or stock of goods,
— to provide customer and guarantee services,
— to employ staff having specialized or technical training.

Article 3

Article 1 shall not apply where:

(a)   manufacturers of identical goods or of goods which are considered by users as equivalent in view of their characteristics, price and intended use enter into reciprocal exclusive purchasing agreements between themselves in respect of such goods;

(b)   manufacturers of identical goods or of goods which are considered by users as equivalent in view of their characteristics, price and intended use enter into a non-reciprocal exclusive purchasing agreement between themselves in respect of such goods, unless at least one of them has a total annual turnover of no more than 100 million ECU;

(c)   the exclusive purchasing obligation is agreed for more than one type of goods where these are neither by their nature nor according to commercial usage connected to each other;

(d)   the agreement is concluded for an indefinite duration or for a period of more than five years.

TITLE II

Special provisions for beer supply agreements

Article 6

1.   Pursuant to Article 85(3) of the Treaty, and subject to Articles 7 to 9 of this Regulation, it is hereby declared that Article 85(1) of the Treaty shall not apply to agreements to which only two undertakings are party and whereby one party, the reseller, agrees with the other, the supplier, in consideration for the according of special commercial or financial advantages, to purchase only from the supplier, an undertaking connected with the supplier or another undertaking entrusted by the supplier with the distribution of his goods, certain beers, or certain beers and certain other drinks, specified in the agreement for resale in premises used for the sale and consumption of drinks and designated in the agreement.

2.   The declaration in paragraph 1 shall also apply where exclusive purchasing obligations of the kind described in paragraph 1 are imposed on the reseller in favour of the supplier by another undertaking which is itself not a supplier.

Article 7

1.   Apart from the obligation referred to in Article 6, no restriction on competition shall be imposed on the reseller other than:

(a)   the obligation not to sell beers and other drinks which are supplied by other undertakings and which are of the same type as the beers or other drinks supplied under the agreement in the premises designated in the agreement;

(b)   the obligation, in the event that the reseller sells in the premises designated in the agreement beers which are supplied by other undertakings and which are of a different type from the beers supplied under the agreement, to sell such beers only in bottles, cans or other small packages, unless the sale of such beers in draught form is customary or is necessary to satisfy a sufficient demand from consumers;

(c)   the obligation to advertise goods supplied by other undertakings within or outside the premises designated in the agreement only in proportion to the share of these goods in the total turnover realised in the premises.

2.   Beers or other drinks are of different types where they are clearly distinguishable by their composition, appearance or taste.

Article 8

1.   Article 6 shall not apply where:

(a)   the supplier or a connected undertaking imposes on the reseller exclusive purchasing obligations for goods other than drinks or for services;

169

(b)   the supplier restricts the freedom of the reseller to obtain from an undertaking of his choice either services or goods for which neither an exclusive purchasing obligation nor a ban on dealing in competing products may be imposed;

(c)   the agreement is concluded for an indefinite duration or for a period of more than five years and the exclusive purchasing obligation relates to specified beers and other drinks;

(d)   the agreement is concluded for an indefinite duration or for a period of more than 10 years and the exclusive purchasing obligation relates only to specified beers;

(e)   the supplier obliges the reseller to impose the exclusive purchasing obligation on his successor for a longer period than the reseller would himself remain tied to the supplier.

2.   Where the agreement relates to premises which the supplier lets to the reseller or allows the reseller to occupy on some other basis in law or in fact, the following provisions shall also apply:

(a)   notwithstanding paragraphs (1)(c) and (d), the exclusive purchasing obligations and bans on dealing in competing products specified in this Title may be imposed on the reseller for the whole period for which the reseller in fact operates the premises;

(b)   the agreement must provide for the reseller to have the right to obtain:

—drinks, except beer, supplied under the agreement from other undertakings where these undertakings offer them on more favourable conditions which the supplier does not meet,

—drinks, except beer, which are of the same type as those supplied under the agreement but which bear different trade marks, from other undertakings where the supplier does not offer them.

Miscellaneous provisions

Article 14

The Commission may withdraw the benefit of this Regulation, pursuant to Article 7 of Regulation No. 19/65/EEC, when it finds in a particular case that an agreement which is exempted by this Regulation nevertheless has certain effects which are incompatible with the conditions set out in Article 85(3) of the Treaty, and in particular where:

(a)   the contract goods are not subject, in a substantial part of the common market, to effective competition from identical goods or goods considered by users as equivalent in view of their characteristics, price and intended use;

(b)   access by other suppliers to the different stages of distribution in a substantial part of the common market is made difficult to a significant extent;

(c)   the supplier without any objectively justified reason:

(1)   refuses to supply categories of resellers who cannot obtain the contract goods elsewhere on suitable terms or applies to them differing prices or conditions of sale;

(2)   applies less favourable prices or conditions of sale to resellers bound by an exclusive purchasing obligation as compared with other resellers at the same level of distribution.

APPENDIX THREE

HEARING OFFICERS AND COMMISSION POLICY ON ACCESS TO THE FILE

A3.1 Extracts from Commission Decision 94/810 on the Terms of Reference for Hearing Officers in Competition Procedures before the Commission

THE COMMISSION OF THE EUROPEAN COMMUNITIES,

Having regard to the Treaty establishing the European Community,

Whereas the treaties establishing the Communities and the rules implementing those treaties in relation to competition matters provide for the right of the parties concerned and of third parties to be heard before a final decision affecting their interests is taken;

Whereas the Commission must ensure that that right is guaranteed in its competition proceedings;

Whereas it is appropriate to entrust the organisation and conduct of the administrative procedures designed to protect the right to be heard to an independent person experienced in competition matters, in the interest of contributing to the objectivity, transparency and efficiency of Commission's competition proceedings; ...

HAS DECIDED AS FOLLOWS:

Article 1

1. The hearings provided for in the provisions implementing Articles 65 and 66 of the ECSC Treaty, Articles 85 and 86 of the EC Treaty and Council Regulation (EEC) No. 4064/89 shall be organised and conducted by the Hearing Officer in accordance with Articles 2 to 10 of this Decision.
...
3. Administratively the Hearing Officer shall belong to the Directorate-General for Competition. To ensure the independence of the Hearing Officer in the performance of his duties, he has the right of direct access, as defined in Article 9, to the Member of the Commission with special responsibility for competition.

Article 2

1. The Hearing Officer shall ensure that the hearing is properly conducted and thus contribute to the objectivity of the hearing itself and of any decision taken subsequently. The Hearing Officer shall seek to ensure in particular that in the preparation of draft Commission decisions in competition cases due account is taken of all the relevant facts, whether favourable or unfavourable to the parties concerned.
2. In performing his duties the Hearing Officer shall see to it that the rights of the defence are respected, while taking account of the need for effective application of the competition rules in accordance with the regulations in force and the principles laid down by the Court of First Instance and the Court of Justice.

Article 3

1. Decisions as to whether third parties, be they natural or legal persons, are to be heard shall be taken after consulting the Director responsible for investigating the case which is the subject of the procedure.

2. Applications to be heard on the part of third parties shall be submitted in writing, together with a written statement explaining the applicant's interest in the outcome of the procedure.

3. Where it is found that an applicant has not shown a sufficient interest to be heard, he shall be informed in writing of the reasons for such finding. A time limit shall be fixed within which he may submit any further written comments.

Article 4

1. Decisions whether persons are to be heard orally shall be taken after consulting the Director responsible for investigating the case which is the subject of the procedure.

2. Applications to be heard orally shall be made in the applicant's written comments on letters which the Commission has addressed to him and shall contain a reasoned statement of the applicant's interest in an oral hearing.

3. The letters referred to in paragraph 2 are those:
— communicating a statement of objections,
— inviting the written comments of a natural or legal person having shown sufficient interest to be heard as a third party,
— informing a complainant that in the Commission's view there are insufficient grounds for finding an infringement and inviting him to submit any further written comments,
— informing a natural or legal person that in the Commission's view that person has not shown sufficient interest to be heard as a third party.

4. Where it is found that the applicant has not shown a sufficient interest to be heard orally, he shall be informed in writing of the reasons for such finding. A time limit shall be fixed within which he may submit any further written comments.

Article 5

1. Where a person, an undertaking or an association of persons or undertakings who or which has received one or more of the letters listed in Article 4(3) has reason to believe that the Commission has in its possession documents which have not been disclosed to it and that those documents are necessary for the proper exercise of the right to be heard, he or it may draw attention to the matter by a reasoned request.

2. The reasoned decision on any such request shall be communicated to the person, undertaking or association that made the request and to any other person, undertaking or association concerned by the procedure.

3. Where it is intended to disclose information which may constitute a business secret of an undertaking, it shall be informed in writing of this intention and the reasons for it. A time limit shall be fixed within which the undertaking concerned may submit any written comments.

4. Where the undertaking concerned objects to the disclosure of the information but it is found that the information is not protected and may therefore be disclosed, that finding shall be stated in a reasoned decision which shall be notified to the undertaking concerned. The decision shall specify the date after which the information will be disclosed. This date shall not be less than one week from the date of notification.

5. Where an undertaking or association of undertakings considers that the time limit imposed for its reply to a letter referred to in Article 4(3) is too short, it may, within the original time limit, draw attention to the matter by a reasoned request. The applicant shall be informed in writing whether the request has been granted.

A3.2 Commission Notice on the Internal Rules of Procedure for Processing Requests for Access to the File in Cases Pursuant to Articles 85 and 86 of the EC Treaty

INTRODUCTION

Access to the file is an important procedural stage in all contentious competition cases (prohibitions with or without a fine, prohibitions of mergers, rejection of complaints, etc.). The Commission's task in this area is to reconcile two opposing obligations, namely that of safeguarding the rights of the defence and that of protecting confidential information concerning firms.

The purpose of this notice is to ensure compatibility between current administrative practice regarding access to the file and the case-law of the Court of Justice of the European Communities and the Court of First Instance, in particular the 'Soda-ash' cases. The line of conduct thus laid down concerns cases dealt with on the basis of the competition rules applicable to enterprises, Articles 85 and 86 of the EC Treaty, Regulation (EEC) No. 4064/89 (hereinafter 'the Merger Regulation'), and Articles 65 and 66 of the ECSC Treaty.

Access to the file, which is one of the procedural safeguards designed to ensure effective exercise of the right to be heard provided for in Article 19(1) and (2) of Council Regulation No. 17 and Article 2 of Commission Regulation No. 99/63/EEC, as well as in the corresponding provisions of the Regulations governing the application of Articles 85 and 86 in the field of transport, must be arranged in all cases involving decisions on infringements, decisions rejecting complaints, decisions imposing interim measures and decisions adopted on the basis of Article 15(6) of Regulation No. 17.

The guidelines set out below, however, essentially relate to the rights of the undertakings which are the subject of investigations into alleged infringements; they do not relate to the rights of third parties, and complainants in particular.

In merger cases, access to the file by parties directly concerned is expressly provided for in Article 18(3) of the Merger Regulation and in Article 13(3)(a) of Regulation (EC) No. 3384/94 ('the Implementing Regulation').

I. SCOPE AND LIMITS OF ACCESS TO THE FILE

As the purpose of providing access to the file is to enable the addressees of a statement of objections to express their views on the conclusions reached by the Commission, the firms in question must have access to all the documents making up the 'file' of the Commission (DG IV), apart from the categories of documents identified in the Hercules judgment, namely the business secrets of other undertakings, internal Commission documents and other confidential information.

Thus not all the documents collected in the course of an investigation are communicable and a distinction must be made between non-communicable and communicable documents.

A. Non-communicable documents

1. Business secrets

Business secrets mean information (documents or parts of documents) for which an undertaking has claimed protection as 'business secrets', and which are recognised as such by the Commission.

The non-communicability of such information is intended to protect the legitimate interest of firms in preventing third parties from obtaining strategic information on their essential interests and on the operation or development of their business.

The criteria for determining what constitutes a business secret have not as yet been defined in full. Reference may be made, however, to the case-law, especially the Akzo and the BAT and Reynolds judgments, to the criteria used in anti-dumping procedures, and to decisions on the subject by the Hearing Officer. The term 'business secret' must be construed in its broader sense: according to Akzo, Regulation No. 17 requires the Commission to have regard to the legitimate interest of firms in the protection of their business secrets.

Business secrets need no longer be protected when they are known outside the firm (or group or association of firms) to which they relate. Nor can facts remain business secrets if, owing to the passage of time or for any other reason, they are no longer commercially important.

Where business secrets provide evidence of an infringement or tend to exonerate a firm, the Commission must reconcile the interest in the protection of sensitive information, the public interest in having the infringement of the competition rules terminated, and the rights of the defence. This calls for an assessment of:

    (i)   the relevance of the information to determining whether or not an infringement has been committed;

    (ii)   its probative value;

    (iii)   whether it is indispensable;

    (iv)   the degree of sensitivity involved (to what extent would disclosure of the information harm the interests of the firm?);

    (v)   the seriousness of the infringement.

Each document must be assessed individually to determine whether the need to disclose it is greater than the harm which might result from disclosure.

2.   Confidential documents

It is also necessary to protect information for which confidentiality has been requested.

This category includes information making it possible to identify the suppliers of the information who wish to remain anonymous to the other parties, and certain types of information communicated to the Commission on condition that confidentiality is observed, such as documents obtained during an investigation which form part of a firm's property and are the subject of a non-disclosure request (such as a market study commissioned by the firm and forming part of its property). As in the preceding case (business secrets), the Commission must reconcile the legitimate interest of the firm in protecting its assets, the public interest in having breaches of the competition rules terminated, and the rights of the defence. Military secrets also belong in the category of 'other confidential information'.

As a rule, the confidential nature of documents is not a bar to the disclosure if the information in question is necessary in order to prove an alleged infringement ('inculpatory documents') or if the papers invalidate or rebut the reasoning of the Commission set out in its statement of objections ('exculpatory documents').

3.   Internal documents

Internal documents are, by their nature, not the sort of evidence on which the Commission can rely in its assessment of a case. For the most part they consist of drafts, opinions or memos from the departments concerned and relating to ongoing procedures.

The Commission departments must be able to express themselves freely within their institution concerning ongoing cases. The disclosure of such documents could also jeopardise the secrecy of the Commission's deliberations.

It should, moreover, be noted that the secrecy of proceedings is also protected by the code of conduct on public access to Commission and Council documents as set out in Commission Decision 94/90/ECSC, EC, Euratom, as amended by Decision 96/567/ECSC, EC, Euratom as are internal documents relating to inspections and investigations and those whose disclosure could jeopardise the protection of individual privacy, business and industrial secrets or the confidentiality requested by a legal or natural person.

These considerations justify the non-disclosure of this category of documents, which will, in future, be placed in the file of internal documents relating to cases under investigation, which is, as a matter of principle, inaccessible (see point II.A.2).

B.   *Communicable documents*

All documents not regarded as 'non-communicable' under the abovementioned criteria are accessible to the parties concerned.

Thus, access to the file is not limited to documents which the Commission regards as 'relevant' to an undertaking's rights of defence.

The Commission does not select accessible documents in order to remove those which may be relevant to the defence of an undertaking. This concept, already outlined in the Court of First Instance judgments in Hercules and Cimenteries CBR, was confirmed and developed in the Soda-ash case, where the Court held that 'in the defended proceedings for which Regulation No. 17 provides it cannot be for the Commission alone to decide which documents are of use for the defence.... The Commission must give the advisers of the undertaking concerned the opportunity to examine documents which may be relevant so that their probative value for the defence can be assessed' (Case T-30/91, paragraph 81).

Special note concerning studies:

It should be stressed that studies commissioned in connection with proceedings or for a specific file, whether used directly or indirectly in the proceedings, must be made accessible irrespective of their intrinsic value. Access must be given not only to the results of a study (reports, statistics, etc.), but also to the Commission's correspondence with the contractor, the tender specifications and the methodology of the study.

However, correspondence relating to the financial aspects of a study and the references concerning the contractor remain confidential in the interests of the latter.

II.   *PROCEDURES FOR IMPLEMENTING ACCESS TO THE FILE*

A.   *Preparatory procedure Cases investigated under Articles 85 and 86*

1.   *Investigation file*

1.1   *Return of certain documents after inspection visits*

In the course of its investigations under Article 14(2) and (3) of Regulation No. 17, the Commission obtains a considerable number of documents, some of which may, following a detailed examination, prove to be irrelevant to the case in question. Such documents are normally returned to the firm as rapidly as possible.

1.2   *Request for a nonconfidential version of a document*

In order to facilitate access to the file at a later stage in proceedings, the undertakings concerned will systematically be asked to:

detail the information (documents or parts of documents) which they regard as business secrets and the confidential documents whose disclosure would injure them; substantiate their claim for confidentiality in writing; give the Commission a nonconfidential version of their confidential documents (where confidential passages are deleted).

As regards documents taken during an inspection (Article 14(2) and (3)), requests are made only after the inspectors have returned from their mission.

When an undertaking, in response to a request from the Commission, claims that the information supplied is confidential, the following procedure will be adopted:

(a)   at that stage of the proceedings, claims of confidentiality which at first sight seem justified will be accepted provisionally. The Commission reserves the right, however, to reconsider the matter at a later stage of the proceedings;

(b)   where it is apparent that the claim of confidentiality is clearly unjustified, for example where it relates to a document already published or distributed extensively, or is excessive where it covers all or virtually all the documents obtained or sent without any plausible justification, the firm concerned will be informed that the

Commission does not agree with the scope of the confidentiality that is claimed. The matter will be dealt with when the final assessment is made of the accessibility of the documents (see below).

1.3   Final assessment of the accessibility of documents

It may prove necessary to grant other undertakings involved access to a document even where the undertaking that has issued it objects, if the document serves as a basis for the decision or is clearly an exculpatory document.

If an undertaking states that a document is confidential but does not submit a nonconfidential version, the following procedure applies:

the undertaking claiming confidentiality will be contacted again and asked for a reasonably coherent nonconfidential version of the document;

if the undertaking continues to object to the disclosure of the information, the competent department applies to the Hearing Officer, who will if necessary implement the procedure leading to a decision pursuant to Article 5(4) of Commission Decision 94/810/ECSC, EC of 12 December 1994 on the terms of reference of hearing officers in competition procedures before the Commission. The undertaking will be informed by letter that the Hearing Officer is examining the question.

1.4   Enumerative list of documents

An enumerative list of documents should be drawn up according to the following principles:

(a)   the list should include uninterrupted numbering of all the pages in the investigation file and an indication (using a classification code) of the degree of accessibility of the document and the parties with authorised access;

(b)   an access code is given to each document on the list:
— accessible document
— partially accessible document
— non-accessible document;

(c)   the category of completely non-accessible documents essentially consists of documents containing 'business secrets' and other confidential documents. In view of the 'Soda-ash' case-law, the list will include a summary enabling the content and subject of the documents to be identified, so that any firm having requested access to the file is able to determine in full knowledge of the facts whether the documents are likely to be relevant to its defence and to decide whether to request access despite that classification;

(d)   accessible and partially accessible documents do not call for a description of their content in the list as they can be 'physically' consulted by all firms, either in their full version or in their non-confidential version. In the latter event, only the sensitive passages are deleted in such a way that the firm with access is able to determine the nature of the information deleted (e.g. turnover).

2.   File of internal documents relating to ongoing cases

In order to simplify administration and increase efficiency, internal documents will, in future, be placed in the file of internal documents relating to cases under investigation (non-accessible) containing all internal documents in chronological order. Classification in this category is subject to the control of the Hearing Officer, who will if necessary certify that the papers contained therein are 'internal documents'.

The following, for example, will be deemed to be internal documents:
(a)   requests for instructions made to, and instructions received from, hierarchical superiors on the treatment of cases;
(b)   consultations with other Commission departments on a case;
(c)   correspondence with other public authorities concerning a case;
(d)   drafts and other working documents;
(e)   individual technical assistance contracts (languages, computing, etc.) relating to a specific aspect of a case.

B. Preparatory procedure — Cases examined within the meaning of the Merger Regulation

1. Measures common to the preparatory procedure in cases investigated pursuant to Articles 85 and 86

(a) Return of certain documents after an inspection

On-the-spot inspections are specifically provided for in Article 13 of the Merger Regulation: in such cases, the procedure provided for in point II.A.1.1 for cases examined on the basis of Articles 85 and 86 is applicable.

(b) Enumerative list of documents

The enumerative list of the documents in the Commission file with the access codes will be drawn up in accordance with the criteria set out in point II.A.1.4.

(c) Request for a non-confidential version of a document

In order to facilitate access to the file, firms being investigated will be asked to:
—detail the information (documents or parts of documents) they regard as business secrets and the confidential documents whose disclosure would injure them,
—substantiate their requests for confidentiality in writing,
—give the Commission a reasonably coherent non-confidential version of their confidential documents (where confidential passages are deleted).
This procedure will be followed in stage II cases (where the Commission initiates proceedings in respect of the notifying parties) and in stage I cases (giving rise to a Commission decision without initiation of proceedings).

2. Measures specific to preparatory procedures in merger cases

(a) Subsequent procedure in stage II cases

In stage II cases the subsequent procedure is as follows.
Where a firm states that all or part of the documents it has provided are business secrets, the following steps should be taken:
—if the claim appears to be justified, the documents or parts of documents concerned will be regarded as non-accessible to third parties,
—if the claim does not appear to be justified, the competent Commission department will ask the firm, in the course of the investigation and no later than the time at which the statement of objections is sent, to review its position. The firm must either state in writing which documents or parts of documents must be regarded as confidential, or send a non-confidential version of the documents.
If disagreement regarding the extent of the confidentiality persists, the competent department refers the matter to the Hearing Officer, who may if necessary take the decision provided for in Article 5(4) of Decision 94/810/ECSC, EC.

(b) Specific cases

Article 9(1) of the Merger Regulation provides that 'the Commission may, by means of a decision notified without delay to the undertakings concerned ... refer a notified concentration to the competent authorities of the Member State concerned'. In the context of access to the file, the parties concerned should, as a general rule be able to see the request for referral from a national authority, with the exception of any business secrets or other confidential information it may contain.
Article 22(3) of the Merger Regulation provides that 'If the Commission finds, at the request of a Member State, that a concentration (...) that has no Community dimension (...) creates or strengthens a dominant position (...) it may (...) adopt the decisions provided for in the second subparagraph of Article 8(2), (3) and (4)'. Such requests have the effect of empowering the Commission to deal with mergers which would normally fall outside its powers of review. Accordingly, the parties concerned

should be granted right of access to the letter from the Member State requesting referral, after deletion of any business secrets or other confidential information.

C. Practical arrangements for access to the file

1. General rule: access by way of consultation on the Commission's premises

Firms are invited to examine the relevant files on the Commission's premises.

If the firm considers, on the basis of the list of documents it has received, that it requires certain non-accessible documents for its defence, it may make a reasoned request to that end to the Hearing Officer.

2. If the file is not too bulky, however, the firm has the choice of being sent all the accessible documents, apart from those already sent with the statement of objections or the letter rejecting the complaint, or of consulting the file on the Commission's premises.

As regards Articles 85 and 86 cases, contrary to a common previous practice, the statement of objections or letter of rejection will in future be accompanied only by the evidence adduced and documents cited on which the objections/rejection letter is based.

Any request for access made prior to submission of the statement of objections will in principle be inadmissible.

D. Particular questions which may arise in connection with complaints and procedures relating to abuse of a dominant position (Articles 85 and 86)

1. Complaints

While complainants may properly be involved in proceedings, they do not have the same rights and guarantees as the alleged infringers. A complainant's right to consult the files does not share the same basis as the rights of defence of the addressees of a statement of objections, and there are no grounds for treating the rights of the complainant as equivalent to those of the firms objected to.

Nevertheless, a complainant who has been informed of the intention to reject his complaint may request access to the documents on which the Commission based its position. Complainants may not, however, have access to any confidential information or other business secrets belonging to the firms complained of, or to third-party firms, which the Commission has obtained in the course of its investigations (Articles 11 and 14 of Regulation No. 17).

Clearly, it is even more necessary here to respect the principle of confidentiality as there is no presumption of infringement. In accordance with the judgment in Fedetab, Article 19(2) of Regulation No. 17 gives complainants a right to be heard and not a right to receive confidential information.

2. Procedures in cases of abuse of a dominant position

The question of procedures in cases of abuse of a dominant position was referred to by the Court of First Instance and the Court of Justice in the BPB Industries and British Gypsum v Commission case.

By definition, firms in a dominant position on a market are able to place very considerable economic or commercial pressure on their competitors or on their trading partners, customers or suppliers.

The Court of First Instance and the Court of Justice thus acknowledged the legitimacy of the reluctance displayed by the Commission in revealing certain letters received from customers of the firm being investigated.

Although it is of value to the Commission for giving a better understanding of the market concerned, the information does not in any way constitute inculpatory evidence, and its disclosure to the firm concerned might easily expose the authors to the risk of retaliatory measures.

APPENDIX FOUR

EXTRACTS FROM REGULATION 3385/94: FORM A/B

Commission Regulation 3385/94

[Regulation No. 3385 of the Commission of 21 December 1994]
(form, content and other details of applications and notifications provided for in Council Regulation No. 17)

THE COMMISSION OF THE EUROPEAN COMMUNITIES,

Having regard to the Treaty establishing the European Community,

Having regard to the Agreement on the European Economic Area,

Having regard to Council Regulation No. 17 of 6 February 1962, First Regulation implementing Articles 85 and 86 of the Treaty, as last amended by the Act of Accession of Spain and Portugal, and in particular Article 24 thereof,

Whereas Commission Regulation No. 27 of 3 May 1962, First Regulation implementing Council Regulation No. 17, as last amended by Regulation (EC) 3666/93, no longer meets the requirements of efficient administrative procedure; whereas it should therefore be replaced by a new Regulation;

Whereas, on the one hand, applications for negative clearance under Article 2 and notifications under Articles 4, 5 and 25 of Regulation No. 17 have important legal consequences, which are favourable to the parties to an agreement, a decision or a practice, while, on the other hand, incorrect or misleading information in such applications or notifications may lead to the imposition of fines and may also entail civil law disadvantages for the parties; whereas it is therefore necessary in the interests of legal certainty to define precisely the persons entitled to submit applications and notifications, the subject matter and content of the information which such applications and notifications must contain, and the time when they become effective;

Whereas each of the parties should have the right to submit the application or the notification to the Commission; whereas, furthermore, a party exercising the right should inform the other parties in order to enable them to protect their interests; whereas applications and notifications relating to agreements, decisions or practices of associations of undertakings should be submitted only by such association;

Whereas it is for the applicants and the notifying parties to make full and honest disclosure to the Commission of the facts and circumstances which are relevant for coming to a decision on the agreements, decisions or practices concerned;

Whereas, in order to simplify and expedite their examination, it is desirable to prescribe that a form be used for applications for negative clearance relating to Article 85(1) and for notification relating to Article 85(3); whereas the use of this form should also be possible in the case of applications for negative clearance relating to Article 86;

Whereas the Commission, in appropriate cases, will give the parties, if they so request, an opportunity before the application or the notification to discuss the intended agreement, decision or practice informally and in strict confidence; whereas, in addition, it will, after the application or notification, maintain close contact with the *parties to the extent necessary to discuss with them any practical or legal problems which it discovers on a first examination of the case and if possible to remove such problems by mutual agreement;*

Whereas the provisions of this Regulation must also cover cases in which applications for negative clearance relating to Article 53(1) or Article 54 of the EEA Agreement, or notifications, relating to Article 53(3) of the EEA Agreement are submitted to the Commission,

HAS ADOPTED THIS REGULATION:

Article 1   Persons entitled to submit applications and notifications

1.   The following may submit an application under Article 2 of Regulation No. 17 relating to Article 85(1) of the Treaty or a notification under Articles 4, 5 and 25 of Regulation No. 17;

    (a)   any undertaking and any association of undertakings being a party to agreements or to concerted practices; and

    (b)   any association of undertakings adopting decisions or engaging in practices; which may fall within the scope of Article 85(1).

Where the application or notification is submitted by some, but not all, of the parties, referred to in point (a) of the first subparagraph, they shall give notice to the other parties.

2.   Any undertaking which may hold, alone or with other undertakings, a dominant position within the common market or in a substantial part of it, may submit an application under Article 2 of Regulation No. 17 relating to Article 86 of the Treaty.

3.   Where the application or notification is signed by representatives of persons, undertakings or associations of undertakings, such representatives shall produce written proof that they are authorised to act.

4.   Where a joint application or notification is made, a joint representative should be appointed who is authorised to transmit and receive documents on behalf of all the applicants or notifying parties.

Article 2   Submission of applications and notifications

1.   Applications under Article 2 of Regulation No. 17 relating to Article 85(1) of the Treaty and notifications under Articles 4, 5 and 25 of Regulation No. 17 shall be submitted in the manner prescribed by Form A/B as shown in the Annex to this Regulation. Form A/B may also be used for applications under Article 2 of Regulation No. 17 relating to Article 86 of the Treaty. Joint applications and joint notifications shall be submitted on a single form.

2.   Seventeen copies of each application and notification and three copies of the Annexes thereto shall be submitted to the Commission at the address indicated in Form A/B.

3.   The documents annexed to the application or notification shall be either originals or copies of the originals; in the latter case the applicant or notifying party shall confirm that they are true copies of the originals and complete.

4.   Applications and notifications shall be in one of the official languages of the Community. This language shall also be the language of the proceeding for the applicant or notifying party. Documents shall be submitted in their original language. Where the original language is not one of the official languages, a translation into the language of the proceeding shall be attached.

5.   Where applications for negative clearance relating to Article 53(1) or Article 54 of the EEA Agreement or notifications relating to Article 53(3) of the EEA Agreement are submitted, they may also be in one of the official languages of the EFTA States or the working language of the EFTA Surveillance Authority. If the language chosen for the application or notification is not an official language of the Community, the applicant or notifying party shall supplement all documentation with a translation into an official language of the Community. The language which is chosen for the translation shall be the language of the proceeding for the applicant or notifying party.

Article 3   Content of applications and notifications

1.   Applications and notifications shall contain the information, including documents, required by Form A/B. The information must be correct and complete.

2.   Applications under Article 2 of Regulation No. 17 relating to Article 86 of the Treaty shall contain a full statement of the facts, specifying, in particular, the practice concerned and the position of the undertaking or undertakings within the common market or a substantial part thereof in regard to the products or services to which the practice relates.

3.   The Commission may dispense with the obligation to provide any particular information, including documents, required by Form A/B where the Commission considers that such information is not necessary for the examination of the case.

4.   The Commission shall, without delay, acknowledge in writing to the applicant or notifying party receipt of the application or notification, and of any reply to a letter sent by the Commission pursuant to Article 4(2).

Article 4   Effective date of submission of applications and notifications

1.   Without prejudice to paragraphs 2 to 5, applications and notifications shall become effective on the date on which they are received by the Commission. Where, however, the application or notification is sent by registered post, it shall become effective on the date shown on the postmark of the place of posting.

2.   Where the Commission finds that the information, including documents, contained in the application or notification is incomplete in a material respect, it shall, without delay, inform the applicant or notifying party in writing of this fact and shall fix an appropriate time limit for the completion of the information. In such cases, the application or notification shall become effective on the date on which the complete information is received by the Commission.

3.   Material changes in the facts contained in the application or notification which the applicant or notifying party knows or ought to know must be communicated to the Commission voluntarily and without delay.

4.   Incorrect or misleading information shall be considered to be incomplete information.

5.   Where, at the expiry of a period of one month following the date on which the application or notification has been received, the Commission has not provided the applicant or notifying party with the information referred to in paragraph 2, the application or notification shall be deemed to have become effective on the date of its receipt by the Commission.

Article 5   Repeal

Regulation No. 27 is repealed.

Article 6   Entry into force

This Regulation shall enter into force on 1 March 1995.

This Regulation shall be binding in its entirety and directly applicable in all Member States.

Done at Brussels, 21 December 1994.

FORM A/B
INTRODUCTION

Form A/B, as its Annex, is an integral part of the Commission Regulation (EC) 3385/94 of 21 December 1994 on the form, content and other details of applications and notifications provided for in Council Regulation No. 17 (hereinafter referred to as 'the Regulation'). It allows undertakings and associations of undertakings to apply to the Commission for negative clearance agreements or practices which may fall within the prohibitions of Article 85(1) and Article 86 of the EC Treaty, or within Articles 53(1) and 54 of the EEA Agreement or to notify such agreement and apply to have it exempted from the prohibition set out in Article 85(1) by virtue of the provisions of Articles 85(3) of the EC Treaty or from the prohibition of Article 53(1) by virtue of the provisions of Article 53(3) of the EEA Agreement.

To facilitate the use of the Form A/B the following pages set out:

— in which situations it is necessary to make an application or a notification (Point A),

— to which authority (the Commission or the EFTA Surveillance Authority) the application or notification should be made (Point B),

181

—*for which purposes the application or notification can be used (Point C),*
—*what information must be given in the application or notification (Points D, E and F),*
—*who can make an application or notification (Point G),*
—*how to make an application or notification (Point H),*
—*how the business secrets of the undertakings can be protected (Point I),*
—*how certain technical terms used in the operational part of the Form A/B should be interpreted (Point J), and*
—*the subsequent procedure after the application or notification has been made (Point K).*

A IN WHICH SITUATIONS IS IT NECESSARY TO MAKE AN APPLICATION OR A NOTIFICATION?

I. PURPOSE OF THE COMPETITION RULES OF THE EC TREATY AND THE EEA AGREEMENT

1. Purpose of the EC competition rules

The purpose of the competition rules is to prevent the distortion of competition in the common market by restrictive practices or the abuse of dominant positions. They apply to any enterprise trading directly or indirectly in the common market, wherever established.

Article 85(1) of the EC Treaty (the text of Articles 85 and 86 is reproduced in Annex I to this form) prohibits restrictive agreements, decisions or concerted practices (arrangements) which may affect trade between Member States, and Article 85(2) declares agreements and decisions containing such restrictions void (although the Court of Justice has held that if restrictive terms of agreements are severable, only those terms are void); Article 85(3), however, provides for exemption of arrangements with beneficial effects, if its conditions are met. Article 86 prohibits the abuse of a dominant position which may affect trade between Member States. The original procedures for implementing these Articles, which provide for 'negative clearance' and exemption pursuant to Article 85(3), were laid down in Regulation No. 17.

2. Purpose of the EEA competition rules

The competition rules of the Agreement on the European Economic Area (concluded between the Community, the Member States and the EFTA States) are based on the same principles as those contained in the Community competition rules and have the same purpose, i.e., to prevent the distortion of competition in the EEA territory by cartels or the abuse of dominant position. They apply to any enterprise trading directly or indirectly in the EEA territory, wherever established.

Article 53(1) of the EEA Agreement (the text of Articles 53, 54 and 56 of the EEA Agreement is reproduced in Annex I) prohibits restrictive agreements, decisions or concerted practices (arrangements) which may affect trade between the Community and one or more EFTA States (or between EFTA States), and Article 53(2) declares agreements or decisions containing such restrictions void; Article 53(3), however, provides for exemption of arrangements with beneficial effects, if its conditions are met. Article 54 prohibits the abuse of a dominant position which may affect trade between the Community and one or more EFTA States (or between EFTA States). The procedures for implementing these Articles, which provide for 'negative clearance' and exemption pursuant to Article 53(3), are laid down in Regulation No. 17, supplemented for EEA purposes, by Protocols 21, 22 and 23 to the EEA Agreement.

II. THE SCOPE OF THE COMPETITION RULES OF THE EC TREATY AND THE EEA AGREEMENT

The applicability of Articles 85 and 86 of the EC Treaty and Articles 53 and 54 of the EEA Agreement depends on the circumstances of each individual case. It presupposes that the arrangement or behaviour satisfies all the conditions set out in the relevant provisions. This question must consequently be examined before any application for negative clearance or any notification is made.

1. Negative clearance

The negative clearance procedure allows undertakings to ascertain whether the Commission considers that their arrangement or their behaviour is or is not prohibited by Article 85(1), or Article 86 of the EC Treaty or by Article 53(1) or Article 54 of the EEA Agreement. This procedure is governed by Article 2 of Regulation No. 17. The negative clearance takes the form of a decision by which the Commission certifies that, on the basis of the facts in its possession, there are no grounds pursuant to Article 85(1) or Article 86 of the EC Treaty or under Article 53(1) or Article 54 of the EEA Agreement for action on its part in respect of the arrangement or behaviour.

There is, however, no point in making an application when the arrangements or the behaviour are manifestly not prohibited by the abovementioned provisions. Nor is the Commission obliged to give negative clearance. Article 2 of Regulation No. 17 states that '. . . the Commission may certify . . .'. The Commission issues negative clearance decisions only where an important problem of interpretation has to be solved. In the other cases it reacts to the application by sending a comfort letter.

The Commission has published several notices relating the interpretation of Article 85(1) of the EC Treaty. They define certain categories of agreements which, by their nature or because of their minor importance, are not caught by the prohibition.

2. Exemption

The procedure for exemption pursuant to Article 85(3) of the EC Treaty and Article 53(3) of the EEA Agreement allows companies to enter into arrangements which, in fact, offer economic advantages but which, without exemption, would be prohibited by Article 85(1) of the EC Treaty or by Article 53(1) of the EEA Agreement. This procedure is governed by Articles 4, 6 and 8 and, for the new Member States, also by Articles 5, 7 and 25 of Regulation No. 17. The exemption takes the form of a decision by the Commission declaring Article 85(1) of the EC Treaty or Article 53(1) of the EEA Agreement to be inapplicable to the arrangements described in the decision. Article 8 requires the Commission to specify the period of validity of any such decision, allows the Commission to attach conditions and obligations and provides for decisions to be amended or revoked or specified acts by the parties to be prohibited in certain circumstances, notably if the decisions were based on incorrect information or if there is any material change in the facts.

The Commission has adopted a number of regulations granting exemptions to categories of agreements. Some of these regulations provide that some agreements may benefit from exemption only if they are notified to the Commission pursuant to Article 4 or 5 of Regulation No. 17 with a view to obtaining exemption, and the benefit of the opposition procedure is claimed in the notification.

A decision granting exemption may have retroactive effect, but, with certain exceptions, cannot be made effective earlier than the date of notification (Article 6 of Regulation No. 17). Should the Commission find that notified arrangements are indeed prohibited and cannot be exempted and, therefore, take a decision condemning them, the participants are nevertheless protected, between the date of the notification and the date of the decision, against fines for any infringement described in the notification (Article 3 and Article 15(5) and (6) of Regulation No. 17).

Normally the Commission issues exemption decisions only in cases of particular legal, economic or political importance. In the other cases it terminates the procedure by sending a comfort letter.

B TO WHICH AUTHORITY SHOULD APPLICATION OR NOTIFICATION BE MADE?

The applications and notifications must be made to the authority which has competence for the matter. The Commission is responsible for the application of the competition rules of the EC Treaty. However there is shared competence in relation to the application of the competition rules of the EEA agreement.

The competence of the Commission and of the EFTA Surveillance Authority to apply the EEA competition rules follows from Article 56 of the EEA Agreement. Applications and notifications relating to agreements, decisions or concerted practices liable to affect trade between Member States should be addressed to the Commission unless their effects on trade between Member States or on competition within the Community are not appreciable within the meaning of the Commission notice of 1986 on agreements of minor importance. Furthermore, all restrictive agreements, decisions or concerted practices affecting trade between one Member State and one or more EFTA States fall within the competence of the Commission, provided that the undertakings concerned achieve more than 67% of their combined EEA-wide turnover within the Community. However, if the effects of such agreements, decisions or concerted practices on trade between Member States or on competition within the Community are not appreciable, the notification should, where necessary, be addressed to the EFTA Surveillance Authority. All other agreements, decisions and concerted practices falling under Article 53 of the EEA Agreement should be notified to the EFTA Surveillance Authority (the address of which is given in Annex III).

Applications for negative clearance regarding Article 54 of the EEA Agreements should be lodged with the Commission if the dominant position exists only in the Community, or with the EFTA Surveillance Authority, if the dominant position exists only in the whole of the territory of the EFTA States, or a substantial part of it. Only where the dominant position exists within both territories should the rules outlined above with respect to Article 53 be applied.

The Commission will apply, as a basis for appraisal, the competition rules of the EC Treaty. Where the case falls under the EEA Agreement and is attributed to the Commission pursuant to Article 56 of that Agreement, it will simultaneously apply the EEA rules.

C   THE PURPOSE OF THIS FORM

Form A/B lists the questions that must be answered and the information and documents that must be provided when applying for the following:
—a negative clearance with regard to Article 85(1) of the EC Treaty and/or Article 53(1) of EEA Agreement, pursuant to Article 2 of Regulation No. 17, with respect to agreements between undertakings, decisions by associations of undertakings and concerted practices,
—an exemption pursuant to Article 85(3) of the EC Treaty and/or Article 53(3) of the EEA Agreement with respect to agreements between undertakings, decisions by associations of undertakings and concerted practices,
—the benefit of the opposition procedure contained in certain Commission regulations granting exemption by category.
This form allows undertakings applying for negative clearance to notify, at the same time, in order to obtain an exemption in the event that the Commission reaches the conclusion that no negative clearance can be granted.
Applications for negative clearance and notifications relating to Article 85 of the EC Treaty shall be submitted in the manner prescribed by form A/B (see Article 2(1), first sentence of the Regulation).
This form can also be used by undertakings that wish to apply for a negative clearance from Article 86 of the EC Treaty or Article 53 of the EEA Agreement, pursuant to Article 2 of Regulation No. 17. Applicants requesting negative clearance from Article 86 are not required to use form A/B. They are nonetheless strongly recommended to give all the information requested below to ensure that their application gives a full statement of the facts (see Article 2(1), second sentence of the Regulation).
The applications or notifications made on the form A/B issued by the EFTA side are equally valid. However, if the agreements, decisions or practices concerned fall solely within Articles 85 or 86 of the EC Treaty, i.e., have no EEA relevance whatsoever, it is advisable to use the present form established by the Commission.

D   WHICH CHAPTERS OF THE FORM SHOULD BE COMPLETED?

The operational part of this form is sub-divided into four chapters. Undertakings wishing to make an application for a negative clearance or a notification must complete Chapters I, II and IV. An exception to this rule is provided for in the case where the application or notification concerns an agreement concerning the creation of a cooperative joint venture of a structural character if the parties wish to benefit from an accelerated procedure. In this situation Chapters I, III and IV should be completed.

In 1992, the Commission announced that it had adopted new internal administrative rules that provided that certain applications and notifications — those of cooperative joint ventures which are structural in nature — would be dealt with within fixed deadlines. In such cases the services of the Commission will, within two months of receipt of the complete notification of the agreement, inform the parties in writing of the results of the initial analysis of the case and, as appropriate, the nature and probable length of the administrative procedure they intend to engage.

The contents of this letter may vary according to the characteristics of the case under investigation:

— in cases not posing any problems, the Commission will send a comfort letter confirming the compatibility of the agreement with Article 85(1) or (3),

— if a comfort letter cannot be sent because of the need to settle the case by formal decision, the Commission will inform the undertakings concerned of its intention to adopt a decision either granting or rejecting exemption,

— if the Commission has serious doubts as to the compatibility of the agreement with the competition rules, it will send a letter to the parties giving notice of an in-depth examination which may, depending on the case, result in a decision either prohibiting, exempting subject to conditions and obligations, or simply exempting the agreement in question.

This new accelerated procedure, applicable since 1 January 1993, is based entirely on the principle of self-discipline. The deadline of two months from the complete notification — intended for the initial examination of the case — does not constitute a statutory term and is therefore in no way legally binding. However, the Commission will do its best to abide by it. The Commission reserves the right, moreover, to extend this accelerated procedure to other forms of cooperation between undertakings.

A cooperative joint venture of a structural nature is one that involves an important change in the structure and organisation of the business assets of the parties to the agreement. This may occur because the joint venture takes over or extends existing activities of the parent companies or because it undertakes new activities on their behalf. Such operations are characterised by the commitment of significant financial, material and/or non-tangible assets such as intellectual property rights and know how. Structural joint ventures are therefore normally intended to operate on a medium- or long-term basis.

This concept includes certain 'partial function' joint ventures which take over one or several specific functions within the parents' business activity without access to the market, in particular research and development and/or production. It also covers those 'full function' joint ventures which give rise to coordination of the competitive behaviour of independent undertakings, in particular between the parties to the joint venture or between them and the joint venture.

In order to respect the internal deadline, it is important that the Commission has available on notification all the relevant information reasonably available to the notifying parties that is necessary for it to assess the impact of the operation in question on competition. Form A/B therefore contains a special section (Chapter III) that must be completed only by persons notifying cooperative joint ventures of a structural character that wish to benefit from the accelerated procedure.

Persons notifying joint ventures of a structural character that wish to claim the benefit of the aforementioned accelerated procedure should therefore complete Chapters I, III and IV of this form. Chapter III contains a series of detailed questions necessary for the Commission to assess the relevant market(s) and the position of the parties to the joint venture on that (those) market(s).

Where the parties do not wish to claim the benefit of an accelerated procedure for their joint ventures of a structural character they should complete Chapters I, II and IV of this form. Chapter II contains a far more limited range of questions on the relevant market(s) and the position of the parties to the operation in question on that *(those) market(s), but sufficient to enable the Commission to commence its examination and investigation.*

E THE NEED FOR COMPLETE INFORMATION

The receipt of a valid notification by the Commission has two main consequences. First, it affords immunity from fines from the date that the valid notification is received by the Commission with respect to applications made in order to obtain exemption (see Article 15(5) of Regulation No. 17). Second, until a valid notification is received, the Commission cannot grant an exemption pursuant to Article 85(3) of the EC Treaty and/or Article 53(3) of the EEA Agreement, and any exemption that is granted can be effective only from the date of receipt of a valid notification. Thus, whilst there is no legal obligation to notify as such, unless and until an arrangement that falls within the scope of Article 85(1) and/or Article 53(1) has not been notified and is, therefore, not capable of being exempted, it may be declared void by a national court pursuant to Article 85(2) and/or Article 53(2).

Where an undertaking is claiming the benefit of a group exemption by recourse to an opposition procedure, the period within which the Commission must oppose the exemption by category only applies from the date that a valid notification is received. This is also true of the two months' period imposed on the Commission services for an initial analysis of applications for negative clearance and notifications relating to cooperative joint ventures of a structural character which benefit from the accelerated procedure.

A valid application or notification for this purpose means one that is not incomplete (see Article 3(1) of the Regulation). This is subject to two qualifications. First, if the information or documents required by this form are not reasonably available to you in part or in whole, the Commission will accept that a notification is complete and thus valid notwithstanding the failure to provide such information, providing that you give reasons for the unavailability of the information, and provide your best estimates for missing data together with the sources for the estimates. Indications as to where any of the requested information or documents that are unavailable to you could be obtained by the Commission must also be provided. Second, the Commission only requires the submission of information relevant and necessary to its inquiry into the notified operation. In some cases not all the information required by this form will be necessary for this purpose. The Commission may therefore dispense with the obligation to provide certain information required by this form (see Article 3(3) of the Regulation). This provision enables, where appropriate, each application or notification to be tailored to each case so that only the information strictly necessary for the Commission's examination is provided. This avoids unnecessary administrative burdens being imposed on undertakings, in particular on small and medium-sized ones. Where the information or documents required by this form are not provided for this reason, the application or notification should indicate the reasons why the information is considered to be unnecessary to the Commission's investigation.

Where the Commission finds that the information contained in the application or notification is incomplete in a material respect, it will, within one month from receipt, inform the applicant or the notifying party in writing of this fact and the nature of the missing information. In such cases, the application or notification shall become effective on the date on which the complete information is received by the Commission. If the Commission has not informed the applicant or the notifying party within the one month period that the application or notification is incomplete in a material respect, the application or notification will be deemed to be complete and valid (see Article 4 of the Regulation).

It is also important that undertakings inform the Commission of important changes in the factual situation including those of which they become aware after the application or notification has been submitted. The Commission must, therefore, be informed immediately of any changes to an agreement, decision or practice which is the subject of an application or notification (see Article 4(3) of the Regulation). Failure to inform the Commission of such relevant changes could result in any negative clearance decision being without effect or in the withdrawal of any exemption decision adopted by the Commission on the basis of the notification.

F THE NEED FOR ACCURATE INFORMATION

In addition to the requirement that the application or notification be complete, it is important that you ensure that the information provided is accurate (see Article 3(1) of the Regulation). Article 15(1)(a) of Regulation No. 17 states that the Commission may, by decision, impose on undertakings or associations of undertakings fines of up to ECU 5,000 where, intentionally or negligently, they supply incorrect or misleading information in an application for negative clearance or notification. Such information is, moreover, considered to be incomplete (see Article 4(4) of the Regulation), so that the parties cannot benefit from the advantages of the opposition procedure or accelerated procedure (see above, Point E).

G WHO CAN LODGE AN APPLICATION OR A NOTIFICATION?

Any of the undertakings party to an agreement, decision or practice of the kind described in Articles 85 or 86 of the EC Treaty and Articles 53 or 54 of the EEA Agreement may submit an application for negative clearance, in relation to Article 85 and Article 53, or a notification requesting an exemption. An association of undertakings may submit an application or a notification in relation to decisions taken or practices pursued into in the operation of the association.

In relation to agreements and concerted practices between undertakings it is common practice for all the parties involved to submit a joint application or notification. Although the Commission strongly recommends this approach, because it is helpful to have the views of all the parties directly concerned at the same time, it is not obligatory. Any of the parties to an agreement may submit an application or notification in their individual capacities, but in such circumstances the notifying party should inform all the other parties to the agreement, decision or practice of that fact (see Article 1(3) of the Regulation). They may also provide them with a copy of the completed form, where relevant, once confidential information and business secrets have been deleted (see below, operational part, question 1.2).

Where a joint application or notification is submitted, it has also become common practice to appoint a joint representative to act on behalf of all the undertakings involved, both in making the application or notification, and in dealing with any subsequent contacts with the Commission (see Article 1(4) of the Regulation). Again, whilst this is helpful, it is not obligatory, and all the undertakings jointly submitting an application or a notification may sign it in their individual capacities.

H HOW TO SUBMIT AN APPLICATION OR NOTIFICATION

Applications and notifications may be submitted in any of the official languages of the European Community or of an EFTA State (see Article 2(4) and (5) of the Regulation). In order to ensure rapid proceedings, it is, however, recommended to use, in case of an application or notification to the EFTA Surveillance Authority one of the official languages of an EFTA State or the working language of the EFTA Surveillance Authority, which is English, or, in the case of an application or notification to the Commission, one of the official languages of the Community or the working language of the EFTA Surveillance Authority. This language will thereafter be the language of the proceeding for the applicant or notifying party.

Form A/B is not a form to be filled in. Undertakings should simply provide the information requested by this form, using its sections and paragraph numbers, signing a declaration as stated in Section 19 below, and annexing the required supporting documentation.

Supporting documents shall be submitted in their original language; where this is not an official language of the Community they must be translated into the language of the proceeding. The supporting documents may be originals or copies of the originals (see Article 2(4) of the Regulation).

All information requested in this form shall, unless otherwise stated, relate to the calendar year preceding that of the application or notification. Where information is not reasonably available on this basis (for example if accounting periods are used that are not based on the calendar year, or the previous year's figures are not yet available) the most recently available information should be provided and reasons given why figures on the basis of the calendar year preceding that of the application or notification cannot be provided.

Financial data may be provided in the currency in which the official audited accounts of the undertaking(s) concerned are prepared or in Ecus. In the latter case the exchange rate used for the conversion must be stated.

Seventeen copies of each application or notification, but only three copies of all supporting documents must be provided (see Article 2(2) of the Regulation).

The application or notification is to be sent to:

Commission of the European Communities,
Directorate-General for Competition (DG IV),
The Registrar,
200 Rue de la Loi,
B-1049 Brussels

or be delivered by hand during Commission working days and official working hours at the following address:

Commission of the European Communities,
Directorate-General for Competition (DG IV),
The Registrar,
158 Avenue de Cortenberg,
B-1040 Brussels.

I CONFIDENTIALITY

Article 214 of the EC Treaty, Article 20 of Regulation No. 17, Article 9 of Protocol 23 to the EEA Agreement, Article 122 of the EEA Agreement and Articles 20 and 21 of Chapter II of Protocol 4 to the Agreement between the EFTA States on the establishment of a Surveillance Authority and of a Court of Justice require the Commission, the Member States, the EEA Surveillance Authority and EFTA States not to disclose information of the kind covered by the obligation of professional secrecy. On the other hand, Regulation No. 17 requires the Commission to publish a summary of the application or notification, should it intend to take a favourable decision. In this publication, the Commission '... shall have regard to the legitimate interest of undertakings in the protection of their business secrets' (Article 19(3) of Regulation No. 17; see also Article 21(2) in relation to the publication of decisions). In this connection, if an undertaking believes that its interests would be harmed if any of the information it is asked to supply were to be published or otherwise divulged to other undertakings, it should put all such information in a separate annex with each page clearly marked 'Business Secrets'. It should also give reasons why any information identified as confidential or secret should not be divulged or published. (See below, Section 5 of the operational part that requests a non-confidential summary of the notification.)

J SUBSEQUENT PROCEDURE

The application or notification is registered in the Registry of the Directorate-General for Competition (DG IV). The date of receipt by the Commission (or the date of posting if sent by registered post) is the effective date of the submission (see Article 4(1) of the Regulation). However, special rules apply to incomplete applications and notifications (see above under Point E).

The Commission will acknowledge receipt of all applications and notifications in writing, indicating the case number attributed to the file. This number must be used in all future correspondence regarding the notification. The receipt of acknowledgement does not prejudge the question whether the application or notification is valid.

Further information may be sought from the parties or from third parties (Articles 11 to 14 of Regulation No. 17) and suggestions might be made as to amendments to the arrangements that might make them acceptable. Equally, a short preliminary *notice may be published in the C series of the Official Journal of the European Communities, stating the names of the interested undertakings, the groups to which they belong, the economic sectors involved and the nature of the arrangements, and inviting third party comments (see below, operational part, Section 5).*

Where a notification is made together for the purpose of the application of the opposition procedure, the Commission may oppose the grant of the benefit of the group exemption with respect to the notified agreement. If the Commission opposes the claim, and unless it subsequently withdraws its opposition, that notification will then be treated as an application for an individual exemption.

If, after examination, the Commission intends to grant the application for negative clearance or exemption, it is obliged (by Article 19(3) of Regulation No. 17) to publish a summary and invite comments from third parties. Subsequently, a preliminary draft decision has to be submitted to and discussed with the Advisory Committee on Restrictive Practices and Dominant Positions composed of officials of the competent authorities of the Member States in the matter of restrictive practices and monopolies (Article 10 of Regulation No. 17) and attended, where the case falls within the EEA Agreement, by representatives of the EFTA Surveillance Authority and the EFTA States which will already have received a copy of the application or notification. Only then, and providing nothing has happened to change the Commission's intention, can it adopt the envisaged decision.

Files are often closed without any formal decision being taken, for example, because it is found that the arrangements are already covered by a block exemption, or because they do not call for any action by the Commission, at least in circumstances at that time. In such cases comfort letters are sent. Although not a Commission decision, a comfort letter indicates how the Commission's departments view the case on the facts currently in their possession which means that the Commission could where necessary — for example, if it were to be asserted that a contract was void under Article 85(2) of the EC Treaty and/or Article 53(2) of the EEA Agreement — take an appropriate decision to clarify the legal situation.

K   DEFINITIONS USED IN THE OPERATIONAL PART OF THIS FORM

Agreement: The word 'agreement' is used to refer to all categories of arrangements, i.e., agreements between undertakings, decisions by associations of undertakings and concerted practices.

Year: All references to the word 'year' in this form shall be read as meaning calendar year, unless otherwise stated.

Group: A group relationship exists for the purpose of this form where one undertaking:

—owns more than half the capital or business assets of another undertaking, or

—has the power to exercise more than half the voting rights in another undertaking, or

—has the power to appoint more than half the members of the supervisory board, board of directors or bodies legally representing the undertaking, or

—has the right to manage the affairs of another undertaking.

An undertaking which is jointly controlled by several other undertakings (joint venture) forms part of the group of each of these undertakings.

Relevant product market: questions 6.1 and 11.1 of this form require the undertaking or individual submitting the notification to define the relevant product and/or service market(s) that are likely to be affected by the agreement in question. That definition(s) is then used as the basis for a number of other questions contained in this form. The definition(s) thus submitted by the notifying parties are referred to in this form as the relevant product market(s). These words can refer to a market made up either of products or of services.

Relevant geographic market: questions 6.2 and 11.2 of this form require the undertaking or individual submitting the notification to define the relevant geographic market(s) that are likely to be affected by the agreement in question. That definition(s) is then used as the basis for a number of other questions contained in this form. The definition(s) thus submitted by the notifying parties are referred to in this form as the relevant geographic market(s).

Relevant product and geographic market: by virtue of the combination of their replies to questions 6 and 11 the parties provide their definition of the relevant market(s) affected by the notified agreement(s). That (those) definition(s) is (are) then used as the basis for a number of other questions contained in this form. The definition(s) thus submitted by the notifying parties is referred to in this form as the relevant geographic and product market(s).

Notification: this form can be used to make an application for negative clearance and/or a notification requesting an exemption. The word 'notification' is used to refer to either an application or a notification.

Parties and notifying party: the word 'party' is used to refer to all the undertakings which are party to the agreement being notified. As a notification may be submitted by only one of the undertakings which are party to an agreement, 'notifying party' is used to refer only to the undertaking or undertakings actually submitting the notification.

OPERATIONAL PART

PLEASE MAKE SURE THAT THE FIRST PAGE OF YOUR APPLICATION OR NOTIFI-CATION CONTAINS THE WORDS 'APPLICATION FOR NEGATIVE CLEARANCE/ NOTIFICATION IN ACCORDANCE WITH FORM A/B'

CHAPTER I   SECTIONS CONCERNING THE PARTIES, THEIR GROUPS AND THE AGREEMENT (TO BE COMPLETED FOR ALL NOTIFICATIONS)

Section 1   Identity of the undertakings or persons submitting the notification

1.1   Please list the undertakings on behalf of which the notification is being submitted and indicate their legal denomination or commercial name, shortened or commonly used as appropriate (if it differs from the legal denomination).

1.2   If the notification is being submitted on behalf of only one or some of the undertakings party to the agreement being notified, please confirm that the remaining undertakings have been informed of that fact and indicate whether they have received a copy of the notification, with relevant confidential information and business secrets deleted.[1] (In such circumstances a copy of the edited copy of the notification which has been provided to such other undertakings should be annexed to this notification.)

1.3   If a joint notification is being submitted, has a joint representative[2] been appointed?[3]

If yes, please give the details requested in 1.3.1 to 1.3.3 below.

If no, please give details of any representatives who have been authorised to act for each or either of the parties to the agreement indicating who they represent.

1.3.1   Name of representative.

1.3.2   Address of representative.

1.3.3   Telephone and fax number of representative.

1.4   In cases where one or more representatives have been appointed, an authority to act on behalf of the undertaking(s) submitting the notification must accompany the notification.

Notes

1.   The Commission is aware that in exceptional cases it may not be practicable to inform non-notifying parties to the notified agreement of the fact that it has been notified, or to provide them a copy of the notification. This may be the case, for example, where a standard agreement is being notified that is concluded with a large number of undertakings. Where this is the case you should state the reason why it has not been practicable to follow the standard procedure set out in this question.

2.   For the purposes of this question a representative means an individual or undertaking formally appointed to make the notification or application on behalf of the party or parties submitting the notification. This should be distinguished from the situation where the notification is signed by an officer of the company or companies in question. In the latter situation no representative is appointed.

3.   It is not mandatory to appoint representatives for the purpose of completing and/or submitting this notification. This question only requires the identification of representatives where the notifying parties have chosen to appoint them.

Section 2 Information on the parties to the agreement and the groups to which they belong

2.1 State the name and address of the parties to the agreement being notified, and the country of their incorporation.

2.2 State the nature of the business of each of the parties to the agreement being notified.

2.3 For each of the parties to the agreement, give the name of a person that can be contacted, together with his or her name, address, telephone number, fax number and position held in the undertaking.

2.4 Identify the corporate groups to which the parties to the agreement being notified belong. State the sectors in which these groups are active, and the world-wide turnover of each group.

Section 3 Procedural matters

3.1 Please state whether you have made any formal submission to any other competition authorities in relation to the agreement in question. If yes, state which authorities, the individual or department in question, and the nature of the contact. In addition to this, mention any earlier proceedings or informal contacts, of which you are aware, with the Commission and/or the EFTA Surveillance Authority and any earlier proceedings with any national authorities or courts in the Community or in EFTA concerning these or any related agreements.

3.2 Please summarise any reasons for any claim that the case involves an issue of exceptional urgency.

3.3 The Commission has stated that where notifications do not have particular political, economic or legal significance for the Community they will normally be dealt with by means of comfort letter. Would you be satisfied with a comfort letter? If you consider that it would be inappropriate to deal with the notified agreement in this manner, please explain the reasons for this view.

3.4 State whether you intend to produce further supporting facts or arguments not yet available and, if so, on which points.

Section 4 Full details of the arrangements

4.1 Please summarise the nature, content and objectives pursued by the agreement being notified.

4.2 Detail any provisions contained in the agreements which may restrict the parties in their freedom to take independent commercial decisions, for example regarding:
  — buying or selling prices, discounts or other trading conditions,
  — the quantities of goods to be manufactured or distributed or services to be offered,
  — technical development or investment,
  — the choice of markets or sources of supply,
  — purchases from or sales to third parties,
  — whether to apply similar terms for the supply of equivalent goods or services,
  — whether to offer different services separately or together.

If you are claiming the benefit of the opposition procedure, identify in this list the restrictions that exceed those automatically exempted by the relevant regulation.

4.3 State between which Member States of the Community and/or EFTA States trade may be affected by the arrangements. Please give reasons for your reply to this question, giving data on trade flows where relevant. Furthermore please state whether trade between the Community or the EEA territory and any third countries is affected, again giving reasons for your reply.

Section 5 Non-confidential summary

Shortly following receipt of a notification, the Commission may publish a short notice inviting third party comments on the agreement in question. As the objective pursued by the Commission in publishing an informal preliminary notice is to receive third party comments as soon as possible after the notification has been received, such a notice is usually published without first providing it to the notifying parties for their comments. This section requests the information to be used in an informal preliminary notice in the event that the Commission decides to issue one. It is important, therefore, that your replies to these questions do not contain any business secrets or other confidential information.

1. *State the names of the parties to the agreement notified and the groups of undertakings to which they belong.*
2. *Give a short summary of the nature and objectives of the agreement. As a guideline this summary should not exceed 100 words.*
3. *Identify the product sectors affected by the agreement in question.*

CHAPTER II   SECTION CONCERNING THE RELEVANT MARKET (TO BE COMPLETED FOR ALL NOTIFICATIONS EXCEPT THOSE RELATING TO STRUCTURAL JOINT VENTURES FOR WHICH ACCELERATED TREATMENT IS CLAIMED)

Section 6   The relevant market

A relevant product market comprises all those products and/or services which are regarded as interchangeable or substitutable by the consumer, by reason of the products' characteristics, their prices and their intended use.

The following factors are normally considered to be relevant to the determination of the relevant product market and should be taken into account in this analysis:[1]
— *the degree of physical similarity between the products/services in question,*
— *any differences in the end use to which the goods are put,*
— *differences in price between two products,*
— *the cost of switching between two potentially competing products,*
— *established or entrenched consumer preferences for one type or category of product over another,*
— *industry-wide product classifications (e.g., classifications maintained by trade associations).*

The relevant geographic market comprises the area in which the undertakings concerned are involved in the supply of products or services, in which the conditions of competition are sufficiently homogeneous and which can be distinguished from neighbouring areas because, in particular, conditions of competition are appreciably different in those areas.

Factors relevant to the assessment of the relevant geographic market include[1] the nature and characteristics of the products or services concerned, the existence of entry barriers or consumer preferences, appreciable differences of the undertakings' market share or substantial price differences between neighbouring areas, and transport costs.

6.1   In the light of the above please explain the definition of the relevant product market or markets that in your opinion should form the basis of the Commission's analysis of the notification.

In your answer, please give reasons for assumptions or findings, and explain how the factors outlined above have been taken into account. In particular, please state the specific products or services directly or indirectly affected by the agreement being notified and identify the categories of goods viewed as substitutable in your market definition.

In the questions figuring below, this (or these) definition(s) will be referred to as 'the relevant product market(s)'.

6.2   Please explain the definition of the relevant geographic market or markets that in your opinion should form the basis of the Commission's analysis of the notification. In your answer, please give reasons for assumptions or findings, and explain how the factors outlined above have been taken into account. In particular, please identify the countries in which the parties are active in the relevant product market(s), and in the event that you consider the relevant geographic market to be wider than the individual Member States of the Community or EFTA on which the parties to the agreement are active, give the reasons for this.

In the questions below, this (or these) definition(s) will be referred to as 'the relevant geographic market(s)'.

Note
1. *This list is not, however, exhaustive, and notifying parties may refer to other factors.*

Section 7   Group members operating on the same markets as the parties

7.1   For each of the parties to the agreement being notified, provide a list of all undertakings belonging to the same group which are:

7.1.1   active in the relevant product market(s);
7.1.2   active in markets neighbouring the relevant product market(s) (i.e., active in products and/or services that represent imperfect and partial substitutes for those included in your definition of the relevant product market(s)).

Such undertakings must be identified even if they sell the product or service in question in other geographic areas than those in which the parties to the notified agreement operate. Please list the name, place of incorporation, exact product manufactured and the geographic scope of operation of each group member.

Section 8   The position of the parties on the affected relevant product markets

Information requested in this section must be provided for the groups of the parties as a whole. It is not sufficient to provide such information only in relation to the individual undertakings directly concerned by the agreement.
8.1   In relation to each relevant product market(s) identified in your reply to question 6.1 please provide the following information:
8.1.1   the market shares of the parties on the relevant geographic market during the previous three years;
8.1.2   where different, the market shares of the parties in (a) the EEA territory as a whole, (b) the Community, (c) the territory of the EFTA States and (d) each EC Member State and EFTA State during the previous three years.[1] For this section, where market shares are less than 20%, please state simply which of the following bands are relevant: 0 to 5%, 5 to 10%, 10 to 15%, 15 to 20%.

For the purpose of answering these questions, market share may be calculated either on the basis of value or volume. Justification for the figures provided must be given. Thus, for each answer, total market value/volume must be stated, together with the sales/turnover of each of the parties in question. The source or sources of the information should also be given (e.g., official statistics, estimates, etc.), and where possible, copies should be provided of documents from which information has been taken.

Note
1.   I.e. Where the relevant geographic market has been defined as world wide, these figures must be given regarding the EEA, the Community, the territory of the EFTA States, and each EC Member States. Where the relevant geographic market has been defined as the Community, these figures must be given for the EEA, the territory of the EFTA States, and each EC Member State. Where the market has been defined as national, these figures must be given for the EEA, the Community and the territory of the EFTA States.

Section 9   The position of competitors and customers on the relevant product market(s)

Information requested in this section must be provided for the group of the parties as a whole and not in relation to the individual companies directly concerned by the agreement notified.
For the (all) relevant product and geographic market(s) in which the parties have a combined market share exceeding 15%, the following questions must be answered.
9.1   Please identify the five main competitors of the parties. Please identify the company and give your best estimate as to their market share in the relevant geographic market(s). Please also provide address, telephone and fax number, and, where possible, the name of a contact person at each company identified.
9.2   Please identify the five main customers of each of the parties. State company name, address, telephone and fax numbers, together with the name of a contact person.

Section 10   Market entry and potential competition in product and geographic terms

For the (all) relevant product and geographic market(s) in which the parties have a combined market share exceeding 15%, the following questions must be answered.
10.1   Describe the various factors influencing entry in product terms into the relevant product market(s) that exist in the present case (i.e., what barriers exist to prevent undertakings that do not presently manufacture goods within the relevant product

market(s) entering this market(s)). In so doing take account of the following where appropriate:

—to what extent is entry to the markets influenced by the requirement of government authorisation or standard setting in any form? Are there any legal or regulatory controls on entry to these markets?

—to what extent is entry to the markets influenced by the availability of raw materials?

—to what extent is entry to the markets influenced by the length of contracts between an undertaking and its suppliers and/or customers?

—describe the importance of research and development and in particular the importance of licensing patents, know-how and other rights in these markets.

10.2 Describe the various factors influencing entry in geographic terms into the relevant geographic market(s) that exist in the present case (i.e., what barriers exist to prevent undertakings already producing and/or marketing products within the relevant product market(s) but in areas outside the relevant geographic market(s) extending the scope of their sales into the relevant geographic market(s)?).

Please give reasons for your answer, explaining, where relevant, the importance of the following factors:

—trade barriers imposed by law, such as tariffs, quotas etc.,

—local specification or technical requirements,

—procurement policies,

—the existence of adequate and available local distribution and retailing facilities,

—transport costs,

—entrenched consumer preferences for local brands or products,

—language.

10.3 Have any new undertakings entered the relevant product market(s) in geographic areas where the parties sell during the last three years? Please provide this information with respect to both new entrants in product terms and new entrants in geographic terms. If such entry has occurred, please identify the undertaking(s) concerned (name, address, telephone and fax numbers, and, where possible, contact person), and provide your best estimate of their market share in the relevant product and geographic market(s).

CHAPTER III SECTION CONCERNING THE RELEVANT MARKET ONLY FOR STRUCTURAL JOINT VENTURES FOR WHICH ACCELERATED TREATMENT IS CLAIMED

[Not reproduced here.]

CHAPTER IV FINAL SECTIONS (TO BE COMPLETED FOR ALL NOTIFICATIONS)

Section 16 Reasons for the application for negative clearance

If you are applying for negative clearance state:

16.1 why, i.e. state which provision or effects of the agreement or behaviour might, in your view, raise questions of compatibility with the Community's and/or the EEA rules of competition. The object of this subheading is to give the Commission the clearest possible idea of the doubts you have about your agreement or behaviour that you wish to have resolved by a negative clearance.

Then, under the following three references, give a statement of the relevant facts and reasons as to why you consider Article 85(1) or 86 of the EC Treaty and/or Article 53(1) or 54 of the EEA Agreement to be inapplicable, i.e.:

16.2 why the agreements or behaviour do not have the object or effect of preventing, restricting or distorting competition within the common market or within the territory of the EFTA States to any appreciable extent, or why your undertaking does not have or its behaviour does not abuse a dominant position; and/or

16.3 why the agreements or behaviour do not have the object or effect of preventing, restricting or distorting competition within the EEA territory to any appreciable extent, or why your undertaking does not have or its behaviour does not abuse a dominant position; and/or

16.4 why the agreements or behaviour are not such as may affect trade between Member States or between the Community and one or more EFTA States, or between EFTA States to any appreciable extent.

Section 17 Reasons for the application for exemption

If you are notifying the agreement, even if only as a precaution, in order to obtain an exemption under Article 85(3) of the EC Treaty and/or Article 53(3) of the EEA Agreement, explain how:

17.1 the agreement contributes to improving production or distribution, and/or promoting technical or economic progress. In particular, please explain the reasons why these benefits are expected to result from the collaboration; for example, do the parties to the agreement possess complementary technologies or distribution systems that will produce important synergies? (if so, please state which). Also please state whether any documents or studies were drawn up by the notifying parties when assessing the feasibility of the operation and the benefits likely to result therefrom, and whether any such documents or studies provided estimates of the savings or efficiencies likely to result. Please provide copies of any such documents or studies;

17.2 a proper share of the benefits arising from such improvement or progress accrues to consumers;

17.3 all restrictive provisions of the agreement are indispensable to the attainment of the aims set out under 17.1 (if you are claiming the benefit of the opposition procedure, it is particularly important that you should identify and justify restrictions that exceed those automatically exempted by the relevant Regulations). In this respect please explain how the benefits resulting from the agreement identified in your reply to question 17.1 could not be achieved, or could not be achieved so quickly or efficiently or only at higher cost or with less certainty of success (i) without the conclusion of the agreement as a whole and (ii) without those particular clauses and provisions of the agreement identified in your reply to question 4.2;

17.4 the agreement does not eliminate competition in respect of a substantial part of the goods or services concerned.

Section 18 Supporting documentation

The completed notification must be drawn up and submitted in one original. It shall contain the last versions of all agreements which are the subject of the notification and be accompanied by the following:

> *(a) sixteen copies of the notification itself;*
>
> *(b) three copies of the annual reports and accounts of all the parties to the notified agreement, decision or practice for the last three years;*
>
> *(c) three copies of the most recent in-house or external long-term market studies or planning documents (for the purpose of assessing or analysing the affected markets) with respect to competitive conditions, competitors (actual and potential), and market conditions. Each document should indicate the name and position of the author;*
>
> *(d) three copies of reports and analyses which have been prepared by or for any officer(s) or director(s) for the purposes of evaluating or analysing the notified agreement.*

Section 19 Declaration

The notification must conclude with the following declaration which is to be signed by or on behalf of all the applicants or notifying parties.[1]

> *The undersigned declare that the information given in this notification is correct to the best of their knowledge and belief, that complete copies of all documents requested by form A/B have been supplied to the extent that they are in the possession of the group of undertakings to which the applicant(s) or notifying party(ies) belong(s) and are accessible to the latter, that all estimates are identified as such and are their best estimates of the underlying facts and that all the opinions expressed are sincere.*
>
> *They are aware of the provisions of Article 15(1)(a) of Regulation No. 17.*
>
> *Place and date:*
>
> *Signatures:*

Please add the name(s) of the person(s) signing the application or notification and their function(s).

Note

1. *Applications and notifications which have not been signed are invalid.*

APPENDIX FIVE

GLOSSARY

Absolute territorial protection

A clause in a distribution agreement whereby a supplier agrees not to supply to others who will sell in the same territory as the first buyer. This is usually accompanied by another clause in the agreement, defining the territory within which the first buyer will operate. This type of protection may involve a ban on passive as well as active sales.

Chiselling

When an individual covertly undercuts the prices agreed by an unlawful cartel of producers/ sellers. It is sometimes suggested that the likelihood of chiselling is so great that cartels do not pose a long-term threat to competition. Since, the theory goes, the cartel members are necessarily prepared to act in an underhand fashion and rip off their customers (in the form of agreed higher prices), they will feel little hesitation in ripping off their fellow cartel members (e.g., by offering secret discounts to customers) and thereby increasing their market share.

Competition

A perfectly competitive market is unattainable in practice. It is a situation towards which one can aim without ever getting there. In a competitive market, no single producer can influence the price of the product: there are enough competitors or competing products to ensure that the quantity sold by a producer does not affect the price. The lack of influence which an individual firm has in a competitive market is best illustrated by the demand curve for a firm in a competitive industry (see **Figure A** below). This shows that for this firm there is effectively a set price for the product. As long as it does not try to sell above this price, it can sell as much of the product as it can produce. Once it puts its price above the level indicated, it will sell nothing as there are plenty of available and acceptable substitutes around. Note that for a competitive *industry*, the demand curve will be like that in **Figure B** (see demand curve over). See also **Marginal costs and revenue, Figure C.**

Figure A — Output of a firm in a competitive industry

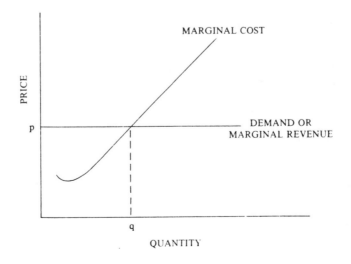

Demand curve

Economists are often concerned about the 'demand' for a product. When determining levels of demand, a demand curve is usually constructed. This is simply a graph illustrating the relationship between the number of items that a consumer will buy and the price charged for the item. The demand curve is usually on a negative slope (see **Figure B**) because the more you get, the less you want. For example, as the price of coats drops, so the number of coats sold increases, but if you bought, say, two coats at £100 each, you are unlikely to buy yourself another coat unless the price drops. Thus, in order to sell more coats, the seller has to reduce the price. If he charges £150, you'll buy one; if he drops the price to £100, you'll buy two; but you'll only buy three if he drops the price to £70.

Figure B — The demand curve

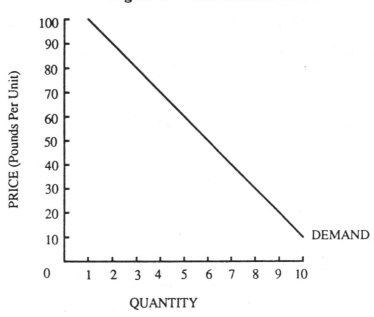

DG IV

The department of the Commission which deals with competition matters, especially investigations. In 1999, the long-term Commissioner in charge of competition matters, Karel Van Miert, of Belgium, was replaced by Mario Monti, of Italy, as part of large-scale changes to the membership of the Commission.

DG XV

The department of the Commission which deals with the single market. In particular, it is responsible for industrial and intellectual property rights, and issues concerning the free movement of goods. In 1999, its Commissioner, Mario Monti, switched to become the Commissioner for Competition.

Exclusionary rebates and discounts

Fidelity rebates (i.e. keep buying from me and you get a rebate); rebates based on improving your volume of purchases from a particular supplier above last year's levels. Basically, financial incentives to stay with a particular supplier and even buy more of his product. These tactics tie up distributors and make it difficult for other suppliers to find an outlet for their products.

Exclusive dealer/distributor

This is an independent distributor who agrees to stock the goods of a particular supplier in return for a promise that the supplier will not supply those goods to another distributor within a defined territory. The distributor is restricted to that territory for his sales. The distributor may also agree to stock the full range of the supplier's goods and not to stock any competing products. Such agreements are regarded by the European Commission as having competitive advantages in certain circumstances: this has led the Commission to issue block exemptions in this field, notably Regulation 1983/83.

Exclusive purchase

Originally exclusive distribution and exclusive purchasing were treated by the Commission as a single form of business conduct — exclusive dealing (see Regulation 67/67). Since 1983, two block exemptions have existed in this field, with Regulation 1984/83 covering exclusive purchasing agreements. As the Commission has observed,

> Regulations ... 1983/83 and ... 1984/83 are both concerned with exclusive agreements between two undertakings for the purpose of the resale of goods.

In an exclusive purchase agreement, the purchaser (or reseller) agrees to buy the relevant goods only from that supplier. Unlike exclusive distribution, the purchaser has no exclusive territory and this has two effects. First, the supplier can supply the same goods to others operating in the vicinity of the exclusive purchaser; secondly, the purchaser is not restricted to a particular area for his sales efforts.

Two particular types of exclusive purchase agreement which are especially dealt with in Regulation 1984/83 are those for the supply of beer in pubs etc. and of petrol in service stations.

Export bans

A contract clause forbidding the purchaser from reselling outside his territory (which may be anything from a 100-metre radius around his shop to the territory of a member state). Such bans may be on active sales only or passive sales, or both. A ban on active sales outside one's territory would prevent the opening of additional shops, for example. A ban on passive sales would prevent one from selling to a customer who came in from outside the allotted territory.

Geographical market

Relevant to the issue of whether there is an effect on trade between Member States. See also **Market share analysis**.

Horizontal agreement

Simply an agreement between companies operating at the same level of the market, e.g., manufacturers of a product (as in *ICI* v *Commission* (48/69) [1972] ECR 619). Compare **Vertical agreement.**

Marginal costs and revenue

These terms refer to the additional costs incurred or revenue raised by producing and selling each additional item. Profits are maximised if one sells the quantity at the price indicated by the place where marginal costs and revenue are equal. See **Figure C**.

Figure C — Profit maximisation by a firm

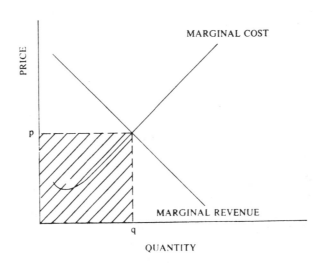

Market share analysis

When determining, for example, whether a company has a dominant position in a market (for use in proceedings under Article 82 (ex 86), EC Treaty), it is necessary to decide on the nature of both the product market and the geographical market. In *United Brands* v *Commission* (27/76) [1976] ECR 425 the relevant product was bananas, not all soft fruits and certainly not all fruits; in *Michelin* v *Commission* (322/81) [1983] ECR 3461 the relevant product was tyres for heavy trucks, not all truck tyres and not all motor vehicle tyres. The geographical market in *Michelin* was The Netherlands, rather than, say, the Benelux countries; in *United Brands* sales of bananas in France, the UK and Italy were excluded from consideration because of different trading conditions from the other six Member States.

Once the relevant product and geographical markets have been determined, one can gather evidence on the percentage share (either in terms of finance or volume) of that market held by the suspect firm. This is commonly used by the Commission as an indicator of the presence (or absence) of a dominant position. In *United Brands*, the company was found to possess a significant market share and hold a dominant position, even though for at least some of the time it had been incurring losses.

Monopoly

In very simple terms, a monopolist has freedom to charge a price he chooses for his product and (usually) sell less of it, regardless of his competitors' actions and the demands of consumers: he is independent of the other 'players' in that market. One evil of such domination, according to economic theory, is that resources will be misused: higher prices will be charged by the monopolist and some potential customers will either go unsatisfied or will buy inappropriate substitutes. Either way, there is an inefficient allocation of resources ('welfare loss'). Also, the lack of any competition means that the monopolist has less incentive to improve his product or be innovative: this is a disadvantage to consumers.

Some economists argue that monopolies are not necessarily all bad. For example, the greater profits generated may lead both directly and indirectly to more investment in research and development, either by the monopolist or by potential competitors who would like to enter the market and share the profits.

Figure D — Comparing monopoly with a competitive industry

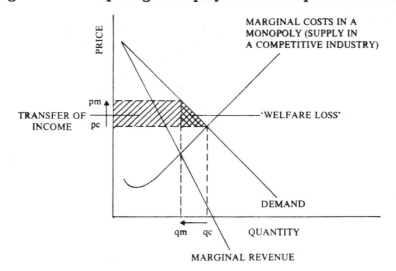

Figure D represents the situation in a perfect monopoly. Note that price and quantity are determined by the spot where marginal costs equal marginal revenue (because this is where profits are maximised). In a competitive industry, marginal revenue and the demand curve are the same so that demand is satisfied. In a monopoly the marginal revenue is always lower than the demand so that when the monopolist maximises profits there is an unsatisfied demand.

The EC prohibits abuse, but not the mere attainment, of a dominant position. Dominant position is not necessarily the same as a monopoly — if a company has a monopoly, then almost certainly it will have a dominant position; but there have been cases in the EC where a company does not seem to have a monopoly but has nevertheless been held to be dominant (see *United Brands*).

New agreement

One made since March 1962, when the competition rules took effect. Alternatively, one made after the date of accession of a Member State if one of the parties operates in the new Member State and the agreement took effect there. They are specifically dealt with in Article 4, Regulation 17/62, and should be compared with **'old' agreements**.

Non-challenge clause

Basically, this concerns the licensing of intellectual property rights (e.g., patents). (See, e.g., *Bayer AG* v *Sullhofer* (65/86) [1988] ECR 5249.) The licensor permits the licensee to have access to his patent and manufacture the patented goods, subject to the requirement not to challenge the grant of the patent to the licensor. A licensee might want to do this because, if he could show the patent was invalid, he could make the goods without having to pay a royalty to the licensor. This type of clause is often seen as anti-competitive, although it may not be where the patent licence was granted compulsorily rather than voluntarily.

Non-competition clause

A contract clause requiring one party not to compete with the other or sometimes with third parties. An example is a standard franchise agreement. It may last for the duration of the agreement or extend beyond the lifetime of the agreement. Essentially, the longer it lasts, the more it is likely to be regarded as anti-competitive. Such clauses were considered by the Court of Justice in *Kai Ottung* v *Klee & Weillback A/S and Thomas Schmidt A/S* (320/87) [1990] 4 CMLR 67 in the context of a licence for a patented invention. The Court observed that if the licensee was prohibited from manufacture and marketing after termination of the licence, he would be at a disadvantage because, once the patent had expired, others would be free to make and market the product. In such circumstances, the clause would be anti-competitive. It might be saved, though, if the clause were limited in time to the duration of the patent. See also Regulation 240/96, the block exemption on technology transfers.

Old agreement

One which was made between undertakings prior to March 1962 and therefore predated the operation of the EC competition rules. See Article 5 of Regulation 17/62 and **provisional validity**.

Predatory pricing

This is the name given to a theory that a company will reduce the price of its product to below its marginal costs (i.e. deliberately make a loss on each sale) in order to attract many customers to it. In order for its competitors to survive, they too will have to slash prices and face losses. Sooner or later, one of the companies will either go out of business or get out of that product. Either way, that leaves the market free of competition for the survivor who can then charge a monopoly price for the product. After a while, the survivor will recoup his losses and start to make monopoly profits.

This theory has been the subject of some debate. Some economists consider that the theory is unrealistic — once monopoly prices were charged, other companies would be attracted to enter the market. The consequence would then be a drop in price towards that originally charged and the survivor would be unable to recoup the losses in full or make monopoly profits. These views seem to be accepted in the USA (see e.g, *Matsushita Electrical Industries Co.* v *Zenith Radio Corp.* (1986) 106 S Ct 1348). In the European Community, predatory behaviour (including pricing policy) is acknowledged as a fact. See, e.g., the investigation of AKZO Chemie by the European Commission (1986), and the 1989 report on predatory pricing by the OECD.

Price fixing

Price fixing has traditionally been condemned by both the Commission and the ECJ. They are often concerned with agreements between competitors (i.e. horizontal agreements or cartels) to sell their products at the same prices: this may occur with homogenous products (like chemical dyes) or similar products (like personal stereos). Such agreements usually cover the whole range of the parties' relevant products. The theory is that such agreements are anti-competitive because the consumer cannot benefit from competition on prices: he cannot purchase the goods cheaper in the store down the road. If the Commission finds competitors even exchanging information about their respective future prices, it may suspect (at the least) a concerted practice which infringes Article 81 (ex 85).

Such horizontal agreements may occur at the level of manufacturers (see, e.g., *ICI* v *Commission* (48/69) [1972] ECR 619; *Ahlström Oy* v *Commission* (C-89, 104, 114, 116–7/85, C-125-129/85) [1993] 4 CMLR 407); or distributors; or retailers. The economic impact of a similar (but vertical) agreement between, say, a manufacturer and one of its distributors to fix the resale prices for the distributor is likely to be less than if all distributors of competing products agree on prices: that single distributor will face price competition from other distributors. One can distinguish vertical agreements from horizontal ones and argue that price fixing is less significant in vertical arrangements.

However, one manufacturer may fix the resale prices for all of its distributors: this entirely removes competition on prices for that product, although it may still face such competition from distributors of substitute products. This control over resale prices is still forbidden by the Commission and the ECJ, and they will be alert to find even indirect control being exercised over prices. See, for example, *Pronuptia de Paris* (161/84) [1986] ECR 353, where the ECJ stated that for a franchisor to *merely* recommend prices to its franchisee was acceptable; what would infringe Article 85 would be where a concerted practice existed between franchisor and franchisee (vertical) or between franchisees (horizontal) to apply the 'recommended' prices as actual prices. A concerted practice of this sort between franchisor and franchisee might be found to exist where the franchisor maintained control over the franchisee's publicity and promotional material (including statements about prices). See also **Chiselling**.

Product market
See **Market share analysis**.

Provisional validity
A term applied to 'old' agreements, referring to a form of prima facie legality which they have. See Regulation 17/62.

Royalties
Often used in patent licences. Considered by the Court of Justice in *Kai Ottung* where it was held that generally a royalty clause which required payments to continue after expiry of the patent would infringe Article 81(1) (ex 85(1)). However, if the licensee could freely terminate the licence agreement on reasonable notice, an obligation to continue paying for the duration of the licence (i.e. for an indeterminate period) was not prohibited by Article 81(1) (ex 85(1)).

Selective distribution systems
As the name implies, what is involved in this type of business is the appointment of several distributors to a network, who are engaged in reselling a product. The distributor must meet certain criteria, imposed by the supplier, in order to qualify for appointment. These criteria might include fitting out a retail shop in a specific way (e.g., *Yves Rocher* shops: see OJ 1987 L8/49), or giving specific training to sales staff, or providing an after-sales service to customers. Such networks may fall foul of Article 81(1) (ex 85(1)), in particular if the supplier requires distributors to satisfy quantitative criteria in order to be appointed, rather than qualitative criteria.

Ties

The notion that a seller with market power can force an unwilling buyer to buy more products than are actually wanted. So if seller S has a monopoly in, say, nail guns (maybe a patent for them) and requires every purchaser of nail guns to buy their supply of nails from him too, even though they could get the nails from another supplier, this represents a tie-in. This type of requirement is often seen as anti-competitive.

Vertical agreement

An agreement made between undertakings operating at different levels of the market, e.g., a manufacturer makes an agreement with a distributor to distribute his products.

APPENDIX SIX

OVERVIEW OF EUROPEAN COMMUNITY LAW

The information which follows is designed only as an introduction to European Community law. It merely outlines the basic concepts, structure and operation of the Community legal order and gives extracts from some source material.

A6.1 The Importance of European Community Law to the UK Practitioner

European Community law became enforceable law in the UK by virtue of the European Communities Act 1972 (ECA 1972). Every year, thousands of decisions based on the Community treaties are made by Community institutions which affect the Member States and the lives of their citizens. An individual citizen of a Member State is not only subject to national law but is also affected by European Community law. Practitioners should be well-informed about the Community legal order as well as the national law which affect their clients. For example, in a recent case involving the Tipp-Ex Company, the company was fined heavily for a breach of Community law notwithstanding its illegal action had been approved (wrongly) by their lawyer!

A barrister will be expected to advise on a point of European Community law when it arises in a case, to decide if the client or his opponent can rely on it in their claim or defence and perhaps to deal with the point in the national court or before the European Court.

A Community law point may arise in a variety of topics with which the ordinary legal practitioner has to deal and is not limited to the commercial sphere only. The practitioner is expected to recognise that a European Community matter has arisen, know where to go to obtain further information about it, how to handle it in person or when to seek specialist advice in relation to it.

A6.2 The Community is a Supranational Legal Order

The Community is often described as a supranational legal order. This is because it is an association of states endowed with autonomous legal authority. Although it was created like a traditional international organisation by international treaties, it is more developed. The same founding documents which established the Community bestowed on it its own sovereign rights and competence. The Community legal system is independent of and superior to those of the Member States. In exchange for membership to the Community, Member States have relinquished some of their own legislative powers and transferred them to the Community institutions which are empowered to enact an autonomous body of Community law. Member States and their citizens are subject to Community law in matters over which the Community has competence. The objectives of the Community are pursued by means of Community legislation and case law and enforced by both the ECJ, the Court of First Instance and the national courts (*Van Gend en Loos* (26/62) [1963] CMLR 105).

A6.3 Legislative Powers of the Community Institutions

The EC Treaty sets out the Community's aims. The Community institutions are left to fill in the details by enacting legislation. As the EC Treaty covers a wide variety of matters, an almost unlimited potential exists for Community legislation (subject to the requirement that the Community institutions may only act within the areas and power laid down by the EC Treaty).

Some Treaty provisions are precise enough not to need further implementation (e.g., the competition rules, Articles 81 (ex 85) and 82 (ex 86)). Others specifically call for, or simply require, further measures to be passed. The Council, acting in conjunction with the Commission and the Parliament, has an implicit power to legislate if action by the Community should prove necessary to attain one of the objectives of the Community and the Treaty has not provided the necessary powers (Article 308 (ex 235), EC Treaty).

To facilitate the Community in carrying out its policies towards third countries, the EC Treaty bestows legal personality on the Community (Article 281 (ex 210)), enables the Commission to negotiate on its behalf and the Council, after consulting with the Parliament where so required by the Treaty, to conclude Treaties between the Community and third countries or international organisations (Article 300 (ex 228)).

By reason of the broad power of the Community institutions to legislate in many areas covered by the EC Treaty, the practitioner has to be constantly alert to keep up to date with the legislation being passed. The best way to do so is through the Official Journal (OJ), published by the Community. Ignorance of EC law is no defence — *Tipp-Ex* case (C-279/87) [1990] ECR I-261).

Member States must be vigilant that they are not breaking Community legislation so that an infringement action is not brought against them. The practitioner may need to advise on such a matter also.

A6.4 How is Legislation Made in the Community?

The legislative process in the Community is based on a division of power between the Commission and the Council. There are only a few cases in which the Commission alone may exercise legislative power. In most cases the Commission proposes and the Council disposes. Before the Council can take a final decision, depending on the subject-matter of the measure, it has to consult the Parliament and sometimes the Economic and Social Committee. The Treaty of European Union strengthened the legislative powers of the Parliament considerably. It acquired a power of 'co-decision' with the Council on areas such as health, culture and research. Under the 'cooperation procedure' the Parliament is able to amend draft legislation sent by the Council (the result is that unanimity is then required in the Council to pass the legislation, rather than a qualified majority). Under further changes, contained in the Amsterdam Treaty 1997, co-decision will become the norm in many areas. However, in the key fields of economic and monetary union, the cooperation procedure will continue to define the roles of the Parliament and Council.

Although the Council is in the strongest position in the decision-making process, the Commission has some tactical advantages. No decision can be taken by the Council without the Commission taking the initiative by proposing the draft Community measure in question. The Commission can amend its proposal up to the time the final decision is made; the Council can only do so by unanimous vote.

A6.5 Legislative Measures that the Community Institutions can Make

The legislative measures or acts which the Community institutions have power to enact are regulations, directives, decisions, recommendations and opinions. Only the first three are legally binding. All five are described in Article 249 (ex 189), EC Treaty:

> *In order to carry out their task and in accordance with the provisions of the Treaty, the European Parliament acting jointly with the Council and the Commission shall make regulations and issue directives, take decisions, make recommendations or deliver opinions.*
>
> *A regulation shall have general application. It shall be binding in its entirety and directly applicable in all Member States.*
>
> *A directive shall be binding, as to the result to be achieved, upon each Member State to which it is addressed, but shall leave to the national authorities the choice of form and methods. A decision shall be binding in its entirety upon those to whom it is addressed.*
>
> *Recommendations and opinions shall have no binding force.*

A Regulation is best described as a normative measure, laying down general rules which apply to anyone who falls within their scope (like a public Act of Parliament in the UK). They do not need additional implementation to take effect.

A directive may be addressed to all Member States, or an individual Member State. It requires implementation by the Member State(s) before it has the force of law, unless it meets the criteria for direct effect. See **A6.9**. The method of implementation is left to the Member State but the result to be achieved is binding.

A decision is an individual act addressed to a specific person or to a Member State. It has the force of law without further enactment. Its nature is essentially administrative, usually affecting just the addressees. It can have judicial undertones, too: see Article 230 (ex 173).

The EC Treaty lays down safeguards in the adoption of these measures. The measures must state the reasons on which they are based and refer to any proposals or opinions which were required to be obtained by the Treaty (Article 253 (ex 190)). Any act which fails to follow this procedural requirement is at risk of annulment (see Article 230 (ex 173)). Another safeguard is publication: see Article 254 (ex 191) for details.

Despite Article 249 (ex 189), the ECJ has held that the true nature of an act is determined by its substance and object, and not its form and label (*Confédération Nationale des Producteurs de Fruits et Legumes* v *Council* (C-16 and 17/62) [1963] CMLR 160); *International Fruit Co. NV* v *Commission (No. 1)* (C-41-4/70) [1975] 2 CMLR 515). The ECJ will re-classify specific measures according to their nature, as distinct from the description applied by the Commission or Council. The ECJ has also developed a category of EC acts which are *sui generis* and not in Article 249 (ex 189) at all. (See *Commission of the European Communities* v *Council of the European Communities* (22/78) [1971] ECR 263, [1971] CMLR 335.)

A6.6 Sources of Community Law

The sources of law, in the sense of the legal rules that form the Community legal order and bind the Community, its institutions, the Member States and (in some instances) individuals, are the following: the founding treaties; the legal acts of the Community; international agreements entered into by the Community institutions on behalf of the Community; the judgments of the ECJ (and the Court of First Instance) and general principles of law. Member States are obliged by Article 10 (ex 5) (see **1.2.3.1** above) to 'take all appropriate measures, whether general or particular, to ensure fulfilment' of the obligations which these sources of law impose.

A6.6.1 THE FOUNDING TREATIES

The founding treaties are a primary source of Community law. They were created directly by the Member States themselves. They are the EC Treaty and Protocols as amended by subsequent Treaties: the Merger Treaty 1965; Acts of Accession 1972 (UK, Ireland, Denmark), 1979 (Greece), 1985 (Spain, Portugal), 1995 (Austria, Finland and Sweden); Budgetary Treaties 1970, 1975; Single European Act 1986; the Treaty on European Union 1992; and the Treaty of Amsterdam 1997. They form a constitutional skeleton for the Community by setting out the objectives of the Community, its mechanisms, the timetable within which the objectives are to be achieved, and setting up its institutions and conferring on them legislative and administrative powers.

A6.6.2 SECONDARY LEGISLATION OF THE COMMUNITY

The acts of the Community institutions form an important source of Community law (see **A6.5**). Note that:

(a) Regulations are directly applicable in national legal systems and apply throughout the Community in all the Member States. Many have direct effect, conferring rights and duties on individuals who can rely on them in the same way as domestic law in their national courts. Unlike national law, however, they have not been passed by the national legislature.

(b) Directives are often used for coordinating the laws of Member States (Article 94 (ex 100), EC Treaty). Member States may be obliged to introduce new legislation or redraft or amend existing national legislation and administrative rules to conform to the objectives of a directive. They may have direct effect in certain circumstances.

(c) Decisions are administrative measures. Sometimes the Community institutions themselves are responsible for implementing the treaties or regulations. They can make decisions binding on individuals, firms or Member States. A directive usually requires the addressee to perform some action or refrain therefrom. It also may confer rights or impose obligations on those to whom it is addressed.

A6.6.3 INTERNATIONAL AGREEMENTS BETWEEN THE EC AND NON-MEMBER STATES

The international agreements that the Community enters into with non-Member States and other international organisations on behalf of the Community are a third source of Community law. Such agreements may be new, such as the Rome Convention 1979, or existing agreements for which the Community takes responsibility from Member States on their accession to the Community, such as the General Agreement on Tariffs and Trade (GATT). This agreement was established before the Community existed, but all the Member States were parties to it and it concerned matters over which the Community has competence. 'In so far as the Community has assumed the powers previously exercised by Member States in the area governed by the General Agreement, the provisions of that agreement have the effect of binding the Community' (*Third International Fruit Company* case (C-21-4/72) [1972] ECR 1439, para. 18).

A6.6.4 INTERNATIONAL AGREEMENTS BETWEEN MEMBER STATES

International agreements between Member States may be concluded on any topic, within or without the scope of Community law only if their subject-matter is within the jurisdiction of the Community, as defined by the Treaty of Rome and subsequent legislation.

Member States may be under an obligation to reach agreement on a topic as part of a programme determined by the Treaty of Rome. In certain cases these additional conventions are intended to supplement its provisions. For example, Article 293 (ex 220), EC Treaty enables the Member States to enter into treaties and conventions on specific matters listed in the Article. Two conventions have been concluded: one on the

Mutual Recognition of Companies and Legal Persons and a second, on Jurisdiction and the Enforcement of Judgments in Civil and Commercial Matters (both 1968). These agreements are regarded as Community law.

Alternatively, the States may achieve a binding consensus on a topic entirely of their own choosing. If this has no connection with the work of the Community, then it should not be regarded as a source of Community law. As the Community institutions draw on the fundamental aims and objectives set out in the Treaty of Rome (e.g. in the Single European Act), the topics where Member States have a 'free hand' will be restricted.

In some areas, the Member States seem to have accepted the desirability of broadening the application of European Community law. For example, the Member States have set out to create new intellectual property rights, the Community patent and the Community trademark, which are closely connected to the concept of a single community.

The Treaty of Rome imposes no obligation on Member States to create these new property rights and it might be thought that they are, therefore, no part of Community law. However, the relationship with the Community is clear.

The geographical limit of these intellectual property rights is defined as that of the Community's Member States; the right is described in the agreement as a Community patent (for example). The countries which are involved are all of the existing Member States (and no one else); the European Commission was brought in to advise on the proposed agreement; the European Court of Justice is given jurisdiction over the agreement; and there is a clear connection between the aims of the Community on free movement of goods and services around the common market (and fair competition) and the establishment of a single Community-wide patent together with the single application needed to obtain it. This type of international agreement should clearly be seen as a source of Community law, although subordinate to the Treaty of Rome and its subsequent secondary legislation.

A6.7 Judicial Legislation

The entire jurisprudence of the ECJ, including the general principles of law it has recognised and the doctrines it has developed, forms an important source of Community law. This has recently been enlarged by the developing case law of the Court of First Instance.

A6.7.1 GENERAL PRINCIPLES OF LAW

The notion of general principles of law has been developed by the ECJ in its judgments; they are often regarded as a separate source of Community law and are based on concepts of law and justice found in most legal systems.

The EC Treaty makes indirect reference to general principles of law in several of its articles. For example:

(a) Article 220 (ex 164) states that the 'Court of Justice shall ensure that in the interpretation and application of this Treaty the law is observed'. 'Law' here suggests a law which transcends the text of the EC Treaty itself. The practical application of this abstract notion is shown in (b) and (c).

(b) Article 230 (ex 173) permits the Court of Justice to declare Community acts illegal if, e.g., an act infringes a rule of law relating to the application of the Treaty. This has meant that private or legal persons (if they have locus standi) may challenge a Commission decision on the ground that it infringes a general principle of law, such as equality or legitimate expectations.

(c) Article 288(2) (ex 215(2)) provides that the non-contractual liability of the Community shall be based on 'the general principles common to the law of the Member States'. For example, the Community is only liable for unlawful acts of a legislative nature (i.e. regulations) if the Court of Justice decides that the act infringed a 'superior rule of law' which was intended to protect the individual, since this is a common basis for state liability for such acts in national courts of the Member States (*Aktien-Zuckerfabrik Schöppenstedt* v *Council* (5/71) [1971] ECR 975).

The particular principles are inspired by those common to the legal systems of Member States and are recognised or developed by the ECJ when required in cases before it. Although the categories of general principles which the ECJ will use are not closed, those which have been considered by the ECJ in its case law, and thus recognised as sources of Community law, have arisen in an *ad hoc* fashion.

(a) The restrictive nature of the Community's non-contractual liability for legislative acts of its institutions (see *Schöppenstedt*).

(b) Legality in administration (i.e., the institutions comply with the set procedures and act reasonably).

(c) Proportionality: action must be proportionate to the end it seeks to achieve. See *Internationale Handelsgesellschaft* (11/70) [1970] ECR 1125 and *Bela-Muhle Josef Bergman* v *Grows-Farm* (114/76) [1977] ECR 1211.

(d) Legal certainty. See *Germany* v *Commission* (44/81) [1982] ECR 1855 and *Simmenthal* (92/78) [1979] ECR 811.

(e) Protection of legitimate expectations. See *Amylum* v *Council* (108/81) [1982] ECR 2107, para. 4-17 and *CNTA* v *Commission* (74/74) [1975] ECR 533.

(f) Non-discrimination and equality of treatment. See *Sabbatini* v *European Parliament* (20/71) [1972] ECR 345, *Prais* v *Council* (130/75) [1976] ECR 1589 and *Bela-Muhle Josef Bergman* v *Grows-Farm* (114/76) [1977] ECR 1211.

(g) Entitlement to a hearing. See *Transocean Marine Paint* v *Commission* (17/74) [1974] ECR 1063.

(h) Professional legal privilege in anti-competition investigations by the Commission. See *AM & S* (155/79) [1982] ECR 1575.

(i) The right to be assisted by counsel. See *Demont* (15/80) [1981] ECR 3147.

(j) The fundamental human rights upon which the constitutional law of Member States is based. See *Stauder* v *City of Ulm* (29/69) [1969] ECR 419, *Internationale Handelsgesellschaft* (11/70) [1970] ECR 1125 and *Nold* v *Commission* (4/73) [1974] ECR 491.

It is not possible to explain all of these principles here. An explanation of two will illustrate their use.

A6.7.1.1 Equality
The principle of equality or non-discrimination means that the Community institutions must act without regard to sex or nationality.

Mrs Sabbatini challenged the Community staff regulation which provided that only 'a head of family' was entitled to an expatriation allowance. The regulation defined this phrase in such a way that only men could receive the allowance. Her claim, based on the general principle of equality, succeeded. Ms Prais challenged the Council's decision to hold a competitive examination on the date of a Jewish festival as religious discrimination. The ECJ held that religious freedom was a general principle of law but on the facts discrimination had not been made out in Ms Prais' case. In *Bela-Muhle Josef Bergman* v *Grows-Farm* (otherwise known as the *Skimmed Milk Powder* case) the Council passed a measure to force animal feed producers to use skimmed milk in their feed rather than soya. The result of this was to increase the price of animal feed thus harming livestock farmers. The only farmers who benefited from this were dairy farmers as their product was being used in the feedstuffs. The claim that the policy was discriminatory between the two categories of farmers succeeded.

Specific non-discrimination is mentioned in two important EC Treaty Articles. Article 12 (ex 7) prohibits discrimination on the ground of nationality in the application of the Treaty. (This has especially been relied on in relation to the free movement of workers (Article 39 (ex 48)) and services (Article 49 (ex 59)).) Article 141 (ex 119) provides for equal pay for men and women who do equal work. (Directives also specifically deal with equal treatment between men and women in social security matters, occupational pension schemes and in self-employment.)

A6.7.1.2 Human rights

There is no written list of fundamental rights and freedoms in Community law. Some basic rights however were mentioned in the original EC Treaty: freedom of movement of workers (Article 39 (ex 48)); the right of establishment (Article 43 (ex 52)); the freedom to provide services (Article 49 (ex 59)); the freedom of movement of goods (Article 23 (ex 9)); the right of association (Article 140 (ex 118(1))); the protection of business and professional secrets (Article 287 (ex 214)); and numerous prohibitions on discrimination (Articles 12, 13, 39, 43, 50, 81 and 141 (ex 7, 48, 52, 60, 85 and 119)).

However, the ECJ has developed the Community's unwritten fundamental rights in its case law.

Stauder was the first case in which it declared that a respect for human rights was a fundamental general principle of Community law that the ECJ would safeguard. In *Internationale Handelsgesellschaft* the ECJ made clear that Community measures would not be judged by the human rights concepts of the national constitutions of Member States, but would be judged by its own concept of human rights. However, Community concepts which the ECJ will protect are those which are common to the constitutions of Member States. These act as inspiration to the development of the Community's concepts (*Nold*). International conventions concerning the protection of human rights to which Member States are parties or have acceded also serve as guidelines for the Community concepts *(Nold)*. In *Rutili* v *Minister for the Interior* (36/75) [1975] ECR 1219 specific reference in this respect was made to the European Convention on Human Rights.

Examples of human rights concepts that the ECJ has recognised, in addition to the ones which overlap with some of the general principles already listed and discussed above, are the right of ownership, the general right of privacy, freedom to engage in business and to choose and practise a profession, freedom of association, privacy and correspondence.

The ECJ's process of evolving 'European fundamental rights' is a continuing and piecemeal process. The ECJ has been unable to develop rights for all areas in which this might be necessary or desirable because its judgments are confined to the particular cases which are brought before it. In this context, one should see now also Article 6 (ex F) of the Treaty on European Union (**1.2.1**). It should be noted that, in an Opinion delivered on 28 March 1996 (2/94), the ECJ responded to a request from the Council of Ministers, which sought advice on whether accession by the European Community to the European Convention on Human Rights would be compatible with the EC Treaty. The ECJ stated that, in the present state of Community law, the Community would have 'no competence' to accede to the ECHR. Subsequently, the EU has embraced both the concept of human rights and the ECHR itself, through changes wrought by the Treaty of Amsterdam. See Articles 6 (ex 3c) and 46 (ex 56), EC Treaty.

A6.8 Community Law in our National Legal System

A6.8.1 INTERNATIONAL LAW AND THE ENGLISH LEGAL SYSTEM

Under English law, international laws (specifically treaties) may be binding on the State and subject to enforcement by legal process. An example is the European Convention on Human Rights and Fundamental Freedoms (ECHR). But international law is unlikely to create rights for individuals which can be enforced through our own courts or tribunals. Again, using the example of the ECHR, a complainant must use the procedures and institutions established by the ECHR in order to complain about a violation of the Convention.

An English court might take note of the principles of the ECHR, especially when interpreting an Act of Parliament as our Parliament is not to be understood as passing legislation which is contrary to the international obligations of the UK unless the Act expresses this intention. But if the victim of an act which was contrary to the ECHR seeks relief from the English courts, the cause of action must be one known to English law (e.g., assault; false imprisonment; a claim for judicial review based on a denial of natural justice): a writ which simply alleges an infringement of the Convention will be struck out as disclosing no cause of action.

So, international laws generally have no effect on individuals in the UK: they give no rights, impose no obligations, which can be relied on in our courts. These laws bind only the State and are enforceable against the State through procedures totally distinct from our legal system. European Community law is different: it can give rights to individuals or impose obligations on individuals and the State which are enforceable through our courts. It does this by virtue of the European Communities Act 1972 (ECA). Since this was originally written, the UK Parliament has passed the Human Rights Act 1998. How this potentially momentous piece of legislation will impact on the matters addressed above remains to be seen.

A6.8.2 THE EUROPEAN COMMUNITIES ACT 1972

The laws of the European Community became a part of our domestic legal system as a result of the European Communities Act 1972. So, the articles of the EC Treaty and the secondary legislation of the Community institutions are as much a part of our legal system as is an Act of Parliament, an Order in Council or a decision of the House of Lords.

Under s. 2(1) of the ECA 1972:

> all such rights, powers, obligations and restrictions from time to time created or arising [from the EC Treaty, amongst others], and all ... remedies and procedures [provided for by the Treaty] as in accordance with [the Treaty] are without further enactment to be given legal effect or used in the United Kingdom shall be recognised and available in law, and be enforced ... and followed accordingly ...

The important element here is that some Community laws may give rights and obligations without further enactment, that is they become a part of our laws without any statute or Order in Council to implement them.

By s. 2(2) of the ECA 1972, the Government is empowered to pass secondary legislation, when appropriate, to implement any Community obligation of the UK. By s. 2(4) any such legislation (and Acts of Parliament) passed or to be passed 'shall be construed and have effect subject to the foregoing provisions of this section'. This subsection is often relied on as implicitly establishing the supremacy of Community law over English law by 'entrenching' its position.

A6.8.3 THE EUROPEAN COMMUNITIES ACT AND ENGLISH COURTS

Whenever a question arises in legal proceedings as to the interpretation or effect of the EC Treaty (or as to the validity, effect or interpretation of EC secondary legislation), this shall be treated as a question of law, not of fact. The question should either be referred to the European Court of Justice (ECJ) for its opinion or determined by the English judge 'in accordance with the principles laid down by and any relevant decision of the European Court' (s. 3(1) of the ECA 1972). This seems to establish the primacy of the ECJ and its case law in relation to our own courts.

In a similar vein, s. 3(2) requires an English judge to take judicial notice of (i.e. be bound by):

(a) the Community Treaties;

(b) the Official Journal of the Communities; and

(c) 'any decision of, or expression of opinion by, the European Court' on the questions of law referred to in s. 3(1).

The two most important 'decisions' by the ECJ, which English judges are bound by are: (a) that Community law takes precedence over national law where the two are in conflict; and (b) that some Community laws give rights or obligations to individuals which can be enforced in our courts without the need for implementing legislation. These two decisions are examined below.

A6.9 The Direct Effect of Community Law

Under Article 249 (ex 189) of the EC Treaty, regulations are directly applicable in the Member States. No other type of Community law is thus described. But the ECJ has evolved a concept of 'direct effect': by this it means that Community laws which meet certain criteria may be used by individuals in national courts. Sometimes such laws may only be used against the State (i.e. they impose no obligation on individuals) — perhaps to claim damages or *certiorari*; other laws proscribe certain conduct — they may be used by one individual to sue another or as a defence to litigation. Some examples may help.

A6.9.1 SOME EXAMPLES

A6.9.1.1 Example 1
A UK Government minister bans imports of French turkeys. His action is designed to support UK turkey breeders at the expense of French producers. Article 28 (ex 30) of the EC Treaty establishes the principle of free circulation of goods between the Member States of the Community. The ECJ has held this article to be directly effective. The French turkey producers sue the minister in the English High Court for damages, relying on his alleged infringement of Article 30 (now 28). They establish the right to a declaration that the ban is illegal but the remedy of damages is denied by the court. The case is subsequently settled out of court.

See *Bourgoin v Ministry of Agriculture, Fisheries and Food* [1986] QB 716.

A6.9.1.2 Example 2
A woman works for a local health authority. When she reaches the age of 62, she is dismissed from her job. There is no reason for this, other than her age. The policy of the health authority is to dismiss female staff when they reach 60, male staff at age 65. She makes a claim in the Employment Tribunal, alleging that her dismissal contravenes a Community Directive, No. 76/207. This provides that male and female employees shall receive equal treatment in their conditions of work, including dismissal. The question of whether the directive is directly effective is referred to the ECJ. The ECJ decides that it is enforceable against the state (in this case represented by the

health authority). The Employment Tribunal then upholds her claim and awards her several thousand pounds compensation.

See *Marshall* v *Southampton and SW Hants AHA* [1986] QB 401.

A6.9.1.3 Example 3
A French national gets a place at an English university to read for a degree in electrical engineering. His application to the relevant UK Government department for payment of his tuition fees and maintenance grant is refused because he does not meet the requirements for foreign students' grants. He sues the responsible Government minister, claiming that the requirements discriminate against him on the ground of his nationality, contrary to Articles 12 (ex 6) and 39 (ex 48) of the EC Treaty. Both Articles are directly effective, according to the case law of the ECJ. During the proceedings, the Government changes the rules regarding payment of tuition fees for EC nationals; a reference to the ECJ establishes the right of EC workers to move to another Member State and get a maintenance grant from their 'host' country.

See *Brown* v *Secretary of State for Scotland* [1988] ECR 3237.

A6.9.1.4 Example 4
An English company makes dairy products, using milk supplied by the Milk Marketing Board (MMB). The MMB announces it will no longer sell directly to the company; the company must now buy from a middle man with higher prices. The company sues the MMB in the High Court for damages, alleging breach of Article 82 (ex 86) of the Treaty (anti-competitive conduct). The ECJ has held previously that Article 82 is directly effective. The English courts hold that a breach of Article 82 is actionable (as a breach of statutory duty) and can be used to claim damages.

See *Garden Cottage Foods* v *Milk Marketing Board* [1984] AC 130.

A6.9.1.5 Example 5
An English company owns the patent in a pharmaceutical substance 'S'. Another company applies for a licence to import 'S' into the UK from another Member State (Italy). Before the licence is granted (or refused), the applicant starts importing 'S'. The patentee sues in the High Court, alleging infringement of its patent. It claims an injunction to stop the imports. The importer's defence states that its imports have been bought quite lawfully in Italy, although 'S' is not patented there, and it relies on Article 28 (ex 30) of the Treaty (free circulation of goods). A reference to the ECJ makes it clear that the injunction would contradict Article 28 so the English court refuses to grant the injunction.

See *Allen & Hanburys Ltd* v *Generics (UK) Ltd* [1989] 1 WLR 414.

A6.9.1.6 Example 6
Two men are prosecuted for breaking the laws on importation of obscene material. They have imported pornographic literature from another Member State where it is lawfully on sale. Their defence is that they bought the literature legitimately and, under Article 28 (ex 30) of the Treaty, are allowed to export it to any other Member State. This would have succeeded, as Article 28 is directly effective, save that there is an exception to the basic right of free circulation, contained in Article 30 (ex 36). This allows States to derogate from the right on the ground of public morality.

See *R* v *Henn and Darby* [1981] AC 850.

A6.9.2   WHICH COMMUNITY LAWS ARE DIRECTLY EFFECTIVE?

A list of all the Treaty Articles and secondary legislation that have been held to be directly effective would be too long for insertion here. The ECJ has held that several articles of the Treaty are directly effective; also certain regulations, directives and decisions. However, each article, regulation, etc. will be examined individually by the ECJ to see whether it meets the criteria for direct effect. Thus, the contents of a list of directly effective laws is governed by which measures have been referred by national courts to the ECJ for its opinion on the matter. The criteria are examined in **A6.9.3** onwards.

A6.9.3   DIRECTLY EFFECTIVE ARTICLES OF THE TREATY

The following Articles have been held to be of direct effect:

(a) Article 12 (ex 6) (non-discrimination between EC nationals on grounds of nationality); *Gravier* v *City of Liege* [1985] ECR 593.

(b) Article 25 (ex 12) (ban on introduction of new customs duties on imports from one Member State to another); *Van Gend en Loos* [1963] ECR 1.

(c) Article 28 (ex 30) (elimination of quantitative restrictions on the free movement of goods between Member States); *Ianelli & Volpi Spa* v *Ditta Paola Meroni* [1977] ECR 557.

(d) Article 39 (ex 48) (freedom of workers who are EC nationals to move to another Member State to work there); *Van Duyn* v *Home Office* [1974] ECR 1337.

(e) Article 43 (ex 52) (freedom of EC nationals who are self-employed or members of a profession, or EC companies, to set themselves up in another Member State); *Reyners* v *Belgian State* [1974] ECR 631.

(f) Article 49 (ex 59) (freedom of EC nationals to move temporarily to another Member State in order to provide (or receive) a service there); *Van Binsbergen* [1974] ECR 1299.

(g) Articles 81 (ex 85) and 82 (ex 86) (prohibition on conduct which restricts or distorts competition in the common market); *BRT* v *SABAM* [1974] ECR 51.

(h) Article 141 (ex 119) (equal pay for male and female staff who do equal work); *Defrenne* v *Sabena* [1976] ECR 455.

The criteria for Articles to be directly effective were first established by the ECJ in the *Van Gend en Loos* case (26/62) and have since been modified. The wording of the Article must be:

(a) clear and unambiguous;

(b) unconditional (on the exercise of a power or discretion by, for example, a Member State or the European Commission);

(c) not dependent on further action.

Clarity and lack of ambiguity are not features of Community law that the man in the street might subscribe to. These features can by supplied by the ECJ, though, often when an EC measure is referred to it for interpretation under Article 234 (ex 177) of the Treaty. The ECJ has also occasionally interpreted an Article in such a way that it has direct effect in certain circumstances but not others. A typical example of this is the litigation between Ms Defrenne and the Belgian national airline, *Sabena* (43/75). The ECJ was concerned to interpret Article 141 (ex 119) regarding the principle of equal pay for equal work. The ECJ held that it was directly effective so far as 'direct' discrimination was concerned but not for 'indirect' discrimination. The distinction was based on the premise that in some situations discrimination could be determined simply on a legal analysis (direct discrimination) while in others a more complex determination would be required which a court might be ill-equipped to perform (indirect discrimination). So, if Miss A works alongside Mr B doing the same job, they should both receive the same wage, subject to proper reasons for distinction like seniority. On the other hand, if Miss A is a canteen assistant in a shipyard, while Mr

B is a welder there, a job evaluation scheme is required to see if their jobs are of equal value; or Miss A may do a job which only women have done for that employer but seeks to argue that, if a man had the job, he would be paid more. Both of the latter examples are indirect discrimination according to the ECJ and Article 141 (ex 119) will not help.

If an Article requires further action, for example by a Member State, then usually it has no direct effect. However, in this situation the Member State would not be allowed to reap the benefit of its own inaction. If a time limit was expressed in the Article (or could be implied) for the further action to be taken but none was, the ECJ is likely to hold that (subject to the first two criteria being satisfied) the Article is now directly effective insofar as it may be enforced against the defaulting Member State. In such circumstances, the Member State might be liable to compensate individuals for any losses caused by its default: see *Brasserie du Pêcheur SA v Germany* (C-46/93) [1996] 2 WLR 506.

A6.9.4 DIRECTLY EFFECTIVE REGULATIONS

Similar provisions have been held by the ECJ to exist for regulations as have been considered in **A6.9.3** for Articles of the Treaty. The regulation must be clear and unambiguous, it must be unconditional and not require further action to be taken.

A6.9.5 DIRECTLY EFFECTIVE DIRECTIVES AND DECISIONS

The ECJ has held that directives can have direct effect, a good example being the *Marshall* case, referred to above. Unlike regulations, which are not meant to require any action on the part of Member States to implement them into national law, directives usually specify an aim or general principles and leave choices to the Member States. A good example is the Commission's Directive on Product Liability which allowed Member States to take several different options as to liability. The UK enacted the Consumer Protection Act 1987 to implement it.

This might be thought to indicate that a directive should not have direct effect but the ECJ has said that to deprive directives of direct effect would lead to their avoidance by Member States, again through inactivity. This has led the ECJ to declare that once the time limit for implementation of a directive has passed without any (or any proper) implementation, an individual may rely on the directive against the Member State, providing it is clear and precise. The idea is that the Member State cannot rely on its own failure to deprive the individual of a right or remedy. However, the same policy argument cannot be used against another individual; it is not Mr Brown's fault if the UK Parliament has not enacted Directive 90/123, for example. This has led the ECJ to declare that directives have vertical direct effect (i.e., impose obligations on the State, give rights to individuals) but not horizontal direct effect (i.e., do not impose obligations on individuals). This view was recently reaffirmed by the ECJ in *Paola Faccini Dori v Recreb Srl* [1995] All ER (EC) 1. The obligation imposed on the Member State may include a liability to pay damages to individuals: see *Francovich v Italy* (C-6/90) [1991] ECR I-5357.

One result has been several cases in the UK where individual litigants have tried to rely on EC directives against a defendant arguing that the defendant is an 'emanation of the State' and thus subject to vertical direct effect. Two notable cases involved a (then) nationalised corporation, British Gas, and a company wholly-owned by the British Government, Rolls-Royce. They were sued by their employees, who relied on EC directives about equal pay or treatment. Both employees lost since the courts decided that neither organisation represented the State (unlike the area health authority in the *Marshall* case).

Lastly, decisions may have direct effect. The criteria are the same as for directives. See, for example, the case of *Grad v Finanzamt Traunstein* (9/70) [1971] CMLR 1.

For further reading, see Josephine Steiner, 'Coming to Terms with EEC Directives' (1990) 106 LQR 144.

A6.10 Supremacy of Community Law

There are two points of view to be considered here. First, that of the European Community, second, that of the Member State. The European Community has always taken the view that its law takes precedence over any conflicting national law (see, e.g., the second *Simmenthal* case (*Amministrazione delle Finanze dello Stato* v *Simmenthal SpA* (106/77) [1978] ECR 629)), whether the national law is precedent in time or not. The ECJ is firmly of the opinion that national courts should not apply national law on an issue where a Community measure could be applied.

The doctrine developed by the ECJ is that Community law has primacy over national law. The doctrine of Community primacy was first clarified by the ECJ in a preliminary ruling on a reference from a Milan Justice of the Peace in *Costa* v *ENEL* (6/64) [1964] ECR 585.

When Italy nationalised the production and supply of electricity and transferred the management of it to ENEL, Mr Costa, a shareholder in the Edison Volta company felt that his interests had been adversely affected. He refused to pay his electricity bill which was only a few hundred lire. His defence before the Milan justice was, inter alia, that the nationalisation of the electricity industry infringed several articles of the EC Treaty. When asked to interpret these Articles in a preliminary reference by the justice, the ECJ used the opportunity to stress that:

> The integration into the Laws of each Member State of provisions which derive from the Community, and more generally the terms and spirit of the Treaty, make it impossible for the States, as a corollary, to accord precedence to a unilateral and subsequent measure over a legal system accepted by them on a basis of reciprocity. The executive force of Community law cannot vary from one State to another in deference to subsequent domestic laws, without jeopardising the attainment of the objectives of the Treaty set out in Article 5(2) [now 10(2)] and giving rise to discrimination prohibited by Article 7 [now 12].

Another important ECJ case on this concept is *Internationale Handelsgesellschaft* (11/70) [1970] ECR 1125.

The doctrine of supremacy of EC law has found expression in the Member States in different ways according to their different constitutions (Trevor Hartley's book, *Foundations of European Community Law* has a good chapter reviewing the Member States' constitutions). In the UK s. 2(4) of the ECA 1972 seems to establish the supremacy of Community law. Sometimes this concept has been accepted with apparent enthusiasm by English courts (see, e.g., *Pickstone* v *Freemans plc* [1988] 3 WLR 265), but on other occasions a rather narrower view has prevailed (e.g., *Duke* v *GEC Reliance Systems Ltd* [1988] 2 WLR 359). One way to encourage acceptance is through preliminary references by national courts to the ECJ under Article 234 (ex 177) of the EC Treaty. A problem exists with this, though. Such references are usually made at the discretion of the court then dealing with the case; they cannot be insisted upon by the parties to litigation. The more xenophobic a State's judges are, the less likely is any reference to the ECJ where a ruling on supremacy (or at least on an interpretation inconsistent with national law) might emerge. In the long term, the European community can really only rely on the States and all their institutions (including the courts) being 'communautaire' and embracing the philosophy of the supranational single common market, with all the consequent loss of national sovereignty which that implies.

APPENDIX SEVEN

THE COURT OF JUSTICE OF THE EUROPEAN COMMUNITIES

The Treaties, the Statutes of the Court annexed as Protocols to the Treaties, and the Rules of Procedure of the Court provide the framework in which the European Court operates. Originally, the EC Treaty created the European Court of Justice (ECJ). More recently, an inferior court has also been created: the Court of First Instance (CFI). The June 1996 issue of *European Law Review* (Vol. 21 No. 3) contains several articles with radical proposals for the future of the European Court.

A7.1   The Jurisdiction of the European Court

The supranational aspect of the Community constitution is safeguarded by the ECJ. For the purposes of this appendix, the two courts of the Community — the Court of Justice and the Court of First Instance — have not usually been differentiated. The ECJ ensures that Community law is interpreted and applied uniformly throughout the Member States of the Community. It has sole jurisdiction to decide on the validity of Community legislation. It acts as referee in disputes between the institutions *inter se*, between the Community and Member States, and protects the rights of the individual against the Community bureaucracies, an important role as the democratic element is still quite weak within the Community.

The EC Treaty gives the ECJ a general duty to ensure that, in the interpretation and application of the EC Treaty, Community law is observed (Article 220 (ex 164)). This does not mean that the ECJ has a general power to determine any case submitted to it. It has jurisdiction only in the specific topics and procedures which the Treaty has indicated. The kinds of proceedings that may be dealt with by the ECJ are:

(a) Infringement actions brought against Member States for failing to fulfil their obligations under the EC Treaty or the law derived therefrom (Articles 226–227 (ex 169-170)).

(b) Annulment actions (Article 230 (ex 173)). The ECJ can review the legality of the acts of the institutions on the grounds mentioned in Article 230 (ex 173). If the act is found to be illegal, the European Court can declare it void (Article 231 (ex 174)). The institution concerned is required to take the necessary measures to comply with the Court's judgment (Article 233 (ex 176)).

(c) An action for failure of an institution to act (Articles 232 (ex 175) and 233 (ex 176)).

(d) An action for damages for the non-contractual liability of the Community (Articles 235 (ex 178) and 288(2) (ex 215(2))).

(e) A reference by a national court or tribunal for a preliminary ruling on the interpretation and validity of Community provisions (Article 234 (ex 177)).

(f) The adjustment of penalties provided for in Council regulations. For example, Regulation 17/62 (on competition), allows the European Court to adjust fines or periodic penalties imposed by the Commission for infringements of the competition rules.

(g) Staff cases. The European Court has jurisdiction to resolve disputes between the Community institutions and its servants (Article 236 (ex 179)).

(h) Contractual liability of the Community (Articles 238 (ex 181) and 288 (ex 215)). A contract concluded by the Community may give the ECJ jurisdiction to hear disputes arising in relation to the contract.

(i) Opinions pursuant to Article 300(1) (ex 228(1)) (e.g., the ECJ may give an opinion as to whether a proposed agreement to be concluded by the Community with a third country or international organisation is compatible with EC law).

The SEA 1986 provided for a Court of First Instance to determine certain classes of action or proceedings brought by national or legal persons. The Court first sat in September 1989. The actions it hears are staff cases, competition and coal and steel cases brought by individuals under Article 230 (ex 173) or 232 (ex 175). Actions started by Member States or the Community institutions and preliminary rulings are expressly excluded from the jurisdiction of the Court of First Instance.

The Court of First Instance looks at the facts in each case in greater detail than formerly happened in the ECJ. An illustration can be found in the *BASF AG* v *Commission* case (T-79/89 etc.) where the annulment of a Commission decision was sought before the Court. The application was dismissed as inadmissible because the decision was so flawed in content and creation as to be legally non-existent thus rendering any annulment unnecessary. The case went on appeal to the ECJ. The ECJ disagreed with the CFI and quashed the Commission's decision on the ground of infringement of an essential procedural requirement (see (137/92) [1994] ECR I-2555).

The Court of First Instance is perhaps intended to be less 'judicially creative' than the ECJ, although the Decision of the Council which established the Court recited that:

> in respect of actions requiring close examination of complex facts, the establishment of a second court [Court of First Instance] will improve the judicial protection of individual interests.

A7.2 The Composition and Organisation of the European Court

The ECJ has 15 judges and nine Advocates-General. The qualifications for appointment are similar for both. They must be

> *persons whose independence is beyond doubt and who possess the qualifications required for appointment to the highest judicial offices in their respective countries or who are jurisconsults of recognised competence.* (Article 223 (ex 167).)

Jurisconsults can include academic lawyers. Appointment is 'by common accord of the Governments of the Member States' for a period of six years and is renewable. In practice one Judge is appointed from each Member State; traditionally there is an additional post which is rotated between the different Member States. Every three years there is a partial replacement of six or seven judges and three Advocates-General. A President of the Court is elected by the judges themselves.

An Advocate-General is not a judge but he has equal status. After parties' written and oral submissions have been given in a case and before the judges deliberate, the Advocates-General appointed to the case gives an Opinion in open court. His Opinion on the case is fully reasoned, impartial and independent and recommends to the judges the decision to take. It need not be followed by the judges but it often is. It is published together with the judgment in the law reports and may be cited by counsel and Advocates-General in future cases.

A Judge Rapporteur is chosen by the President of the Court for each case. The Judge Rapporteur has the responsibility of seeing the case through the various stages of the proceedings and preparing reports on the case at different stages. After the Advocate-General's Opinion, the Judge Rapporteur drafts a judgment on which the other judges deliberate before a final, collective, judgment is reached by them.

The Registrar of the ECJ is responsible for the administration of the court and the reception, transmission and custody of documents relating to the cases.

Cases are decided either in plenary session (i.e. a quorum of nine judges) or in Chambers of three or five judges.

The Court of First Instance consists of 15 members, but has no permanent Advocates-General. Instead, any member of the Court may be called upon to perform the task of an Advocate-General in each case (he may not then participate in judging that case). The Court sits in chambers of three or five judges and their decisions may be the subject of an appeal to the ECJ. The Fifth and Sixth Chambers consist of seven judges each (of whom, five will sit in a given case), while the First, Second, Third and Fourth Chambers sit with three judges each. The first UK appointment to the Court of First Instance was David Edward QC, a Scots advocate. Following the appointment of Sir Gordon Slynn as a Law Lord, David Edward was appointed as a judge of the ECJ and Christopher Bellamy QC replaced him in the Court of First Instance.

A7.3   The Practice and Procedure of the European Court

The rules of procedure of the ECJ in relation to its jurisdiction under the EC Treaty can be found in the Protocol on the Statute of the Court of Justice, which is annexed to the EC Treaty, and in the Rules of Procedure of the Court.

The ECJ has jurisdiction over two types of action: direct and indirect. Direct actions commence and end in the ECJ, subject to the work of the Court of First Instance. References for preliminary rulings are indirect actions, which begin and end in the national court. The preliminary ruling of the ECJ is only a step in the proceedings before the national court.

In both types of action greater emphasis is placed on written procedure than oral hearings and the approach at the relatively short oral stage is inquisitorial, not adversarial.

An extremely informative article on the working of the Court of Justice has been written by David Edward and can be found in (1995) *European Law Review* 539.

A7.3.1   DIRECT ACTIONS

A7.3.1.1 Written procedure
Direct actions are initiated by a written application addressed to the President and Members of the ECJ, which is sent to the Registrar of the ECJ. The content of the application is governed by Article 38 of the Rules. Its main function is to define the issues between the parties, set out the grounds on which the application is based, the form of order sought and the nature of evidence relied upon. The Registrar effects service of the documents. The defendant must lodge a defence within a month of the application being served. A default judgment can be obtained. The defendant can contest the admissibility of an action as a preliminary objection by making a separate application to the ECJ. Further optional pleadings can be made, e.g., a reply by the applicant and a rejoinder by the defendant.

A7.3.1.2 Fact finding

The ECJ may decide that a preparatory inquiry is necessary to clarify issues of fact. Article 45 of the Rules provides for various 'measures of inquiry', in practice the most usual being written questions devised by the Court and sent to the parties concerned. The parties reply in writing.

A7.3.1.3 The oral hearing

A public hearing is held at which oral submissions are made by representatives of the parties. These are relatively short as the Court has already studied the more lengthy written submissions. Members of the Bench sometimes interrupt counsel's speeches to ask questions. Usually their questions are put after all the submissions have been made.

A7.3.1.4 The opinion of the Advocate-General

The Advocate-General then delivers his Opinion which can be either *ex tempore* or delivered in open court at a later date.

A7.3.1.5 Deliberation and judgment

The Court deliberates in secrecy. Its decision may be taken by majority vote although it is always presented as a collective judgment with all the judges signing it. No individual judgments, e.g., dissenting judgments, are given. As compromises have to be made this may explain why a judgment (or parts of it) sometimes lacks clarity and cohesion.

A judgment usually has three parts: the first contains a statement of the facts and a summary of the arguments of the parties; the second contains the reasons for the judgment in numbered paragraphs; and the third is the actual decision. The form of the judgment is terse, formal and abstract like a French court judgment. The short operative third part of the judgment is delivered in open court.

A7.3.1.6 Interim relief

The ECJ can provide interim relief (Articles 242 (ex 185) and 243 (ex 186)). In practice it is sought most often when a company challenges a Commission decision that the company has infringed the Community rules on competition (*United Brands* v *Commission* (27/76) [1978] ECR 207). The rules governing interim measures are found in the Rules of Court (especially Articles 83 and 85) and in ECJ case law (e.g., *Camera Care* v *Commission* (792/79R) [1980] ECR 119, *Ford of Europe Inc and Forde Werke AG* v *Commission* (228/82) [1982] ECR 3091, *Finsider SPA* v *Commission* (392/85) [1986] 2 CMLR 290, *Brass Band Instruments Ltd* v *Boosey and Hawkes Plc* [1988] 4 CMLR 67).

A7.3.1.7 Intervention

Member States and institutions of the Community have a right to intervene in proceedings between other parties. Private parties may intervene in an action brought by another private party for annulment, failure to act or for damages, if the private intervener has an interest in the outcome of the case itself (Article 37 of the Statute).

A7.3.2 REFERENCES FOR PRELIMINARY RULINGS

Article 20 of the Statute and Article 103 of the Rules govern the procedure before the ECJ.

A7.3.2.1 Making the reference

The parties to the national proceedings cannot initiate proceedings for preliminary rulings. The national court can alone make an order for reference. It will ask questions on the interpretation or validity of Community law. In the English High Court, see RSC O. 114, CPR Sch. 1.

A7.3.2.2 Written procedure

There are no formal pleadings as the proceedings are not contentious. The ECJ is not asked to decide the merits of the dispute between the parties. Its function is simply to assist the national court on the questions asked. It makes no inquiry as to the facts.

A statement of agreed or decided facts should be found in the reference for the order or the national court's file on the case.

The Registrar will transmit copies of the preliminary reference to the parties in the national proceedings, to the Member State, the Commission (and to the Council, if the reference concerns an act of the Council). Those notified may submit written observations to the ECJ but there is no obligation on them to do so.

A7.3.2.3 Oral procedure
Those notified may also attend the oral hearing and make submissions. The procedure is similar to that for direct actions. After the Advocate-General's Opinion the oral proceedings are closed.

A7.3.2.4 Deliberations and judgment
The procedure is the same as for direct actions.

When the preliminary ruling is sent back to the national court, the case before the national court is resumed (proceedings having usually been suspended, pending the outcome of the preliminary reference).

A7.3.3 THE LANGUAGE OF THE CASE

The language of the case (i.e. that in which the proceedings should be drafted) may be any one of the eleven official Community languages and Irish. In a direct action the applicant can choose the language of the case. However, where the action is brought against a Member State, it is the official language of that State. In references for preliminary rulings the language of the case is the language of the referring court (Rules, Article 29).

The working language of the ECJ is French, although the Advocates-General draft and deliver their Opinions in their own languages. The judgments are drafted and deliberated in French but the authentic version of the judgment will be in the language of the case. If that is not French, it will be a translation into that language from French.

A7.3.4 REPRESENTATION BEFORE THE EUROPEAN COURT

Member States and Community institutions are represented by an agent who is often assisted by an advisor or lawyer entitled to practise before a Court in a Member State (e.g., an agent from the Treasury Solicitor's Department, assisted by a barrister). Other parties in direct actions are represented by a lawyer entitled to practise in the courts of a Member State (Article 17 of the Statute). In preliminary rulings the ECJ is to take account of the rules of procedure of the national court making the reference (Rules, Article 194(2)).

A7.3.5 COSTS

In direct actions the unsuccessful party shall be ordered to pay costs, if these have been asked for in the pleadings. A successful party may however be ordered to pay costs which the ECJ considers to have been unreasonably or vexatiously caused to the opponent (Rules, Article 69).

In references for preliminary rulings the question of costs is to be determined by the national court or tribunal in question (Rules, Article 104(3)). However, costs incurred by Community institutions or Member States which intervene in such proceedings are not recoverable, i.e. they must be borne by the intervener.

A7.3.6 LEGAL AID

In direct actions the ECJ may grant legal aid to a party 'who is wholly or in part unable to meet the cost of the proceedings' (Rules, Article 76).

In references for a preliminary ruling, parties to the national proceedings may be eligible under national law for legal aid in respect of proceedings before the ECJ. For example, in *R v Marlborough Street Stipendiary Magistrates, ex parte Bouchereau* [1977] ECR 1999 an existing legal aid certificate for the case before the national court was held to cover proceedings for a preliminary reference. In exceptional cases the ECJ may also grant legal aid.

A7.4 Interpretation of the Treaties and Community Legislation by the European Court

The ECJ in some ways takes the same approach as an English court: it looks at the words used. It also considers their meaning in the context of the instrument as a whole (contextual interpretation). However, where the contextual interpretation is not helpful it uses the teleological method of interpretation. This means that the ECJ interprets the provision so that it fits into the general aims of the Community legal order, what the Court thinks the Community should be trying to achieve and the needs of the Community. The ECJ differs from the English courts in the extent to which it readily departs from the literal meaning and resorts to the teleological approach and the use of policy in arriving at its decisions.

A7.5 Policy and Decision-Making in the European Court

One of the distinguishing features of the ECJ is the extent to which the ECJ relies on policy considerations in its decisions. Its policy is the promotion of European integration by:

(a) strengthening the Community and its supranational elements;

(b) developing the scope and effectiveness of Community law;

(c) increasing the powers of the Community institutions.

For example, in *Parti Ecologiste 'Les Verts' v European Parliament* (294/83) [1987] 2 CMLR 343, the ECJ extended its power of judicial review to cover the legality of acts of the European Parliament as well as those of the Commission and the Council, the only institutions actually mentioned in Article 230 (ex 173), EC Treaty. It did this because it thought that such acts ought to be reviewable.

The principle of effectiveness (i.e. a provision is to be interpreted in the way that enables it to achieve its objective as effectively as possible), has been used by the ECJ to develop the doctrine of direct effect for directives.

Sometimes the Advocates-General make a comparative study of national provisions in order to find a solution which best fits the purposes of Community law (e.g., *AM & S Europe Ltd v Commission* (155/79) [1982] ECR 1575).

The ECJ introduces new doctrines gradually, initially as a general principle subject to qualifications. In later cases it re-affirms the principle and slowly decreases the qualifications. This was its approach to the treaty-making power of the Community and the doctrine of direct effect (e.g., *Defrenne v Sabena* (43/75) [1976] ECR 455).

The original EC Treaty had little to say on the subject of human rights. The subject had been covered already, in the European Convention on Human Rights and Fundamental Freedoms of 1950, and the EC Treaty was more concerned with economic matters. Following amendments to the EC Treaty by the Treaty of Amsterdam (effective from 1 May 1999), the European Court is now required to respect fundamental rights, as guaranteed by the European Convention on Human Rights. This enshrines in the Treaty what had been developed gradually in the case-law of the European Court over many years. In fact, other amendments of the EC Treaty expand upon this formalisation of the role of human rights within the European Union. Article 6 (ex 12) EC states clearly that the EU is based upon principles of liberty, democracy, respect for human rights and fundamental freedoms, and the rule of law. Article 46 (ex 56) EC places responsibility on the European Court to ensure that the acts of the Community institutions show respect for fundamental rights.

A7.6   The Doctrine of Precedent in the European Court

There is no formal doctrine of *stare decisis* but the ECJ tends to follow its previous decisions in most cases. Its case law is instrumental in developing Community law. Only rarely does it refer to previous cases in its judgment, although sometimes it may repeat parts of a previous judgment without quotation marks or without mentioning the name of the case. On rare occasions it may not follow precedent, e.g., where the circumstances have changed or the views of the judges have altered. In such situations the ECJ does not overrule or distinguish the previous case. It merely ignores it. The Opinions of Advocates-General are often cited by lawyers appearing before the ECJ.

APPENDIX EIGHT
FLOWCHARTS

The following flowcharts are provided as a quick and simple aid to analysis, when using the competition rules. You may find it useful to see if you can improve them or devise new ones.

A8.1 Is the Behaviour Prohibited by Article 81(1)?

START

```
Is this an          NO    Is this a decision    NO    Is it a        NO    The activity is
agreement          ──►    by associations of   ──►    concerted     ──►    outside the scope
between                   undertakings?               practice?            of Article 81(1)
undertakings?                                                               (ex 85(1))

  │ YES                     │ YES                      │ YES                     ▲
  ▼                         ▼                          ▼                         │
  └─────────────────────────┘──────────────────────────┘                        │
                  │                                                              │
                  ▼                                                              │
          May it affect trade                    NO                             │
          between Member     ──────────────────────────────────────────────────┤
          States?                                                               │
                  │                                                             │
                  │ YES                                                         │
                  ▼                                                             │
          Is its object          NO    Is its effect                NO         │
          the prevention,       ──►     the prevention,            ───────────┤
          restriction or                restriction or
          distortion of                 distortion of
          competition                   competition
          within the                    within the
          common market?                common market?

                  │ YES                         │ YES
                  ▼                             ▼
                  └──────────────┬──────────────┘
                                 ▼
                        Prima facie, the
                        agreement is prohibited
                        by Article 81(1) (ex 85(1))
```

A8.2   Is the Behaviour Rendered Void by Article 81(2)?

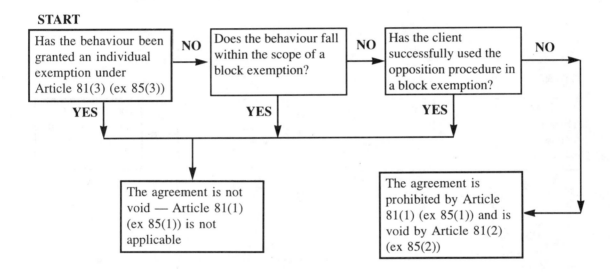

A8.3   Individual Exemption: Article 81(3)

START

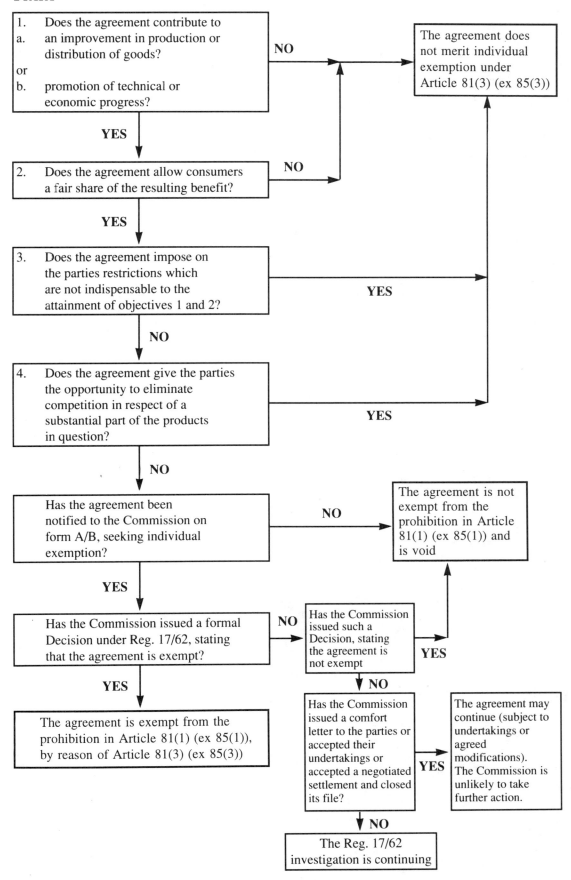

1.   Does the agreement contribute to
a.   an improvement in production or
        distribution of goods?
or
b.   promotion of technical or
        economic progress?

NO

The agreement does not merit individual exemption under Article 81(3) (ex 85(3))

YES

2.   Does the agreement allow consumers a fair share of the resulting benefit?

NO

YES

3.   Does the agreement impose on the parties restrictions which are not indispensable to the attainment of objectives 1 and 2?

YES

NO

4.   Does the agreement give the parties the opportunity to eliminate competition in respect of a substantial part of the products in question?

YES

NO

Has the agreement been notified to the Commission on form A/B, seeking individual exemption?

NO

The agreement is not exempt from the prohibition in Article 81(1) (ex 85(1)) and is void

YES

Has the Commission issued a formal Decision under Reg. 17/62, stating that the agreement is exempt?

NO

Has the Commission issued such a Decision, stating the agreement is not exempt

YES

YES

NO

The agreement is exempt from the prohibition in Article 81(1) (ex 85(1)), by reason of Article 81(3) (ex 85(3))

Has the Commission issued a comfort letter to the parties or accepted their undertakings or accepted a negotiated settlement and closed its file?

YES

The agreement may continue (subject to undertakings or agreed modifications). The Commission is unlikely to take further action.

NO

The Reg. 17/62 investigation is continuing

APPENDIX NINE

BIBLIOGRAPHY

A9.1 Treaties, Statutes, Protocols, Rules

Treaties establishing the European Communities: e.g. The European Economic Community Treaty 1957.
The Single European Act 1986.
Protocol of the Statute of the Court of Justice of the European Economic Community.
Rules of Procedure of the Court.
The European Communities Act 1972.
Rules of Civil Procedure, Sch. 1, ord. 114.
Treaty on European Union, Maastricht 1992.
Treaty of Amsterdam 1997.

A9.2 Books on Competition Law

There are both specialist and general books which deal with EC competition law. In the following selection, (G) indicates a book containing a section on competition law, (S) indicates a book devoted to competition law.

Bellamy and Child, *Common Market Law of Competition* 4th edn, 1993, Sweet & Maxwell. (S)
Craig and De Burca, *EC Law: Text, Cases and Materials*, 1995, OUP. (G)
Goyder, J., *EEC Competition Law*, 1988, Clarendon Press. (S)
Green, N., *Commercial Agreements and Competition Law*, 1986, Graham & Trotman. (S)
Hawk, B., *United States, Common Market and International Antitrust — a Comparative Guide* (especially vol. II), Law & Business Inc./Harcourt Brace Jovanovich. (S)
Kapteyn and Verloren van Themaat, *Introduction to the Law of the European Communities: after the coming into force of the Single European Act*, 1989, Kluwer Publishers. (G)
Korah, V., *An Introductory Guide to EC Competition Law and Practice*, 6th edn, 1997, Hart Publishing. (S)
Slot, P.-J., and McDonnell, A. (eds), *Procedure and Enforcement in EC and US Competition Law*, 1993, Sweet & Maxwell. (S)
Steiner, J., and Woods, L., *Textbook on EC Law*, 6th edn, 1998, Blackstone Press. (G)
Van Bael, I. and Bellis, J.-F., *Competition Law of the EEC*, 1995, CCH Illinois. (S)
Vaughan, D. (ed.), *Law of the European Communities*, 2 vols, 1997, Butterworths. (G)
Weatherill, S. and Beaumont, P., *EC Law*, 1995, Penguin. (G)
Whish, R., *Competition Law*, 1997, Butterworths. (S)
Wyatt and Dashwood, *The Substantive Law of the EEC* 3rd edn, 1993, Sweet & Maxwell. (G)

A9.3 Practitioners' Works

Anderson, *References to the European Court*, 1995, Sweet & Maxwell.
Halsbury's Laws, Vols 51 and 52.
Vaughan, *The Law of the European Communities* (1986) 2 vol. (reprint of the relevant volumes of *Halsbury's Laws*), Butterworth & Co.
Lasok, *The European Court of Justice: Practice and Procedure*, 2nd edn, 1994, Butterworth & Co.
Usher, *European Court Practice*, 1983, Sweet & Maxwell Ltd.
Kapteyn and Verloran Van Themaat, *Introduction to the law of the European Communities*, 2nd edn, Kluwer.
D'Sa, *European Community Law and Civil Remedies in England and Wales*, 1994, Sweet & Maxwell Ltd.
Brealey & Hoskins, *Remedies in EC Law: Law and Practice in the English and EC Courts*, 1994, FT Law & Tax.

A9.4 Periodical Reports and Journals (English Language)

Common Market Law Reports (much more up-to-date than the European Court Reports), published by European Law Centre Ltd monthly. Has a special series devoted to competition matters. Reports cases in the Court of Justice and cases in national courts which have a EC significance.

Common Market Law Review, covers the whole spectrum of Community affairs; often very good articles on competition matters.

European Competition Law Review, good articles on competition and free movement of goods; good case digests.

European Court Reports (official law reports of the Court of Justice), English-language version is always about two years behind; off-prints of individual cases are usually available from the Court (usually in French) after date of judgment until publication in the ECR.

European Intellectual Property Review, a specialist journal which deals with Community competition matters via case summaries, reports of Community press releases, articles. Also deals with issues concerning free movement of goods.

Official Journal (often abbreviated to OJ, or JO in French texts), this is the organ through which official announcements are made. These may be formal notices in a competition investigation, a declaration of a decision to exempt a company from Article 85(1), or other, legislative, matters. Series L covers the legislation of the Community, divided into those measures which must be published and those which need not be but are published; Series C covers everything else.

A9.5 Journal Articles on Competition Law

Easterbrook, Frank H., On identifying exclusionary conduct, [1986] Notre Dame LR 972: an article by a judge on the 7th Circuit Court of Appeals; a radical look at the abuse of a dominant position in US terms.
Farr, Sebastian, Abuse of a Dominant Position — the *Hilti* case [1992] 4 ECLR 174.
Fox, Eleanor M., Monopolization and dominance in the United States and the European Community: efficiency, opportunity and fairness, [1986] Notre Dame 981: a good comparative study, of use when looking at Article 86, EC Treaty.
Furse, Mark, Fines and the Commission's discretion [1995] ECLR 1A9.
Green, Nicholas, Article 85 in perspective: stretching jurisdiction, narrowing the concept of a restriction and plugging a few gaps, [1988] ECLR 190: looks at actual

and potential developments in the application of Article 85.

Hawk, Barry, The American (anti-trust) revolution: lessons for the EEC? [1988] ECLR 53: deals with the changes in competition law enforcement in the USA caused by new economic ideas, and their potential impact for the European Community.

Maitland-Walker, Julian, A Step Closer to a Definitive Ruling on a Right in Damages for Breach of the EC Competition Rules [1992] 1 ECLR 3.

Oliver, Peter, Enforcing Community rights in the English Courts, (1987) 50 MLR 881: looks at some aspects of the use of EC rights in English courts. One case dealt with in some detail is *Bourgoin* v *MAFF* [1986] QB 716.

Robertson, Aiden and Williams, Mark, An Ice-Cream War: The Law and Economics of Freezer Exclusivity [1995] 1 ECLR 7.

Smith, Helen, The *Francovich* Case: State Liability and the Individual's Right to Damages [1992] 3 ECLR 129.

Steiner, Josephine, How to make the action suit the case — domestic remedies for breach of EEC Law, (1987) 12 *European Law Review* 102: examination of the remedies available in English courts when an alleged breach of EC law is used as a cause of action.

Van Bael, IVO, Fining à la carte: the lottery of EU competition law [1995] 4 ECLR 237.

Whish, Richard, The enforcement of EC competition law in the domestic courts of Member States [1994] 2 ECLR 60.

N.B. Other articles are referred to in relevant chapters.

A9.6   Other Sources on Competition Law

Areeda & Turner, *Antitrust Law: an analysis of antitrust principles and their application*: regarded as an authority on the economic thinking behind the laws on competition; an American work.

Bork, R., *The Antitrust Paradox*: further reading on American challenges to traditional economic thinking; a representative of the 'Chicago' school of economic theory.

Celex: a computer database, available on subscription from the EC itself.

European Commission, *Competition Law in the EEC and in the ECSC:* a collection of the secondary legislation in competition law.

European Communities Legislation Current Status, Butterworth, updated work.

Foster, Nigel, *Blackstone's EC Legislation* 9th edn, 1998, Blackstone Press: an abundance of primary and secondary legislation in the main 'European' areas, including competition and industrial/intellectual property.

Gellhorn, Ernest, *Antitrust Law and Economics* (in the US 'Nutshell' series): concentrates on competition law and economic theory in the USA but with good, concise sections on basic economic concepts. Available in London through Hammicks

Justis: an electronic database, available on CD-rom. Contains extensive material, including the recent case-law of the Court of Justice.

Internet sites:
- europa — this takes you into an enormous range of sites and information about everything connected with the EU — http://europa.eu.int.
- particular sites of interest to competition lawyers are the DG IV site (for competition matters) — http://europa.eu.int/comm/dg04/index–en.htm and DG XV site (free movement of goods and intellectual property rights) — http://europa.eu.int/comm/dg15/en.
- for national competition matters, refer to the UK Office of Fair Trading — http://www.open.gov.uk/oft/oft home.htm.

LEXIS: another database, supplied by Butterworth Telepublishing and available through their dedicated terminals. Try your law library.

Rudden & Wyatt, *Basic Community Laws* 5th edn, 1994, OUP: a materials book containing significant secondary legislation.

A9.7   Student Textbooks

Hartley, *The Foundation of European Community Law*, 3rd edn, 1994, Oxford University Press.

Steiner and Woods, *Textbook on EC Law*, 6th edn, 1998, Blackstone Press Ltd.

Weatherill and Beaumont, *EC Law*, 2nd edn, 1996, Penguin.

Wyatt and Dashwood, *The Substantive Law of the EEC*, (1993), Sweet & Maxwell Ltd.

INDEX